D0026173

www.wadsworth.com

wadsworth.com is the World Wide Web site for Wadsworth Publishing Company and is your direct source to dozens of online resources.

At wadsworth.com you can find out about supplements, demonstration software, and student resources. You can also send e-mail to many of our authors and preview new publications and exciting new technologies.

wadsworth.com
Changing the way the world learns®

Basic Skills in Psychotherapy and Counseling

CHRISTIANE BREMS, PH.D., ABPP
University of Alaska Anchorage

BROOKS/COLE

THOMSON LEARNING

Australia • Canada • Mexico • Singapore • Spain
United Kingdom • United States

BROOKS/COLE

TM

THOMSON LEARNING

Counseling Editor: Julie Martinez
Editorial Assistant: Marin Plank
Marketing Manager: Caroline Concilla
Signing Representative: Tony Holland
Project Editor: Tanya Nigh
Print Buyer: Tandra Jorgensen
Permissions Editor: Joohee Lee

Production Service: G & S Typesetters, Inc.
Text Designer: Janet Wood
Copy Editor: Carolyn S. Russ
Cover Designer: Laurie Anderson/
                        Yvo Riezebos
Cover Printer: Phoenix Color
Compositor: G & S Typesetters, Inc.
Printer: Maple Vail

COPYRIGHT © 2001 Wadsworth,
Brooks/Cole Counseling is an imprint of Wadsworth,
a division of Thomson Learning, Inc. Thomson
Learning™ is a trademark used herein under license.

ALL RIGHTS RESERVED. No part of this work
covered by the copyright hereon may be reproduced
or used in any form or by any means—graphic, elec-
tronic, or mechanical, including photocopying,
recording, taping, Web distribution, or information
storage and retrieval systems—without the written
permission of the publisher.

Printed in the United States
  2 3 4 5 6 7 04 03 02 01

For permission to use material from this text,
contact us by **Web:** http://www.thomsonrights.com
  Fax: 1-800-730-2215 **Phone:** 1-800-730-2214

Wadsworth/Thomson Learning
10 Davis Drive
Belmont, CA 94002-3098
USA

For more information about our products, contact us:
Thomson Learning Academic Resource Center
1-800-423-0563
http://www.wadsworth.com

International Headquarters
Thomson Learning
International Division
290 Harbor Drive, 2nd Floor
Stamford, CT 06902-7477
USA

UK/Europe/Middle East/South Africa
Thomson Learning
Berkshire House
168-173 High Holborn
London WC1V 7AA
United Kingdom

Asia
Thomson Learning
60 Albert Street, #15-01
Albert Complex
Singapore 189969

Canada
Nelson Thomson Learning
1120 Birchmount Road
Toronto, Ontario M1K 5G4
Canada

Library of Congress Cataloging-in-Publication Data
Brems, Christiane.
    Basic skills in psychotherapy and counseling / Christiane Brems.
        p.   cm.
    Includes bibliographical references and index.
    ISBN 0-534-54942-X
    1. Counseling.   2. Psychotherapy.   I. Title.
  BF637.C6 B722   2000
  616.89'14—dc21

                                            00-057972

This book is printed on acid-free recycled paper.

To the women who have shaped my life —
My beloved mother, Rosemarie Brems
My adorable grandmother,
  Carolina Hilsheimer
My caring sister, Gabriele Strubel
and in the memory of Emmi Brems

Contents

Chapter Two

Self-Awareness Skills 38

Chapter Three

Self-Care Skills 70

Part Four

SKILLS FOR AFFECTIVE AWARENESS IN PSYCHOTHERAPY AND COUNSELING   289

Chapter Ten

Working with Affect and Emotion: Overview and Basic Skills   291

Chapter Eleven

Working with Affect and Emotion: Focus on the Body   320

Chapter Twelve

Working with Affect and Emotion: Focus on Feelings   366

Listing of Figures and Tables

Preface

> I have just three things to teach:
> Simplicity, patience, compassion.
> These three are our greatest treasures.
> Simple in actions and in thoughts,
> You return to the source of being.
> Patient with both friends and enemies,
> You accord with the way things are.
> Compassion toward yourself,
> You reconcile all beings in the world.
>
> *The Tao Te Ching*

Dear Reader:

Thank you very much for holding this book in your hands and reading these words, regardless of whether you have already purchased the text or whether you are still evaluating if you would like to buy it. It was my pleasure to write this book and I would like to take this opportunity to share why I made the decision to write it and why it may be useful to you, the reader.

Why Did I Write This Book?

As you and I are well aware, many books are on the market today that teach about basic skills in counseling and psychotherapy. Was there really a reason for yet another? The answer to this question in my mind was an unequivocal "Yes," for a number of reasons. For years I have been searching for a book that would be useful for a beginning course in psychotherapy or counseling that would be sophisticated yet pragmatic, dense with knowledge yet readable, and comprehensive yet appropriate for a single semester. Clearly there are sophisticated, comprehensive, and fact-packed books on this topic; I own many of them and treasure them. However, for a simple beginner's course, these large volumes are often overwhelming and so theoretical that the novice becomes flooded with detail and in the process loses the human connection with the material and the client. There are also books that are simple and straightforward, as well as easy to read. Unfortunately, many of these texts fail to provide a clear framework for the simple skills they present, leaving students with fragments of skills and without a context in which to apply them.

Thus, I have been searching for a book that would provide students with all the basic information and knowledge necessary to engage in safe beginning practice of counseling and psychotherapy; a book that would provide a context or framework along with skills and detailed application. I was looking for a book that would achieve this goal of giving context and application without forcing students to sort through reams of research literature, which while certainly invaluable and important to a student's overall education, may detract from the purpose of the type of course for which this book is written. Over and over again I failed in my search. Finally, since I knew what I was looking for, I began to shape a text that would have these very features. What grew out of this desire of mine for a simple yet sophisticated, scientific yet pragmatic book is the product you now hold in your hands. It is a book that hopes to help students deal with the most basic of issues of mental health practice by introducing them to the basic skills necessary in counseling and psychotherapy work, embedding these skills in a clear and logical framework that can be applied within virtually any counseling or psychotherapy theory.

For Whom Did I Write This Book?

The audience for this book is upper-level undergraduate or graduate students who are about to embark on a career in the mental-health professions. A wide range of students can benefit from this text, including students in all of the following mental-health-care fields:

- psychology
- counseling
- social work
- psychiatric nursing
- psychiatry
- marriage and family or relationship therapy or counseling
- child psychotherapy or counseling
- human relations and
- any other mental-health-care field

The book is targeted towards beginning students in any one of these mental-health fields. It is conceptualized as the primary text that would accompany a basic course in psychotherapy or counseling skills. It will be invaluable to novices in the mental-health field, but may also be a great resource for more advanced students who seek a summary text with many examples and sample transcripts useful in direct client work. The book is best absorbed in its entirety before the first client contact. Once the skills addressed in this book are mastered, the reader will be ready to see a first client. I would invite readers at that point to turn to two of my other books to facilitate the continued journey in the mental-health field. The two other books represent the sequels to this text and build upon the basic skills presented here. They are *Psychotherapy: Processes and Techniques* (Brems, 1999) and *Dealing with Challenges in Psychotherapy and Counseling* (Brems, 2000). For readers who are interested in work with children, *A Comprehensive Guide to Child Psychotherapy* (Brems, 1993; revision to be released 2001) may be helpful.

What Is in This Book?

This book will prepare readers for beginning mental-health practice by giving them an overall appreciation of counseling and psychotherapy, while also providing all the microskills necessary to apply this deeper knowledge pragmatically and directly with clients. The book deals with all the critical topics that need to be thought through by a counselor or therapist before embarking upon therapeutic work with clients. As such, it covers the following basic areas of information and skills:

- choosing a career in mental health: *disciplines, degrees, motivations*
- personal traits: *traits that help, traits that hurt*
- countertransferences: *dangers, uses*
- values clarification: *personal and interpersonal self-awareness*
- cultural sensitivity: *awareness, knowledge, skills*
- self-care: *inner work, nutrition, health, exercise, relationships*
- communication skills: *nonverbal communication, listening, attending*
- understanding affect and emotion: *awareness, experience, expression*
- dealing with affect and emotion: *dealing with crisis, catharsis*
- working with affect and emotion: *using the body, using feelings*
- understanding thought and cognition: *normal cognitive development, cognitive processing levels*
- dealing with thought and cognition: *dealing with crisis*
- working with thought and cognition: *simple strategies, advanced interventions*

The text provides an overall easy-to-understand framework for mental-health practice, in a fresh format. Within that framework it deals with many basic building blocks of counseling and psychotherapy that traditional texts have included for decades. Some of the traditional approaches covered in the text include:

- nonverbal communication
- listening skills
- attending skills
- use of silence
- encouragers
- restatements and paraphrases
- reflections
- summarizations
- open-ended questions
- systematic inquiry
- breathing exercises
- relaxation exercises
- reframing and relabeling
- normalization
- pointing out patterns
- confrontation
- here-and-now process
- interpretation

The conceptualization of therapeutic competence that underlies this book emphasizes the interplay between therapeutic skills and personal traits and abilities. Figure 1-1 (in Chapter One) provides an overview of how personal-awareness skills, communication skills, affective skills, and cognitive skills interact and work together to create a competent counselor or therapist. Both instructors and students will benefit from the reality that students will not only be exposed to basic skills, as listed above, but will receive a solid framework within which to apply these skills. They will benefit from the many case examples and instructions that help them translate technical information into practical terms and application. The clear and jargon-free writing, along with the many summaries and tables, should help students easily understand information presented and locate details needed at a later time. Finally, the many Skills Development Recommendations provided throughout will help instructors structure course work and will encourage students to practice and explore the new skills to be learned.

How Is This Book Special?

To summarize, this book has many special features that make it the perfect accompaniment for basic counseling and psychotherapy skills courses. These features include, but may not be limited to, the following advantageous characteristics:

- clear and useful theoretical framework for all presented skills
- presentation of all traditional basic skills

- presentation of many basic skills not traditionally covered in basic-skills books
- attention to personal issues relevant to counselors and therapists
- many examples and session transcripts
- clear instructions for skills and exercises
- many transcripts for exercises that can be used as written with clients
- self-contained sections that can be read in any needed sequence to adapt to reader preferences
- scores of tables and lists that clearly summarize material for easy and quick reference
- clear and uncomplicated writing style
- no ties to a particular conceptual approach to counseling or psychotherapy
- tailored Skills Development Recommendations to help students practice and master basic skills
- thorough subject and author indexes

Thank you for selecting or considering this book. I wish you an enjoyable career in mental-health care and hope this text will prove to be a helpful companion.

Sincerely,
Christiane Brems, Ph.D., ABPP

Acknowledgments

There are always many people to thank when a book comes to fruition. I want to start by expressing my undying gratitude to the love of my life and my best friend, Mark E. Johnson. Thank you for reading every draft of every page of this project and for your patience with my preoccupations and obsessions in writing this and other books. Thank you for being the centering presence in my life.

My appreciation also goes as always to my wonderful German family, who has supported me all of my life, even after I moved thousands of miles away to a new life in a new country. Your love and caring mean the world to me. I am grateful to all of you: Bernhard Brems, Rosemarie Brems, Lina Hilsheimer, Gabriele Strubel, Hans Juergen "Floh" Strubel, and Jan Strubel. Thanks for being who you are.

Thank you, the students in the clinical-psychology program at the University of Alaska Anchorage, who have helped create a joyous and stimulating world of teaching. My gratitude goes to all of you for your enthusiasm for doing therapy, your enjoyment of learning, and your wide-eyed excitement for what I had to offer you. I know you will go on to do great things!

Finally, my appreciation goes to the editing and proofreading team that helped shape this book into its final form. Thank you, Julie Martinez and Carolyn S. Russ. And to the reviewers for their helpful and insightful feedback. Thank you, Rachell N. Anderson, The University of Illinois at Springfield; Alisabeth Buck, Tacoma Community College; Bob Egbert, Southern Adventist University; Harold Engen, University of Iowa; Joshua Gold, University of Southern Carolina; Jeffery S. Haber, Metropolitan State College of Denver; and Martha Sauter, McLennan Community College. This book could not have become what it is without your help.

PRELIMINARY ISSUES

Traits of Successful Therapists and Counselors

CHAPTER

1

This is what should be done
By one who is skilled in goodness,
And who knows the paths of peace:
Let them be able and upright,
Straightforward and gentle in speech.
Humble and not conceited,
Contented and easily satisfied.
Unburdened with duties and frugal in their ways.
Peaceful and calm, and wise and skillful,
Not proud and demanding in nature.
Let them not do the slightest thing
That the wise would later reprove.

From the Buddha's Metta Sutra

The field of mental-health care offers many exciting career paths, as well as the potential for great personal career satisfaction. However, it is not an easy life-work to choose as the professional will be invariably and profoundly affected by this type of work on a personal and professional level. There are probably few careers that affect their practitioners as profoundly and personally as does a career in mental health. Equally, few career choices are as affected by personal aspects of the practitioner. Given the great importance of the personal to the professional and the professional to the personal, an in-depth exploration of the person who is considering a career in mental health is in order.

ISSUES IN CHOOSING A CAREER IN MENTAL HEALTH

Careers in mental health are quite diverse. An informed decision as to which career path to follow will be based on a study of the academic fields devoted to psychotherapy and counseling, terminal-degree requirements, credentialing

3

requirements, and the student's motivations for choosing a career in the helping professions. The major fields that have devoted themselves to psychotherapy and counseling are psychology, psychiatry, counseling, and social work. At least two important offshoots of these primary fields that have gained independence over the years are the fields of marriage and family counseling or therapy, and human services. Different disciplines within the area of mental health have different graduation and credentialing requirements. Graduation requirements are generally driven by terminal degrees within a field as well as highly idiosyncratic variations in curricula across states and schools. Credentialing requirements (certifications and licensure) similarly differ greatly depending on where practitioners set up a practice and what degree path they chose originally. The motivation students have for choosing a career in the helping professions is equally important to explore. Despite the clear need for such exploration, this is a practice that does not seem to happen automatically. This chapter will guide students toward a thorough exploration of their career choice as well as personal issues that may enter the practice of their careers once they have made a conscious choice about which particular route to choose.

Disciplines, Degrees, and Related Credentials Relevant to a Career in Mental Health

It is not the purpose of this book to help mental-health professionals choose the best career path; it is, however, devoted to providing the tools for a successful career as a psychotherapist or counselor. Fundamental to their success is making appropriate academic choices. It is not uncommon for young professionals to choose an academic path based on guidance from important external sources such as parents, teachers, and college professors, without careful review of all the options. Some graduates may choose psychology because their local university does not offer a counseling degree program; some may choose social work because a parent was a social worker. Choosing the academic field of study—that is, psychology versus social work and so on—can have major implications about the terminal degree to strive for. In some disciplines, such as social work, the master's degree is an excellent option as it is the accepted terminal degree within that profession. In other disciplines, such as psychology, a doctorate may be required to carry out certain functions, whereas a master's degree may suffice to engage in other duties. In yet other fields, the differentiation between the master's degree and doctorate in terms of implications for mental-health practice may be rather vague or may merely set apart the practitioner from the teacher or researcher. This is true, for example, in counseling and marriage and family work.

It is not uncommon for graduate students to have certain career aspirations that are not entirely commensurate with their degree choices. For example, frequently graduate students in psychology want to work strictly as counselors or psychotherapists in a general mental-health setting such as a community mental-health center. Yet these very same future professionals are enrolled in rigorous doctoral programs training them also to be researchers and teachers. Such individuals might be better served in a rigorous master's program in psychology or counseling that trains them to do what it is they aspire to. These students may never have understood their options or alternatives. Table 1-1 outlines the major disciplines that train mental-health professionals. Within each discipline, the table breaks out various degree options (if applicable), as well as possible licenses and credentials compatible with the degree choice. It also shows the ultimate responsibilities that can be carried out by professionals in these fields of interest, again differentiating levels of education. The table is strictly concerned with post-baccalaureate training and career choices requiring a graduate education, hence it does not include paraprofessional counseling fields.

The reader will notice in Table 1-1 that social work, marriage and family training (counseling or therapy), and counseling as professions have strongly endorsed and supported the master's degree as one of two terminal degrees (the other being the doctorate). In all three disciplines, master's degrees lead to nationally accepted (though state-granted) licenses, namely, the licensed clinical social worker (LCSW), licensed marriage and family therapist (MFT), and licensed professional counselor (LPC), respectively. Psychology, on the other hand—or, perhaps more accurately, the American Psychological Association (APA)—has rejected the master's as a terminal degree for purposes of independent licensure and practice in psychology. Despite this official stance of the American Psychological Association, however, many states in the United States and provinces in Canada have developed licenses for psychological practice at the master's level. Yet, there is no standard label for this master's level license (examples including psychological associate and psychometrician), nor a standard for scope of practice of these providers. Some states, such as Alaska, allow the care provider to practice completely independently after a certain number of years; some require irregular supervision regardless of how long the master's level provider has been in practice; some (in fact, perhaps most) require weekly supervision of master's level practitioners. This reality has made the master's degree a more desirable degree in the disciplines of social work, counseling, and marriage and family, where this level of education leads to clear and undisputed licenses.

It is an unfortunate reality for the discipline of psychology that the master's degree is not an officially endorsed degree. Movements are under way to change that. For example, the Northamerican Association of Masters in Psychology (NAMP) has developed and implemented accreditation procedures for academic programs in psychology at the master's level. It is not yet clear how successful this movement will be in elevating the master's in psychology to terminal-degree status or to the equivalent of the LCSW, but it appears to be a

TABLE
1-1

CAREER OPTIONS FOR MENTAL-HEALTH-CARE PROVIDERS

Discipline and Degree	Typical Position or Job Title	Typical License or Certification	Possible Job Duties	Typical Job Settings	Special Notes
Clinical Psychology					
Ph.D. or Psy.D.	Psychologist	Psychologist license, board certification	Research and evaluation, teaching, testing and assessment, therapy, supervision, administration	Academia, research institute, clinic/hospital, private practice	Cannot prescribe medications
M.S. or M.A.	Therapist, clinician	Psychological associate, psychometrician, many other labels	Therapy, case management	Clinic/hospital, private practice	Not considered a terminal degree; not licensable for independent practice in all states
Counseling Psychology					
Ph.D. or Psy.D.	Psychologist	Psychologist license, board certification	Research and evaluation, teaching, testing and assessment, counseling, supervision, administration	Academia, research institute, counseling center, clinic/hospital, private practice	Cannot prescribe medications
M.S., M.A., or M.Ed.	Counselor, clinician	Psychological associate, psychometrician, many other labels OR licensed professional counselor	Counseling, case management	Counseling center, clinic/hospital, private practice	Not considered a terminal degree; not licensable in psychology for independent practice in any state

School Psychology

Degree	Title	License/Certification	Roles	Settings	Notes
Ph.D. or Ed.D.	School psychologist	Psychologist license, board certification	Research and evaluation, teaching, testing and assessment, counseling, supervision, administration	Schools, academia, counseling center, clinic/hospital	Cannot prescribe medications
M.S., M.A., or M.Ed.	School counselor, school psychologist	School psychologist, psychometrician, perhaps other labels	Counseling, academic testing, vocational testing	Schools, counseling center, clinic/hospital	In some states considered a terminal degree and licensable as a school psychologist

Counseling

Degree	Title	License/Certification	Roles	Settings	Notes
Ed.D. or Ph.D.	Counselor	Licensed professional counselor	Counseling, teaching, research and evaluation, supervision, administration	Counseling center, private practice, academia, clinic/hospital	Cannot prescribe medications; generally not licensable as a psychologist
M.S., M.A., or M.Ed.	Counselor	Licensed professional counselor	Counseling, case management	Counseling center, private practice, clinic/hospital	Terminal degree; same license as doctoral-level counselor

Social Work

Degree	Title	License/Certification	Roles	Settings	Notes
D.S.W. or Ph.D.	Social worker	Licensed clinical social worker	Administration, teaching, research and evaluation, counseling or therapy, supervision	Clinic/hospital, social-service agency, counseling center, private practice, academia	Cannot prescribe medications; cannot do psychological assessment
M.S.W.	Social worker	Licensed clinical social worker	Case management, counseling or therapy	Social-service agency, clinic/hospital, counseling center, private practice	Terminal degree; with license often treated as equivalent to doctorate in psychology

TABLE 1-1 (CONTINUED)

Discipline and Degree	Typical Position or Job Title	Typical License or Certification	Possible Job Duties	Typical Job Settings	Special Notes
Human Services					
Ph.D. or Ed.D.	Counselor (no discipline-specific label)	No discipline-specific license exists—licensed professional counselor may be an option	Administration, teaching, research and evaluation, counseling or therapy, supervision	Social-service agency, clinic/hospital, counseling center, academia	Cannot prescribe medications; cannot do psychological assessment
M.S., M.A., M.Ed.	Counselor (no discipline-specific label)	No discipline-specific license exists—licensed professional counselor may be an option	Case management, counseling or therapy	Social-service agency, counseling center, clinic/hospital	Not a clearly defined degree for licensing purposes
Medicine					
M.D.	Psychiatrist	Medical license, board certification	Research and evaluation, administration, pharmacotherapy, psychotherapy, teaching, supervision	Medical school or academia, research institute, private practice, hospital	Prescription and hospital privileges; cannot do psychological assessment
R.N.	Psychiatric nurse or psychiatric nurse-practitioner	Psychiatric nurse-practitioner license	Pharmacotherapy, psychotherapy, administration	Clinic/hospital, private practice (some states only)	Licensing options vary from state to state and define private-practice options

step in the right direction (see also Brems and Johnson, 1996a). For the time being, LCSWs enjoy many privileges and advantages from which master's level practitioners in psychology tend to be barred. Most importantly, LCSWs are generally fully reimbursable by third-party sources such as insurance and Medicaid, tend to hold high-responsibility administrative positions, and can practice independently without supervision. Even LPCs and MFTs have more freedom than master's level psychological associates, though they do not enjoy some of the privileges of LCSWs. For example, third-party payment eligibility differs from state to state.

Another interesting development is reflected less obviously in Table 1-1. Although there are still two primary fields within the discipline of psychology that provide mental-health services—namely, clinical and counseling psychology (the latter not to be confused with degree programs in counseling)—the actual practice and career paths of the graduates from these two fields differ very little. The differences between clinical and counseling psychology appear relatively minor and the similarities are growing. Both have similar curricula, career paths, and clienteles. One of the few major differences that appears to remain is the fact that most doctoral programs in counseling psychology prefer for their applicants to have completed a master's degree, whereas most clinical-psychology programs prefer their applicants to apply straight out of an undergraduate program. Another minor difference emerges with regard to career counseling, which appears to remain largely within the realm of counseling psychology. The interested reader should peruse the extensive literature about clinical versus counseling psychology before making a final decision about which to choose (for example, Brems and Johnson, 1996b, 1997; Brems, Johnson, and Galluchi, 1996; Johnson and Brems, 1991).

It is also notable that both social work and psychology have discipline-specific (D.S.W., Psy.D.) as well as generic (Ph.D.) doctorates. There is generally no difference with regard to licensure or other certification eligibility between a discipline-specific and generic doctorate (especially if granted by a professionally accredited program). However, within psychology, it appears to be true anecdotally that Psy.D.s may have more difficulty than Ph.D.s in being hired for academic positions in traditional Ph.D.-granting psychology doctoral programs. Like medical professionals, psychologists have the option for board certification by the American Board of Professional Psychology (ABPP). Unfortunately, unlike in psychiatry, only a small percentage of psychologists choose to pursue board certification, which involves a rigorous examination process. Psychologists (this label always implying a doctorate) are always eligible for third-party reimbursement. In some states or communities, they may have hospital privileges and may be able to initiate hospitalization. This is also true for D.S.W.s and, in some states, for LCSWs. Only psychiatrists, however, are able to prescribe medications. Only psychologists are fully trained to conduct independent psychological assessments (testing batteries).

Motivations Underlying the Choice of a Career in Mental Health

The relatively objective and informed selection of discipline and educational level does not suffice in and of itself to assure a successful career in the field of mental health care. It will be equally important to take a look at more personal issues that may ultimately affect each individual's success as a counselor, social worker, or psychotherapist. One basic question deals with why, beyond the objective criteria covered in Table 1-1, an individual has chosen to enter a helping profession. Personal motivations for entering the mental health field can be helpful or harmful; most importantly, a practitioner must be clear as to why the choice was made and how those personal reasons may enter into the work itself.

All career choices involve an underlying set of motivators that steer the individual in a certain professional direction. Students interested in the workings of nature or with a curiosity about what makes things work may be motivated to focus their careers on physics, geology, or similar disciplines. Students with a history of medical concerns or with family experiences that involved illness and perhaps death are often drawn to the medical profession. Individuals who have always enjoyed and been rewarded for artistic self-expression may choose theater or music. What then are typical motivations for people who choose a career in mental health? A few motivations emerge on a regular basis. It is important to recognize how different motivations may affect the choice and practice of the profession; some motivations may affect the practice of helping in positive ways, some in negative ones. Equally important, the same motivator in two different care providers may manifest in uniquely different ways in their work, being conducive to good work in one and intrusive for the other. Thus, as the reader peruses the various motivations offered below, the main issue is to evaluate each with regard to its truth for that individual and with its potential impact on her or his relationship with clients. The Skill Development Recommendations later in this chapter will revisit this issue further; a helpful summary, addressing issues useful to self-appraisal, is provided in Table 1-2.

As indicated in Table 1-2, one important motivator that commonly emerges is the desire to help. This motivator may have developed in various ways, but often harks back to a helping role within the practitioner's family of origin. In other words, the career choice is often based on continuing a role that is familiar and perhaps enjoyed by the individual. If enjoyed, the desire to help can be a powerful positive influence in the practitioner's career; if perceived as burdensome, it will certainly get in the way. For some clinicians, the original desire to help was a positive force early in the career; as successes and burdens mount, however, the stresses of always being in the helping role may become overwhelming. If the desire to help is the main motivating force in the choice of this career path, it will be important for the mental-health-care provider to choose self-care skills outside of work that recharge and rejuvenate. Practitioners motivated by this desire may be advised to avoid doing a lot of volunteer work in their spare time.

Another common motivator is the desire to change the world. Although this desire is often accompanied by the desire to help, the two are not entirely synonymous. The desire to change the world implies that the clinician wants to have an impact on a wide range of people and wants to create change that ripples through the social structure and system on a grander scale. This desire can affect work positively and negatively. It may lead a clinician to work with huge caseloads to bring a message to as many individuals as possible. This approach to changing the world one person at a time is a recipe for burnout. Other mental-health-care providers may be able to find paths that are less stressful, working in administrative or political-action settings that by definition affect more people but no longer involve direct work with individual clients. One danger in the desire to change the world rests in the failure to do so on a large scale, which to individual practitioners may feel like a failure in their careers.

The desire to have a purpose or to be needed can be another powerful motivator for choosing a mental-health career. The creation of meaning in life is a powerful force that is met for many through their work. Individuals who consider entering a helping profession often perceive the field as a means of fulfilling their desire to be needed and to have a purpose. The sense of being needed, in turn, is often perceived as a means of assuring that a practitioner's existence on earth has meaning and purpose. However, being needed can, in the long run, become draining and exhausting. If the mental-health-care provider always gives and never receives, burnout is inevitable. What may have seemed a way to achieve a sense of purpose and meaning may in the end be the opposite, leading the clinician to a sense of loss and disillusionment. On the other hand, for many helping professionals, it is the desire to be needed and the creation of meaning in their lives through their work that brings them the greatest satisfaction. These caring individuals thrive on providing for others and are true expressions of altruism and compassion in action. What tends to mark these successful professionals is their ability to create support and compassion for themselves through meaningful relationships and activities in their private lives.

Another powerful motivator for entering the mental-health field is a personal struggle with emotional or psychological problems. There are practitioners who enter the field to heal themselves, though this motivation may be hidden even from their own awareness. They seek to find the solution to their unhappiness through the educational and later the professional process, only to find that this may not be the answer. This motivation is very similar to what Day (1995) called the desire to do for clients what clinicians wish someone had done for them. No doubt, entering a graduate education in mental health challenges the student to explore the self and personal history. However, this

TABLE

1-2 **MOTIVATORS FOR ENTERING A CAREER IN THE HELPING PROFESSIONS**

Motivator for Profession	Positive Consequences	Potential Negative Consequences	Cautions / Recommendations
Desire to help	Caring, sensitivity, altruism, other-focus, life satisfaction	Burnout, lack of self-care, dissatisfaction if not acknowledged for contributions, create dependency in client, helper/caretaker countertransference	Use many self-care strategies that are rejuvenating and recharging; evaluate needs to caretake others
Desire to change the world	Caring, contributions to individuals and society, creation of change in social structure and system, altruism, and leaving of a legacy	Inappropriately large caseload, burnout, feelings of being a failure without large-scale impact of work, pushing clients beyond their capabilities, social arbiter countertransference	Choose job positions with responsibilities beyond individual counseling or therapy that are commensurate with larger social or political goals
Desire to create purpose and meaning	Altruism, compassion, satisfaction with personal life, self-esteem and satisfaction derived from being needed, dedication to clients or a cause	Exhaustion and burnout from always being the giver and never the receiver of care, unself-aware due to seeking of meaning or life purposes through external means only	Engage in introspection to assure that meaning is not entirely externally derived (i.e., not derived only from being needed)

Desire for self-help	Exquisite sensitivity and understanding for clients, enhanced empathy from personal experience	Sympathy (not empathy), inability to tolerate pressures of graduate training and/or job, countertransference due to overidentification	Develop a healthy integrated self through self-care and/or treatment before making a decision about a career in mental health
Desire to control or tell others what to do	Willingness to take charge or responsibility and the desire to be helpful	Forgetting to explore how the client may want to solve a problem, not allowing the client to take charge and take ownership of solutions, being overbearing or controlling	Explore options with the client not for the client, be willing to listen without jumping to conclusions or solutions, put the client's preferences ahead of personal preferences
Desire to share the experience of recovery	Exquisite sensitivity and understanding for clients, enhanced empathy from personal experience	Pushing of a single approach that was successful for self, inability to differentiate client from self, countertransference due to overidentification or due to forcing client into a mold	Be open to diverse approaches and interventions, tailor treatment to each individual client, seek supervision if recognizing a strong pattern of uniformity in work across all clients
Desire to share personal insights or wisdom	Excellent knowledge base and range of practical advice and intervention strategies	Coercing a single or specific agenda or means of approaching life and treatment, without the ability to listen to and recognize the client's needs and desires; demanding certain behaviors from clients; advice-giving	Be open to tailoring treatment to each individual client, taking time to listen and to hear what the client wants and needs, seek supervision if recognizing a strong pattern of uniformity in work across all clients or if giving too much advice
Desire for financial freedom and status	Motivation for hard work, academic and career achievement	Disillusionment or dissatisfaction with achievements and accomplishments, domination of or disrespect for clients, countertransference related to keeping clients in treatment	Evaluate motives for keeping clients in treatment long-term, generate alternative sources of income, derive pleasure from accomplishments in other areas of life

self-exploration is most successful if based upon a solid foundation of a relatively healthy and integrated self. Those students who enter with fragile selves may not be able to withstand the pressures of graduate school or the real world once engaged in practice. The issue of wounded healers has come to the forefront in recent years, and most associations of mental-health professionals have begun to address this concern. Entry into these professions based on the desire for self-help may not be sound decision making.

Closely related to the desire to heal the self is the desire to enter the profession to give to others what was personally experienced. Day (1995) called this motivation the desire to do for others what someone else has done for the clinician in the past. These individuals enter the mental-health field because they have had emotional or psychological problems in the past, which they have mastered through some form of counseling or therapeutic intervention. They are now motivated to give back to others what they believe has saved them. This motivation is noble indeed and can provide practitioners with exquisite sensitivity for their clients. The potential pitfall is that these clinicians may push the approach that worked for them, not recognizing that it may not be optimal for all clients.

Another related motivator for choosing a mental health profession may be the desire to share knowledge and wisdom. This desire is closely related to the wish to be helpful, but is guided primarily by the belief of clinicians that they have special insights or awareness that are useful not only in their personal lives but also in the lives of others. This motivation can be powerfully useful if applied in an open-minded and exploratory manner. The clinician may function from an excellent base of knowledge and may indeed have developed many useful insights and a great deal of wisdom. However, if the clinician believes that the personal insight or awareness has to be applied in a certain way (that is, in the way it worked for her or him), this motivation can lead to rigidity and the imposition of goals and solutions that are not necessarily shared by or helpful to the client. This clinician may coerce certain behaviors in the client or end up giving advice. Failures on the part of the client to then follow through with the clinician's suggestions may lead the mental-health-care provider to feel frustrated and angry with the client.

Not easily admitted to self and others is the desire to enter the helping profession to gain control and to tell others what to do. Nevertheless, this is a powerful motivator for some mental-health professionals. This motivator can take a positive shape when the provider offers clear structure and guidance for clients but the pitfalls are obvious. Clients do not need to be controlled and they do not come to treatment for advice. They need to be understood and supported in their own right and given permission to unfold their lives in their own desired direction. A controlling clinician who thinks the answers are clear and has a specific piece of advice or a solution for every problem may not give the client space to engage in this type of work and growth.

Skill Development Recommendations

Recommendation 1-1 *Using Table 1-2, explore each motivation with regard to its likelihood of being true for you. Journal about how this motivation has already manifested in your life, both positively and negatively. Think about the worst-case scenario of this motivation playing itself out in your clinical work and develop strategies of prevention.*

Recommendation 1-2 *Pick two of the professions listed in Table 1-1 that most appeal to you and that most likely reflect your future career choices. Then identify one professional in your community for each of these professions (by means of the Yellow Pages, for example, or recommendations from your professors). Call each person and ask for an interview. Interview them about the profession to explore whether your impression of and hopes about the profession match with its reality. Then reconsider your career choices, either affirming your goals or revising them as needed.*

Not often admitted, the desire for status and financial freedom can also enter into the decision to become a mental-health-care provider. Status is often tied to advanced degrees, especially doctorates. This may lead students to choose doctoral careers for all the wrong reasons. Financial gain is a potential motivator for many professions. While many practicing mental-health-care providers may laugh at the suggestion that financial gain is a motivator to enter this field, the innocent student may make assumptions about money and prestige that are not entirely grounded in the reality of the profession. Not surprisingly, these practitioners will be disillusioned and dissatisfied when their careers fail to provide for this basic need for recognition and advancement. A more devastating outgrowth of this desire is the impact it may have on the practitioner's relationship with clients. If prestige is not forthcoming outside the therapy room, these practitioners may dominate and demand a respect from their clients that is excessive. If financial freedom is threatened, these clinicians may choose to keep a client in counseling, not because the person is still in need, but because she or he has a great insurance company that keeps paying!

Most likely there are many other motivators that direct individuals to a career in mental health. Again, no single motivation is bad or good in and of itself. Each merely has potential positive and negative impacts that need to be clear in the clinician's mind. Any motivation, however positive, if misapplied can lead to "pride rather than humility, insistence rather than invitation, telling rather than listening, demanding rather than believing, or making and coercing rather than letting" (Cormier and Cormier, 1998, p. 12). As will be noted below, almost nothing about a provider is entirely positive or negative; what counts is the level of self-awareness the individual professional has about personal motivations, traits, and countertransferences. With good self-awareness, clinicians can learn to make positive use of motivators and traits and can learn to transcend negative aspects of both. Given the importance of self-awareness, self-awareness skills will be dealt with in great detail later. However, now that the reader has explored how personal motivations may play a role in career choice and how they potentially affect the client-clinician relationship, it is important to turn to an exploration of how other personal traits can enter into mental-health work.

Personal Traits Relevant to the Practice of Psychotherapy and Counseling

The process of becoming a mental-health-care provider is challenging, representing a path of development that can be highly intellectually stimulating, personally gratifying, and interpersonally satisfying, on the one hand; and emotionally draining, personally devastating, and cognitively exhausting on the other. The process of learning in the mental-health field progresses through four stages, outlined beautifully by Lauver and Harvey (1997) as follows:

Stage One: Unconscious Incompetence   At this stage the trainee is not yet aware of the extent of the knowledge and skills required to become an effective mental-health-care provider and blissfully moves along in training, unaware of personal shortcomings and gaps in knowledge. Students at this stage often demonstrate a syndrome that could be called "I already know all of this." Their mind is often somewhat closed as they believe that their common sense and pure motivation are sufficient to do the job of counseling or therapy. Being at this stage is relatively easy for trainees because they have not yet come face to face with their shortcomings and still feel blissfully happy about their career path and choice. Fortunately for their clients, and for the clinicians and their supervisors, this stage invariably comes to an abrupt end as counselors or therapists begin to recognize (or have pointed out to them by their supervisors) the limits of their personal knowledge, skills, and abilities. As limitations and countertransferences (to be discussed in more detail below) rear their ugly heads, clinicians recognize that there are things they need to learn, insights they need to develop, and processes they need to become aware of. They are now entering the painful Stage Two of the learning process.

Stage Two: Conscious Incompetence   At this stage the trainee is aware of limitations, both in the realm of knowledge and personality. Many students actually begin the learning process at Stage Two, not Stage One (in a way missing out on the blissful state of unconscious incompetence). Clinicians at this stage are very vulnerable and need to be supervised with care and caring as they consolidate skills and form a professional self-image during a time of great self-doubt. Conscious incompetence means being painfully aware of mistakes, cringing when reviewing video- or audiotapes of sessions with clients, admitting errors in judgment, becoming aware of missed opportunities for interventions, recognizing poor choices of strategies, and most of all, realizing personal traits that may hinder the work. This stage is painful, can lead to self-doubt, and represents a true trial by fire. This stage, however, is also the experience that leads students to a hunger for learning and a desire for good guidance and supervision that is the mark of a healthy professional. A student in this stage, while introspective and not always happy, is usually a pleasure to work with, seeking new knowledge, reading, and consolidating learning almost twenty-four hours a day. Clinicians who survive this stage with the help of a healthy foundation of an integrated self and calming and supportive guidance from teachers and supervisors are then ready to consolidate their learning into a budding sense of competence, the basis of Stage Three.

Stage Three: Conscious Competence At this stage, clinicians have learned a lot, have developed a solid base of intervention skills, and have memorized the basics necessary to do good therapeutic work. They begin to be able to tailor helpful treatment plans, and their interventions begin to be well-chosen and well-timed. All this work, however, is done with great concentration and effort; most choices and decisions are made deliberately and consciously. This repetitive decision making and pondering leads the clinician to the point where skills slowly begin to be integrated into a repertoire of strategies, and personal traits begin to be tailored and modified into a useful way of being with clients. The conscious effort and concentration required at this stage of learning means a high expenditure of energy, and clinicians at this stage often leave work exhausted but happy. They have worked hard with their clients, but they have done well and feel that something was accomplished. Where Stage Two was emotionally draining and challenging, Stage Three is cognitively exhausting and stimulating. At some point, trainees will recognize that the work gets easier; some skills begin to come almost automatically and not every intervention has to be pondered and thought through in detail before being used. The clinician is about to enter Stage Four.

Stage Four: Unconscious Competence At this stage, the mental-health-care provider has consolidated learning, has reached a healthy level of self-awareness, has developed open-mindedness and flexibility, and no longer is afraid of possible challenges presented by clients. Learning has become so ingrained and automatic that the work with clients is now second nature for the clinician. Decisions are self-evident, and treatment plans easily emerge from the data collected from clients. The work with clients becomes a pleasure for the clinician, and the strain and concentration of Stage Three begin to disappear. Clinicians can now work from a healthy emotional and cognitive plane. The biggest threat in this stage is that the clinician may slip into automatic pilot. Unconscious competence and automatic pilot are not the same thing. An unconsciously competent clinician continues to seek out supervision or consultation, engages in careful self-care, reevaluates treatment decisions regularly, and reviews client charts on an ongoing basis. This clinician makes sure that the ease of work is not confused with sloppiness or carelessness, nor with a routine imposed on all clients regardless of their idiosyncratic needs and backgrounds. The positive traits a clinician brings to the profession will separate the unconsciously competent care provider from the automatic pilot. Ongoing self-awareness work is one aspect of the healthy clinician and will be addressed in detail later. First, an overview of counselor traits is in order.

Each individual who chooses a mental-health career comes equipped with personal traits and characteristics that influence the work to be done with clients. Some of these influences may move the therapeutic process along (that is, may be facilitators), whereas others may interfere. This exploration will begin by highlighting traits that tend to be useful, if not critical, to success. It is important for students to be honest in their assessment of the degree to which they possess these particular traits. The glaring absence of several traits may point toward the potential for problems. The occasional doubt about one or two, on the other hand, may merely suggest that some personal work is needed.

It is important to note that this chapter differentiates skills from traits. *Traits* are those characteristics mental-health-care providers bring with them at the outset of their careers; they are the character traits and personal expressions developed over a lifetime of experience and interaction with others. Traits may be innate, consciously developed, or inadvertently learned; they are what is present and expressed right now. *Skills,* on the other hand, are those behaviors (and possibly characteristics) that will be learned by the student over the course of being in a mental-health training program (regardless of discipline). They are the expressions and capacities of successful professionals that no instructor will take for granted in a student, but instead will work consciously and with effort to instill and teach.

Occasionally, it is difficult on the surface to differentiate a trait from a skill. Empathy is an important case in point. Empathy will be presented in this chapter as a trait. However, it will also be dealt with in an entire chapter on empathy as a skill. In other words, there are basically two forms of empathy: the raw trait that is incidentally developed (and thus preexisting) in the student, and the refined set of techniques and conscious interventions that will be learned over time. Most commonly, however, traits are clearly and easily differentiated from skills. It is important to note that traits are not necessarily unalterable. They are, though, somewhat ingrained and will be acquired or eliminated only with conscious work and effort.

Facilitating Traits of Mental-Health-Care Providers

A wide array of traits exists that can be very helpful to the therapeutic or counseling exchange between clients and clinician when present abundantly and automatically. In turn, absence of these personal characteristics in the care provider can have negative consequences for the client's treatment or the clinician's level of career satisfaction and success. Table 1-3 gives an overview of the most important personal characteristics a clinician can bring to therapy or counseling. This table outlines how these traits can facilitate the process as well as how their absence may negatively affect it. It needs to be reiterated that not all clinicians will possess all of these traits to the same degree. Doubt about a few can be overcome; the absence of several, on the other hand, is probably a red flag for the student. A few of the more important traits will also be discussed below.

Self-esteem is an important trait as clients are not always enamored with a clinician's techniques and procedures and may make their displeasure known verbally by attacking the therapist. The insecure therapist may be worn down by negative clients, whereas a healthy (and realistic) dose of self-esteem makes the therapist less vulnerable to transferential and otherwise undeserved personal attacks by clients (Brems, 1994). A therapist who cannot deal with the temporary assault on her or his self-esteem in a session is bound for failure or burnout (Kottler and Brown, 1992). An overall *sense of competence* is important as well (Cormier and Cormier, 1998), especially as clinicians experience the self-imposed assault on their competence through increasing awareness of what they do not yet know. A solid sense of general life competence is an excellent trait to help beginning mental-health-care providers pass through the stage of conscious incompetence. They will be able to recognize their continuing competence in other areas of their lives and can thus emerge into Stage Three with healthy self-esteem and a heightened experience of competence and clarity.

Self-respect is an important trait that assists clinicians in setting appropriate therapeutic boundaries with the client. Only self-respecting clinicians are able to adhere to the agreed-upon time frame for a session without feeling guilty, request payment as agreed upon, and refrain from accepting unnecessary calls or contacts from clients between sessions. Such appropriate setting of boundaries is actually very important for clients as it communicates control and safety of the therapeutic setting. It is likewise crucial for mental-health-care providers, as it takes care of their needs for a predictable schedule and private life outside of the clinic (cf., Herlihy and Corey, 1997, for a very complete discussion of boundary issues).

TABLE
1-3

PERSONAL TRAITS THAT FACILITATE MENTAL-HEALTH TREATMENT AND RAPPORT

Personal Trait	Sample of Possible Positive Effects of Presence	Sample of Potential Negative Effects of Absence
Self-esteem and competence	• ability to tolerate criticism from clients • ability to tolerate treatment failure • feelings of security and self-assurance	• self-doubt • permission for clients to manipulate or take advantage • inability to express strength and safety, especially during crises • externalization of blame for failures or perceived failures • burnout or wounded-healer symptoms
Self-respect and appropriate use of power	• ability to set safety limits and boundaries • ability to keep treatment structured and predictable • ability to take care of personal needs • ability to deal with crises • ability to work with challenging or difficult clients	• tendency to be taken advantage of or manipulated • inability to keep treatment from spinning out of control • tendency to direct clients rather than allowing them to choose their own path • inability to manage crisis situations
Willingness for introspection and self-exploration	• awareness of countertransference • self-awareness of strengths and weaknesses • awareness of potential blind spots • ability to track and recognize interpersonal process in treatment • ability to take responsibility for own errors	• intrusion of countertransference into treatment • lack of awareness of personal issues intruding on conceptualization and intervention • poor self-care • externalization of blame for problems in treatment or with rapport
Acceptance and open-mindedness	• openness to values, behaviors, and approaches to life that differ from personal choices • acceptance of diverse lifestyles and preferences • compassion and caring • nonjudgmental attitudes	• imposition of personal values, standards, and beliefs • proneness to -isms (e.g., racism, sexism, heterosexism) • rigidity and intolerance • passing of judgment
Cultural sensitivity	• awareness of presence and impact of prejudice and stereotypes • valuing of variety and diversity • recognition of many truths and realities • acceptance of differing opinions	• prejudice • stereotyping • squelching of diversity and variety • lack of awareness of impact of own behavior and beliefs • sense of threat derived from differences

Characteristic	Positive	Negative
Respect for others	• honoring of clients' wishes and needs • appropriate use of language • practice of equality • practice of patience to accommodate to client's pace in treatment	• offensive language (e.g., sexist, racist) • authoritarian attitude • one-upping • imposition of personal sense of timing rather than adjusting to client needs
Empathy	• caring and understanding • honoring each client's unique history and approach to life • willingness to listen • ability to communicate concern	• lack of emotional availability • inability to grasp the client's experience of the world • poor communication skills
Tolerance for ambiguity	• ability to revise treatment plans as needed • ability to tolerate and embrace the need for change • ability to function well in the absence of a single right answer or truth • ability to function in the absence of clarity	• overwhelmed by complexity • overwhelmed by crises • inability to change course in treatment if needed • inability to accommodate change and adjust to new data • fear of the unknown
Cognitive complexity	• ability to be insightful • ability to think quickly • ability to problem-solve creatively • ability to diagnose and conceptualize • ability to respond to outpouring of data	• overwhelmed by information • inability to understand underlying dynamics of a client's behavior, feelings, thoughts, and relationships • potential for misdiagnosis • inability to form meaningful conceptualizations
Capacity for intimacy	• ability to relate to clients as human beings • capacity to express warmth and caring • ability to develop a sense of emotional support and closeness	• aloofness or distancing • fear of rejection leading to being easily manipulated by clients • inability to develop therapeutic rapport • inability to develop empathic concern and understanding
Flexibility	• ability to "roll with the punches" • ability to make appropriate accommodations for client's needs and wishes • tolerance	• rigidity in thought and practice • paralysis when faced with change or challenge • intolerance and lack of acceptance
Sense of ethics and professionalism	• ethical treatment of clients • keeping up-to-date with the profession • responsibility for personal growth and continuing education • practice within the scope of educational background/limits	• violation of ethical codes • unprofessional behavior with clients • lack of self-care • lack of professional growth and self-care

TABLE 1-3 (CONTINUED)

Personal Trait	Sample of Possible Positive Effects of Presence	Sample of Potential Negative Effects of Absence
Awareness and expression of personal style	• congruence • authentic behavior • intervention choices that fit personal style • expression of humanity • extension of common human courtesy to clients	• incongruence or phoniness • lack of genuineness • awkwardness in implementation of strategies incompatible with personal style • overdoing of therapeutic neutrality
Good personal boundaries	• recognition of treatment as being for the client • setting of appropriate treatment limits	• inappropriate self-disclosure • movement of therapeutic focus away from the client to the self • countertransference
Ability to delay gratification of needs	• ability to retain focus on client in all (or most) circumstances • lack of self-preoccupation during sessions • ability to keep personal life out of the treatment room	• putting own needs ahead of clients' • allowing personal needs to intrude upon treatment (e.g., smoking in a client's presence) • inappropriate self-disclosure
Ability to delay expression of affect	• ability to keep strong (countertransference) reactions from intruding at inopportune moments • ability to keep affects stemming from personal life out of the treatment room • ability to cancel sessions when not entirely mentally or physically healthy	• countertransference expressed impulsively • bringing in of personal feelings with clients • failure to cancel sessions during time of personal distress, crisis, or illness
Personal mental health	• sense of humor • ability not to take self too seriously • wisdom • creativity • enjoyment and contentment in personal life • desire to give to others	• countertransference • inappropriate boundaries • inappropriate self-disclosure • boredom • burnout • sense of being burdened and exhausted • wounded-healer symptoms

The structuring of therapy or counseling is also related to clinicians' healthy expression of power. Power, or *expertness,* is an important and useful trait if wielded carefully and respectfully. Clearly, this trait can turn negative quickly if over- or misused. Appropriate use of power means setting safety limits and clear treatment boundaries. A balanced use of power means that the clinician knows when to take responsibility and to create limits, boundaries, and structure, and when to relinquish control so as not to coerce, manipulate, or force clients (Cormier and Cormier, 1998). The trait becomes negative when it is used to justify paternalism. The clinician is a guide, not a director, who functions on behalf of the client. Power is being abused if clinicians find themselves directing their clients instead of allowing them to choose their own paths.

Therapists and counselors must have a high level of *cognitive complexity.* Their work requires that they be able to conceptualize client cases and respond quickly to situational issues. Clinicians must truly be able to "think on their feet." They must be knowledgeable and have the desire and ability to assimilate new information quickly and to reason abstractly. Only a bright clinician can respond quickly enough to the quick outpouring of data that can occur in therapy and keep up with the client in terms of conceptualizing and revising treatment plans effectively (Cormier and Hackney, 1987).

Additionally, continuing to learn about therapy and related strategies is essential as the field changes continually (Egan, 1994). Striving for excellence is how Kottler and Brown (1992) refer to the process of constantly learning and increasing the therapist's sense of awareness and therapeutic skill. Each new client is viewed as a new learning opportunity that will stretch the therapist's limits and broaden his or her horizons.

The clinician must also be fully competent in the *ethical* sense. Most, if not all, mental-health professions have a code of ethics that requires that care providers be fully trained, up to date, and generally competent at what they do (Swenson, 1997). Counselors must know their professional limits and when to refer to another provider when these limits have been reached by the demands of a case or client. Further, new information emerges constantly as work progresses. This requires *flexibility* that results in positive revisions of treatment plans and conceptualizations, and adaptability of treatment strategies in a meaningful manner (Morrison, 1995). Not all human beings are capable of functioning in such an environment of ambiguity and tentativeness. Some will attempt to make counseling or therapy fit a rigid model. No client, no family, no therapy fits a specific mold (Land, 1998). In fact, the whole therapeutic process relies upon change, upheaval, tentativeness, and not uncommonly, ambiguity. Related to the concept of flexibility is the idea that a good therapist must have *patience* (Strupp, 1996). Counseling cannot be rushed, and counselors cannot expect clients to follow a particular time line.

Mental-health-care providers need to possess a high level of willingness to self-explore and a certain level of *emotional maturity.* Clinicians who fail to have introspective abilities or tendencies are very prone to feelings and attitudes that may confound the treatment process (cf., Knobel, 1990). *Self-exploration,* entered into willingly and regularly, helps prevent inappropriate countertransference reactions and helps the mental-health-care provider respond out of concern for the client, not for the self. Self-exploration is crucial to the ability to recognize when a clinician's personal needs have been mobilized in a therapeutic relationship and to keep these needs out of the therapy room. Emotional maturity helps counselors recognize that their own personal needs may need to be addressed, and keeps them from doing so in the presence of the client (Kottler and Brown, 1992). Willingness to self-explore and introspect also helps clinicians recognize the need to seek supervision and consultation. Emotional maturity allows mental-health-care providers to improve and enhance self-knowledge by seeking supervision and consultation, not only when personal needs and limitations obviously rise to the surface (Strupp, 1996), but on a regular basis to prevent inappropriate expression of personal needs in therapy sessions (Basch, 1980). Seeking self-knowledge through ongoing introspection and self-exploration also means that clinicians practice what they preach, looking at themselves regularly with caring and realistic criticism (Egan, 1994).

Related to self-exploration and the ensuing higher level of self-awareness is a clinician's ability to recognize when personal values may have intruded upon treatment or the evaluation of a client. Since it is desirable not to impose values on clients, the ability to recognize that it is happening, coupled with acceptance and flexibility, is crucial to successful mental-health work (Choca, 1988; Cormier and Cormier, 1998; Knobel, 1990).

Open-mindedness is an essential trait that helps clinicians welcome even those clients whose values may differ from their own. Open-minded therapists will not inadvertently or deliberately force personal values onto clients, especially clients who grew up in an environment that was significantly different from that of the therapist (Castillo, 1997; Pinderhughes, 1983). A difference in backgrounds will not threaten treatment as long as the mental-health-care provider can keep an open mind and is able to see the client's life from the client's unique perspective. What the clinician may need to understand is that some behaviors of the client that would be considered maladaptive or questionable in the therapist's personal background, may have had great adaptive value in the client's environment. Clearly, counseling cannot be entirely free of values and value judgments (Lewis and Walsh, 1980; Pinderhughes, 1997). However, the counselor is encouraged to be as flexible and open-minded as possible, and to recognize personal values and how they may collide with the values of a client. Remaining as nonjudgmental and compassionate about clients' realities as possible certainly facilitates the therapeutic relationship and enhances the likelihood of being able to help clients help themselves (Reid, 1998). Being nonjudgmental and open-minded also suggests and requires *respectfulness* vis-à-vis the client, as well as a stance of egalitarianism that eliminates power differentials between client and provider (Land, 1998).

As reflected in the need for flexibility, counselors and therapists need to be able to deal with unknowns and to be willing to take risks and explore new ground. Being able to deal with ambiguity is a critical skill of every counselor (Kottler and Brown, 1992). All therapists have to be capable of *epistemological feeling* (Knobel, 1990, p. 61), that is, they must have the ability to listen empathically and to alter their assessments of a client's situation flexibly and appropriately in changing contexts (Cormier and Cormier, 1998). Unwillingness to follow intuitions can result in leaving facets of the client undiscovered that might otherwise prove crucial to growth and change. In the therapy setting, risk-taking has to be weighed against the possible consequences of making a mistake, but it is rare that one failed or inappropriate treatment intervention derails the entire therapeutic process. Indeed, some clinicians believe that the occasional empathic failure of the therapist is crucial to successful treatment (Kohut, 1984; Wolmark and Sweezy, 1998). Only repeated failures are likely to have an impact, not one unfortunate choice of wording or behavior. It is often preferable for the counselor to follow an intuition and risk a new intervention that seems right than to adhere rigidly to one that has already proven less than successful.

In facilitating the therapeutic process, it is important that counselors allow their own selves to come through, to be authentic (Knobel, 1990), and genuine (Egan, 1994). It is quite impossible for clinicians to deny who they really are outside of the therapy room, as personality can neither be hidden nor camouflaged (Chrzanowski, 1989). The clinician must recognize, however, that *authenticity* does not equal self-disclosure. The therapy is there for the client; it is not intended to give the therapist the opportunity to self-disclose or deal with personal psychological or emotional issues. All therapists and counselors have a certain interpersonal style: Some are extroverted and active; others are introverted and observing. This general pattern shows through in the types of interventions a clinician chooses (cf., Keinan, Almagor, and Ben-Porath, 1989; Kolevzon, Sowers-Hoag, and Hoffman, 1989), and finding a way of doing therapy that fits with the clinician's general style of being and life values is critical (Dorfman, 1998). Only if the style fits the clinician will she or he be able to muster the enthusiasm that is so crucial to the treatment of any client. It is impossible for counselors to deny who they are in the way they greet their clients, sit in the room, and interact throughout the session. Being themselves expresses their humanity and allows them to extend common human courtesies to their clients.

Adapting one's therapeutic style and technique to personal traits is not the same as abandoning the *therapeutic neutrality*. It is still important to be nonjudgmental and not to impose certain opinions or outcomes on a client (Kottler and Brown, 1992). However, a clinician takes neutrality too far if it translates into sterile and impersonal ways of relating to clients. Even psychoanalytic therapists have come to recognize that remaining anonymous does not mean being nonresponsive (cf., Basch, 1980; Wolf, 1988) or having no personality. It merely means maintaining clear boundaries and retaining the focus of the session on the client, not the therapist (Brems, 1999; Morrison, 1995). In this regard, immediate needs of the mental-health-care provider are kept out of the therapy session. For example, if clinicians are hungry or upset, they delay gratification of these needs and feelings while with the client (Kottler and Brown, 1992). This may be one of the greatest challenges for the new practitioner, but becomes second nature as time wears on. It also makes self-care outside of the therapy room an even more important component of therapists' lives so as not to become a human being who is full of denial of personal needs and feelings.

Another important personal characteristic of the successful counselor is *empathy*. Each therapist strives to understand how a client feels in a given situation, given that client's specific and unique experiences, history, and background (cf., Kohut, 1984; Shulman, 1988). Empathy, thus defined, requires the therapist to listen carefully and to hear or see not only the overt content of what is being expressed either verbally or behaviorally, but also to listen to the latent message that is contained within the client's expression. Such empathy, also termed vicarious introspection (Kohut and Wolf, 1978), is more than the warm, fuzzy feeling of caring; it is an artful and scientific approach to better understanding. Empathy is incomplete if it ends with the internal or private understanding of the client by the therapist. Empathy only serves a positive therapeutic purpose if the therapist is able to communicate understanding back to the person (Brems, 1999). Once counselors have listened carefully and believe they have empathically understood the communication of the client, this understanding is communicated back to the client. Only when the client receives the message of understanding and feels the therapist's empathic concern is the interpersonal cycle of empathy complete (cf., Barrett-Lennard, 1981; Brems, 1989).

The ability to enter *intimate and caring relationships* is a prerequisite that almost needs no mention. Clinicians clearly have to be able to enter into a meaningful dialogue with other human beings, need to be able to exude warmth and caring, must not fear rejection or closeness, and must be open to the humanity in all people (Cormier and Cormier, 1998). A clinician who is aloof or excessively distancing will likely have some trouble developing therapeutic rapport. As with genuineness and authenticity, the clinician needs to walk a fine line. Social relationships with clients are inappropriate, as are intimate or sexual ones. Interpersonal warmth and caring must be expressed in a therapeutically appropriate manner to help the client feel cared for without violating treatment boundaries.

Finally, there is the issue of the *mental health* of the clinician. By definition, mentally healthy individuals have many of the traits that make a human being successful in the helping professions. Mentally healthy people are capable of empathic attunement, have the wish and the ability to understand the needs of others, understand their own needs, are capable of delaying their own needs to meet the needs of others, are realistically self-confident with a clear acceptance of personal flaws and shortcomings, have little fear of rejection or humiliation, possess a certain amount of creativity, have a sense of humor, and are wise (Rowe and MacIsaac, 1986). The latter three concepts beg some definition. *Creativity* refers to a person's ability to derive pleasure from problem solving. This pleasure in coming up with solutions to tough situations and circumstances is reinforcing for clinicians and continues to propel them toward finding options and alternatives, both in their own lives and in the lives of clients. Creativity is one of the most important traits in successfully dealing with challenges and crises of clients and of daily living. A *sense of humor* is defined as the ability to laugh at oneself. It excludes biting sarcasm or vicious irony, instead referring to the capacity to make light of past failures and minor imperfections, and not to take life or oneself too seriously. Finally, *wisdom* is characterized by the acceptance of personal limitations and frailties. Wise persons can forgive mistakes and lack of ability, accepting self and others fully. Wisdom dictates that parents, teachers, and clinicians can be forgiven and accepted even if they have made mistakes in the past and can be respected and cared for nevertheless. True wisdom is achieved if this capacity is present in relation to others and the self.

In summary, many personal traits can greatly facilitate the therapeutic or counseling process through their mere presence. They are the traits graduate-level instructors look for in their new students as they are often the very things that will differentiate the successful from the unsuccessful therapist. Although all of these traits can be fostered and developed, their preexistence is a great asset, their absence often a warning sign. Absence of these traits generally requires that the student take some personal time to develop and foster them. Often this can involve personal therapy or counseling; it always involves engaging in the self-care skills that are outlined in a later chapter (and also in Brems, 2000). Ultimately, management of these personal traits determines not only the success of the clinician with clients, but also the clinician's ability to sustain his or her own mental health throughout a career.

Hindering Traits of Mental-Health-Care Providers

The presence of traits that tend to be less than therapeutic is often more problematic than the absence of some of the positive traits mentioned. Given the fact that these traits share some of the same qualities, that is, they are preexisting, ingrained, and habitually present in the individual, the potential for negative influence is great. Elimination of negative traits will have to be addressed by as many avenues as possible, including through self-care, personal counseling or therapy, and careful supervision. It is impossible to mention all possibly hindering personal traits, just as it was impossible to identify all facilitating traits. It is important to note that in the discussion of positive traits, the absence of any of the positive traits by definition implies the presence of a hindering trait. Thus, the mere opposites of positive traits—for example, absence of self-esteem, intolerance, lack of flexibility—will not be addressed again here. What follows is a discussion of a few additional personal traits that can interfere with therapeutic process or rapport.

One important trait that can interfere with good mental-health service delivery is *fear of failure*. Fear of failure can lead clinicians to take the safe approach, never taking risks or following intuitions, and may result in allowing the client to "run the show." Fear of failure can force the client into false mental health as the client will pick up on the clinician's great need for the client to improve. This flight into health has been talked about in the psychoanalytic and psychodynamic literature (for example, Kohut, 1984; Wolf, 1988), but is not often mentioned in this context.

Another fear that gets in the way of good therapeutic work is the *fear of reaching out* to other resources. Such clinicians believe that they have to solve all the problems in the world alone and should never have to rely on other resources in helping a client heal or grow. The ensuing lack of referral for additional assistance can leave the client vulnerable and can lead to inappropriate treatment. Failing to refer a client with a possible medical condition is only one such example. Less egregious examples of a clinician's unwillingness to draw on other resources include the inability to refer to support groups or to ask for help from a consultant or supervisor, and similar omissions. This fear can be related to arrogance in the clinician, but this is not always the case. Sometimes mental-health-care providers who fear reaching out are just shy and have the idea that they *ought* to know everything. More devastating are those clinicians who do not reach out because they think they *do* know all the answers. Their overcertainty leads them to make diagnoses and treatment plans that are less than optimal, and may also lead to misinterpretations and misunderstandings. Clearly, counseling does not tend to be successful when an overly certain clinician fails to seek input and moves ahead with a chosen treatment even in the face of evidence that it is not working.

A third fear that can get in the clinician's way is the *fear of newness*. These are the clinicians who do the same thing day in and day out; they use the same intervention with each client, whether it is relevant and effective or not. Often these clinicians are afraid to try anything new; sometimes they are unwilling. When they are unwilling, their fear of the new is often coupled with arrogance or overcertainty. Sometimes these clinicians are merely bound to the tradition in which they were trained. They adhere strictly to the principles of their former supervisors or the books they studied. They do not realize that the field advances, new developments can help speed up treatment, or their personal style may be better accommodated by an alternative approach. Over-adherence to tradition is highly problematic and can make the clinician rigid and inflexible.

Also problematic can be *needs* of clinicians that are carried into the therapy or counseling setting. Such needs include the need to be admired, the need to be accepted, the need for respect, and the need for awe. Mental-health-care providers with these needs will feel dissatisfied if their clients cannot provide admiring or sustaining responses, which is more likely than not. Since clients come to treatment to work on emotional problems, they are highly unlikely to want to provide positive feedback to their clinician, nor should they ever be expected to do so. The clinician who needs to have these needs met in the counseling setting is prone to burnout and dissatisfaction. The counselor who has these needs may well perceive the client in a negative light when no admiration is forthcoming. Coming to treatment with needs is a setup for clinicians; counselors and therapists need to make sure first that all their needs are healthy and developmentally appropriate; and second that their needs are met outside of the therapy room.

Another hindering set of traits is the *lack of a sense of humor or lightness,* and the inability to be anything but severe and serious. Taking everything overly seriously and never being able to laugh with a client can create a very heavy or burdening environment. Sometimes the best thing to do in a crisis is to diffuse some of the seriousness with lightness, to allow some of the sorrow to be lifted by optimism. This is not to say that clinicians have license to make light of their clients' concerns. It merely suggests that the inability to let up can become quite burdening and depressing.

A final hindering trait that will be mentioned here is actually a collection of traits. It is the clinician's *inability to access a certain aspect of the human experience* either in the self or in the client. One way this problem may manifest is as an inability to feel—either in the form of being completely unaware of personal emotions or in the form of not being able to tolerate affect in clients. Similarly, but in a different realm of human experience, it is problematic if a clinician is cut off from cognitions. This may mean the clinician is unaware of personal cognitive process or may manifest as an inability to understand the thought process of clients, perhaps because of an overemphasis on emotion—the clinician whose answer to everything is to explore how the client feels.

The third realm of human experience refers to the clinician's behavior. Unawareness of personal behavior could mean being significantly overweight and not recognizing what this may communicate to the client about personal impulse control. Using drugs or alcohol or engaging in other detrimental behaviors would also suggest that the clinician is unable to exert proper self-regulation in the realm of behavior. Clinicians unable to recognize the need for self-regulation in their own lives may likewise be unable to identify problem behaviors in clients and may fail to recognize where proper intervention needs to take place.

The final example of this type of negative trait is if the clinician's blind spot is in the area of relationships. A clinician who cannot access personal needs for relatedness and human contact (that is, one who is truly schizoid or avoidant) will have a hard time making contact with a client in any realm (affect, thought, or behavior). Similarly, this clinician may not recognize a client's devastating relationship patterns and may intervene in ways that lead to the reinforcement of unhealthy relatedness patterns.

All hindering traits, whether the ones noted above, or others, will manifest in the client-clinician relationship in some form. One common way in which the literature has dealt with hindering traits is through the discussion of countertransference, since that is the way in which hindering traits most commonly reveal themselves. Following is a discussion of countertransference and how to deal with it.

Countertransference Issues

It is generally agreed that countertransference enters therapy or counseling through lack of self-awareness and usually presupposes that the clinician is not cognizant of the fact that the therapeutic process or rapport is beginning to be influenced by his or her personal beliefs, needs, traits, and attitudes (Holmquist and Armelius, 1996). Countertransference is most traditionally defined as a therapist's response to a client that is based upon the therapist's unconscious in general, and unconscious anxieties and conflicts in particular (cf., Freud, 1949, 1959; Webb, 1989). However, this definition is very global and does not differentiate the different manifestations countertransference can take in actual treatment. Hence, further definition has resulted in the identification of four types of countertransferences: issue-specific, stimulus-specific, trait-specific, and client-specific countertransference (Brems, 1994). The first three types tend to be disruptive to treatment and always arise out of a lack of self-awareness. The fourth type of countertransference does not fit the traditional criteria of countertransference in that it can actually serve a therapeutic purpose and generally arises because the clinician is keenly self-aware and introspective. It is often discussed in the context of countertransference, but not always with the recognition that it has an appropriate and rightful place in counseling and therapy and serves a useful purpose.

A few red flags that negative countertransference may have been stimulated in a client-clinician relationship are shown in Table 1-4 and should alert the clinician to engage in self-exploration or to seek supervision.

TABLE 1-4 RED FLAGS FOR ISSUE-SPECIFIC, TRAIT-SPECIFIC, OR STIMULUS-SPECIFIC COUNTERTRANSFERENCE

Red Flag	Possible Types of Countertransference That Are Being Stimulated
Avoidance of certain topics	Issue-specific
Negative reactions to certain topics	Issue-specific
Heightened emotionality around certain topics	Issue-specific
Tendency toward overreaction to certain topics	Issue-specific
Stereotyped or predictable reaction to certain topics	Issue-specific, trait-specific
Avoidance of certain types of clients	Stimulus-specific
Rejection of certain types of clients	Stimulus-specific
Negative reactions to certain types of clients	Stimulus-specific
Heightened emotionality around certain types of clients	Stimulus-specific
Tendency toward overreaction to certain types of clients	Stimulus-specific
Stereotyped or predictable reaction to certain types of clients	Stimulus-specific, trait-specific
Overidentification with certain types of clients	Stimulus-specific, issue-specific
Sexual or romantic feelings for certain types of clients	Stimulus-specific, trait-specific
Sexual or romantic feelings for a particular client	Issue-specific, stimulus-specific, trait-specific
Overprotectiveness with certain types of clients	Stimulus-specific, trait-specific
Overprotectiveness with a particular client	Issue-specific, stimulus-specific, trait-specific
Desire for a social relationship with certain types of clients	Stimulus-specific, trait-specific
Desire for a social relationship with a particular client	Issue-specific, stimulus-specific, trait-specific
Rejection of a particular client	Issue-specific, stimulus-specific, trait-specific
Seeking of or need for approval or admiration from clients	Trait-specific
Advice-giving or directing clients	Trait-specific
Encouragement of dependence	Trait-specific
Paternalism or fostering of inequality between client and clinician	Trait-specific

Issue-Specific Countertransference

Issue-specific countertransference arises as a reaction resulting from the stimulation of unexplored (unaware or unconscious) aspects of the clinician in response to specific behaviors, feelings, and needs expressed by a client. In other words, the clinician's reactions to a client's issues are flavored by personal needs, attitudes, values, beliefs, or traits that the clinician is generally not aware of. This reaction is often referred to as unresolved conflicts of the clinician (for example, Corey, Corey, and Callanan, 1998). For instance, a therapist who has anxieties about sexuality may be particularly threatened and may respond negatively to the discussion of sexual issues by a young client, especially if that client has learned and incorporated seductive behaviors. Another therapist who is free of unconscious sexual values or beliefs may respond to the same client in an entirely different manner. Such clinicians may be entirely capable of treating other clients, that is, those clients who do not present with issues that tap into a clinician's own personal (unconscious) needs, beliefs, and attitudes. A clinician's success with some clients does not justify failure to resolve unexplored areas of self that can get in the way of counseling or therapy because of their likelihood to pop up in a countertransferential manner. The crux of this type of countertransference is the coincidental and unfortunate coming together of a counselor's and client's issues that are incompatible, too similar, or too threatening. When mental-health-care providers begin to realize that certain topics or issues stimulate heightened feelings or specific reactions on their part, it behooves them to seek some guidance in trying to figure out what is creating their excessive or inappropriate response. Self-exploration and consultation are helpful avenues to pursue in this regard.

Stimulus-Specific Countertransference

A second type of countertransference has been labeled stimulus-specific countertransference. In this case, the reaction is not stimulated by a client's expressed therapy issues, but rather arises in response to an external or personality feature in the client that stimulates material in the clinician that is irrelevant to the client's presenting concerns. In fact, any individual, client or not, would stimulate this (over)reaction in the mental-health-care provider. For instance, clinicians with yet-to-be-explored issues around sibling rivalry with a brother may respond inappropriately or inexplicably to all male clients who remind them of this brother. Stimulus-specific countertransference reactions are usually to blame if a clinician (or anyone for that matter) reacts inappropriately to all clients or human beings who share a particular physical, psychological, or emotional trait (such as excessive weight, a particular skin color, or a stern demeanor) because that stimulus taps into (unconscious) emotions or beliefs in the clinician that have not been adequately explored. The crux of this countertransference is the therapist's unconscious and immediate reaction to an external stimulus that is independent of the client's treatment needs or presenting concerns.

Trait-Specific Countertransference

Trait-specific countertransference is even more global and has also been referred to as a clinician's "habitual modes of relating" (Sandler, 1975, p. 415, as quoted in Bernstein and Glenn, 1988, p. 226), or the care provider's "expression of character traits" (Lilleskov, 1971, p. 404, as quoted in Bernstein and Glenn, 1988, p. 226). This type of countertransference reaction implies that clinicians respond to clients as they tend to respond to anyone at any time in their life. For instance, a therapist with rigid morals, who tends to be condescending and judgmental in general, will bring this attitude into the treatment room. Clearly, such an habitual way of relating is dangerous as it not only is automatic and unconscious, but will potentially and profoundly influence the clinician's therapeutic work with any client, regardless of issues presented or stimuli expressed. Trait-specific countertransferences not uncommonly arise out of the various motivations of clinicians to seek a career in mental health (see above). For example, if a clinician is motivated by the need to control and influence, a likely trait-specific countertransference is a controlling and advice-giving therapeutic stance. This clinician is likely to attempt to exert control in all relationships, including those with significant others, friends, and clients. A clinician who is motivated by the desire to help, on the other hand, will likely evidence a caregiver, enabler, or rescuer countertransference, again generally, not only in relationships with clients, but in most if not all interpersonal settings. The crux of this type of countertransference is the mental-health-care provider's habit-driven, characteristic manner of relating to all people in many if not all contexts, including the therapy or counseling setting. The clinician's lack of awareness about this interpersonal style and habitual self-expression allows the treatment to become distorted and driven by clinician, not client, needs.

Client-Specific Countertransference

Client-specific countertransference is a reaction in the clinician to a client that occurs only with that client. In fact, if the clinician begins to explore the client's relationships, it often becomes evident that the client elicits this or a similar reaction in most, if not all, adult relationships. The reason this type of countertransference is included as a countertransference at all is the reality that in the past any emotional reaction on the part of a clinician was considered unusual (even inappropriate). It has since been recognized that reactions in clinicians to clients can be useful therapeutic tools as long as the clinician is aware of the reaction and can understand it as being specific to the client. It is critical for clinicians to explore whether their reaction is genuinely stimulated by a pattern in the client—or by one of the three prior types of countertransferences discussed thus far. The best way to double-check this is to carefully explore what

Skill Development Recommendations

Recommendation 1-3   *Using Table 1-3, evaluate yourself on each of the listed traits, thinking about feedback you have received about yourself in a variety of interpersonal settings. Also, interview someone close to you about his or her perceptions of you with regard to each of these traits. Pick this person carefully for their honesty, good will, and knowledge of you.*

types of reactions the client tends to elicit in others. If a similar pattern emerges, most likely a true client-specific countertransference is taking place. If the client reports no such reactions in others, the clinician needs to explore whether a countertransference based on issue, trait, or stimulus better explains the reaction. If this is the case, the clinician will most likely note a similar reaction with other clients; in other words, the pattern follows the clinician, not the client.

To give an example of a client-specific countertransference, a very oppositional and demanding client with poor self-esteem and strong attention-seeking behavior may overwhelm and alienate adults after prolonged contact. The mental-health-care provider may experience the same frustration in sessions that others encounter with the client outside of counseling. Hence, this reaction is not due to the clinician's lack of self-awareness, but rather is specific to the client's behavior. The crux of this countertransference is the client's eliciting of a consistent (for example, negative or protective) response from the environment, shared by the clinician.

Client-specific countertransference, unlike the other types, provides the self-aware clinician with added insight and empathy about the client. Such a countertransference reaction can be used therapeutically and purposefully with the client. It provides information about the client and can provide excellent feedback about the client's impact on the environment, as well as providing information about why this client elicits a similar response in so many contexts. It provides insight regarding target behaviors of the client that may need to be modified quickly to help the client improve interpersonal relationships.

THE NEXT STEP: NECESSARY SKILLS FOR MENTAL-HEALTH PRACTICE

This chapter has outlined the great importance of taking stock of personal issues that may enter into the decision to make a career in the mental-health field and that may influence actual professional practice once a clinician works with clients. Self-awareness clearly is the key to success. It is therefore critical that clinicians learn self-awareness skills during their graduate education. Self-awareness skills can be conceptualized rather broadly as including

- individual self-awareness (addressing issues such as personal traits, values, attitudes, and beliefs)
- interpersonal self-awareness (addressing issues such as needs in relationships and effects on others)
- cultural self-awareness (addressing issues such as prejudice, bias, and stereotyping)
- physical self-awareness (addressing issues such as body language, nonverbal communication, and voice quality)
- professional self-awareness (addressing issues such as learning skills and strategies, choosing skills and strategies, and individualizing counseling or therapy to client needs)

Self-awareness skills defined in such a manner comprise the full spectrum of skills that are the basis of counseling and therapy. They range from the personal to the professional and include not only personal self-exploration, but also professional development and learning. Even the necessary communication and therapeutic or counseling skills that will ensure success with a wide range of clients can be conceptualized as being part of developing self-awareness. The remainder of this book concerns itself with assisting students in the mental-health field to acquire self-awareness skills in all personal and professional areas relevant to the practice of counseling and therapy.

Chapter One served to set the reader on the path of personal self-exploration by asking her or him to take a look at individual traits and countertransferences. Chapter Two continues the work on the development of individual self-awareness skills, but also addresses interpersonal and cultural self-awareness. In that context, it will raise issues such as values clarification and development of cultural competence. Chapter Three will address preventive self-care, an important aspect of individual self-awareness training and an excellent means of impairment prevention.

The remainder of the book will deal with physical and professional self-awareness. Part Two begins this process through exploration of physical self-awareness and will be devoted to communications skills. These chapters will address issues such as attending and listening skills; nonverbal communication; enhancing communication and data gathering through the skilled use of questions; and facilitating self-disclosure through encouragers, restatements, paraphrases, reflections, and summarization. Part Two ends with a discussion of empathy, the bridge between simple communication skills and skills that encourage growth and healing.

The third part of the book concludes the professional self-awareness development process by concerning itself with the creation of insight or cognitive

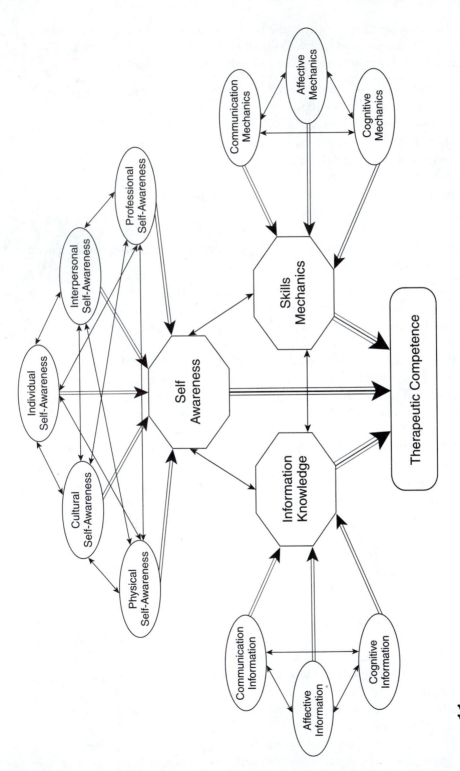

FIGURE 1-1

Diagram of Therapeutic Competence

self-awareness in clients. Topics will include an overview of types of cognitive interventions to use and a variety of strategies ranging from simple imparting of information to complex cognitive interventions that require great cognitive flexibility on the part of the clinician.

The fourth part of the book, continuing the development of professional self-awareness, will deal with facilitating affective self-awareness in clients. These chapters will present issues such as recognizing what level of affective intervention is needed, empathy as a process and its specific application, and a variety of exercises that can be used with clients to help them work with feelings, moods, and emotions. Before moving on to the next chapter, it is recommended that readers thoroughly review and engage in the Skill Development Recommendations.

In summary, therapeutic competence is a combination of self-awareness, knowledge, and application of skills. Self-awareness reflects the personal aspect the clinician brings to the therapeutic encounter. Knowledge is comprised of the wealth of information the mental-health-care provider accumulates through education and training. Application of skills refers to the translation of awareness and knowledge into action. All three aspects of therapeutic competence have to be attended to, for successful counseling or therapy to take place. Ignoring the personal aspects by not engaging in self-exploration and introspection can allow knowledge to be undermined by automatic reactions that make the application of information less than skillful. On the other hand, self-awareness alone does not suffice to make a good clinician. Knowledge and information are essential for the mental-health-care provider to know what to do when and why. Practicing interventions and strategies contributes to skill development. However, the simple carrying-out of skills in a mechanical or uninformed way, that is, in a manner that is informed neither by self-awareness nor knowledge, will leave the client feeling less than cared for. Competence thus defined can be diagrammed as shown in Figure 1-1 and represents the foundation of this text.

CHAPTER 2

SELF-AWARENESS SKILLS

2

Self-knowledge is an anchor that makes
unpredictability tolerable.

Deepak Chopra

Work with clients in counseling or therapy can be enjoyable and rewarding as
well as taxing and exhausting. This chapter explores how counselors and therapists can develop self-exploration and introspection skills that can facilitate
good therapeutic rapport and clear understanding of the process that unfolds
between client and clinician. First, attention is focused on exploring values that
clinicians endorse personally and professionally, to show how values enter
treatment and the therapeutic relationship. Awareness of personal values is
crucial to recognizing when they may distort—or enhance—what transpires
between client and clinician. Attention then turns to an exploration of cultural sensitivity and competence. Counselors and therapists need to have
knowledge about, awareness of, and skills for culturally competent and sensitive practice, given that in today's world many clients differ in background from
their mental-health-care provider. These differences are not only ethnic or
racial, but also include a diversity of other cultural backgrounds that will be
dealt with in this discussion. Once values have been clarified and cultural competence has been developed, mental-health-care providers are in a much better place to begin work with clients in a manner less likely to reflect biases or
countertransferences.

Developing individual and interpersonal self-awareness is not an easy task.
It requires openness and willingness to find out less than flattering facts about
the self, both personally and in relationships. Creating self-awareness can be uncomfortable, can result in self-consciousness and self-doubt, and may lead to
inhibition and pain (Sommers-Flanagan and Sommers-Flanagan, 1999). Fortunately, these negative effects of self-exploration are temporary and lead to positive outcomes that will benefit both clinician and client. As pointed out in Chap-

ter One, self-awareness needs to be sought in at least five areas: individual, interpersonal, cultural, physical, and professional. The issues relevant to individual, interpersonal, and cultural functioning usually involve preexisting clinician traits. As defined in Chapter One, traits preexist, while skills need to be developed. As such, the self-awareness work in these three realms involves exploration of existing counselor or therapist characteristics, a process that has been referred to as values clarification. The issues relevant to physical and professional self-awareness generally involve skills that have to do with communication (verbal and nonverbal) and intervention strategies in counseling and therapy. As such, they require not so much a process of clarification as of learning (of course all learning also involves some component of clarification or exploration). This chapter concerns itself with exploration of traits, though it will also make some suggestions for new learning, especially in the realm of cultural self-awareness.

VALUES CLARIFICATION

Ethical, professional, moral, and legal behavior presupposes that clinicians are individually and interpersonally self-aware, knowledgeable, open-minded, and well informed. "Counselors are required to distinguish their personal moral codes from and reconcile them with the profession's values to behave in an ethical manner" (Cottone and Tarvydas, 1998, p. 123). Being able to do so clearly hinges on exploring and identifying personal values that underlie one's moral beliefs. Perhaps some definitions are in order first. *Morals* refer to an individual's beliefs about what is good or bad behavior. They are standards used as guides for conduct, especially in social contexts (Steinman, Richardson, and McEnroe, 1998). They reflect the individual's "perspectives of right and proper conduct" (Corey, Corey, and Callanan, 1998, p. 3), and are usually grounded in the standards of a broader cultural group (including religious groups). *Values*, on the other hand, are less social, and more individually formed and based. They are the "beliefs and attitudes that provide direction in everyday living" (Corey, Corey, and Callanan, 1998, p. 3), and reflect priority systems people use to guide their personal decision making and choices (Steinman, Richardson, and McEnroe, 1998). *Ethics* reflect "beliefs . . . about what constitutes right conduct" (Corey, Corey, and Callanan, 1998, p. 3), based on an understanding of a set of guidelines or an ethical code, often developed by a professional group to guide professional behavior. A code of ethics judges human actions based on a hierarchy of values that makes the evaluation of behavioral choices supposedly objective and rational (as opposed to morals, which are personal and less than objective or rational; Cottone and Tarvydas, 1998). Laws arise from the morals of a social system or cultural group; professionalism reflects right conduct given a profession's requirements and parameters. Thus, values are personally, morals are socially, laws are societally, and ethics are professionally based. Values, morals, ethics, laws, and professionalism interact and at times can require the same outcome or render the same evaluation. However, behavior can also be ethical or legal yet unprofessional (for example, lateness to sessions by a clinician is unprofessional but not unethical or illegal); legal but not ethical (accepting large gifts from clients may be legal, but it is neither ethical nor professional); rooted in personal values or social mores, but not ethical (creating client dependency on the clinician may be personally preferred by the clinician, perhaps even condoned by the culture, but is not ethical); and so forth.

To make ethical, legal, and professional decisions, counselors and therapists not only have to be aware of and knowledgeable about the codes of conduct that regulate their profession, but also about their personal values and socially based morals. A thorough discussion of the ethical standards developed by the various associations of the mental-health professions, such as the National Association of Social Workers, the American Psychological Association, and the American Counseling Association, is beyond the scope of this book. This issue has been dealt with in a variety of texts, including those by Anderson (1996); Canter, Bennett, Jones, and Nagy (1994); Corey, Corey, and Callanan (1998); Cottone and Tarvydas (1998); Herlihy and Corey (1992, 1996); Steinman, Richardson, and McEnroe (1998); and Swenson (1997); and through the ethical codes established by the relevant professional associations (American Psychological Association [APA, 1992]; National Association of Social Workers [NASW, 1993]; American Counseling Association [ACA, 1995]). What will be provided below is a general review of the moral principles that underlie most if not all ethical codes, and a discussion of how personal values relate to these issues. This is followed by suggestions on how clinicians can gain the necessary individual and interpersonal self-awareness to behave ethically, professionally, and legally.

Mandatory Versus Aspirational Ethics

Many ethical guidelines are actually documents that contain within them two sets of ethics: mandatory ethics and aspirational ethics. Mandatory ethics are much easier to deal with as they are usually relatively clear in their application, strictly enforced, have clear consequences for violation, and are written in such a way that all mental-health-care providers for whom the ethical guidelines are written must comply with them. Mandatory ethics are often called a standard of practice; they may be incorporated into a profession's ethical guidelines or may be presented in a separate document. An example of a mandatory ethic that cuts across all ethical guidelines of the mental-health professions is the prohibition against sexual relationships with clients. This is a clear guideline with no gray area: Sex with current clients is forbidden and will carry consequences for the provider who violates this mandatory ethic. Aspirational ethics represent the ideal professional behavior. They describe optimal practice, the best possible standard for behavior among the mental-health-care providers within a given profession. These ethics are not mandatory and have many more gray areas. Violation or noncompliance may be more difficult to establish, and because of this difficulty enforcement is not a given. An example of an aspirational ethic that is found in all ethical guidelines for mental-health-care providers is the provision of pro bono services. All professions appear to suggest that their providers provide some of their service on a sliding-fee scale or at no cost to needy clients. This aspirational ethic is an ideal, a standard that is difficult to enforce. A provider who has not or is not currently providing pro bono service is generally not vulnerable to a charge of ethical violation.

If personal values lead a practitioner to violate a standard of practice (mandatory ethics), the consequences are generally clear and enforced. The violation of aspirational ethics, on the other hand, bearing no clear and direct consequences in many instances (though they will in some), is thus often left to the individual practitioner to determine and rectify. It is in the area of aspirational ethics that personal values and morals enter most profoundly. Only excellent self-monitoring and self-awareness may keep clinicians on the path of remaining true to the aspirational ethics of the profession. For example, clinicians may need to evaluate regularly their purposes in keeping some clients in treatment for longer periods than others. Should they realize that clients who pay more or who have better third-party reimbursement tend to have more sessions, it will strictly be clinicians' personal values that will steer them back on the correct path. The decision making process regarding ethical behavior (mandatory and aspirational) is based on six moral principles that become most useful in evaluating gray areas of conduct. They are autonomy, beneficence, nonmaleficence, justice, fidelity, and veracity (the latter two are sometimes collapsed into one and referred to simply as fidelity).

Autonomy refers to the clinician's willingness to honor the right of individuals to make their own decisions. This principle is occasionally translated as self-determination, individualism, or independence (for example, Corey, Corey, and Callanan, 1998). However, the better understanding truly has to do with free choice, the right to decide one's own fate, and to choose one's own life direction. This right suggests that independence or individualism does not have to be the choice, that is, this definition is more culturally sensitive in that it allows clients the autonomy to decide not to be autonomous. The main issue from the clinician's perspective about autonomy as an ethical principle is that the client has the right to choose and the clinician does not make determinations for the client about the direction of treatment or the nature of the solutions.

Beneficence refers to the commitment to do good to others. This principle speaks to the promotion of clients' welfare, dignity, and respect. It is concerned with assuring that the goals set in treatment, the strategies chosen for intervention, and the outcomes achieved are for the good of the client. This is a highly individualized principle in that what is for the good of one client may not be for the good of another. One example of this specificity or tailoring of treatment to the welfare of the client occurred in Alaska several years ago. As part of a master's thesis, a trainee set out to teach assertiveness skills in the schools in Anchorage. Assertiveness training is generally thought of as being good for clients; it reflects a value that is highly regarded in Western society. However, Anchorage has a diverse ethnic population, and Alaska Native culture has a different standard for assertiveness, especially in the home. The Alaska Native students exposed to assertiveness training through this trainee's program began reporting greater trouble at home and their parents were not pleased. The skills taught, which truly were for the good of the European American and African American students in the classroom, were not for the good of the Alaska Native pupils. Thus, beneficence has to be individually determined and assessed within the context of each client.

Nonmaleficence refers to the understanding that the utmost concern of the mental-health-care provider has to be to do no harm. Clearly related to beneficence, it nevertheless deserves separate mention and definition. Doing no harm refers to intentional or purposeful behaviors and interventions as well as unintentional ones. Nonmaleficence implies that clinicians need to be respectful of their clients, need to consider cultural differences and expectations, need to take into account individual differences and needs, and need to tailor treatment idiosyncratically to the unique presentation of each client. One example of an unintentional, thoughtless violation of the principle of nonmaleficence is the inappropriate (less than sensitive) use of diagnostic labels. Diagnoses can profoundly affect clients' perception of self and may label them inappropriately for many years to come. The misuse of diagnostic labels has been pointed out repeatedly in the literature, especially with regard to inappropriate diagnostic labeling of non-White ethnic groups (see Brems, 1999).

Justice refers to the fair and equal treatment of and access to services for all clients. Also called distributional justice, this principle requires nondiscrimination in service delivery, fairness in eligibility criteria, and equal distribution of resources across actual and potential clientele. It is this principle that drives consideration in professional codes for pro bono work with needy clients who would otherwise not be able to receive services. It is also this principle that underlies demands for flexible clinic hours and interventions tailored to the individual, social, socioeconomic, and cultural circumstances of all clients. Equal access, equal treatment, and fairness are the essence of this principle.

Fidelity refers to honesty, loyalty, and the commitment to keep promises. According to this principle, the work of clinician and client represents a social contract that must be honored by the clinician. The counselor must uphold all promises made within this contract and must honor all commitments. Much of what is promised in the clinician-client relationship is spelled out in the informed consent signed by the client at the beginning of treatment. Given that this informed consent is a binding social contract, it is the clinician's responsibility to follow through on any promises and commitments outlined in this document. Fidelity most specifically refers to aspects of the informed consent that are not legally based (veracity covers those; see below). As such, it relates to issues such as what to expect from treatment (for example, how often do client and counselor meet, for how long each time, what is the average cost), risks and benefits (for example, improved relationships, feeling better, possible changes in relationships), and procedural issues of the clinic (for example, video- or audiotaping, payment schedule, record-handling). Trust in the therapeutic relationship is based on this principle of fidelity. Only when the therapist is trustworthy is the client able to trust the therapist sufficiently to reveal painful life stories and work on personally painful and sensitive issues.

Veracity refers to the legal aspects of mental-health care and to the honoring of all contracts made with clients. It addresses issues of confidentiality, limits to confidentiality, release of information, legal aspects of record keeping, legal aspects of payment arrangements, third-party-reimbursement issues, and similar legally based concerns. In inpatient settings, veracity also is the principle that underlies least-restrictive-treatment alternatives as well as regulating medication rules when clients refuse this route of treatment. Veracity thus assures that the legal rights of clients are respected and granted. Most clinics and hospitals have brochures that spell out the legal rights of clients. Veracity is granted to clients as long as the items in such brochures and in the informed consent are respected by the institution. Clearly, fidelity and veracity are related; violation of either will have a negative impact upon the clinician-client relationship in that the client will feel violated and will perceive the clinician as less than trustworthy.

Individual Self-Awareness

How a clinician views and applies the six ethical or moral principles is obviously going to be guided by personal values, beliefs, attitudes, and interpretations and hence requires good individual self-awareness. As indicated above, values guide personal preferences and decision making; they reflect an individual's feelings or attitudes about something and translate into preferred actions or behaviors. Rokeach, one of the early and foremost researchers into values, defined them as "an enduring belief that a specific mode of conduct or end-state of existence is personally or socially preferable to an opposite or converse mode of conduct or end-state of existence" (1973, p. 5). However, a value is often actually comprised of more than a simple preference or one single belief but rather is made up of a complex set of beliefs that affect choices from at least one of three perspectives: evaluative, emotional, and existential. Evaluation refers to a judgment of right versus wrong or good versus bad. It is related to morality in that sense. It is important to note, however, that although values and morality influence each other, they are not the same. Some values can be intensely moral (that is, driven by the evaluative perspective), whereas others reflect choices that have nothing to do with morality. For example, an individual chooses a vegan lifestyle for moral (evaluative) reasons if the choice is based upon a belief that veganism protects the environment and the rights of animals; it is not based on a moral decision if the choice is made strictly due to the belief that this lifestyle is more conducive to the health of the individual. Obviously, in many cases values such as this one reflect a combination of reasons, leading the discussion to a definition of the emotional and existential dimensions of values.

The emotional dimension refers to decisions based on whether the choice helps the individual feel positive rather than negative emotions. For example, a clinician may choose a location for a practice based on where she or he feels better. A sunny southern-exposure office may be chosen over a different locale because the clinician enjoys the sunlight pouring into the therapy office. This decision may be made even though the office is on the third floor and has no elevator. Such a location is in violation of the Americans with Disabilities Act and may well reflect a choice that is unethical according to some professional ethical codes. In other words, the value, if it were based on the evaluative dimension, would be bad, not good. Finally, the existential dimension of values or preferences refers to the likelihood of the choice creating meaning for the decision maker. Often clinicians have made the choice to pursue a career in the mental-health professions because they hope that this professional path will lead to a meaningful life. The decision has less to do with whether it is the right or wrong choice from a moral perspective, and may not even involve a conscious emotional dimension, though it is likely that the clinician will also feel good as a result of the work.

It is clear at this juncture that values are intensely personal and are driven by highly idiosyncratic perceptions of reality and backgrounds. Values develop in a social, cultural, socioeconomic, and even geographical context. They are profoundly influenced by parents, families, communities, cultural groups, religious affiliations, societal forces, friends, mentors; the list goes on. They reflect the individual's worldview that grew out of these experiences and influences, as well as the person's philosophy about life and understanding of the world. The more similar two individuals' life experiences are, the more similar their values will be. This includes client and clinician: If client and clinician have highly dissimilar backgrounds, chances are that they will also hold dissimilar values. Research has shown that client-clinician value similarity leads to better and faster treatment outcomes (Cottone and Tarvydas, 1998). This finding suggests that dissimilar values can hinder or slow treatment. However, in all likelihood this is true only for dissimilar values of which the clinician is not aware. An excellent means of keeping values dissimilarity from adversely affecting treatment is the process of values clarification, or the exploration and achievement of individual self-awareness.

Individual self-awareness about values is important because clinicians cannot hide their values from their clients. Values are reflected in too many ways, including nonverbal behavior, office setup, location, and dress. Even choice of theoretical orientation reflects values. For example, choice of Adlerian intervention reflects a value of social interest and social striving; reality therapy is based on a value system of individual responsibility and quality of the individual lifestyle; rational emotive therapy values the rational; existential treatment is based on values of self-determination and freedom with responsibility (Cottone and Tarvydas, 1998). It is for this reason that some writers endorse including a clinician's theoretical orientation and its meaning in the informed consent (for example, Cottone and Tarvydas, 1998). Clients are exposed to clinician values at all times, in subtle and not so subtle ways. Values will enter treatment through numerous subtle and obvious routes, including through the clinician's language, differing responses to various client statements, pushing of agendas (also called indoctrination), failure to inform clients of alternatives to suggested solutions or interventions, imposition of personal views, and others. Values also affect all aspects of treatment, including data collection, diagnosis, treatment planning, relationship and rapport, goal setting, perceptions of solutions, choices of topics in session, selection of intervention strategies, differential reinforcement of clients, messages of agreement and disagreement with the client, termination decisions, and more. Only through self-awareness and self-exploration will individual clinicians be able to identify how their values enter all of these interactions and processes.

Identifying personal values that may or may not be relevant to treatment is a difficult process. Research has indicated that, in general, mental-health-care providers share belief in the following rights and responsibilities of clients (Cottone and Tarvydas, 1998):

- the right to personal freedom
- responsibility toward others
- responsibility for personal decision making within the confines of capacity
- the right to respect for their individuality
- the right not to be dominated, manipulated, or indoctrinated
- the right to make and learn from their own mistakes

An exploration of personal values can begin there, but must not end there. An infinite array of values may enter the client-therapist relationship. Additionally, there is an infinite array of choices that at first glance would not appear to have an impact on the professional relationship. Even some of these, however, may at times and in subtle ways influence therapeutic rapport. For example, on the surface, it would appear that a choice of owning a cat should not in any way become an issue in the treatment of a client. What if a client presents who hates cats, makes fun of people who own cats, has killed cats, and so on? How will the clinician react? This may seem like a silly example, but this is indeed how values can enter treatment in unexpected ways. Other values, choices, and preferences are much more likely to cause concerns; many of these are rooted in issues of religion or spirituality, sexuality, parenting, and similarly highly emotionally and morally charged topics. It is precisely these values that beg questions of whether clinicians should habitually refer certain clients, should work only with clients who share certain life experience, should work only with clients with similar backgrounds, and so forth. Each clinician will have to make personal choices about this. Following are some topics that tend to raise the issue of value similarity or difference between client and clinician. Knowing where the clinician stands with regard to these and similar topics will help in the decision making process about what to do with a client who holds opposing values.

Common Therapy and Counseling Topics That Involve Values:

- abortion
- alternative health care choices
- animal rights
- assisted suicide
- birth control choices
- career choices
- child abuse
- child neglect
- childlessness by choice
- conduct vis-à-vis authority figures
- criminal activity
- death and dying
- dietary choices
- disrespect of others
- domestic violence
- elder abuse
- educational aspirations
- gang membership
- health care choices
- infertility
- issues of power in intimate relationships
- marriage and cohabitation
- organized religion
- parenting
- personal responsibility
- politics
- premarital sex
- racism, sexism, other -isms
- religious practices
- religious preferences
- sexual orientation
- sexual practices
- substance use—legal drugs
- substance use—illegal drugs
- suicide
- traditional sex role orientation
- unsafe sex practices
- weight and weight loss
- working parents

Many other personal values need to be clarified in the clinician's mind before working with clients. The values clarification process begins with an exploration of areas where values enter, which is in virtually all aspects of human life. Once areas and options have been explored, choices are made about which values to endorse. Of course, this is not a static process. People have the right to change their minds and opinions about matters. However, it is important at least to think about where a clinician seems to stand at this moment in time. If no firm stand is taken after careful deliberation, that is a stand as well. It merely implies that the clinician is undecided and will have to see how she or he will react when a given value comes up in treatment. Once choices about values have been made, the crucial third step in the process is to act in accordance. It is certainly admirable to have chosen a value, for example, of protecting and respecting all life. However, if the clinician then goes out and kills an animal and mounts the head to display on a wall, a certain level of incongruence has entered this person's life. In other words, once values have been explored and chosen, authentic living will require the clinician to live by these values. Not living by a value may make it so subtly present in a clinician's life that it is not recognized as a value and enters treatment inadvertently and in an unexplored manner. Having clarified and lived by certain values will help the clinician become quickly aware of those instances when clinician and client values conflict and may cause problems in the therapeutic relationship. There may be some values that will lead the clinician to make referrals if clients strongly endorse the opposite. For example, a mental-health-care provider who firmly believes in the sanctity of life and hence opposes all suicides would have great difficulty helping a client who enters therapy to prepare for an assisted suicide. Table 2-1 provides a few individual self-awareness areas that can be explored by trainees in an attempt to clarify their values. The items included are based on the thirty-six values identified by Rokeach (1973) as essential or central life values. Of these values, half represent terminal values, that is, values that are relevant to choices central to a person's end-state of existence; half represent instrumental values, that is, values relevant to choices about mode of conduct. For each instrumental value the clinician can clarify where on a continuum personal preference might fall. For example, the continuum for ambitious to unambitious could be broken into numerical subcategories ranging from *1 = very ambitious* to *7 = very unambitious* and levels of ambitiousness in between. It can be further broken down into topical subcategories such as ambitiousness in the context of work, family life, hobbies, housing, car selection, with level of ambition differing depending on the area of life to which it is applied. The listing in Table 2-1 is not to suggest that these are the only values clinicians need to clarify; it is merely included as an impetus or starting point for self-exploration.

TABLE 2-1	ROKEACH'S CENTRAL LIFE VALUES	
	Instrumental Values	**Terminal Values**
	Ambitious to Unambitious	Comfortable Life
	Broad-Minded to Narrow-Minded	Sense of Accomplishment
	Capable to Incapable	World at Peace
	Clean to Unclean	World of Beauty
	Courageous to Cowardly	Exciting Life
	Forgiving to Unforgiving	Equality
	Helpful to Unhelpful	Family Security
	Honest to Dishonest	Freedom
	Imaginative to Unimaginative	Health
	Independent to Dependent	Inner Harmony
	Intellectual to Nonintellectual	Maturity
	Logical to Illogical	National Security
	Loving to Unloving	Pleasure
	Loyal to Disloyal	Salvation
	Obedient to Disobedient	Self-Respect
	Polite to Impolite	Social Recognition
	Responsible to Irresponsible	True Friendship
	Self-Controlled to Impulsive	Wisdom

Interpersonal Self-Awareness

Once clarity about individual values has been gained to at least some degree, attention can be turned toward values that are implied and choices that are made in interpersonal contexts. Interpersonal self-awareness relates to all six of the moral or ethical principles outlined above (that is, autonomy, beneficence, and so on) in that all of these principles are clearly applied in an interpersonal context when related to counseling or therapy. The granting of autonomy may be affected by a mental-health-care provider's interpersonal stance of creating dependency. If creating dependency is a value of the clinician, it is likely that this value may be imposed on clients to the detriment of granting autonomy and self-determination. Similarly, thinking that the clinician always has all the answers in relationships and knows better than the client what needs to be done may result in violations of beneficence. Decisions may be made that are good for the client from the clinician's perspective but bad for the client given the client's preferences and familial or cultural context. An interpersonal stance

Skill Development Recommendations

Recommendation 2-1   *Using the list of therapy topics that invite value judgments, determine your stance on each. Then think about how you would feel about a client holding an opposite value. Given your reaction to such a client, what would be your best course of action (for example, referral, collaboration, supervision)?*

Recommendation 2-2   *Using Table 2-1, rate each instrumental value on a scale of 1 to 7 (as defined in above) and sort the terminal values in order of their importance to you. Look at your results. What do they suggest about how your values may hinder or support your career choices in the mental-health field?*

---

of distrust and lack of loyalty on the part of a clinician can affect fidelity and veracity in that this clinician may be less than truthful or reliable. Given that interpersonal beliefs, attitudes, and values can enter the ethical and professional relationship with clients, clinicians need to explore how they behave and what they prefer in relationships. A variety of interpersonal dynamics needs to be explored in this context to gain interpersonal self-awareness.

Some of the more important and obviously applicable interpersonal dynamics are listed in Table 2-2. These may not be the only interpersonal values that enter into the therapy relationship and into ethical decision making. However, they give the reader a starting point, as well as an idea about what kinds of interactions and patterns to explore. Many additional interpersonal values may emerge for a given counselor or therapist. These are best explored as they arise, either in therapeutic or other relationships. Their impact on how the clinician relates to a client needs to be evaluated as objectively as possible. Sometimes such objective evaluation may require the seeking out of a consultant or supervisor who can help the counselor realize blind spots. The reality is that every human being has developed a certain interpersonal style over a lifetime. This style is not static and continuously evolves as new experiences accumulate. How clinicians relate in their personal life will greatly influence or be mirrored by how they relate to their clients. A clinician who has problems with intimacy in life in general may have difficulty developing an empathic relationship with a client that feels sufficiently supportive and caring for the client to feel secure and willing to self-disclose. A counselor who is uncomfortable around people may communicate this interpersonal awkwardness to clients who in turn may feel as though they are causing the clinician discomfort and may search for the reasons within themselves. A therapist with poor social skills

TABLE
2-2

INTERPERSONAL PATTERNS TO EXPLORE TO GAIN INTERPERSONAL SELF-AWARENESS

Interpersonal Issue	Possible Patterns or Manifestations (excessive, insufficient, healthy)
Intimacy needs	Seeking excessive closeness; inability to establish intimate relationships; healthy capacity for intimacy
Need for approval from others	Excessive need for approval; indifference to others' level of approval; appreciation of approval from others but not dependent on it
Importance of relationships in life	Relationships unimportant; relationships the only priority; relationships ranked somewhere in the middle of the individual's list of priorities
Preoccupation with relationships	Thoughts dominated by occurrences in relationships; relationships and occurrence within them not given a second thought; relationships thought about to the extent necessary to keep them healthy and functional
Need for relationships	Inability to function outside of relationships; relationships dismissed as unnecessary to life; importance of relationships recognized without being incapacitated by their temporary absence
Level of trust	Inability to trust others; overly trusting and perhaps gullible; trusting within reasonable limits of exploration
Level of trustworthiness in relationships	Cannot be trusted because of violations of agreement and promises; always true to one's word even to the detriment of the self; generally trustworthy
Level of confidence in relationships	Self-doubt about own ability to relate well in intimate relationships; overly confident about being right and knowing what is best for relationships; confident that can remain healthy through collaboration relationships
Dependency needs	Excessively dependent to the point of not being able to function without the other; counterdependent denial of any interpersonal dependency needs; a balance of dependency needs and independence with mutuality in the relationship
Self-versus-other orientation in relationships	Preoccupied and concerned only with personal needs in relationships; preoccupied and concerned only about the needs of the relationship partner; aware of and concerned about the needs and wishes of both partners

Comfort with asking for help	Inability to ask for help under any circumstances; quick to ask for help without attempt to solve problems alone first; healthy balance of self-reliance and asking for assistance
Importance given to feedback from others	Dismisses feedback from relationship partners; overly concerned with and reactive to feedback; weighs feedback respectfully and carefully, then draws conclusions
Level of self-versus-other absorption	Completely self-absorbed and alienated; completely other-absorbed and overinvolved; able to shift focus as needed for healthy relating
Approach-avoidance behaviors	Approach only; avoidance only; some approach, some avoidance as appropriate to the circumstances
Level of value granted to relationships	Overvalues all relationships; undervalues all relationships; realistically values relationships on their individual merit
Social skills	Absence of social skills with lack of self-efficacy about social relating; sense of overconfidence in social skills; appropriate social skills
Comfort in new relationships	Uncomfortable and self-conscious around strangers; overly confident and boisterous around strangers; comfortable but appropriately cautious in new relationships
Center of attention	Needs to be the center or focus of attention in social settings; always shrinks from being the center or focus of attention in social settings because of embarrassment; can shift in and out of focus or center of attention as dictated by healthy social relating
Self-disclosure in relationships	Never self-discloses, even in intimate relationships where disclosure is appropriate; self-discloses prematurely and inappropriately in all relationships or relationships where disclosure is not appropriate; carefully discriminates where and when self-disclosure is appropriate
Emotional expressiveness in relationships	Never expresses affect or tenderness; overly emotional and sympathetic in all relationships; can discriminate when and with whom expression of affect is appropriate and necessary
Identification with others	Overidentifies with everyone by losing sense of separate identity; stays entirely distanced, never being able to relate to anyone's experience; identifies as appropriate and fitting, and tailors expression to situation
Conflict with authority figures	Oppositional with and dismissive of superiors or perceived authority figures; overly submissive and guided by real or perceived authority figures; respectful of authority without compromising personal values and ethics
Stance toward equality in relationships	Always seeks to be one-up and in charge; always feels inferior and compelled to be one-down; views all humans as equal

may be unsuccessful in establishing therapeutic rapport not because of insufficient caring or empathy, but because of interpersonal mannerisms that are offensive or uncomfortable for the client.

The first step in developing interpersonal self-awareness is to recognize what interpersonal patterns are possible; Table 2-2 will help the clinician get started with this step. The second step has to do with identifying how, in each category of relating, the counselor or therapist actually behaves in relationships. Table 2-2 provides possible patterns for each interpersonal issue, providing the pattern first as it may manifest if there is an over-expression, then an under-expression, and finally a healthy expression of a given trait. Third, the mental-health-care provider then has to evaluate how this pattern of behavior may affect clients and influence the therapeutic relationship. Fourth, choices may need to be made to alter certain interpersonal patterns before beginning to engage in counseling or therapy. If such alterations are necessary, it will behoove the clinician to seek out personal counseling or therapy for some assistance.

CULTURAL COMPETENCE AND SENSITIVITY

All mental-health-care providers must develop cultural self-awareness. Development of cultural self-awareness requires clinicians to evaluate their level of cultural sensitivity and competence, that is, their perceptions of and attitudes about other cultural groups. In fact, gaining the skills and knowledge necessary to deal with a racially, ethnically, and culturally diverse clientele, through introspection and learning, is deemed as important to a clinician's education as gaining the basic skills and knowledge of counseling or therapy (Iijima Hall, 1997). Perhaps the best place to start is by looking at how a cultural group is defined. Traditionally, when members of society think of cultural groups, they think of labels such as race and ethnicity. Culture, however, is actually a broader term that is inclusive of more groupings than those based on race and ethnicity.

In thinking about cultural diversity, the term *race* is often used. *Race,* however, refers strictly to a biological classification that is based on physical and genetic characteristics, with only three primary races identified, namely, Caucasoid, Mongoloid, and Negroid. *Ethnicity,* a slightly more inclusive label, refers to a shared social and cultural heritage as may be identified, for example, for Asian Americans or Alaska Natives. Clearly many more than three groups exist that would fit this definition. *Culture,* the broadest term, refers to any group that shares and transmits within it a certain set of values, beliefs, and/or learned behaviors. Such transmission can occur across generations through the teaching, both advertent and inadvertent, of shared values and rules, or can be conducted purposefully and planfully with new members, as occurs in gay and lesbian cultures. For example, members of the Jewish faith constitute an ethnic group with a shared social, cultural, and religious heritage; however, they do not constitute a race. Within the Jewish faith, a number of cultural subgroups may exist depending on the level of orthodoxy of their religious beliefs and practices. Similarly, White members of society constitute an ethnic group that has a number of cultures (or cultural subgroups) within it, such as Irish Americans, Italian Americans, German Americans, and so forth, each of which shares a learned set of values, attitudes, beliefs, or behaviors.

In other words, race breaks down further to ethnicity, which in turn may cross racial boundaries (for example, a Native American individual who has a biological race combining Mongoloid and Negroid). Similarly, ethnicity breaks down further into cultures, which in turn may cross ethnic boundaries (for example, a gay individual who has an African American and Alaska Native ethnic identification). Individuals can belong to several cultural groups at once (for example, one may be upper-middle class, Caribbean African American, and physically challenged), they may have varied ethnic backgrounds and identify with more than one ethnic group (for example, a person may be Italian American and Navajo, identifying primarily with a Navajo upbringing but also incorporating Italian American values), and they may be biologically racially mixed (for example, an individual may have one Caucasoid and one Negroid parent). In fact, in modern society, most clients will have such multiple identifications and diverse backgrounds. Clearly, race, ethnicity, and culture are not identifiable by looking at the outside of a person or even at easily observed behaviors, an assumption often made in day-to-day life. To understand a client's racial, ethnic, and cultural identity, careful questioning is needed to assess that person's identification and perception. The group with which the client identifies most (in which the client claims heritage) becomes that individual's reference group and will have the strongest impact with regard to having shaped behaviors, attitudes, and values (Phinney, 1996).

Although ethnic or cultural status often overlaps with minority status of a group of people, this is not always so. Minority status as relevant in the counseling or therapy context has nothing to do with the actual number of people within a specific group. Instead, a minority group has been most fittingly defined as

> A group of people who, because of physical or cultural characteristics, are singled out from others in the society in which they live for differential and unequal treatment, and who therefore regard themselves as objects of collective discrimination. . . . Minority status carries with it the exclusion from full participation in the life of the society (Wirth, 1945, p. 347).

This definition characterizes a number of groups in American society who experience oppression and, as a result, are not able to participate fully in society as a whole. It also separates the conceptual identification of what constitutes a minority from the numerical concept. For example, in many countries, women suffer oppression at the hands of males, rendering them a conceptual

minority, despite the fact that they are a numerical majority. Using this definition, other minorities may include individuals with physical disabilities, the el-
derly, gays and lesbians, and individuals who are economically disadvantaged,
depending on whether, as a cultural group, they perceive themselves as receiving differential or unequal treatment. Thus, clinicians in a culturally diverse society work not only with individuals who are diverse in terms of their ethnic or
cultural backgrounds, but possibly also in terms of other avenues of oppression.

In recognition of the diversity of the population inside and outside of the
United States and the need to provide adequate and appropriate mental-health
services to all ethnic, cultural, and minority members of a given society, the
American Psychological Association, the American Counseling Association,
and the National Association for Social Workers, along with other professional
organizations, have expressed strong support of the need for mental-health-
care providers to be culturally sensitive, and for training programs to help meet
this need. For example, the American Psychological Association's ethical guidelines clearly state that "psychologists are aware of cultural, individual, and role
differences, including those due to age, gender, race, ethnicity, national origin, religion, sexual orientation, disability, language, and socioeconomic status"
(American Psychological Association, 1992, p. 1599). Similarly, the need for in-
clusion of cultural issues in the training of all therapists was advanced by the
National Conference on Graduate Education in Psychology (American Psychological Association, 1987) when this committee stated that "psychologists must
be educated to realize that all training, practice, and research in psychology are
profoundly affected by the cultural, subcultural, and national contexts within
which they occur" (p. 1079). Obviously then, there is growing pressure from
professional organizations, as well as from individual practitioners, for therapists to become culturally sensitive to meet the needs of a culturally diverse
population and clientele (cf., Iijima Hall, 1997; Ponterotto, Casas, Suzuki, and
Alexander, 1995).

Cultural sensitivity and competence are developed through introspective
work and require a great deal of self-exploration and personal openness on the
part of the developing mental-health-care professional (Singelis, 1998). This
effort is not only worthwhile but also meets the spirit of contemporary professional ethical codes for the mental-health professions. It is best applied toward
the development of cultural competence that has three major components: cultural awareness, cultural knowledge, and cultural skills. Simply put, cultural
awareness is gained through self-reflection and respect for others, as well as
through the strong recognition of and belief in the notion that difference does
not equal deviance (Namyniuk, 1996); cultural knowledge can be accumulated
via familiarization with cultural, anthropological, historical, and related events
involving or affecting all cultural and ethnic groups with whom a clinician anticipates working (cf., chaps. 5–9 in Ponterotto, Casas, Suzuki, and Alexander,
1995); and cultural skill is developed through learning about alternative ap-

proaches to intervention, reduction in prejudicial or stereotyped use of language, and political activism (Ivey, 1995). Clinicians who strive to be culturally sensitive and competent need to be able to claim all three of these traits as a part of their repertoire of skills and beliefs. Entire books have been written to help mental-health-care providers develop these sensitivities (for example, Hogan-Garcia, 1999; McGrath and Axelson, 1993; Singelis, 1998). Each of the three categories deserves further exploration, and an overview is provided in Table 2-3 (adapted from Johnson, 1993).

It is worth noting that cultural sensitivity not only can be learned, it can also be measured (Ponterotto and Alexander, 1996). This measurement is based in the belief that regardless of how well trained a counselor is in certain multicultural skills or how well he or she chooses techniques or tests based on the client's cultural and ethnic background, ultimately any tool is only as good (that is, as multiculturally competent) as the person using it. In other words, "what is of paramount importance is the clinician's multicultural awareness, knowledge, and interpretive skill" (Ponterotto and Alexander, 1996, p. 651). A number of instruments—for example the Cross-Cultural Counseling Inventory-R (LaFramboise, Coleman, and Hernandez, 1991), the Multicultural Awareness-Knowledge-and-Skills Survey (D'Andrea and Daniels, 1991; D'Andrea, Daniels, and Heck, 1991), and the Multicultural Counseling Inventory (Sodowsky, Taffe, Gutkin, and Wise, 1994)—exist for this purpose. The interested reader is referred to Suzuki, Meller, and Ponterotto (1996) and McGrath and Axelson (1993) for more detail as well as exercises and self-report measures.

Cultural Awareness

Cultural awareness refers to the process of recognizing personal biases, prejudicial beliefs, and stereotypic attitudes or reactions. Gaining awareness has to precede modification of behavior and attitudes, and can be a painful effort as clinicians begin to recognize that they are not free of recalcitrant prejudicial behaviors and beliefs. Later, the Skill Development Recommendations will concretize this process, which will also be described briefly in the following paragraphs. A good first step toward gaining awareness involves taking a look at the cultures and minority groups of which clinicians are a member to review personal cultural backgrounds, cultural assumptions, and cultural stereotypes. This may involve taking a look at country of origin, gender, sexual preference, language, skin color, physical limitations, cultural practices, and any other personal traits that may be cultural in nature or that may have resulted in the differential, perhaps unequal treatment by the clinician. In so doing, clinicians need to recognize that while there have been some consistent recipients of oppression, over the years the focus of prejudice has shifted from culture to culture. Further, the degree of bias against a given culture may have waxed and waned, but may have remained present at all times in one form or another. As

TABLE
2-3

TRAITS OF A CULTURALLY SENSITIVE MENTAL-HEALTH-CARE PROVIDER

Cultural Awareness

- Awareness of and sensitivity to clinician's personal cultural heritage
- Consciousness and embracing of all minority groups of which the clinician is a member
- Awareness of personal reactions to and behaviors with members of differing cultural backgrounds
- Attribution of value to and respect for all cultural differences
- Seeking-out of experiences involving members of differing cultural backgrounds
- Awareness of clinician's personal values and biases and their effect on therapy
- Development of awareness of use of personal language
- Sensitivity to neither overemphasizing nor underemphasizing clinician-client cultural differences
- Awareness of personal cultural identity and level of acculturation
- Feelings of comfort regarding cultural differences between clinician and client
- Awareness of within-group differences to respect the individuality of all people
- Demonstration of sensitivity to situations that may require referral of a culturally different client to a member of the same cultural heritage

Cultural Knowledge

- Understanding of how the sociopolitical system in the United States treats minorities
- Knowledge of U.S. history, especially as relevant to various cultural groups
- Knowledge about the history, presence, and various manifestations of racism, sexism, and heterosexism and their effects on members of various cultural groups
- Knowledge of political, social, and economic pressures that come to bear on various cultural groups

- Familiarity with the history of mental-health treatment for minority- and cultural-group members
- Recognition of potential biases of traditional psychotherapy theories
- Awareness of cultural definitions of mental illness and perspectives on mental-health services
- Knowledge about cultural and minority groups in the United States
- Knowledge about particular groups with whom the clinician anticipates or is working
- Clear and explicit knowledge about and understanding of the generic characteristics of therapy
- Familiarity with cross-cultural applications of psychotherapy skills
- Awareness of the effects of the therapy setting and office on clients from various minority or cultural groups
- Knowledge about institutional barriers that prevent members of various cultural or minority groups from using mental-health services
- Knowledge of clients' native language

Cultural Skill

- Adeptness at adjusting communication and therapeutic style to match individual clients' needs
- Skillful use of nonverbal communication and silence
- Use of language that is devoid of prejudice and bias
- Knowledge of a variety of intervention strategies that may be appropriate to clients of differing cultural backgrounds
- Knowledge about how to give the appropriate amount of attention to the role of culture
- Avoidance of categorization of individuals according to stereotypes and prejudices
- Development of ethnorelativism
- Respect and flexibility in providing services to meet the individual needs of clients
- Selection and application of intervention skills as client needs dictate and as appropriate to clients' personal contextual background
- Action as a social-change agent to help reduce or eliminate racism, sexism, and heterosexism

trainees begin to identify the minority, ethnic, or cultural groups of which they are members, they must contemplate the experiences and influences that were the result of being a member in that group.

Once identification of personal backgrounds has taken place, new mental-health-care providers can shift to assessing their day-to-day reactions to different situations and different people to determine their biases and prejudices. As such, as trainees go through their day, they may begin to make an effort to become aware of personal reactions to people from different cultures and minority groups. Most people do not routinely assess such reactions. However, it is an important process on the road to becoming culturally aware. Internal reactions to ethnic jokes, for example, may provide valuable information to help the clinician develop self-awareness. Behavior while interacting with someone who is culturally different from oneself can be attended to and understood with new awareness. Most new therapists may recognize for the first time that they truly react differently with people from other ethnic, cultural, or minority groups, a realization that sometimes causes concern or embarrassment. However, shaming the clinician is not the point of assessing daily reactions. Rather, the point is to help trainees realize that everyone, even the most open-minded individual, has been influenced by societal and familial training. It is highly unlikely that anyone exists who is completely free of biases and differential reactions. The point of assessment is to begin to become conscious of these reactions, not to chastise oneself for them. It can be helpful to attend to any undue generalizations from one member of a group to all members of that group; to take stock of the cultural heritage or ethnic backgrounds of people with whom the therapist in training spends personal time; to evaluate honestly whether friends and acquaintances are primarily of the same culture, and, if so, how this pattern came to pass.

The next step in developing increasing awareness involves the seeking out of experiences with different cultural, ethnic, or minority groups and beginning to identify stereotypic beliefs and biases. In so doing, it is helpful to keep in mind that both positive and negative stereotypes can be destructive because they move the clinician away from interacting with a client as an individual. Once stereotypes have been identified, they can be evaluated for accuracy, since for many stereotypes, a kernel of truth exists that renders them quite compelling. Testing stereotypes can be particularly difficult because it is always possible to think of at least one example to verify a preconceived notion. Therefore, it is important to look at the bigger picture of reality in evaluating stereotypes. For example, there is a prevalent stereotype that minority members in the United States exploit the welfare system. While some minority members may be identified for whom this may hold true, the reality is that the majority of welfare recipients are White, as are the majority of individuals who commit welfare fraud.

As the counselor striving to become culturally aware begins to monitor personal reactions to different situations and people, awareness of personal language will add an important component of self-exploration. Words selected in general discourse (and hence in the therapy room) often are representative of the thought processes underlying them. In addition to tracking the use of blatant ethnic epithets, attention is also directed toward more subtle indicators of bias and prejudice (Sharma and Lucero-Miller, 1998). For instance, the clinician needs to explore the use of language that implies gender bias through choice of nouns (such as chairman, policeman, congressman) or pronouns (such as use of the generic "he"), as well as language that may reflect ethnic bias through inappropriate phrases like "jew me down," being "gypped," "Indian giver," "scotch on a deal," or "Irish temper." The clinician must also explore biased assumptions, for example, explanations or identifications of inappropriate behaviors, such as lateness, seductiveness, anger, untrustworthiness, or thriftiness, based on a person's ethnicity. Another prejudicial use of language is to refer to members of a culture different from one's own as "they" or "them." This depersonalizes and segregates members of that culture only to further perpetuate the separation of groups. Once novice clinicians become aware of linguistic choices that reveal prejudice or bias (whether intentional or inadvertent), they are ready to attempt to select alternatives and to eliminate language that conveys prejudice and bias, no matter how subtle.

Another important insight involves the awareness of the great differences among persons within the same cultural or ethnic group. In fact, differences within a group are often greater than those between cultures. One major within-group difference clinicians must be aware of involves the cultural identity of an individual, that is, the relative importance an individual places on his or her own culture versus other cultures. Cultural-identity development has been conceptualized in a myriad of ways. Although stage models have been criticized, one commonly used way of looking at cultural-identity development involves individuals going through a process of identifying with a number of successive stages. There are several models to describe such developmental stages, including the Minority Identity Model (Atkinson, Morten, and Sue, 1997), Black Identity Development Model (Jackson, 1975), and Negro-to-Black Conversion Experience (Cross, 1971). As an example, Cross's model views the development of an African American's cultural identity as passing through four stages: preencounter, encounter, immersion, and internalization. In the *preencounter* stage, the individual holds disdain and hatred for being Black; in *encounter,* the person begins to value herself or himself for being Black; in *immersion,* the individual rejects and hates all that is not Black; and in the *internalization* stage, the person gains a sense of self-confidence and security in who she or he is and is able to embrace all cultures. A model not tied to any particular group was presented by Phinney (1990), whose stages are labeled *diffuse* (unexplored ethnic identity), *foreclosure* (commitment to a group based not on independent opinion but on parental or similar values), *moratorium* (exploration without commitment), and *achieved* (completed exploration which has resulted in commitment to a group). Although stage models were developed originally to describe the process encountered by minority group members, parallels have emerged for White ethnic identity development (Carter, 1990; Helms, 1990; Helms and Carter, 1990). Stage models may not best capture cultural identity, however, as identity can shift across time and various experience factors (Hayano, 1981), and as individuals may be at different stages with regard to different identifications (Jones, 1990). The process of identifying a cultural identity is valid not only for clients but also for the mental-health-care provider. In recognition of this, to become culturally sensitive, clinicians must explore their own cultural identity. To do so, they will need to examine deeply the sentiments they hold about their own and other cultures to recognize commitments (or lack thereof) to other ethnic groups.

Related to the issue of cultural-identity development, clinicians need to be aware that individuals within a given culture will vary considerably with regard to their level of acculturation. Acculturation is defined as the degree to which individuals adopt the dominant society's social and cultural norms to the exclusion of that of their own (Dillard, 1983). Acculturation is typically not a matter of endorsing one set of cultural norms versus another, but rather refers to the degree of incorporation of values or attitudes derived from both cultures. There are many factors that may affect level of acculturation, including socio-economic status, number of generations that have been in the United States, educational and employment opportunities, and geographical location. Gauging clients' levels of acculturation is an important part of getting to know them and involves an evaluation of several factors, including the degree to which traditional cultural practices are followed and the native language is used in thinking and speaking (cf., Gibbs and Huang, 1989). Four levels of acculturation have been identified (for example, Dana, 1993): *traditional* (adherence to the "birth" culture), *assimilated* or nontraditional (adherence to majority culture), *bicultural* (adherence to birth and majority culture), and *marginal* (lack of adherence to either culture). Level of acculturation will affect how clients interact with members of both cultures and may influence the therapeutic relationship. For example, if a Native American client appears very committed to Native culture, therapy might make use of metaphor and storytelling, a commonly used technique in Native culture, to resolve problems. Once again, clinicians also need to work toward awareness of their own level of acculturation to further clarify personal cultural identity. To assist with the process of clarifying personal cultural identity, several scales have been developed. They are very specific to the cultural background of the client, and they exist for most cultural groups represented with great frequency in the United States. For example, the Developmental Inventory of Black Consciousness (DIB-C; Milliones, 1980) and the Racial Identity Attitude Scale (RIAS; Parham and Helms, 1985; Ponterotto and Wise, 1987) can be used. For Hispanic clients, a variety of scales exist that must be carefully chosen according to the subgroup of American Hispanics to which the client belongs (for example, the Acculturation Scale for Mexican Americans [Cuellar, Harris, and Jasso, 1980]). Unfortunately, some ethnic subgroups exist in the United States for whom satisfactory acculturation scales have not yet been developed, despite a few attempts in the literature. One example of such a subgroup is Alaska Natives of Eskimo descent (for example, Yupik and Inupiat; Dana, 1993). For clients of cultural backgrounds for whom no good acculturation measures exist, a clinical interview that will at least attempt to get at the relevant issues (such as language, lifestyle choices, exposure to majority culture, adherence to traditional ways) is of critical importance (Kohatsu and Richardson, 1996). Clinicians can follow a similar process in their own self-exploration.

Cultural Knowledge

While awareness is being established, the clinician also strives to become more knowledgeable about cultural issues. The definition of cultural knowledge is broad and multidisciplinary, requiring individuals to utilize many resources. Courses, workshops, and seminars are obvious avenues for gaining accurate knowledge about the many issues related to culture. A number of additional possibilities are presented below. Cultural knowledge is critical for many reasons, including the fact that accurate information may help dispute any stereotypes that mental-health-care providers have become aware of about a group, and will lead to better appreciation and understanding of different cultures. In general, if used appropriately, knowledge will assist counselors to be better able to interact effectively with members of other cultures. However, caution must be exercised so that newly acquired knowledge is not represented as the truth about all members of any given group. Such stereotypic or overgeneralized use of knowledge can be destructive and can get in the way of being truly effective and empathic (Namyniuk, 1996).

Knowledge gathered from books is best not limited to a single discipline, and optimally starts with gaining a firm and accurate understanding of the history of the United States in general, and the history of different ethnic and cultural groups in particular (for example, Tataki, 1993; Zinn, 1995). Acquisition of such knowledge may include an investigation of the history of immigration; the introduction, role, and history of slavery; and the conquest of the continent. It is important to remember that history books can be biased and selective in their reporting and that it is often difficult to find books that provide a balanced perspective on history. In addition to gaining a historical perspective on the role of racism in the United States, it is important to recognize the role of racism, sexism, and heterosexism in contemporary society. Integrating historical information with current statistics and data on poverty may provide added insights into the lives of many minority and cultural groups. Further, much has been written about economic and political pressures that come to bear on minorities within the United States. Such reading will help clinicians recognize the adverse effects bias can have on the minority members who believe and adopt (or adapt to) the prejudices toward their groups, as well as other groups within society (Johnson, 1993).

The path toward cultural knowledge includes the reading of books within the mental-health professions, on topics such as the psychology of racism. These readings must also include a review of empirical information about cross-cultural differences within the United States. However, a word of caution about this literature is in order. Some of this research, particularly projects completed prior to the 1980s, focused on comparing different cultural groups with European Americans, implicitly establishing White Americans as the cultural norm against which other cultures were compared to identify differences and similarities. Consequently, the results are frequently (mis)interpreted within a context of Whites as the ideal norm. Clearly, this is an inherent bias against cultural groups other than Whites that must be considered and compensated for when reading such research reports. The reader interested in more information about cultural biases in research is referred to an excellent overview of cross-cultural-therapy research by Ponterotto and Casas (1991) as well as Matsumoto (1994).

In the process of becoming culturally knowledgeable, mental-health-care providers will learn that the dominant theories of counseling and therapy in the United States were developed by White Europeans (predominantly male) and may not have universal applications. Traditional personality theories as currently taught in most mental-health programs emphasize values and world-views that are ethnocentric in nature; specifically, they tend to be Eurocentric, reflecting the European cultural heritage of majority culture. Personality theories were developed to provide a context in which to explore individuals with regard to their behaviors, values, beliefs, attitudes, language, relationship, and so forth. All of these aspects of what it means to be human are entirely culture-bound (Armour-Thomas and Gopaul-McNicol, 1998; Barnouw, 1985). To look at these variables in clients or oneself without knowing the cultural context in which they developed is likely to distort what is expressed. For instance, most primary personality theories focus on the individual and state as a basic premise that it is important for children to individuate and separate from their family. From this perspective of individualism, the indicators for a client's progress toward health would be lessened reliance on family and others along with increased independence. Continued dependence or reliance on family or larger social networks would be viewed as a sign of pathology. Such a viewpoint would clearly not be compatible with cultures (for example, Asian American) that emphasize a perspective of collectivism, that is, the importance of the family or community and the role of the individual within it (Singelis, Triandis, Bhawuk, and Gelfand, 1995).

Further, it is important for mental-health-care providers to realize that mental-health services are not universally held in high regard. Some cultures place greater emphasis on seeking assistance from family members or community elders, while other cultures see any sign of mental illness as a disgrace to the family that must be hidden from all (Suzuki, Meller, and Ponterotto, 1996). Some minority members view mental-health services as either being irrelevant to the everyday struggle for survival they face or as being yet another tool for the White majority to pacify and control minorities. Finally, clinicians also need to become knowledgeable of the institutional barriers that may prevent members of some cultural and ethnic groups from seeking and using mental-health services (LaFramboise and Foster, 1989; Sue, Allen, and Conaway, 1978). There are many possible reasons for the underutilization of mental-health services by minority group members: the perception of some clients that mental-health-care providers are insensitive to diverse needs; fear that clinicians may try to impose personal values upon clients; and inability to accommodate to the hours and days of operation and the amount of charges for services.

The counselor must also become knowledgeable of the fact that there is no single universally accepted definition of "normal" and that the standard of what constitutes acceptable behavior will vary from one culture to another (Lum, 1999). Thus, clinicians need to learn not to rigidly apply one single definition of mental health across all clients and need to recognize that culturally valued traits will play a role in the behavioral manifestation of a client's personality. Cultures vary greatly in what they consider to be a problem or an appropriate strategy for coping within a given situation (cf., Castillo, 1997; Dana, 1993; Iijima Hall, 1997). What may constitute abnormality in one culture may be acceptable, if not mainstream behavior, in another. Different cultures may also express the same type of problem in different ways, choosing different idioms to describe an essentially identical emotional level and type of pain (Matsumoto, 1994a). As such, depression among mainstream White clients may conform to the criteria outlined in the DSM-IV, whereas depression among the Chinese may manifest itself through a different set of highly somatized symptoms, such as constipation, loss of appetite, and fatigue, with little expressed dysphoric affect (Castillo, 1997; Dana, 1993). Some disorders appear to be culture-bound, appearing only (or predominantly) in some, but not all cultures (American Psychiatric Association, 1994; Suzuki, Meller, and Ponterotto, 1996). This latter phenomenon may be explained by the observation that different cultures reinforce different traits and behaviors. As any trait or behavior taken to an extreme may result in pathology, different cultural groups will have different manifestations of pathology based on the types of traits they emphasize in their healthy population (Alarcon and Foulks, 1995; Iijima Hall, 1997).

It is particularly critical to gain extensive knowledge about the primary group or groups with which clinicians anticipate doing the bulk of their work. For example, if a therapist were to conduct therapy in rural Alaska, it would be in the therapist's (and clients') best interest to learn about Alaska Native cultures, particularly about the Native groups who live in neighboring areas. If a counselor were to work in a city with a predominantly Hispanic population, such as El Paso, Texas, it would be in everybody's best interest for the counselor to learn about Hispanic culture and, if at all possible, to speak Spanish. Not only does this knowledge enable the clinician to be more effective with clients from these cultures, but it will also lead to greater credibility. Clinicians must never overlook the most important source of knowledge about their clients' culture: the clients themselves. Clients can be an especially valuable source of information as they will provide the mental-health-care provider with their personal perspective of their culture, information that may prove invaluable in assessment, case conceptualization, and the development of a treatment strategy (Brems, 1998a).

If at all possible, clinicians are encouraged to learn the native language of the clients with whom they will be conducting treatment. Although a difficult task, it will pay considerable rewards in the increased rapport and respect that will be gained from clients. Certainly, learning a language is a difficult process and therapists may never be completely comfortable conducting therapy in their second language. However, as a bare minimum counselors need to learn a few common words of greeting and farewell, as well as commonly used terms or phrases. If nothing else, trying to learn a second language will give mental-health-care providers a better appreciation and empathy for those clients who are themselves learning a second language, namely, English!

Beyond reading and taking classes or workshops, one of the most important avenues to gaining knowledge about different cultures is to become involved in firsthand experience (Lum, 1999). There are many different avenues to gain this experience and trainees are advised to take advantage of as many as possible. One possible approach is to attend various cultural events that are offered by or about the culture. These might include dances, plays, movies, and lectures. A word of caution here is for the clinician to remember that these are merely pieces of the culture, not complete reflections of the entire cultural process and heritage. This caution is necessary because many people will attend cultural events that highlight the artistic or romantic aspects of a culture to the exclusion of other aspects. If these were the only contacts with a given culture, the counselor would derive a highly distorted understanding. Relatedly, it is helpful to seek out opportunities for interaction with members of other cultures, preferably including both professional and personal involvement. For instance, professionally speaking, there may be opportunities to volunteer time at a community mental-health center that offers special programs for members of a specific culture or that is located in a neighborhood that is predominantly comprised of minority members. On a personal level, opportunities need to be sought out for interaction with members of other cultures on a social level. All professional and personal efforts to learn more about a cultural or ethnic group whose members the therapist anticipates treating will not only lead to more knowledge and experience, but will also have the added benefit of increasing visibility, and hence added respect, among the people in that group.

It is presumed that all contemporary graduate programs in the mental-health professions teach cultural competence and sensitivity. Courses and curriculum on these topics can be further enhanced through practica and internships that involve a culturally diverse clientele. If this cannot be achieved solely through careful selection of practicum or internship sites while in graduate school, graduate training can be augmented by additional volunteer experiences, as well as by supervised employment attained upon graduation. Counselors need to take responsibility to encourage their supervisors to challenge them with a culturally diverse clientele, given the limitations and parameters of a specific clinical site. If the choice is available to trainees, they can select a practicum or internship site located within a culturally diverse neighborhood or city. Throughout all of these experiences, culturally sensitive supervision is a critical component. Within supervision, focus should be placed, as appropriate, on the counselor's experience of different types of clients. Through this use of supervision to monitor reactions to culturally different clients, the therapist will learn to avoid repeating any previously learned biases and stereotypes.

Cultural Skills

Clinicians' awareness and knowledge of cultural issues will have to be translated into skills to be of use to clients. The process of becoming culturally competent therefore must include the acquisition of new skills and the possible adaptation of existing skills. Perhaps most importantly, mental-health-care providers need to learn and apply appropriate communication skills that are adapted to meet the needs of each individual client (Kim, 1994). Cultures differ in their emphasis in communication. Some individuals are most concerned about the clarity of their message, some about the relationship between speaker and listener, some about the evaluation they will receive based on their expression, some about the impositions made by their remarks, and some about the effectiveness of their communication (Kim, 1994). Clinicians need to learn to recognize their clients' and their own personal preferences in communication and adjust accordingly. For example, a client who tends to express issues in treatment in a manner that is mostly concerned with how the clinician will respond to the client (that is, is most concerned with being evaluated) may have a tendency to withhold facts that are perceived as potentially leading to negative evaluation. Another client, who is mainly concerned with not hurting the clinician's feelings may not self-disclose information that is perceived as potentially critical of the clinician. Concern for relationship in communication tends to be correlated with cultures that are more collectivistic; concern for communication of facts and effectiveness with cultures that are more individualistic (Triandis, 1989).

Some cultures may place greater emphasis on nonverbal communication; members of these cultures are less likely to view talking therapies as ideal therapeutic modalities. The clinician will have to develop skills that can accommodate these needs (Cargile and Sunwolf, 1998). For example, among some groups, silence may be a sign of respect, not resistance. Skillful use of silence will be a respectful means of expressing cultural competence with such clients. Using a client's native language can be invaluable. Regardless of language, skillful clinicians keep their communication free of bias and prejudice, eliminating inappropriate phrases, terms, and expressions from their vocabularies.

Culturally competent clinicians have to acquire the skills to identify and carry out the techniques that will be most effective with any given client. Rather than approaching each and every client in the same manner, counselors recognize the need to modify their therapeutic approach depending on the needs of each individual client (Ponterotto, Casas, Suzuki, and Alexander, 1995). With increased sensitivity to the differences in how clients from different cultures may express their individuality and connectedness, therapists will not pathologize a client based on such differences (Brislin, 1993; Singelis and Brown, 1995). Skillful mental-health-care providers are also aware that there are marked differences within any given culture and are careful not to make broad generalizations of the types of treatments that will work for all members of that culture (Suzuki, Meller, and Ponterotto, 1996). Thus, therapists need to have the skills to be flexible in their therapeutic approach and use this flexibility in a competent and appropriate manner when dealing with clients from different cultures.

Also crucial is the ability to place the appropriate amount of attention on the role of culture in therapy. That is, clinicians must neither overemphasize nor underemphasize the importance of culture in therapy with a given client. To do so, counselors need to have the skills to evaluate a situation effectively and to assess the level of attention that needs to be given to culture with each client. Therapists recognize that stereotyping and generalizing are acts destructive to the therapeutic process, and that even within a given culture, members will have varying degrees of commitment to traditional cultural values and behaviors. This skill is dependent upon having attained a level of ethnorelativism that helps the counselor to neither overemphasize nor ignore the impact of culture.

Ethnorelativism can be considered the opposite end of a continuum ranging from ethnocentrism to ethnorelativism. Most people develop an ethnorelativistic perspective by passing through a number of fairly predictable stages, formulated originally by Bennet (1986). The starting point for most humans is an *ethnocentric* one; individuals learn through what they are exposed to, which early in the life span is generally their own culture. Once confronted with the diversity of others in the greater environment, Bennet suggests that people's first response is *denial* that the difference exists. This is followed by a *defense* of their own position and characteristics over those of the group perceived as different, since difference is perceived as a threat. Generally, this attempt at defending their position is followed by a *minimization* or trivialization of the differences once they can no longer deny that differences exist and once individuals realize that their own perspective is neither the only one nor necessarily the correct one. At this level, people still believe in a universal law, but recognize that it may manifest or express itself differently among different groups of people. From minimization people generally move to an *acceptance* that others can be different without being worse. They begin to realize that there is no universal truth, but rather that values, attitudes, and beliefs can be completely different and can stem from a different worldview. Such acceptance is followed by an *adaptation* of personal behavior and attitudes, a move that tends to increase flexibility in multicultural contexts and in general. Once individuals have learned to integrate their own experiences, values, attitudes, and beliefs with those of people from cultural backgrounds different than their own, they finally think *ethnorelativistically.* Such individuals begin to recognize that behavior, values, and attitudes have to be understood within a larger context and that people cannot be judged or stereotyped according to worldview perspectives (or based on comparisons with generalized group means). Although some authors (for example, Dana, 1987) suggest that mental-health-care providers in general need to have attained at least Stage Four (acceptance), it appears likely that only clinicians who have at least reached Stage Five will be able to engage in sensitive and competent counseling and therapy (Brems, 1998a). It is possible to accept another person without interacting with her or him; such acceptance is likely to incorporate an air of condescension or arrogance, attitudes that do not appear conducive to rapport.

Ethnorelativistic clinicians will have the skill not to categorize individuals according to their ethnic or cultural background, that is, not to treat all members of any given group as identical (Richardson and Molinaro, 1996). Although the U.S. population is often categorized into five major groups, namely, Whites, African Americans, Hispanic Americans, Asian Americans, and Native Americans, each of these broad categories has within it a number of subcategories. For example, the broad category of Asian Americans contains a number of smaller groupings, each with its own unique cultural background and heritage. The group includes individuals whose cultural background lies in very diverse countries including China, Japan, Samoa, North and South Korea, Vietnam, and Guam. Further complicating this issue is the fact that even within each of these country-based subgroups, there are further subgroups. For example, within Vietnam, there is a significant proportion of ethnic Chinese who have, over the years, maintained great autonomy from other Vietnamese. Further, even within the Chinese-Vietnamese group there may be major differences such as rural versus urban, rich versus poor, gay versus straight, Buddhist versus Christian, and so forth. This example demonstrates how broad categorization of individuals ignores the numerous differences that exist within this larger grouping. The same obviously holds true for other ethnic groups, with variables such as country of origin, sexual orientation, physical abilities, socioeconomic status, religion, and age.

Recognizing that institutional barriers may prevent members of some cultural or minority groups from utilizing mental-health services, clinicians need to learn to become flexible in their provision of services (Namyniuk, Brems, and Clarson, 1997). They recognize that the client cannot control some problems and that nontraditional steps may need to be taken to help resolve the situation (Brems, 1999). For example, if a client presents for therapy due to feelings of inadequacy or depression, the intake interview may reveal that the individual is the only culturally different student in a predominantly White university student body and that White students have been making racist comments. The client, unable to make friends in the new setting and subject to ongoing derogation, soon begins to incorporate many of these negative perceptions into her or his self-concept. In this situation, there is an outside force (racism at school) that has had a direct and adverse impact on the client. Hence, focusing solely on the client in an attempt to improve self-concept will most likely not be the most effective intervention. Instead, therapy will be most effective if a three-pronged intervention is adopted that involves the client, the community, and the university. By including interventions in the university setting, the therapist may be able to make an impact on the client's environment which in turn may have a positive effect on self-esteem.

Consequently, culturally competent clinicians will want to cultivate another important set of skills: being agents for social change (Hogan-Garcia, 1999; Monges, 1998). Clinicians need to learn how to eliminate any form of discrimination, including that based on ethnicity, sexual preference, age, mental or physical limitations, religion, gender, and so forth. Being culturally sensitive, mental-health-care providers act to ensure that everyone has access to the services and resources that are needed. In so doing, they take a proactive advocacy stance to help victims of discrimination. Trainees need to recognize that as clinicians they will be granted a great deal of power by their clients and other community members. They must recognize their responsibility to use this power to help eliminate discrimination in society, both directly and indirectly. Indirectly, the therapists will come to serve as an example of a nonbiased individual. They will learn to be careful of chosen words and actions to convey perceptions of equality of all persons and respect for individuals from all walks of life. Counselors come to recognize that many clients will model their behavior after that of the clinician. With this recognition, they learn to be careful of any interpersonal interactions that might convey prejudice or bias, even of the subtlest kind.

Skill Development Recommendations

Recommendation 2-3   *Choose several or all of the recommendations made in the Cultural Sensitivity section and incorporate them into your daily life. For example, take an inventory of your personal cultural background; explore your circle of friends for its diversity or lack thereof; become aware of your language and any reflections of racism or sexism; open yourself up to your thoughts and feelings as you encounter individuals from other cultures; attend cultural events and evaluate your reactions; volunteer to work with individuals from other cultures; listen to the language and conversations of others with an ear for racism or sexism. In opening yourself up to these experiences, keep a journal of your thoughts and reactions. Review this journal regularly with an open mind to slowly gain awareness of any prejudices, stereotypes, and values that emerge.*

Recommendation 2-4   *Choose a cultural group (other than your own primary group) with whose members you anticipate working in therapy or counseling. Identify a mental-health professional from within that group and ask for an interview. Interview that individual with regard to what you need to know about working with members from that cultural group. Listen openly and do not offend by making stereotypic assumptions.*

When necessary and appropriate, mental-health-care providers will learn ways in which to take direct actions to prevent or eliminate all forms of discrimination. This direct action can range from not condoning racist or sexist jokes told in their presence to using the political system to create positive changes in society. In becoming culturally skillful, therapists recognize that although the primary purpose of therapy or counseling is to help enhance the quality of clients' lives, it is equally important to complement this individual approach to improving life with a more general approach to enhancing the quality of society. Thus, counselors will come to do everything possible to help create a society that is more respectful and humane in its treatment of all persons (Johnson, 1993).

SELF-CARE SKILLS*

> We can shed those layers and layers of habits and
> learned responses that lead to careless action
> and thoughts. We can learn to look before we leap
> and think before we act; we can stop living like moths
> who are inevitably attracted to bright, dangerous
> flames. We can shake free of our knee-jerk behaviors
> and responses to life; we can let go of dissatisfying and
> unhealthy patterns. And, as we become more mindful,
> our innate wakefulness—our spiritual and inner
> wisdom—begins to blaze forth.
>   *Lama Surya Das, 1999, p. 191*

For successful work with clients, counselors and therapists must first of all be able to take care of themselves. Successful mental-health-care providers are mentally healthy individuals who have good personal awareness and the willingness for introspection. Individual and interpersonal self-awareness in the realms of values and cultural sensitivity were dealt with in detail in Chapter Two. This chapter focuses on skills that facilitate broader individual self-awareness, along with good self-care that keeps the clinician safe from the burnout and impairment that can negatively influence therapy and counseling. Personal mental health has to be grounded in good personal habits that honor the needs of mind, body, and spirit. A wide range of self-care skills can help keep clinicians grounded and healthy, physically and emotionally. It is not necessary to select a particular lifestyle or personal health routine that is suggested here. Each individual reader will need to decide whether any of the skills discussed here can be incorporated into her or his personal life. Self-care is by definition highly personal; opinions on what is right and wrong differ greatly and defen-

---

*This chapter represents a minor modification of an excerpt from Chapter 9 in Brems, C. (2000). *Dealing with challenges in psychotherapy and counseling*. Pacific Grove, Calif.: Brooks/Cole.

siveness can occur quickly. It is recommended that readers peruse the self-care chapter with an attitude of suspended disbelief and open-mindedness. None of the suggestions are meant as directives; they are possibilities. It is hoped that every reader will find something useful for her or his life and situation.

The most important goal of this chapter is to help mental-health-care providers recognize the importance and value of tending to their own personal physical and mental health and that such self-care best involves a routine that is followed not rigidly, but with commitment and pleasure. A healthy clinician will model good emotional and physical health for clients and will be more congruent than a practitioner who struggles personally with balancing physical, mental, and spiritual needs and health. Self-care will be addressed from several perspectives: self-exploration and awareness, relaxation and centeredness, personal habits, relationships, and recreation.

SELF-EXPLORATION AND AWARENESS

"The sense of who one is, and of one's empowering life vision, seems to be at the core of long and creative living" (Jevne and Williams, 1998, p. 5). Self-awareness and emotional stability of the care provider are important aspects of good treatment as well as of burnout prevention. Therapists are confronted with difficulties by clients on a daily basis; in addition, they have to be able to cope with their own life challenges. Being able to maintain self-esteem, self-efficacy, and a basic sense of personal competence is critical during periods of challenge (Wheeler, 1997). One important aspect of self-care—self-exploration—is of great assistance in the struggle to become more aware and less prone to overreaction to clients. Self-exploration brings benefits not only to practitioners, but also their clients. It combines with the work clinicians already do around values clarification and cultural sensitivity development, and as such provides additional concrete strategies for the creation of awareness and insight. In general, emotional stability is achieved through the development of self-awareness. Self-awareness can lead to better professionalism; it is also recommended to help therapists "flourish as human beings, who then bring more than the minimum to their therapeutic work" (Johns, 1997, p. 61). Figuring out what really matters in life is an important endeavor that some take more seriously than others (Schwartz, 1995). Clinicians can hardly choose to ignore this very important issue if they want to be aware, unbiased, and effective mental-health-care providers who neither impose biases on their clients nor succumb to impairment. There are many possible avenues toward self-awareness and personal self-development from which clinicians can choose. The following paragraphs focus on a few important strategies, but the list is by no means all-inclusive.

Personal Therapy or Counseling

One obvious strategy that creates self-awareness is, of course, personal therapy or counseling. One may wonder if this strategy even needs mention in a book for mental-health-care providers. Actually, it appears that it does. Although over 80 percent of mental-health-care providers report having been in personal therapy in the past, only 22.2 percent of doctoral-level providers and 38.8 percent of master's-level providers report being currently in therapy. The remainder, a surprisingly large percentage (61.2 to 79.8 percent), rejected the idea of current personal therapy for several reasons, including concern about the value of personal therapy (15 to 17 percent), embarrassment about being a client (13 to 15 percent), concern about confidentiality (12 to 16 percent), and prior negative experiences with therapy (7 to 8 percent) (Mahoney, 1997). Arguments have been made that all therapists in training should be required to be in personal therapy as well. This is a difficult issue that has not been empirically investigated. One can hardly disagree, however, that a counselor or therapist will be more effective and persuasive if personally convinced of the value of personal therapy. To hold such a belief may then translate into practice even without an imposed requirement from a training program or licensing agency. Since readiness for treatment is a critical issue in outcome of therapy, imposed personal therapy may be less effective than personal therapy that is initiated at the discretion of the practitioner. As Johns (1997) points out, therapy's or counseling's "optimal value is likely to emerge at a time of readiness, through reflective self-awareness which identifies a need, triggered by discomfort, uncertainty, the presence or absence of expected or unexpected feelings, unresolved personal issues, challenge of expected beliefs or crisis or developmental transitions in both professional and personal maturity" (p. 64). Each clinician will have to decide which road to choose. If clinicians make the choice not to seek therapy or counseling, they need to question the level of faith they place in the process and whether they communicate that lack of faith to their clients. The potential negative consequences of this are obvious.

Inner Work

Another excellent set of strategies for creating self-awareness is doing inner work through various self-exploratory means such as reading, journaling, and dream work. Reading does not require much explanation. There is a virtually endless supply of books and manuals that help people explore their lives, relationships, selves, dynamics, pasts, futures, feelings, thoughts, behaviors, and on and on. The main caution in this regard is to be a careful consumer and not to believe every self-help book that has ever been published. The Internet may be a good source for interactive reading resources that facilitate self-exploration.

Journaling was made popular as a legitimate strategy for self-exploration by Pennebaker (1990). He conducted a series of fascinating experiments in which he asked participants to write about things that were stressful for them to help them get their emotions out in the open. He found that writing about stressful life events and the emotions surrounding them was not only stress-reducing in and of itself, but also helped participants improve coping ability as well as over-all health. Based on his research findings, Pennebaker has suggested that writing is most helpful if it deals with both the experience and the emotions and deep feeling involved in the experience. Such self-exploration leads to cathar-sis and insight, and has numerous extremely positive consequences for the writer. It helps improve mood, increases coping ability, enhances the immune system, and in general appears to promote better physical and mental health. In other words, journaling appears to be a powerful strategy for clinicians wish-ing to prevent burnout or impairment. It is also an activity that easily fits into a busy schedule as it can be engaged in anywhere and for brief periods of time. There are virtually no drawbacks to this technique, although some have warned that clinicians need to "guard against becoming morbidly introspective or unduly passive by also emphasizing action" (Bayne, 1997, p. 190). This cau-tion, however, applies to most, if not all, self-exploratory strategies.

A third strategy for inner work is dream work, which is a familiar, power-ful strategy for most mental-health-care providers. Exploring one's dreams to achieve insight can be accomplished relatively easily. The best strategy for re-membering dreams is to direct oneself to remember the dream upon awaken-ing. It is helpful to have a tablet of paper and pen or a tape recorder by the bed-side and to record the dream immediately upon waking from it, even if this is in the middle of the night. Analysis of the dream then occurs the next day. It is best to read a few books or take a class to decide which approach for analyzing dreams is best for the individual. Not all approaches rely exclusively on Freud's or Jung's work, although they are certainly the thinkers who have inspired the work on dreams (cf., Freud, 1900; Jung, 1974). Many larger cities have dream work groups that come together for the sole purpose of working on members' dreams. There are several resources that may provide useful starting points for clinicians interested in using this strategy, including books and tapes that can be found in most popular bookstores (for example, Garfield, 1977; Johnson, 1986; Mahrer, 1989; Taylor, 1983; Ullman and Zimmerman, 1979).

Meditation

A final and perhaps most excellent strategy for developing self-awareness is meditation, though this is not the primary purpose of meditation. Meditation is a strategy that could appear equally appropriately in the section about re-laxation and centeredness, or in the section about relationships. It is such a comprehensive and powerful strategy that it touches all aspects of a person's life. The choice to place its discussion in this section was therefore somewhat arbitrary. Meditation is not one thing; it is many things. It has many goals and no goals; it is a difficult process and yet it is easy. Meditation is about finding peace and stillness, about quieting the mind and being in the moment. In Le-Shan's (1974) book on meditation (perhaps the book cited most often as being helpful in learning the process), he describes the goal of meditation as "access to more of our human potential or being closer to ourselves and to reality, or to more of our capacity for love and zest and enthusiasm, or our knowledge that we are a part of the universe and can never be alienated or separated from it, or our ability to see and function in reality more effectively" (p. 1). This is a most complicated sentence for a book that sets out to simplify something, but it is entirely accurate. Meditation returns the practitioner to a state of quiet and calm and connects humans with their roots in the universe. Although it is potentially the most calming practice of any of the self-exploration skills, it can at times leave the practitioner feeling disturbed or confused. The benefits of meditation have been researched and carefully documented in many places (for example, Hirai, 1989; Wilber, 1993, 1997). Lama Surya Das (1999) provides an excellent summary of the inadvertent positive consequences of consistent meditation practice and includes the following:

- it leads to greater calm, peacefulness, and awareness of inner resources
- it helps the mind empty itself of confusion and clutter
- it helps slow down minds that are restless or filled with angry, obsessive, or fearful thoughts
- it brings about a sense of centeredness and balance
- it makes the senses and perception more vivid and powerful
- it assists with gaining greater insight into personal issues
- it reduces egoism and self-centeredness
- it increases the capacity for love, wisdom, and compassion
- it provides health benefits such as facilitating the healing process from various severe illnesses
- it creates greater understanding of personal behavior
- it reconnects body, mind, and soul
- it opens the heart to others

Although some teachers say that meditation is best learned with a qualified instructor, basic meditation technique is easily learned. Knowing basic technique does not mean knowing how to meditate, and even teachers who have meditated for years accede that it is the practice of meditation that is important, not the goal or the outcome. Practiced over the long term, meditation helps the practitioner develop a calmness and serenity that permeates all of life. It is the ultimate technique for finding defenselessness, relaxation, and peacefulness in life, all states of being that are highly related to well-functioning and preventive of burnout and impairment.

There are many forms of meditation. Regardless of which form one chooses, there is significant agreement as to the basic procedure, which is to sit in a quiet place, either cross-legged on the floor with a cushion for support, or on a straight-back chair with feet on the ground. The sitting posture is preferable as alertness is key to successful meditation, and lying down may lead to drowsiness or sleepiness. Most resources recommend closed eyes; some suggest eyes partially open; only a few suggest eyes wide open (for example, Rinpoche, 1995). Posture is erect but not rigid, comfortable but not too relaxed. Most resources recommend a regular meditation schedule, with many recommending at least twenty to thirty minutes (and up to one hour) once or twice per day. Some writers recommend mornings, others evenings. Perhaps the best schedule is one that accommodates the practitioner's life most realistically. If evening meditation means that the practitioner falls asleep, morning practice may be preferable; if morning meditation tends to be interrupted by family members, evening practice may be superior. Some writers recommend timing meditation so that it follows, rather than precedes, exercise. Being in a calm state of mind before engaging in meditation is helpful but not a prerequisite. For some, such calmness is achieved by means of exercise (traditional or meditative, such as yoga or t'ai chi). It is best to learn meditation in a quiet environment that is private and without interruptions. Although advanced practitioners can meditate anywhere, those still learning the practice tend to do better in silence. Setting aside a specific spot for meditation can be helpful as it becomes a conditioned stimulus for relaxation, calm, and introspection. Some practitioners choose to place meaningful objects in this space (such as flowers, candles, statues), whereas others prefer simplicity. Natural settings or a view of nature are very conducive to a meditative state. Wearing comfortable clothing is helpful, especially clothing that does not constrict the waist, ankles, and wrists. Breathing should be regular and tends to become deeper and deeper as well as more rhythmic as one meditates; diaphragmatic breathing (see relaxation section below) is most conducive to reaching a deeply relaxed meditative state.

The simplest form of meditation merely focuses the mind on the breath. LeShan (1974) categorizes this form of meditation as a meditation of the outer way, as attention is focused on a process or item external to the mind. Another meditation of the outer way is to contemplate an object by looking at it intensely from as many angles as possible during the entire meditation time. Meditations of the inner way focus attention on one's own stream of consciousness without altering it. An example of a meditation of the inner way is the bubble meditation described by LeShan (1974). In this meditation, the person envisions the self sitting at the bottom of a pond, observing bubbles floating upward through the water. As thoughts enter the mind, they are placed in such a bubble and are allowed to drift upward through, and ultimately out of, consciousness. Other types of meditations can have other foci, such as the creation of compassion, the expression of lovingkindness (metta meditation), the creation of awareness about feelings, the achievement of centering, or the sending of healing thoughts. Meditation that is focused on observing one's thoughts often is highly conducive to creating insight and self-awareness and in the Buddhist tradition is referred to as vipassana meditation. What all meditations have in common is their focus on the moment; all attention and concentration is continually returned to the present moment as the past and future are allowed to fade.

It is important to note that it is virtually impossible for most practitioners to quiet the mind completely; thoughts will come and go. The successful practitioner is not the one who banishes all thought, but rather the one who is aware of each thought as it arises, acknowledges it without getting caught up in it, and then returns to the focal point of the chosen meditation. In fact, regardless of which type of meditation is chosen, the universal experience is that it is extremely difficult to keep the mind focused, whether the focus is inward as in the observation of one's own thoughts, or outward as in the observation of one's breath or the contemplation of an object. The key to success is to continuously bring the mind back to the breath, to the object, or to the thought bubbles, and most importantly, to calmness. No one can keep the mind quiet for very long; it is the effortless intention to let go of thoughts that brings on the positive effects of meditation. Learning to quiet the mind by coming into the moment is the key to becoming self-aware, connected to a larger cosmos, and defenseless and accepting in relationships. There is no better self-exploratory and calming technique than meditation. It is likely to influence all areas of a practitioner's life almost automatically with regular practice. Mental-health-care providers should be strongly encouraged to begin to meditate and perhaps to seek out a meditation teacher. It will be helpful for the interested reader to read more about meditation by accessing additional resources, recommended samples of which include:

1. Das, L. S. (1999). *Awakening to the sacred: Creating a spiritual life from scratch*. New York: Broadway Books.
2. Goldstein, J. (1976). *The experience of insight*. Boston: Shambhala.
3. Goldstein, J, and Kornfield, J. (1987). *Seeking the heart of wisdom*. Boston: Shambhala.
4. Kabat-Zinn, J. (1994). *Wherever you go, there you are*. New York: Hyperion.
5. Kabat-Zinn, J. (1990). *Full catastrophe living*. New York: Delta.
6. Kornfield, J. (1993). *A path with heart*. New York: Bantam.
7. LeShan, L. (1974). *How to meditate*. New York: Bantam.
8. Rinpoche, A. T. (1995). *Taming the tiger*. Rochester, Va.: Inner Traditions.
9. Suzuki, S. (1998). *Zen mind, beginner's mind*. New York: Weatherhill.

Skill Development Recommendations

Recommendation 3-1   *Choose one of the above-mentioned strategies and read more about it. Once you have a deeper understanding of it, begin practicing it at least once weekly. For example, once per week sit in meditation, explore your inner life, or visit a counselor or therapist. It will be most helpful to journal about this experience. For the greatest likelihood of impact, practice this recommendation at least three months.*

RELAXATION AND CENTEREDNESS

Another important set of self-care skills is that of relaxation strategies. Of all people, mental-health-care providers are probably best informed about this particular approach to self-care as they often incorporate relaxation strategies into client care. They may not, though, apply relaxation strategies in their own life as often as one would hope. The four most common strategies to achieve a state of relaxation are breathing exercises, mindfulness, relaxation strategies proper, and guided imagery. Of these four strategies, most clinicians are well-versed in the latter two, and less familiar with the first two. Thus, breathing and mindfulness will be covered in some detail whereas relaxation strategies and guided imagery will be briefly reviewed.

Breathing Exercises

Deep and conscious breathing is a very simple and straightforward means of achieving relaxation. Improper breathing, on the other hand, is a quick and straightforward way to stress, tension, and uptightness. Many people hold their breath during periods of great stress, and most never breathe consciously at any point in their lives. In fact, most people pay no attention to breath at all; it is an autonomic response they tend to rely on to just happen. Breath, though, is very much affected by tension and stress, and changes and may even seize momentarily in these situations. This sets up a vicious cycle since uptight or improper breathing in turn increases stress in the body even further. Learning to breathe deeply and consciously can be one of the most important components of achieving stress reduction and mental and physical health. No other strategy works better or faster than deep, conscious breathing to induce a state of deep relaxation. Breathing exercises are an excellent prelude to all relaxation strategies, including progressive-muscle-tension relaxation exercises, guided imageries, and other visualizations, both in personal practice and with clients.

To learn healthful deep breathing for relaxation, it is best to watch a baby. Babies automatically breathe in the most efficient and relaxing manner. Their trick is to use their diaphragm as a means of pulling air more fully into the lungs. Most individuals breathe using only their chest muscles (that is, the intercostal muscles between the ribs), an inefficient and less relaxing mode of breathing. A person who breathes in this way has no detectable motion of the abdomen during inhalation; merely the chest expands. Diaphragmatic breathing, which is relied upon during meditation and associated with states of relaxation, serenity, and peace, on the other hand, is detected by observing the rise and fall of the abdomen with each inhalation and exhalation. In diaphragmatic breathing, the diaphragm (the large muscle between the thoracic and abdominal cavity) flattens with inhalation, moving the abdomen forward and creating space for the lungs to expand with air in the thoracic cavity.

The best way to practice diaphragmatic breathing is to lie flat on one's back with a hand (or both hands) on the stomach. As in most, if not all, breathing exercises, it is best to place the tongue on the alveolar ridge (the soft tissue between the roof of the mouth and the upper front teeth) and to exhale once, forcefully and deeply (as well as noisily) through the mouth. All subsequent breathing is done through the nose exclusively (unless engaging in a special breathing exercise that specifies otherwise). To breathe diaphragmatically, on inhalation the focus is on flattening the diaphragm against the abdominal cavity, allowing the belly to rise gently. As this movement occurs, the lungs will naturally fill with air. On exhalation, the diaphragm relaxes, the stomach recedes, and the lungs empty. This type of breathing can be engaged in any rhythm. The slower the breathing the greater the state of relaxation If one gasps for air between breaths, however, the breathing has slowed too much. It is important to find a comfortable speed and rhythm and then to just observe the breath. Once diaphragmatic breathing has been successfully practiced lying down, it can be used in any body position and can be applied as a quick and easy relaxation strategy anytime, anywhere. It can be used in the middle of a stressful lecture, while sitting with a client, or during a job interview, and no one will know. Its power of relaxation, however, will take hold immediately, especially after prolonged practice in a relaxed setting.

Because diaphragmatic breathing is strongly associated with a state of relaxation, it is not the preferred way of breathing during physical activity or exertion. During activity, breathing is best conducted using the entire breathing apparatus. In this type of breathing, the breath starts with the flattening of the diaphragm and expansion of the abdominal cavity. The breath then moves up to the chest with the continued inhalation expanding the lower thoracic cavity and then the upper chest cavity, finally raising the shoulders. Exhalation works in reverse, with the shoulders dropping first, the lungs contracting, and the diaphragm relaxing to flatten the stomach. This very rejuvenating breath is a good breath to use at the end of a relaxation practice to become alert again. It can also be an excellent means of overcoming fatigue and becoming reenergized anywhere, anytime. A variety of other breathing exercises exists (for example, Schiffmann, 1996; Weil, 1995), but these two basic forms will get anyone started on the road to relaxation and better vital capacity.

Mindfulness Practice

Breathing can easily be combined with the practice of mindfulness, and in fact can be a powerful way to begin to learn being mindful. Mindfulness, in turn, is a helpful precursor for relaxation in general, and relaxation exercises in particular. Its application is possible so constantly throughout life that it can be practiced anytime, anywhere, with anyone. It is a mindset that develops and ultimately becomes second nature, and is very useful in coping with stressors of daily life and in keeping focused on what really matters. Mindfulness is the practice of stillness, centeredness, and full awareness in the present moment. It involves conscious living and alert presence of mind; it helps bring awareness into focus and directs attention to present actions and thoughts (Das, 1999). Shantideva is said to have defined it thus: "Again and again, examine every aspect of your mental and physical activities. In brief, that is the very way of observing mindfulness."

The easiest way to begin to learn mindfulness is to sit still and center attention on breath. Centering attention on breath means observing each inhalation and exhalation and their effects on the body—physical sensations in the nose, the larynx, the lungs, the chest, and the abdomen. Full concentration is placed on observing the subtle changes in the body as breath moves in and out. Each small change in the body is noted and attended to with great awareness, but at the same time with total calm and stillness. Being involved with each breath is true mindfulness of the breath, a centering and calming experience that creates a very peaceful feeling of being in the moment.

Mindfully slowing down and centering does not have to involve sitting still and breathing, although this is the easiest way to experience mindfulness and practice it until it takes hold. Mindfulness can be practiced through any familiar skill or activity by simply placing all attention and concentration on the activity. As in the mindful-breathing exercise, every subtle movement and change in the body is noted and appreciated for its complexity. If possible, the activity can be slowed down to more fully appreciate the many subtle muscular movements and their incredible coordination. It is helpful to the generalization of mindfulness into everyday life to pick a regular activity to couple with the practice of mindfulness. Mindfulness provides a model for the feeling of serenity, centeredness, and peacefulness that is so helpful to relaxation. Thich Nhat Hanh has written masterfully about the practice of mindfulness in day-to-day life and teaches workshops on the subject. One of his preferred foci for mindfulness is walking (Hanh, 1975).

The opposite of mindfulness is absent-mindedness and lack of attention. Anyone who has ever left their house and later wondered whether they turned off the stove or locked the door has experienced the opposite of mindfulness. Activities were engaged in without attention to them and hence they were not even consciously registered in awareness. Mindfulness brings a peaceful feeling that clearly focuses the mind on what is important—the present. In mindfulness, attention is concentrated on the moment and all thoughts of the past and future disappear, and along with them the anxiety and stress they may create. Whatever activity one is engaged in at the moment of mindfulness becomes the center and reason of existence and is done for itself, not for an end goal. In other words, what becomes important is the process, not the outcome. If mindfulness is applied to breathing, the focus is to breathe, not to survive or relax. If mindfulness is applied to eating, the purpose is to savor the food, to enjoy every aspect of eating, from chewing to swallowing, not to satisfy hunger or get dinner over with so that something else can be done. Whole books have been written on the topic of mindfulness. It certainly deserves that much attention (Fields, 1985; Hanh, 1975). The few guidelines provided here, however, suffice to initiate the novice into its practice. One final point is of note: Mindfulness is excellent for work with clients as well. Clinicians who are mindful are fully present with their clients and give them the complete and undivided attention they deserve. Being a mindful mental-health-care provider facilitates being an attentive listener, empathic responder, and insightful problem solver.

Relaxation Exercises

Anyone who has achieved relaxed breathing and mindfulness is fully prepared to begin relaxation through other means. Since most health-care professionals are well versed in relaxation strategies, not much effort will be spent on them here. The following quick review of relaxation strategies is meant mainly to remind clinicians to avail themselves of the very strategies they recommend to clients. As mental-health-care providers learn to use this skill with clients, they can also pay attention to how they may practice it in their own lives. (This skill will be discussed in some detail later, in the context of client work.)

The idea of using relaxation strategies per se is based on the principle that a body cannot be relaxed and anxious at the same time. Relaxation strategies have traditionally been employed to reduce general anxiety, induce sleep, produce relaxation to facilitate coping with a specific anticipated event, or reduce phobic reactions in specific situations. The two primary strategies that have been developed are muscle tension relaxation and pure relaxation. In muscle tension relaxation, muscle groups are first tensed through specific suggested motions and then relaxed; the difference between the two states is then noted in a mindful manner for the purpose of inducing relaxation. Simple or pure relaxation exercises will focus attention on the same muscle groups but without the initial experience of tension. The chosen muscle group is focused on with the desire or direction to relax it. In using relaxation, a few cautions apply, both for personal use and use with clients. Most importantly, it is necessary to remember that:

- if pain occurs, the person relaxing may need to take a break from tensing a certain muscle group
- if a floating feeling occurs, this is usually no problem unless the person relaxing is prone to dissociation (which may be a contraindication for use of relaxation)
- a feeling of heaviness is not only normal, but generally desirable unless the person relaxing has a physical problem that is exacerbated by this (for example, fibromyalgia)
- if the person relaxing sees colors or shapes, this is normal, but can be stopped easily if perceived as unpleasant or disruptive by opening the eyes
- if the person relaxing falls asleep (and this was not the purpose of the relaxation exercise), it is best to awaken them (this is of course difficult if the person has no guide; in such cases it is best to practice relaxation sitting up)

Relaxation is best started with deep breathing, combined with mindfulness of the breath. This slows down, centers, and focuses in the present the person relaxing. It generally works best to progress from the periphery of the body to the center. In other words, one's attention should move from the feet, hands, calves, forearms, thighs, upper arms, head, face, neck, shoulders, to the torso, in that order. Relaxation is contraindicated with individuals who are known to have temporal-lobe epilepsy (complex partial seizures) and other seizure disorders. It needs to be used cautiously with people who are prone to dissociation and with individuals who suffer from post-traumatic stress disorder. Debriefing with the person relaxing (that is, the client or oneself) after a relaxation exercise is a helpful process that can make subsequent sessions more efficient and useful through appropriate modification or changes. Various resources, including books, tapes, and scripts, are available to persons who would like to incorporate relaxation strategies into their everyday life.

Guided Imagery

Guided imagery is also known under various other labels, including mental rehearsal, covert modeling, and visualization. It is based on the principles of progressive relaxation and social-learning theory, and can serve many purposes beyond relaxation. Specifically, in addition to being used to induce relaxation, guided imagery has been used for pain management, skills acquisition and enhancement, self-exploration, and healing. The same cautions that apply to the use of relaxation strategies are also relevant to use of guided imagery. Most importantly, caution needs to be applied when using guided imagery with individuals who have a tendency toward dissociation, excessive anxiety, history of trauma, and certain medical conditions (such as seizures, fibromyalgia, and arthritis). For relaxation purposes, the procedure of guided imagery usually starts with deep breathing, mindfulness, and a few simple relaxation commands. Visualizations of pleasant scenery are then used to induce a deeper state of relaxation. It is important to remember that imagery does not have to be limited to the sense of sight, but also involves the senses of hearing, smelling, touching, and tasting. Scenes (including smells, tastes, and so on) work best if individualized for each individual. However, prepared scripts and tapes are also available, as are numerous books on the subject (for example, Adair, 1984; Borysenko, 1987; Fogelsanger, 1994).

Guided imageries will be adapted to suit the purpose for which they are chosen. In the context of clinicians' self-care, the most likely purposes are relaxation and self-exploration. Strictly for the purpose of relaxation, guided imagery will usually focus on the imagery of pleasant scenes that involves all the senses of the practitioner. Such guided imageries can start out with a fairly generic script that can then be modified according to the preferences of the user. As such, once a script has been used once, it is helpful to evaluate what worked and did not work and to make the necessary modifications during the next practice. Once a successful script has been developed, it can be taped individually for the specific user and used again and again. Clinicians using guided imagery for purposes of relaxation can purchase prerecorded tapes or can tape their own in their own voice or that of a friend. Similar scripts exist for purposes of self-exploration. In this area it appears preferable to develop scripts and tapes uniquely for the individual user. However, for novice users of guided imagery for any purpose, it is quite helpful to make use of the many published scripts and to modify them, rather than to start from scratch. Many books and tapes are available. One excellent source for both is the Academy for Guided Imagery in Mill Valley, California (415-389-9325). The Academy is also an excellent training site for mental-health-care providers who want to learn more about imagery. Some helpful books include:

1. Adair, M. (1984). *Working inside out: Tools for change.* Oakland, Calif.: Wingbow Press.

Skill Development Recommendations

Recommendation 3-2   *Every morning upon waking, engage in a breathing exercise to center yourself. You may choose to do this before getting out of bed (though be careful not to fall asleep again), or you may do so after you have gotten up. Practice this skill for at least three months. Journal about your experience with this exercise and evaluate its usefulness to you on a daily, weekly, and monthly basis.*

2. Borysenko, J., and Borysenko, M. (1994). *The power of the mind to heal.* Carson, Calif.: Hay House.
3. Levine, S. (1987). *Healing into life and death.* Garden City, N.Y.: Doubleday.
4. Levine, S. (1989). *A gradual awakening.* Garden City, N.Y.: Doubleday. (accompanying tape available from Warm Rock Tapes, P.O. Box 100, Chamisal, N.M. 87521)
5. Naparstek, B. (1994). *Staying well with guided imagery.* New York: Warner.
6. Rossman, M. (1993). *Mind/body medicine: How to use your mind for better health.* New York: Consumer Reports Books.

HEALTHY PERSONAL HABITS

There is virtually no limit to the number and variety of personal health care habits a person can develop and engage in. The most obvious and essential ones are included here for a brief discussion. There are no definitive answers or recommendations, and advice that has been published elsewhere is often contradictory and confusing. This section attempts to distill this advice down to the components that tend to be fairly universal to most research findings and suggestions in the literature. It addresses diet and nutrition, physical activity, rest, physical self-awareness, and awareness of nature.

Nutrition

Nothing stimulates defensiveness more easily than talking to people about their food choices and eating habits. Very few people, including clients, supervisees, friends, family members, and others, feel completely comfortable with the choices they have made in this regard and hence the defensiveness when the topic is raised. Despite the dangers inherent in raising the topic, diet and nutrition need to be discussed because they are an absolutely essential part of personal well-being and well-functioning. Food choices affect physical and emotional health, a connection not many people seem to make (for example, Null, 1995; Somer, 1995; Werbach, 1999). There are many types of diets people can choose; a simple differentiation is the omnivorous-versus-vegetarian diet. Omnivores eat animal (flesh and dairy) and plant foods; vegetarians avoid flesh foods, but not necessarily all animal products. Specifically, the vegetarian lifestyle has large variation within it, including but certainly not limited to:

- ovo-lacto-vegetarianism (vegetarians eating eggs and dairy products)
- veganism (vegetarians who shun all animal products; some even reject honey)
- pesco-vegetarianism (vegetarians who eat fish; a contradiction in terms since there is no fish that is not an animal)
- part-time-vegetarianism (people who claim to be vegetarians but consume flesh products on occasion)
- macrobiotics (a special vegetarian diet that is largely grain- and vegetable-based with many fermented products, and limited use of spices and herbs)
- raw-food diets (vegetarians who only eat raw foods, including a large variety of nuts, seeds, and sprouts)

Most commonly when people think of a vegetarian diet, they think of the ovo-lacto-vegetarian lifestyle. A vegetarian diet in and of itself is not more or less healthy than a diet that includes meat (that is, an omnivorous diet). Although research has identified longer lifespans and fewer medical problems for certain population groups who live vegetarian lifestyles, such as Seventh-Day Adventists, these populations have *healthy* vegetarian lifestyles. What makes a vegetarian lifestyle healthy is the conscious choice of wholesome, life-sustaining foods. Junk food vegetarians are no healthier than junk food omnivores. The choice to live a healthy vegetarian lifestyle has many implications, ranging from health concerns to political and social statements. Vegetarianism is a choice that can be made for several reasons:

- *health:* This type of diet is healthier in terms of reducing the number of medical problems and extending the lifespan
- *spiritual:* This type of diet is considerate of animal life and animal well-being
- *environmental:* This type of diet supports a more sustainable economy that is easier on the planet in terms of pollution and resource use
- *financial:* This type of diet can be cheaper than a meat-based diet
- *global:* This type of diet requires less acreage than a meat-based diet and could allow ample food supplies for all people on earth if practiced universally

An omnivorous diet can also meet these criteria under certain conditions. Specifically, a subsistence lifestyle as used to be practiced by indigenous populations can be respectful of the land, the earth, the animals who are hunted, and the people who prepare the food. This lifestyle, however, is quickly fading, even in remote areas of the planet. The mainstream American omnivorous diet encourages appalling conditions for animals who are raised for the mere purpose of slaughter. Although important, this issue is beyond the purpose of this section. Readers are referred to John Robbins' *Diet for a New America* (1987), or Michael W. Fox's *Eating with Conscience: The Bioethics of Food* (1997). As alluded to above, even a vegetarian diet can be unhealthy and disrespectful. A maximally healthy and respectful vegetarian diet requires that the practitioner of the lifestyle make certain healthy and important choices in addition to the choice to avoid flesh products. Most importantly, the healthiest diet is one that is whole-foods based and organic. Non-whole-foods vegetarian diets can be junk food diets that have no healthful impact. Typical American processed foods, such as white flours, processed salts, sugars, and unhealthy fats such as hydrogenated oils and transfatty acids, are the greatest obstacles to health next to toxic and polluted foods such as nonorganic vegetables grown with unhealthful fertilizers, herbicides, and pesticides, and nonorganic, non-free-range meats and dairy products.

Nutritional guidelines and choices recommended for use or avoidance are summarized in Table 3-1. Although at first blush this type of diet may seem to require an inordinate amount of time for food preparation, it really does not require much more energy and time than any other type of diet once a routine has been developed. The transition to this way of eating can be mastered in steps, making the adjustment more acceptable and easier for the body.

In addition to making conscious choices about the foods that are consumed, it is helpful to put some thought into eating habits per se. The average American eats more calories per day than are needed to sustain life. In fact, some researchers are beginning to suggest that calorie restriction (which by others has been reframed as a return to normal calorie levels) is the single most important variable in predicting length of lifespan and the only variable that may actually extend the human lifespan. Eating on the run is not a healthful habit. Eating slowly and consciously can be extremely relaxing. Making time to sit down for meals, as opposed to eating in the car, in front of the television set, or while talking on the phone or running errands, is a centering activity that also facilitates proper digestion and absorption of nutrients. Chewing food well is an important and often-overlooked component of the digestive process and its absence can account for a variety of health problems. Eating slowly and enjoying the food that is eaten rather than just wolfing it down results in greater relaxation and better health (Millman, 1993). Taking time between bites and swallowing each bite before taking the next one assures that food is eaten in proper quantities and can be digested well (Reid, 1994). Making eating an

TABLE

3-1

SUGGESTED GUIDELINES FOR HEALTHY NUTRITION

Category	Specifics
Healthful dietary lifestyle choices	• Favor a vegetarian diet, if possible of the vegan variety
	• If following an omnivorous diet, favor organic and free-range flesh and dairy products
	• Eat consciously, slowly, and with gratitude
	• Make eating a special occasion that is relaxing and centering
	• Enjoy mealtime as a time to center and come together with others
	• Reduce overall caloric intake
	• Eat a variety of foods and rotate foods
	• Follow as many of the suggestions provided below as is reasonable and enjoyable given your preferences
	• Enjoy experimenting with new, wholesome foods (e.g., tempeh, tofu, miso, tahini, dulse, nori, kelp, shiitake)
Foods to favor	• If animal products are used, choose organic and free-range varieties
	• Unprocessed whole foods (e.g., whole grains; wholesome sweeteners; fresh, not canned or frozen, vegetable and fruits; freshly baked breads and pastry products; cold-pressed oils)
	• A wide variety of organic fruits and vegetables, preferably locally grown and in season
	• A wide variety of organic grains, rotating to maximize nutrition and minimize allergic reaction (e.g., amaranth, quinoa, spelt, kamut, oats, brown rice, wild rice, barley, wheat)
	• A wide variety of organic legumes, rotating to maximize nutrition and minimize allergic reaction (e.g., black beans, garbanzo beans, kidney beans, white beans, adzuki beans, soy beans, pinto beans, lentils, split peas)
	• Daily portions of soy-based foods (e.g., tofu, tempeh, miso, shoyu sauce)
	• Nondairy "milks" (e.g., rice milk, soy milk, almond milk, grain milk)
	• Raw foods (e.g., uncooked vegetables and fruits, sprouts, rolled grains)
	• Small daily amounts of healthful fats (e.g., flaxseed oil, nuts, seeds, small quantities of cold-pressed extra virgin olive oil or cold-pressed sesame oil sold in opaque glass containers)

- Freshly extracted vegetable juices
- Sea vegetables (e.g., kelp, dulse, nori)
- Mushrooms (e.g., shiitake, maitake)
- Pure water in large quantities
- Herbal teas and green tea

Foods to avoid

- Processed foods (e.g., ready-made freezer or microwave meals; foods with white sugars, salts, or flours; foods with hydrogenated fats or transfatty acids)
- Empty foods (e.g., sodas, candy bars, candies, many cereals, coffee)
- Junk foods (e.g., fast food, fried food, chips)
- Polluted foods (e.g., produce from countries that do not limit use of certain fertilizers and pesticides; nonorganic, hormonally treated flesh products; nonorganic, hormonally treated dairy products)
- Toxic foods (e.g., foods containing additives such as food coloring, foods containing chemical stabilizers or preservatives)
- Excessively concentrated foods (e.g., fruit juices, sweetened drinks)

Helpful hints

- Practice proper food combining (i.e., keep meals simple, not combining too many different foods at once)
- Eat fruits on an empty stomach and by themselves
- Grind your own whole-grain flours to avoid rancidity; if buying whole-grain flours, choose a store that grinds them fresh or stores the flours in the refrigerated section or in vacuum-packed bags
- Flake your own grains for cereals to avoid rancidity
- Sauté vegetables in a bit of shoyu or liquid aminos instead of oil
- Eat the bulk of your foods early in the day, not in the evening
- Listen to your body in terms of how best to distribute your food intake over the course of the day (i.e., several small meals versus a few big meals)
- Go to your local farmer's market for fresh, organic produce
- Talk to your favorite grocery store manager about stocking organic foods and about special orders of wholesome foods not regularly carried
- Bake all of your own pastries, cookies, cakes, and breads to avoid the unhealthful ingredients of packaged products

TABLE 3-1 (CONTINUED)

Category	Specifics
Helpful hints (continued)	• Learn to read labels and always read labels of any prepackaged foods you buy
	• Buy bulk foods whenever possible to save on packaging and cost
	• Grow an organic garden and use as many homegrown foods as possible
	• Always have a cooked grain and a cooked legume in the fridge ready to combine with fresh vegetables for quick meals
	• Make your own convenience or expensive foods such as grain and nut "milks," cereals, pancake mixes, salad dressings, and spice mixes
	• Plan consumption of grains and legumes by soaking them during the day and cooking them in the evening for use the next day
	• Sprout your own sprouts and grow your own herbs indoors all year long
	• Stock a pantry with wholesome foods; do not buy foods you want to avoid so as not to be tempted
	• Make your teas from bulk herbs and bulk tea leaves; collect your own herbs (e.g., red clover, nettles, dandelion) when in season and dry for year-round use
	• Have your water analyzed and install filters as needed in your home
Read and learn about nutrition	• Balch, J. F., & P. A. Balch. 1997. *Prescription for nutritional healing.* 2d ed. Garden City Park, N.Y.: Avery.
	• Crayhon, R. 1994. *Nutrition made simple: A comprehensive guide to the latest findings in optimal nutrition.* New York: M. Evans.
	• Haas, E. M. 1992. *Staying healthy with nutrition.* Berkeley: Celestial Arts.
	• Null, G. 1995. *Nutrition and the mind.* New York: Seven Stories.
	• Pitchford, P. 1993. *Healing with whole foods: Oriental traditions and modern nutrition.* Berkeley: North Atlantic.
	• Pizzorno, J. 1998. *Total wellness.* Rocklin, Calif.: Prima.
	• Reid, D. 1994. *The complete book of Chinese health and healing.* New York: Barnes and Noble.
	• Robbins, J. 1987. *Diet for a new America.* Walpole, N.H.: Stillpoint.
	• Roehl, E. 1996. *Whole food facts: The complete reference guide.* Rochester, Vt.: Healing Arts.
	• Rohe, F. 1983. *The complete book of natural foods.* Boulder: Shambhala.

occasion to be relished is a nice way of centering oneself through an activity that needs to be engaged in anyway.

Physical Activity

Almost as touchy as the topic of food is the issue of exercise. Everyone knows that being active seems to be related to better health. Nevertheless, only a small portion of the American public actually follows this advice. The type and level of activity that is optimal for the average person appears less clear-cut than the generic advice to seek out an active lifestyle. There seems to be agreement around the need for daily exercise. The incorporation of daily exercise is best accomplished by building a routine of exercise into daily life that can be followed even, or especially, on tiresome and stressful days. For physical activity to be healthful, overexercise needs to be avoided as much as underexercise. In other words, it is important to avoid compulsive exercise that stresses the body even further. It is best to choose activities that result in enjoyment and that do not hurt physically. A good balance of aerobic exercise and stretching appears to be useful, and the incorporation of the enjoyment of the outdoors can add a relaxing and rejuvenating component. It is helpful to seek variety in terms of exercising, as this keeps motivation up and repetitive-stress injuries down. In designing a physical fitness plan it is best to keep in mind four aspects of physical activity and health: strength (or muscular power); stamina (or aerobic capacity and endurance); suppleness (or flexibility); and sensitivity (or balance, rhythm, and timing). All four of these components need to be conditioned and attended to. Incorporating exercise that involves strength, stamina, suppleness, and sensitivity into vacations is another excellent way to unwind and keep the body healthy. Hiking, backpacking, kayaking, and similar activities fit the category of exercise while also being extremely pleasurable and relaxing in an outdoor setting that can be healing to mind, spirit, and body.

The three foremost aerobic forms of regular (if not daily) exercise that are relatively safe to engage in and that build strength as well as stamina are walking, swimming, and cross-country skiing. Walking is an excellent exercise that is easy to fit into busy schedules, inexpensive, and possible anywhere and in any weather. Swimming is another form of activity that has a low incidence of injury and can be greatly enjoyable while giving maximum benefits. Cross-country skiing is another aerobic exercise that is easily learned and has great physical benefits. Many other forms of aerobic exercise exist (dancing, tennis, racquetball, running, step classes, and on and on), and it is important to sample several before settling into a routine. Varying these forms of exercise is also a good idea to keep up motivation and enjoyment. Running, one of the more popular forms of aerobic exercise because of its time efficiency, has many drawbacks, as does high-impact aerobics. It is best to consult with a physician before engaging in potentially more injurious forms of aerobic exercise.

The best supplements to aerobic regimens to build suppleness and sensitivity are stretching exercises, mild workouts with free weights, and systematic exercise routines such as t'ai chi, chi gong, and yoga. Most of these require some initial learning curve and lessons until a basic routine has been mastered. Once learned, however, they can be carried out anywhere, anytime, and are extremely flexible. They can easily be engaged in at the office, even for ten minutes between clients. Additionally, exercises such as t'ai chi, chi gong, and yoga have a strong relaxation or even meditative component and can rest the mind while working out the body. Specific yoga and chi gong routines can be developed with an instructor for specific healing purposes and can be extremely useful for dealing with particular ailments or disease/recurrence prevention.

If a person is currently sedentary, it is important to check with a physician before starting a rigorous exercise program. Once the decision is made to incorporate exercise into daily life, it is a good idea to start exercising slowly, gradually increasing length and intensity. The "main principle in physical activity is gradually and comfortably to be more active" (Bayne, 1997, p. 188). Jumping in full force can lead to injury and quick disillusionment. Thirty minutes of exercise per day most days of the week is a good goal to aim for. Some research has suggested that exercise does not have to be done in a continuous period. Instead, exercise can be incorporated into a busy schedule by doing a little bit at a time, several times a day. Thayer, Newman, and McClain (1994) showed that just ten minutes of brisk walking had a positive effect by increasing energy and reducing tension for up to two hours! It is important to let the body dictate what is comfortable, rather than to use some external standard of having to work out for a certain length of time or to go for a certain criterion of distance, weight, or similar standards. Some people can easily engage in strenuous aerobic exercise without negative effects, whereas others are better served by less-stressful activity. One thing to remember while engaging in all forms of exercise is that very strenuous activity increases the number of free radicals in the body and thus increases the need for proper nutrition, especially the intake of antioxidants. Prolonged strenuous exercise can actually damage the body significantly and can leave the exerciser with a weakened immune system that is more vulnerable to colds and other minor ailments. Some sports physicians, for example, indicate that running a marathon can leave the immune system compromised for up to six weeks (K. W. Klingler, personal communication, 8 June 1998).

Rest

Often when lives get very full with activity and commitments, time is taken away from sleep. This is a bad idea as the cost of reducing sleep can be high. The lack of alertness during the day after a sleep-deprived night may undo the time savings of that extra hour of staying awake the day before. Getting plenty of sleep each night is a most important self-care habit. The number of hours required varies greatly from individual to individual. The best sleep routine is one in which the person awakens in the morning without an alarm clock. This may require going to bed earlier or starting the day later than most other people. The development of routines best follows the dictates of the body rather than some external criterion of what "should" or "should not" be done. Some routines, unfortunately, are dictated. If children have to be at school at a certain time or an employer expects an employee at work at a certain hour, then routines have to be adjusted. However, the number of hours of sleep does not need to be compromised even then. Some people like to incorporate a rest period in the middle of the day. For some, this practice causes a sluggish and drowsy response, but for others it is excellent. Experimentation with what works is again the best method of judging whether to incorporate this routine into one's life.

Physical Self-Awareness

It is very important to learn to recognize warning signals and pleasure signals that come from within one's body. Bodies often know before the conscious mind does that stress is mounting and changes need to be made. Paying attention to the body and letting it decide when to slow down is an important self-awareness skill and health issue. Bodily symptoms and changes can give an indication of when someone may need medical attention, when there is a need to change exercise and nutrition routines, or when the need for relaxation has to be met. Regular physical checkups can be useful even when the body appears to be symptom-free. It may be preferable to consult naturopathic physicians for this type of medical care, as they are more attuned to subtle symptoms and bodily changes. Allopathic medicine is still preoccupied with disease and illness as signaled by strong discomfort and overt symptoms. Non-mainstream (and non-Western) medicine instead looks for patterns and changes in functioning that can be early warning signs about disease or less than optimal health (for example, Pizzorno, 1998; Reid, 1994). The definition of health in allopathic medicine is merely the absence of disease; in naturopathic medicine (and in traditional Chinese medicine, for that matter), the definition of health is much broader, involving the well-functioning of body, mind, and spirit. Being in touch with one's body is a good idea, and a few critical health-monitoring routines can be incorporated by everyone, based on need and risk factors. For example, monthly breast self-exams, daily blood pressure checks, and similar simple health care routines can be life-saving skills for those with risk factors for particular diseases (cf., Pizzorno, 1998, for an excellent book on taking charge of monitoring one's own health).

Taking an interest in one's health care during times of disease or symptoms is another important aspect of physical self-awareness. Blind faith in physicians is often misplaced as allopathic medicine often pretends to have the answers to a problem when the suggestion really is at best an educated guess. Being informed about treatment alternatives and not simply accepting every recommendation ever made by a physician is responsible self-care. Medicine has very few definitive answers, and many mild physical problems have a wide range of possible solutions. The overuse of certain medications, such as antibiotics, has resulted in health care crises of frightening proportions (for example, Garrett, 1994). The treatment of symptoms rather than causes is another problem of allopathic medicine that can only be overcome by responsible self-care and active involvement in one's personal health care. Taking a pill to alleviate a symptom may be easier than searching for the cause of the symptom, but in the long term it tends to create more problems. Symptoms are often signals that the body (or mind) is in distress. Covering the symptom merely prolongs the exposure to the cause of the problem. For example, taking medications for heartburn is a sure way of inviting disaster if the root cause of the problem is not addressed (Pizzorno, 1998). Even more invasive medical procedures are often confused with being healing when they are really only palliative. Bypass surgery is an important example. The bypass may fix the clogged artery, but it will not extend life unless substantial lifestyle changes are made that address the root cause of the disease. Removing the symptoms (that is, the arterial clog) does not deliver health. Making responsible choices about risk-benefit ratios of prescribed treatments is another important self-care skill. Chemotherapy for cancer is an example of the cure sometimes being worse than the disease (Moss, 1996). The exploration of treatment alternatives is often left to the patient. This generally means that the patient who is not self-aware will blindly follow the allopathic physician's lead, taking whatever is prescribed without exploring whether preferable alternatives exist (for example, herbal remedies, nutritional interventions, physical therapies).

The relevance of this issue to therapists and counselors rests in the fact that health care is an active skill and perfect health is only obtained if active involvement is part and parcel of physical self-care. Perfect physical health, in turn, is an important prerequisite to mental health. If clinicians cover their own physical symptoms with palliative methods and fail to seek root causes of their ailments, they most likely will model the same passive consumption of health care for their clients. This is dangerous practice and goes against the idea of empowering consumers to take an active and deciding role in their own health care (physical and emotional). The lesson is to practice what is preached.

Involvement with Nature

The final personal-care habit is somewhat related to relaxation and stress reduction. Being in touch with nature is a centering aspect of life. Too many people in modern life spend hardly any time outdoors. The fact that the indoor environment can be perfectly adjusted in terms of warmth, humidity, and simi-

Skill Development Recommendations

Recommendation 3-3   *Choose one of the personal health habits discussed in this section and obtain more information about it. Once satisfied that you have an adequate fund of information, incorporate at least one new self-care strategy into your life each week. For example, cook one healthy, nutritious meal; exercise; commune with nature; get a good night's sleep. Journal about that experience. Engage in this strategy once weekly for one month. Then add a second strategy each week. Keep adding one strategy to your week for four months. Journal about how these self-care skills affect your daily life.*

---

lar variables has made it tempting for many to avoid the outdoors when conditions are perceived as less than perfect. This leads to an alienation from the rest of the world and from the very environment that is the natural ecology of our species (Burns, 1998). Humans did not evolve indoors; they are potentially closely tied to nature and have a strong relationship with it. Many people could obtain incredible physical and emotional healing power from nature if only they exposed themselves to it, given that "unthreatening natural environments tend to promote faster more complete recuperation from stress than do urban environments" (Pigram, 1993, p. 402). Health care for centuries was naturally-based, not only in the sense of physical health, but also in the sense of mental, emotional, and spiritual well-being. Close communion with nature was perceived as conducive to maintaining health, as well as healing in and of itself. Natural phenomena, such as sacred sites or environments where healing has taken place, interactions with nature such as natural rituals or bathing in natural bodies of water, and natural medicines, such as herbs and foods, were the primary healing and preventative forces that human beings relied on for most of their evolutionary process (Burns, 1998).

Modern life has largely superceded humanity's interaction with raw, natural environments. This is an unfortunate reality given the healing power of natural environments that can reduce stress, enhance positive affect, improve parasympathetic-nervous-system functioning, and enhance self-esteem (Ulrich, Dimberg, and Driver, 1991). Having the knowledge that being part of nature can be healing in and of itself gives clinicians a powerful tool for self-rejuvenation, relaxation, disease prevention, and healing. Spending some time outdoors every day in as natural an environment as possible has enormous positive consequences for mind, body, and spirit. This time outdoors does not have to be reserved for weekends or vacations, nor should it be guided by weather. The experience of walking in the rain can be immensely pleasurable and healing. The silence of a remote piece of land that allows the person to escape the hectic pace and noisy background of modern society cannot be surpassed in terms of its positive effects by any therapeutic or counseling intervention in the repertoire of today's mental-health-care providers. Availing oneself of this incredible resource for health and healing means taking care of oneself. Using this resource for clients is, of course, another possibility and one that is beautifully explored in Burns' (1998) book entitled *Nature-Guided Therapy.*

ATTENTION TO RELATIONSHIPS

Attention to relationships is as important as attention to personal health habits. Most humans are highly social creatures who feel best if firmly embedded in an interpersonal matrix of meaningful and sustaining relationships (cf., Kohut, 1984). There are many personal traits that can greatly facilitate positive relationships that sustain health as opposed to creating stress. Although it is impossible to outline all of these traits here, or to even come close to attempting to teach them, a few suggestions will be outlined whose incorporation into personal life tends to be extremely helpful. Paying careful attention and taking responsibility in relationships can reduce stress and create a source of support that is sustaining when work life is difficult.

The most important relationships to attend to are friendships and intimate relationships. However, the few guidelines that follow really apply to all relationships, even those with strangers, clients, bosses, and colleagues. To make positive relationships happen, active work has to take place. This work is applied to self and relationships to harmonize interactions with others. Working on the self is the first step in creating positive relationships. Empathy, tolerance, acceptance, and respectfulness are essential ingredients of healthy relationships and largely depend on personal attitudes and self-awareness (which will be dealt with in more detail below). Thus, working to become a better and more tolerant person is a prerequisite to learning to respect others and to allow them to be different from one's self. It is important not to place personal rights ahead of those of others; to be considerate of others' needs and respect their right to be themselves; and never to try to form anyone in one's own image. If we treat others respectfully, they will treat us respectfully. Polite and respectful interactions reduce stress in day-to-day life, making interactions with those in our interpersonal matrix more positive and enjoyable.

Another helpful trait that tends to keep relationships positive and sustaining is the ability to laugh at oneself. Those individuals who have learned to laugh at themselves and their own shortcomings are rarely quick to jump to conclusions about others and seldom place blame. They are able to put things in perspective with the recognition that everyone makes mistakes and has flaws that are played out in relationships. The ability to laugh at oneself, however,

Skill Development Recommendations

Recommendation 3-4   *For the next month, keep a journal of your inter-personal relationships. Evaluate how you treat people and look at how you prioritize relationships. If you are satisfied with how you relate to others, you are done; if you identify areas of weakness or dissatisfaction, set specific goals about how to go about improving your relationships. Consider personal counseling or therapy to assist you if needed.*

---

must not be mistaken as an excuse not to change and grow; being able to laugh at oneself is the beginning. The next step is to look at whether the situation can be avoided in the future through self-change and growth. The ability to laugh at oneself in and of itself often suffices to defuse potentially conflictual situations in relationships as the other person involved will not feel attacked or blamed.

Very similar to the concept of not taking oneself too seriously and being able to accept one's shortcomings is the notion of defenselessness and detachment from one's personal point of view. People who are not defensive and not overly attached to convincing everyone of their personal point of view tend to have more positive and less conflictual relationships. It is rare that any issue is so important that a relationship needs to be sacrificed over it. There is usually room for compromise; everyone involved can learn to adjust their point of view or opinion somewhat. Further, the ability to not get defensive when challenged can serve to make interactions with others less conflictual and more collaborative or cooperative. All too often people get locked into perceiving a difference in opinions as a personal attack, followed by the need to defend themselves and their point of view. Learning to accept differences of opinion as the expression of different, but equally human, ways of looking at the same situation can free people to let go of the need to defend themselves. This does not mean that people always have to agree with each other. It merely means that everyone needs to recognize that they neither have to get upset nor angry if they perceive a challenge to their actions or beliefs.

One final note is necessary about relationships and their role in the lives of mental-health-care providers. Just simply *having and valuing* relationships is important as their presence appears to mediate a decrease in burnout among clinicians! The quality of the relationships counts, of course, but first of all, they must be in existence. The traits that were discussed above are helpful for maintaining relationships, but also for initiating them. Attention to building a close circle of friends is critical, as is the forging of at least one intimate relationship.

Attending to family relationships cannot be overemphasized as this is the setting where many of us seek support first and most frequently. Relationships help balance our lives and often ensure that we keep events around us in the proper perspective, not overreacting to "small stuff." There are of course many resources and books that can easily be found in any popular bookstore to help clinicians pay attention to this aspect of their lives.

RECREATIONAL ACTIVITIES

Another highly balancing aspect to life is to pay attention to leisure and recreation. Being able to have fun and to enjoy life is often most easily accomplished through recreational activities. The range of activities is literally infinite and the following paragraphs will merely point out some of the possibilities. The main lesson of this section is to attend to leisure and to learn to view it as important and life-sustaining. Ignoring leisure for the sake of making more time for work is not a good idea. Life is short. Who wants to die thinking, "If only I had tried. . . ." Making time for hobbies and interests is an enjoyable way to add spice to life and prevent boredom and burnout. It is best to make leisure skills as different from work as possible. There are unlimited possibilities as far as hobbies are concerned. The only limiting factors are motivation, desire, creativity, interest, and physical capabilities. It is never too late to pick up new hobbies or to try to acquire new skills. Hobbies can include outdoor activities (hiking, backpacking, kayaking, skiing, gardening), introverted activities (painting, writing poetry, composing music, playing music), sociable activities (dancing, playing music for others, leading guided hikes, joining a theater group), sedate activities (reading, knitting, stamp collecting), active activities (sports, performing arts, volunteering), and many more. The most important thing for clinicians appears to be to develop interests and hobbies outside of the mental-health-care field.

Travel is another way of recreating and spending quality leisure time. Not all vacations have to be lengthy or expensive. Vacations can consist of extended weekend trips and can even be taken at home as long as work is honestly avoided. The definition of vacation is really a broad one that is only limited by personal imagination and preferences. The greatest vacation for some people may be a three-day backpacking trip; for others, it may consist of two weeks in Europe. Making vacations fit personal preferences and finances is the most critical piece so that they do not end up creating more stress than pleasure. If a vacation is so expensive that it subsequently requires many extra hours of work, it may not be worthwhile. Similarly, a vacation that is so full of entertainment and activity that the traveler arrives back home feeling overwhelmed and exhausted, did not serve its purpose fully. Striking a balance between nov-

Skill Development Recommendations

Recommendation 3-5   *For the next month, keep a journal of your recreational pursuits. Evaluate how you spend your time and look at how you prioritize your recreational activities. If you are satisfied with how you relax and recreate, you are done; if you identify areas of weakness or dissatisfaction, set some goals about how to go about improving. Consider personal counseling or therapy to assist you if needed.*

---

elty and relaxation, excitement and meditation, learning and stress reduction is best considered while planning a trip.

Another aspect of recreation and leisure is group memberships. This is not for everyone, but can be extremely rewarding for more sociable types. Group membership is best chosen away from the mental-health profession. Reference is not made here to association membership, although that is certainly important to professional self-care (see Brems, 2000). Reference is made instead to making friends and acquaintances in settings that have nothing to do with the mental-health-care profession. This type of interaction is stimulating and exciting because it provides exposure to a broad range of healthy human beings who come together for a shared purpose or interest. These purposes or interests can range widely, including membership in organizations such as environmental groups, religious/spiritual groups, political groups, clubs organized around sports or special interests, and any other interesting groupings of people who come together on a regular basis for some joint endeavor. Some groups also help people reach beyond themselves as they come together for a greater cause. Such volunteer work can be life-enhancing and extremely gratifying.

Finally, also in the category of recreation, there is entertainment. This is the leisure category of least importance, though it too should not be entirely neglected. Entertainment can consist of artistic events, cinema, dinners out, and similar activities. It can be an event for one or two, a family, or a whole group of friends. Most importantly, however, entertainment does not refer to watching TV or going shopping. Entertainment for recreation and leisure refers to an activity that is rejuvenating, stimulating, relaxing, comforting, or otherwise self-enhancing—not to one that is dulling, passive, or mind-numbing. Entertainment can even consist of playing board games with children or party games with a group. In some families, get-togethers often involve games and similar activities that make the meetings more lively, active, and enjoyable.

SKILLS TO FACILITATE COMMUNICATION IN PSYCHOTHERAPY AND COUNSELING

ATTENDING SKILLS

Nonverbal Communication and Listening

> When you listen to someone, you should give up all your preconceived ideas and your subjective opinions; you should just listen to him, just observe what his way is. We put very little emphasis on right and wrong or good and bad. We just see things as they are with them, and accept them. This is how we communicate with each other. Usually when you listen to some statement, you hear it as a kind of echo of yourself. You are actually listening to your own opinion. If it agrees with your opinion you may accept it, but if it does not, you will reject it or you may not even really hear it.
>
> *Shunryu Suzuki, 1998, p. 88*

Attending skills—such a simple phrase for a complex collection of behaviors and abilities. Attending skills are comprised of a series of complex proficiencies that cut across the verbal and nonverbal domains of communication. Attending represents the basis of all therapeutic encounters; without attending skills, the establishment of therapeutic rapport is most likely difficult, if not impossible. Attending refers to the focused attention that is placed on the other person in an interchange between two (or more) people. It is rare that people receive the full attention of their communication partner(s). When it does happen, they are keenly aware and appreciative of this fact. It is rare that people place full attention on themselves; hence, it is not surprising that most clients, and perhaps too many clinicians, are unaware of, or inattentive to, their own metacommunications. Clients are frequently unaware of communications that go beyond the verbal, and clinicians may forget to attend to these nonverbals. Even more importantly, clinicians may forget to pay attention to their own internal dialogs while listening, becoming less-than-aware listeners. It is no surprise that attending skills, specifically, nonverbal communication and listening, need to be developed by clinicians first and foremost in training. Nonverbal communication and

101

listening present challenges and require a complex web of skills and knowledge that need to become second nature to the seasoned clinician.

NONVERBAL COMMUNICATION

Nonverbal communication is important from two perspectives: (1) nonverbal communication expressed by the client and picked up by the clinician and (2) nonverbal communication used by the clinician for therapeutic goals. Attending to nonverbal communication is an excellent means of gaining a clearer understanding of clients as it opens up a major area of metacommunication. Often nonverbals express or suggest hidden meanings and agendas or lead the clinician in a direction of questioning that would not otherwise have been broached. At times, nonverbals are more accurate signposts of where to take a counseling session than is verbal communication, as they may be a less-censored form of communication. All nonverbal communication, whether unconsciously expressed by the client or purposefully used by the mental-health-care provider, interacts with the verbal message being sent. The relationship between nonverbal communication and verbal expressions has been explored and clarified beautifully by Knapp (1978), who identified six ways in which verbal and nonverbal communication can interact. These six ways not only demonstrate the complex interplay between words and bodily expressions, but also point to the importance of recognizing the nonverbal aspects of all communications lest much of the meaning of an exchange be lost.

Interaction of Verbal and Nonverbal Communication

The first means of interaction is *repetition.* In repetition or confirmation, the nonverbal message (such as a gesture or facial expression) repeats the obvious verbal message. In other words, the verbal and nonverbal content of the communication is identical and thus redundant. Despite this redundancy, it tends to be the nonverbal repetition of verbal expression that makes communication seem alive and provides speaker and listener with a sense of connectedness. The absence of nonverbal repetition may explain why it is more difficult to achieve the same level of intimacy in a telephone conversation as in a personal conversation. Many nonverbal aspects of communication are lost in this medium.

The second possible interaction is *contradiction.* Also called denying or confusion, this is essentially the opposite of repetition in that the nonverbal message contradicts the verbalization. The two aspects of communication express opposite meanings. Contradiction is an important interaction to recognize in therapy and counseling, as clients often give mixed messages. If the clinician is skilled in picking up contradictions, many therapeutic processes can be set in motion through the work with these nonverbal aspects of communication, as will be elaborated upon in the chapter dealing with confrontation. Clinicians, of course, need to avoid contradictions as they communicate incongruence or lack of authenticity.

Third, there is *substitution*. In substitution, nonverbals are used to express a response to a verbal question. In other words, in substitution, the nonverbal response literally takes the place of a verbal reaction. Being able to read the nonverbal response is obviously critical; otherwise, the listener and speaker will disconnect in their interaction. Therapists and counselors need to be attuned to clients' nonverbal responses to questions lest they miss important information or deem the client nonresponsive when in actuality a response has been given.

The fourth interaction is called *complementation*. In complementation (also called strengthening), a nonverbal communication serves to elaborate a verbalization, though as in all cases, this is not often done intentionally. The verbal and nonverbal remain congruent but the verbal message is somehow amplified through the nonverbal expressions accompanying it.

The fifth interaction is referred to as emphasizing or *accenting*. In accenting, the nonverbal aspects of the communication emphasize or highlight certain components of the verbalization. Accenting is helpful in determining where the importance of a verbal message may rest by attending to where the person places nonverbal underscoring. Being aware of accents in a client's speech will help clinicians determine where and how to intervene by picking up clues as to what is of utmost importance to the client. In turn, counselors can use accents of their own to emphasize certain points to their clients.

Finally, there is *regulation*, which is also tellingly called control and refers to the nonverbal processes in communication that assist the speaker and listener in timing or pacing their interaction. These are the nonverbal clues accompanying speech that tell the involved parties when to talk, when to stop, when interest has been lost or peaked, and so forth. Regulation is an important component of therapeutic interaction, as the therapist needs to be aware of the client's clues as well as of the clinician's own inadvertent messages. Awareness of how clients use regulation may be particularly important in cross-cultural or cross-gender settings as regulation signs may differ culturally. Regulation will be discussed in more detail below in the context of timing and in the chapter dealing with encouragers of communication. Examples and definitions are provided in Table 4-1 to highlight the complex and helpful interactions between verbal and nonverbal communication.

Components of Nonverbal Communication

All nonverbal communication consists of one or more of five possible components, namely, physical appearance, kinesics, paralinguistics, use of space, and timing. Physical appearance refers to the physical body of the person, along with

TABLE 4-1

KNAPP'S (1978) CONCEPTUALIZATION OF THE INTERACTION BETWEEN VERBAL AND NONVERBAL COMMUNICATION

Type of Interaction	Definition	Common Life Example	Clinician Example	Client Example
Repetition	Nonverbal expressions repeat the verbal message	Saying "hello" and waving when seeing a friend	Leaning forward and saying with lowered voice, "That must have been so painful."	Crying while talking about a sad event
Contradiction	Nonverbal expressions contradict the verbal message	A parent hitting a child while yelling, "It's because I love you very much."	To be avoided by clinicians; saying "I am not angry with you" in a loud and/or aggressive voice	Laughing and smiling while talking about the death of a loved one
Substitution	Making a nonverbal reaction to a verbal communication	Nodding one's head to indicate "yes" in response to a question	Leaning forward and nodding after a client has said, "Do you understand?"	Crying after the therapist has asked a question about current affect
Complementation	Nonverbal response elaborates upon or deepens the verbal message	Smiling and touching a person while saying "I love you"	Slowing down speech and lowering voice while giving relaxation instructions	Fast rate of speech and body movement while talking about an anxiety-provoking event
Accenting	Using nonverbals to emphasize or highlight a certain portion of a long verbal message	Hitting a fist on the table when arriving at an angering point in a speech	Changing pitch of voice and raising head on the word "sad" while saying, "Sounds like a SAD, not a frustrating event!"	Looking away and dropping one's voice when arriving at the most saddening aspect of a long story
Regulation	Nonverbal cues that help listener and speaker regulate the flow of verbal communication	Looking or turning away when feeling bored with a conversation to stop the speaker from talking	Nodding in understanding and maintaining respectful eye contact while the client is speaking to keep the client talking	Pausing and suddenly looking up at the clinician to invite the clinician to say something in response to a verbalization

clothing, grooming, and hygiene. Kinesics refers to the movements of the body as a whole or of various body parts, such as eye contact, leg movements, hand movements, and so forth. Paralinguistics refers to the nonverbal aspects of voice and speech, such as volume and pitch of voice or rate and fluency of speech. Use of space explores the use of personal and environmental space by individuals, including distances they keep from others or positions they choose in relation to objects or other people in the same area. Timing deals with a person's understanding and use of time, as reflected, for example, in tardiness or in timing of certain verbalizations in a temporal context.

Physical Appearance

Clinicians attend to client factors such as height and weight, grooming and hygiene, manner and style of dress, eye and hair color, complexion, level of physical fitness, and physical attributes such as scars, bruises, physical handicaps, and prosthetic devices. Many of these characteristics are simply descriptive, but others are usefully evaluated with regard to their nonverbal-communication value. For example, traits such as eye and hair color are simply noted. Height and weight can be looked at with regard to their relationship to expected healthy or normative ranges. Hygiene and grooming can be rated as to whether they are appropriate given societal health standards and grooming habits. Deficiencies in appearance are assessed to glean information about the adequacy of the client's self-care skills, which in turn may help the clinician make some assessment of the client's social competence and judgment (Beutler and Berren, 1995). Mental-health-care providers need to be cautious not to allow stereotypic assumptions to enter into their evaluation of a client's appearance. Awareness is necessary if a certain style of dress always evokes a particular judgment or response in a counselor or therapist. For example, the use or nonuse of makeup is not to be confused with proper grooming or hygiene among female clients. Many well-groomed women choose not to wear makeup. Noting this feature as unusual is a reflection of the clinician's bias, not the client's self-care.

Appearance of the client is not the only important factor. Appearance of the clinician may be just as important. Clinicians need to be sensitive to the setting in which they work and need to express through their appearance that they can adapt to and understand the clientele with which they work. For example, wearing expensive jewelry in a mental-health clinic in a lower-socioeconomic sector of town may lead to distance between client and therapist. Needless to say, proper grooming and hygiene are as essential as appropriate attire. What constitutes proper clothing, however, is less easily defined. Again, the counselor needs to adapt to the clientele. Wearing high heels and tight skirts when working in play therapy with children is clearly going to get in the way of therapeutic work. Wearing expensive designer suits while working with homeless people may be in poor taste. However, wearing torn, dirty, or very revealing clothing may be equally inappropriate. Clearly, clinicians have to develop good judgment in deciding how to dress each morning.

Kinesics

As shown in Table 4-2, kinesics can emerge from any body part. Some of the most important body features observed involve head, face, eyes, mouth, shoulders, arms, hands, legs, feet, and torso. Motor movement observations about all body parts are important as they can provide a great deal of information about a client's state of alertness and emotionality. They can help the clinician with diagnosis related to alertness (such as delirium and dementia) as well as diagnosis related to psychomotor issues (for example, bipolar disorder). Motor movement overall is often further defined as agitated, fidgety, unusual, normal, or as including tics, tremors, or motor abnormalities. Autonomic responses are also often included, drawing attention to physiological reactions such as rate of breathing, blushing versus paling, or pupil dilation. All motor and facial expressions can be assessed in terms of their congruence with verbal content of conversation as well as the level of activity or agitation they may suggest. Any unusual or characteristic manners and habits of a person are useful to note, such as tics, repetitive verbalizations, or nervous gestures or laughter. Eye contact is also often considered to be an example of kinesics.

Specific meanings can be attached to particular motor expressions and eye contact patterns. Although it is helpful to review the possibilities, clinicians must be aware that not all clients use the same kinesics to express the same thing. For example, unfolded arms used to gesture broadly most commonly means that the client is open and self-disclosing. For the occasional client, however, this same gesture may indicate evasiveness or a hiding behind histrionics. For some clients, consistent eye contact with the clinician is desirable and expresses a good emotional connection, whereas for others, such continual eye contact may be disturbing or upsetting. Generally, the context in which the behavior occurs is very helpful in making the most accurate interpretation. Cultural and gender differences need to be attended to as well, with mental-health-care providers noting that unique differences may exist within and between certain groups of people. Thus, even though Table 4-2 outlines some common interpretations of a range of kinesics, the wise counselor will not mistake this table as being definitive but will use it to glean *ideas* about what certain movements may mean in certain circumstances with certain clients. The most important thing to understand about kinesics is that clients use their bodies to express themselves and that therapists can gain an enormous amount of information about their clients if they bother to learn what these kinesics mean for each individual client.

Kinesics derive additional importance from the reality that they are commonly used as substitutions. In other words, not infrequently clients use their body to respond to a clinician's question. Learning a client's manner of using

TABLE
4-2

SAMPLES OF POSSIBLE INTERPRETATIONS OF COMMON KINESICS

Feature	Nonverbal Expression	Possible Meaning
Eyes	Direct eye contact	• Attentiveness • Readiness for communication • Comfort with setting and clinician
	Lack of eye contact	• Withdrawal • Avoidance of communication • Respect or deference
	Looking down or away	• Preoccupation • Avoidance • Concentrated thought
	Fixed staring	• Preoccupation • Uptightness • Rigidity • Psychosis
	Darting or blinking eyes	• Anxiety • Paranoia • Excitement • Dry contact lenses
	Squinting or furrowed brow	• Thoughtfulness or "aha" experience • Concern • Annoyance
	Teary eyes and/or tears	• Sadness • Happiness • Frustration or anger • Concern or fear
	Dilated pupils	• Alarm • Interest • Recent visit to eye doctor • Under the influence of drugs
	Eyes moving to and away from eye contact	• Recalling a memory • Interest
Mouth	Smiling	• Greeting • Positive mood • Avoidance or denial
	Tight lips	• Stress • Anger or hostility • Concentration
	Quivering lips	• Sadness or crying • Anger • Anxiety
	Biting or chewing of lips	• Anxiety • Bad habit
	Open mouth	• Surprise • Boredom or fatigue or yawning • Having a cold if breathing through open mouth
Facial expressions	Flushed face	• Embarrassment • Anxiety
	Eyes open wide and mouth opening	• Surprise • Startle response • Sudden insight

TABLE 4-2 (CONTINUED)

Feature	Nonverbal Expression	Possible Meaning
Facial expressions (continued)	Furrowed brow with tight mouth	• Deep thought or concentration • Irritation or annoyance • Rejection of a therapist response
	Eyes looking up and mouth pursed	• Memory retrieval • Disagreement • Thoughtfulness or pondering of a suggestion
Head	Nodding up and down	• Agreement • Listening and/or paying attention
	Shaking left to right	• Disagreement • Disapproval
	Hanging	• Sadness • Hopelessness
	Cocked to one side	• Pondering • Listening and/or paying attention
Shoulders and neck	Shrugging	• Uncertainty or ambivalence • Indifference or lack of caring about something
	Slouched	• Sadness • Withdrawal or shyness • Bad posture
	Raised	• Self-protection • Stretching
	Neck rolls	• Tension • Stretching
Arms and hands	Folded arms	• Closed to contact • Dislike or emotional distance • Creating a barrier for self-protection
	Trembling hands	• Anxiety • Anger • Disease process (e.g., hypoglycemia, Parkinson's)
	Clenched fist or tight grasp	• Anger or imminence of acting out • Resistance to disclosure • Intimidation • Bad habit
	Open gesturing	• Openness to disclosure • Willingness to make contact
	Stiff and/or unmoving	• Anger • Anxiety • Reluctance or shyness • Sore muscles
Legs and feet	Crossing and uncrossing	• Anxiety or nervousness • Depression • Self-protection
	Foot tapping	• Anxiety • Impatience
	Stiff and/or controlled movements	• Anxiety • Closed to contact • Repressed attitude • Sore muscles

Feature	Nonverbal Expression	Possible Meaning
Body	Leaning forward	• Attentiveness and interest • Openness • Connectedness
	Leaning away or back	• Withdrawal • Rejection of a clinician verbalization • Relaxation or comfort
	Turned to the side	• Avoidance • Fear or expectation of rejection • Reduced openness
	Rocking or repetitive motion	• Anxiety, nervousness, or worry • Bad habit • Developmental disorder
	Habitual movement (e.g., tapping, hair twirling, squirming)	• Concentration and/or focused attention • Boredom • Impatience • Anxiety or nervousness • Bad habit
Breath	Slow and deep breathing	• Relaxation or attempt at calming down • Comfort • Good breathing habits
	Hyperventilation (overbreathing)	• Anxiety or panic • Loss of emotional control
	Underbreathing	• Anxiety • Depersonalization
	Short, flat, and choppy breathing	• Anxiety • Depression with crying • Poor breathing habits

the body to respond is important for the counselor to understand each individual fully. Similarly, kinesics are an important means through which clients accent their speech. Knowing how to read a client's motor expressions may therefore be very helpful in recognizing where the client places the emphasis in communication and in honing in on the topic most important to the client.

Finally, it is important to note that the use of kinesics is not limited to clients. Clinicians also express nonverbal information through eye contact and body movements. Although it is important for clinicians to understand what clients are attempting to express through kinesics, the same cannot be assumed about clients. Clients make assumptions about the therapist's kinesics based on their own experience with how they express themselves nonverbally; they do not usually attempt to understand the unique expression of the counselor. Aware care providers adapt their personal kinesics to the client, rather than expecting the client to learn the therapist's unique way of using kinesics. This requires self-awareness on the clinicians' part about how they come across to the client and about how the client interprets their nonverbal behavior. One example may be the reduction of eye contact with clients who are clearly uncomfortable with a clinician's usual amount and maintenance of eye contact. Another example may be increased use of hand gestures by the clinician with clients who are very reliant on body signals for accenting speech, to help the client discern more easily where the counselor places emphasis.

Paralinguistics

Nonverbal or metacommunication aspects related to voice and speech have great communication value. Clinicians direct their attention to several aspects of speech, including voice volume and pitch, speech fluency, rate of speech, and pattern of speech. With regard to voice volume and pitch, the client can be better understood if the therapist attends to how high or low the client's volume is when speaking of various contents, and whether volume or inflection changes depending on topic. Very high volume may relate to anger, whereas very low volume may indicate sadness. A high-pitched voice may suggest anxiety; changes in inflection may direct attention to particularly emotional topics. Speech fluency is explored with regard to the intrusion of stuttering or similar speech errors, as well as jerky speech that changes in clarity and fluency across topics. For example, sudden hesitations in speech may indicate anxiety about a topic or second thoughts about self-disclosure. Stuttering that is confined to times when particular topics are broached may give evidence to discomfort or agitation. Speech errors, such as wrong word choice or inability to think of the right word, may suggest anxiety or resistance.

Rate of speech refers to the speed with which the client communicates. It could theoretically be evaluated by looking at the number of words spoken per minute. Most concretely, rate ranges from slow to fast. Rate of speech varies greatly across cultural groups and geographic settings. Thus, interpretative value is derived not from rate of speech in and of itself, but rather from changes in the rate of speech of a given client. In other words, a client who always speaks fast is not perceived as particularly anxious when speech is quick. However, if a client who usually speaks rather slowly suddenly speeds up the rate of speech, such an interpretation is possible. Similarly, if a client who usually speaks at a high rate of word production suddenly slows down and cannot seem to speak more than a few words a minute, the possibility of depression may need to be explored. If the rate of speech always appears unusual, the clinician will evaluate the rate itself. For example, a client who chronically underproduces (that is, has an unusually slowed rate of speech) may be severely depressed; a client who chronically overproduces may be agitated or even manic. Finding out if rate of speech changed over the client's lifetime would be important information in this context, again pointing to the fact that it is indeed the change in rate of speech that is important, but extending the time frame for this temporal exploration.

Patterns of speech refer to any additional changes in speech not captured by the definitions about voice and speech given so far. They draw the clinician's attention to aspects such as silences, pressure (very driven speech that is not only fast in rate but also in thought production), geographic or ethnic accents, or unusual expressions (such as voice breaking, sighing, or gasping breaths that interfere with speech). Sudden silences may signal despair or confusion, or may indicate that clients are digesting an important insight and are collecting their thoughts. Pressure in speech and thought production most commonly reflects agitation of some sort, whether due to anxiety, anger, or excitement. Gasping for breath may signal the onset of panic; a breaking voice may indicate sudden sadness; sighing may indicate discouragement or relief.

It is important to note that, as was true for the interpretation of kinesics, paralinguistics are best understood and interpreted within the individual context of each client. Although a few generic observations were provided above, the most accurate understanding is derived from carefully observing each client and recognizing the most common or usual pattern of paralinguistic expression. Any deviations from the established (baseline) pattern can then be interpreted and used to enhance the understanding of the verbal communication. Voice and speech are also usefully observed with regard to their value in accenting or complementing verbal content. Speech and voice accents can guide the clinician to the most important component of a client's communication and may help the counselor recognize the depth of a client's expression.

The self-aware clinician uses vocal qualities in communicating effectively with a given client. The practice of consciously using paralinguistics for complementation and accenting gives the clinician an added edge in making an important message heard. Further, mental-health-care providers need to be sensitive to the fact that clients may have specific personal reactions to a given clinician's unique way of using voice or speech. Adapting voice quality to match a particular client can be useful in connecting with the client in the early attempts at rapport. However, at times choosing a speech pattern or rate that is very different from the client's may be a useful therapeutic intervention that models a means for calming or relaxing. For example, if a therapist works with a client from an ethnic group that has a much slower rate of speech than that of the clinician, it will behoove the clinician to slow down the rate of speech to match that of the client. If on the other hand, a client has an extremely high rate of speech due to anxiety or agitation, the clinician would model the opposite of the client's rate of speech to help the client gain a modicum of relaxation and calmness. The targeted use of paralinguistics by the therapist can be a powerful therapeutic intervention in its own right.

Use of Space

Observing how clients use personal and environmental space is often a useful way of better understanding them. The two most important aspects of space utilization are distance and position. Distance refers to the amount of personal space a client appears to require. Some clients need significantly more distance from the therapist than others in order to feel comfortable in a counseling setting. They may go to great lengths to move their chairs as far away as possible from the counselor. Other clients may feel most comfortable if the distance between them and their clinician is at an absolute minimum. Although cultural differences exist that may make the need for personal space somewhat predictable, it is generally best just to observe the personal-space needs of each client and then attempt to honor and respect those needs. Gender differences may be observed as well. Difficulty can arise if the personal-space needs of the client and the clinician conflict significantly. For example, if a client has a need to be closer to the therapist than the therapist is comfortable with, the clinician's unconscious reaction of moving a chair away from the client may be interpreted as rejection or aloofness. Thus, clinicians need to be aware of the client's space needs and try to accommodate these as much as possible. The size of a therapy room may have an impact on the space needs of a client and clinician. A small office, overloaded with furniture or other items, may make it impossible for the client to settle into a distance from the clinician that feels comfortable. Therapists who have to use a small space in which to do their work need to think about how to set up chairs and furniture to maximize the use of their limited space. Adding features to the room that create an illusion of more space (such as mirrors) may be of assistance. Also related to distance between the counselor and the client is the issue of touch. Touch closes all distance between two individuals. Although this can be a very human and caring reaction, reaching out and touching a client can also carry negative consequences. Not all clients appreciate touch and some may misinterpret it. The best rule of thumb for beginning clinicians is to refrain from the impulse to touch, especially early on in the work with a given client. If the clinician does not want to refrain from touch, the next-best solution is to ask the client if touch is acceptable. If a client indicates any hint of reticence to this request, the clinician would violate the client's personal boundaries through touch, a disrespectful and perhaps frightening move.

The second aspect of space utilization, positioning, is equally important to understand both from the client's perspective and from the therapist's. Positioning refers to the position a client or clinician chooses relative to other objects in the counseling room. Again, cultural and gender preferences may exist, but individual differences are the most important variation to observe. Positioning is expressed by the clinician in the layout of the therapy office. A therapy office that is set up so that a desk is positioned between client and clinician will communicate something very different from a therapy room in which the client's and clinician's chairs are directly across from each other without obstacles in between. Similarly, the decision about how a client's and counselor's chairs should be arranged in relation to each other communicates different things to different clients. For some, face-to-face arrangements may suggest an attempt at emotional sharing; for others, only side-by-side seating may be acceptable. Observation about how clients react to the layout may be helpful in making necessary revisions or at least discussing the client's comfort level with a given office. If clients make modifications to the therapy environment by changing the prearranged positioning, important information can be gleaned. A client who grabs a pillow and hugs it throughout the session is creating a barrier between self and clinician, perhaps expressing discomfort with excessive perceived closeness to the mental-health-care provider.

Timing

One final nonverbal means of communication available to both clinician and client is that of timing. Timing refers to all time parameters of the session, such as starting and ending on time, as well as the use of time within sessions, such as the timing of important self-disclosures. Timing is an important nonverbal means of regulation, that is, of helping client and clinician negotiate who speaks when. If a client suddenly stops in midsentence and pauses, the timing of this pause suggests that a comment from the clinician about the last expressed thought is expected. If the clinician makes a statement and then is silent, without breaking that silence, a clear communication is offered that invites the client to speak. The timing of certain statements by a client within the context of the therapy hour can give a counselor hints as to whether the client wants to discuss the issue. For example, an important self-disclosure a few minutes before the end of a session may communicate ambivalence on the client's part about whether to discuss this topic. However, it may also be an attempt to extend the therapy hour beyond the established parameters. The clinician's response will have important nonverbal-communication value. If the counselor chooses to extend the session, the nonverbal communication is that the client can manipulate the clinician easily into getting extra time. If on the other hand, the clinician holds fast to the therapeutic hour, a clear communication is made that the counselor has good personal boundaries.

The timing of the beginning and ending of sessions can speak volumes about a clinician's personal and therapeutic boundaries. A clinician who habitually starts late or runs overtime may communicate that personal boundaries are loose. Similarly, a client who comes late for sessions may be testing the counselor's boundaries or may be giving a message about the importance (or lack thereof) of the therapy in the client's life. Timing issues often are best brought from the nonverbal to the verbal realm and are processed as important interpersonal issues between client and counselor. Not addressing some of the examples of behavior given here (such as bringing up important material late in the session or coming late for counseling) means missing important opportunities for process comments. This issue will be revisited in a later chapter.

Helpful Hints for Nonverbal Communication

The therapy or counseling process contains a wealth of nonverbal or meta-communication, expressed by both client and clinician. Understanding nonverbal communication as expressed by the client and using nonverbal communication consciously for therapeutic goals will greatly enhance a clinician's therapeutic skills. A few potential nonverbal pitfalls that are best avoided by mental-health-care providers are illustrated in Table 4-3. These nonverbal expressions tend to put clients off and may lead them to feel unheard and misunderstood. Being self-aware in general has been discussed as an important counselor trait; being self-aware about unconscious nonverbal self-expression cannot be overemphasized with regard to its importance in establishing and retaining therapeutic rapport. In addition to avoiding the nonverbal pitfalls outlined in Table 4-3, three important concepts facilitate good nonverbal communication and thus therapeutic rapport, namely, congruence, sensitivity, and synchrony.

Congruence refers to the clinician's efforts to keep personal verbal and nonverbal expressions in line with each other. Achieving congruence between what a counselor says and does is critical to good therapeutic rapport. Clients are easily confused by incongruence in the clinician and may perceive it, rightly so, as a recapitulation of conflicts or problems they have encountered with others in their lives. Congruence can be practiced; some hints about how to maintain congruence between verbal and nonverbal expression are outlined in Table 4-4.

Sensitivity refers to a mental-health-care provider's ability to receive and understand the client's nonverbal communications. Learning how to interpret the kinesics and paralinguistics of each individual client is a critical component of sensitivity. Recognizing how the client's nonverbal and verbal communications interact (repetition, contradiction, substitution, complementation, accenting, and regulation) will add depth to the counselor's understanding of the client and will facilitate therapeutic responsiveness. Sensitivity also refers to respecting a client's personal-space needs and creating an environment that makes it possible for clients to feel comfortable and heard.

Finally, *synchrony* refers to the clinician's ability to match or oppose the client's nonverbal expressions as therapeutically indicated. Matching is used when the therapist views the client's nonverbal communication as a means of joining with the client and creating an empathic atmosphere. For example, matching a client's lowered voice and lowered rate of speech when the client talks about a sad event will help the client feel heard and understood. Contrarily,

TABLE
4-3

SAMPLE PITFALLS IN NONVERBAL EXPRESSION

Nonverbal Pitfall of the Clinician	Possible Reactions of the Client
Excessive physical closeness at outset of treatment	Feeling crowded or overwhelmed; misunderstanding the behavior as seductiveness by the clinician
Excessive physical distance at outset of treatment	Feeling rejected or at least not accepted; perceiving the clinician as arrogant or standoffish
Distancing movement of body after a client expression	Feeling judged, rejected, or misunderstood; perceiving the clinician as judgmental or reactive for personal reasons
Absent eye contact	Feeling ignored, not feeling cared for; perceiving the clinician as shy or insecure
Jittery or inconsistent eye contact	Not feeling attended to, feeling perceived as boring; perceiving the clinician as distracted
Excessive eye contact	Feeling under scrutiny, feeling uncomfortable and intruded upon; perceiving the clinician as intrusive
Creating barriers out of objects (e.g., desk, pad and pencil)	Feeling rejected, not feeling accepted, feeling unimportant; perceiving the clinician as aloof
Incongruent facial expressions	Confusion, feeling misunderstood, feeling placated, feeling lied to; perceiving the clinician as inconsistent or incongruent
Incongruent gestures	Confusion, feeling misunderstood, feeling placated, feeling lied to; perceiving the clinician as inconsistent or incongruent
Distancing facial expressions (bored look, yawning, lack of consistent eye contact, etc.)	Feeling unimportant, feeling perceived as boring, not being accepted, not feeling liked; perceiving the clinician as emotionally absent
Distancing body movements (crossed arms or legs, bouncing legs, chair moved away, etc.)	Feeling rejected, not feeling heard, not feeling liked, not feeling accepted; perceiving the clinician as emotionally rejecting or cold
Distracting mannerisms (e.g., twirling hair, playing with an earring, scratching, etc.)	Feeling perceived as boring, not feeling attended to, feeling perceived as uninteresting; perceiving the clinician as anxious or inattentive
Excessively loud voice or rapid speech	Feeling bossed around, feeling overwhelmed, being given advice or told what to do; perceiving the clinician as angry or hostile
Excessively low voice or slowed rate of speech	Feeling insecure about the value of treatment; perceiving the clinician as unsure of self
Impatient rate of speech, poor timing (e.g., interrupting client)	Feeling perceived as incompetent, feeling perceived as unimportant, not feeling heard; perceiving the clinician as incompetent or unempathic
Excessively high energy level (e.g., fidgeting, bouncing, talking fast)	Feeling perceived as unintelligent, feeling perceived as boring; perceiving the clinician as impatient
Excessively low energy level (e.g., slowed psychomotor movement, slowed speech)	Feeling unimportant, feeling perceived as boring; perceiving the clinician as depressed or incompetent

TABLE

4-4

CONGRUENCE IN THE VERBAL AND NONVERBAL EXPRESSION OF IMPORTANT CLINICIAN TRAITS

Intended Communication	Nonverbal Expression	Sample Verbalizations
Conveyance of comfort	Calm, soothing voice; relaxed posture; open facial expression	"This is a very safe place" "Please make yourself comfortable"
Conveyance of patience	Slow rate of speech; patient gestures; focused attention	"Take your time" "We have plenty of time"
Welcoming the client	Nodding; smiling; inviting gestures; open body posture	"Welcome; please have a seat" "It's nice to see you again"
Expression of empathy	Leaning forward; sensitive eye contact; matching nonverbals; sensitive timing; appropriate accenting; facing client	"What a frightening experience" "What was that like for you?"
Expression of genuineness	Matched kinesics and paralinguistics; congruence in all aspects of expression; appropriate accenting	"Wow, what a treat for you!" "I am thrilled for you. That was terrific!"
Expression of understanding	Matched paralinguistics and kinesics; appropriate rate of speech; gentle voice; nodding	"Yes, I do understand" "Oh, yes!"
Expression of caring	Warm, soft voice; connected body posture (open seating and leaning forward); open and relaxed facial expressions	"I am so sorry to hear that your mother died" "I truly care about what will happen to you"
Expression of warmth	Warm, soft voice; gentle rate of speech; connected body posture; soft facial expressions	"You really deserved this" "You really need support and guidance from him right now"
Expression of confusion	Open body posture; accenting hand gestures; complement-ing facial expression (e.g., wrinkled forehead, questioning eyes)	"Help me understand this better. . . ." "No, I'm not quite clear on that yet. . . ."

Skill Development Recommendations

Recommendation 4-1   *From now on, while engaging in conversations with family members and friends, begin to focus on their nonverbal expressions of emotions. Note facial features, body posture, gestures, and other bodily clues about how the person with whom you are speaking may be feeling. Do not allow the verbal content to get in the way of your nonverbal listening. Pay careful attention to body language, even if it appears inconsistent with what is being said. Begin to notice if different people have different ways of expressing the same message.*

Recommendation 4-2   *From now on, when you are in a public place with extra time on your hands, become a people watcher. Without hearing their conversations, pay attention to how people express themselves. Try to guess what emotions they are expressing by how they hold their bodies, faces, hands, and so forth.*

when the therapist opposes the client's excessive rate of speech and volume of voice used in a fit of anger, this may help the client get the out-of-control affect under control. Matching of a client's nonverbal expression can occur cross-modally as well. For example, a lowered volume of voice may be matched by the clinician with a lesser production of speech; a high rate of speech production by the client may be cross-modally matched by the therapist who sits up straight and intently. The idea is to match the intensity and quality of the client's expression in some form, whether by imitating the same nonverbal feature of self-expression or by using the same intensity or quality in another nonverbal modality.

LISTENING SKILLS

The second aspect of attending skills is listening. Listening with any degree of accuracy is easiest if the listener focuses attention fully on the speaker. It is further facilitated by the listener's self-awareness, developed through the practice of fully attending to and learning about personal internal processes and reactions in all sorts of situations and circumstances. For listening to take place in therapy or counseling, the clinician and environment are best consciously and psychologically prepared for the therapeutic exchange. This means, but may not be limited to,

- putting aside personal concerns and worries for the extent of the therapy or counseling session
- being fully awake, alert, and focused (that is, not sleepy, fatigued, or sick)
- allowing oneself not to be distracted away from the client even by the most enticing or curious environmental or internal occurrences
- creating an environment that is conducive to a therapeutic exchange (quiet, confidential, sufficiently spacious)
- being sufficiently self-aware to be able to be open to the client's communications
- communicating attentiveness via kinesics (leaning forward, being relaxed and open, and making appropriate eye contact)
- having knowledge of cultural and gender preferences regarding situations that involve the exchange of personal information
- being sufficiently aware of individual differences to adapt rules of the game to the individual needs and preferences of each client
- being aware of and attempting to remove all personal roadblocks to communication

Listening in a therapeutic manner means taking in the client's whole story. The first prerequisite to such complete and active listening is the ability to allow a client to speak uninterruptedly, even if the client takes breaks or pauses between words, sentences, or thoughts. Learning not to speak prematurely, in essence interrupting the client's stream of thought, is one of the most important listening skills. Most people have a tendency to take even the briefest pause as an indication that it is their turn to talk. However, in a therapeutic setting, clinicians have to learn that this is not always the case; it is best for counselors to wait until they are certain that the client has finished before jumping in with a question, comment, or thought. Pauses or silences vary in length from client to client, with gender and cultural differences often being noted. Adapting to a client's speed and use of breaks is the beginning of good listening. Listening to the client's whole story also means taking in all related affects, thoughts, and behaviors in addition to any content that is volunteered by the client. Recognizing the greater context of a client's verbalization and looking for emphasis and meaning are excellent means of assuring good and comprehensive listening. To be able to listen in this manner, certain skills and awareness are necessary. One of the most important issues for beginning clinicians is to learn to recognize barriers to active listening, also referred to as roadblocks.

Roadblocks to Listening

Listening can be interfered with if clinicians are unaware of distortions and interpretations they bring to the therapeutic encounter. The first step in developing accurate active-listening skills is the exploration of a variety of roadblocks or distortions that interfere with effective hearing (Egan, 1994). Six important roadblocks described by Egan are inadequate listening, evaluative listening, filtered or selective listening, fact-centered listening, rehearsing-while-listening, and sympathetic listening.

A clinician who is preoccupied with personal worries or needs will evidence *inadequate listening* due to the inability to redirect the focus of attention to the client. Attention is directed to the self and its worries and needs and distracted away from the client. Hearing a client in this frame of mind is almost impossible as it is flavored so directly by the internal needs of the counselor. Not surprisingly, the therapist does not receive everything the client is saying and mis-hears some of what is voiced. As importantly, attention to kinesics and paralinguistics is distracted and interpretation of these phenomena is inadequate at best, absent at worst.

The clinician who makes judgments about what the client is saying as the client is saying it engages in *evaluative listening*. In this form of listening, objectivity is lost because the mental-health-care provider is making decisions about how to evaluate what the client is saying based on judgment and prejudice. Such evaluation of the client not only misses the point of therapeutic open-mindedness, but it also tends to lead to advice-giving. The clinician who listens evaluatively tends to think of "better solutions" or reactions than those described by the client. The judgmental attitude about the client's choices then tends to come through in the clinician's responses and may be perceived by the client as exactly what it is: evaluative and judgmental.

Some mental-health-care providers hear what they expect to hear or want to hear. They enter the counseling session with certain preconceived notions about the client. These preconceived notions may arise from the client's physical appearance (sloppy dress perhaps leading to the notion that the client is a "slob"), gender (the clinician holds certain sex-role stereotypes that are projected onto the client), ethnicity (the counselor has racial biases or prejudices that emerge), presenting concern (a clinician's belief that all clients with suicidal history are borderline), and so forth. Snap judgments and prejudices intrude on the exchange with the client and result in *selective or filtered listening*. Care providers make the initial assessment of the client, then hear what they expected to hear. For example, a client with a history of suicide may be perceived as fickle, inconsistent in relationships, unclear about future career goals, emotionally labile, and unintegrated. It is certainly possible to frame most clients' stories in such a negative light if that is the expectation that is brought to the session by the clinician. Filtered or selective listening may lead the therapist to hone in on the most pathological aspects of the story and to miss the healthy ones.

When clients come to treatment, they express themselves verbally and nonverbally as discussed previously. They also tell their stories in at least two ways: factual and emotional. A clinician who falls into the trap of *fact-centered listening* will not hear the client's emotional story, and will miss much of the client's metacommunication. Only information or overt content is received; latent, nonverbal, emotional, or personal content that is less obvious is missed. The counselor forgets to listen to all aspects of the client and gets caught up in facts. This creates an experience-distant exchange between clinician and client that will be perceived by the client as unempathic, perhaps even intrusive. It is often the case that fact-centered listening leads to excessive questioning of the client by the clinician, a process called shotgunning (to be explained further in the chapter on questions).

Some therapists, especially those with little experience, are so worried about how to respond to a client that, instead of simply listening, they carry on an internal dialogue formulating what to say next. This preoccupation with finding the perfect response to the client ironically gets in the way of making even a halfway-decent response because in the process of dialoging internally, the client is not heard. This kind of *rehearsing-while-listening* suggests anxiety on the clinician's part, a reality that will be hard to hide from the client. It is preferable to give the client full attention and make a less-than-eloquent remark in response that is at least on target if not beautifully phrased. A nice flow of thought and eloquence in expression will develop with practice and can only be effective if it is to the point and reflects a keen understanding of what the client has said and expressed nonverbally. Rehearsed responses rarely are on target and leave the client feeling misunderstood and not individually responded to or respected.

Sympathetic listening is the kind of listening people engage in in social settings and conversation. On the surface, it may appear to be a fine way of interacting with a client because the counselor responds emotionally and compassionately, but it is not really a therapeutic exchange. The therapist who listens sympathetically gets caught up in the client's story (either its content or its emotional overtones) and overidentifies with the client. Before long, such clinicians feel just as bad as their clients and will have the strong desire to make things better for the client (if only to feel better themselves). Objectivity and therapeutic distance are lost as the counselor is in the middle of the story with the client. Both get caught up in the quagmire of the story and lose sight of how to extract themselves from it. Sympathetic listening does not always have to happen to this full extent. Partial sympathetic listening may reduce a clinician's objectivity, but some distance may be maintained that allows for an appropriate response. Sympathetic listening is hard on the counselor in the long run because it is emotionally draining.

The roadblocks to listening are summarized in Table 4-5. It is important for novice clinicians to be very familiar with them, since these distortions tend to be more prevalent early in professional life. The nervousness and self-

TABLE 4-5 ROADBLOCKS TO EFFECTIVE LISTENING

Roadblocks	Definitions	Potential Consequences
Inadequate listening	Clinician is inattentive or pre-occupied with personal worries or need states	Client will not feel heard; clinician misses important aspects of the client's communication
Evaluative listening	Clinician makes judgments about what is heard and thus loses objectivity	Client feels judged and misunderstood; clinician tends to feel superior and to give advice
Filtered or selective listening	Clinicians hear what they expect or want to hear based on preconceived notions due to prejudice, bias, or stereotypes	Client feels misunderstood and misrepresented; clinician fails to hear the client's true message and misrepresents (often pathologizes) the client's state of being
Fact-centered listening	Clinician only listens to overt content (verbal information) and misses the latent or covert content (personal and emotional message)	Client perceives clinician as experience-distant, non-empathic, and intrusive; clinician tends to overuse questions and shotguns the client
Rehearsing-while-listening	Clinician is preoccupied with how to respond to the client, formulating responses while the client is speaking and thus not attending fully	Client feels misunderstood and disrespected and perceives the clinician as anxious; clinician misses essential aspects of conversation and makes comments that are well-phrased but off-target
Sympathetic listening	Clinician gets caught up in the client's story (content or emotion) and overidentifies with the client	Client may feel heard but not helped; clinician loses objectivity and distance leading to ineffectiveness and burnout

preoccupation of novice clinicians as they see their first clients are perfect breeding grounds for listening roadblocks. Being aware of them helps identify them as they occur and allows the clinician to make changes in listening stance.

Essential Skills for Good Listening

There are other preparations to ensure accurate active listening beyond awareness of roadblocks. First, and perhaps most importantly, clinicians learn to focus their attention in two ways: on the client and on the clinician's immediate personal reactions to the client. This way of focusing attention takes some practice but can be achieved. Second, accurate listening is predicated on the clinician's ability to hear and process not only overt content (information expressed verbally) but also latent content (metacommunications expressed nonverbally and symbolic meanings of verbal expressions).

Focused attention to the client develops with greater practice and ease in therapeutic communication. Early in a clinician's experience, anxiety about the therapeutic exchange leads to occasional inattention and self-focus. As the care provider relaxes and becomes more familiar with therapeutic work, focused attention becomes second nature.

Focusing attention on a communication partner can be practiced in any setting. Allowing others to speak without interrupting, observing their body language while they express themselves, and practicing patience in responding are excellent means of enhancing focused attention. This practice can occur with anyone and often is much appreciated by friends and family of the budding clinician. Focusing attention on the communication partner means taking in every aspect of that person and developing observation skills. Consciously watching communication partners (without making them self-conscious by being obvious about this observation) can be helpful in beginning to learn body language. Making the communication partner the most important focus of the moment is key to turning one's attention to that person completely and skillfully. Clinicians can practice focused attention by listening to their own feelings and thoughts whenever they encounter a novel or challenging exchange. Setting time aside each day to listen to the self (emotions and thought) can be another useful endeavor and is very similar to meditation practice. Focused self-inspection teaches focused attention and increases self-awareness. While with a client, these attention skills can then be practiced by making the client the most important issue in the room. Focused attention skills—listening fully and with conscious awareness, observing carefully but not obviously, and monitoring personal reactions silently but cautiously—lead to clear hearing and openness to receiving all messages sent by the client.

Processing and *understanding overt and latent communication* represent the essence of the second important aspect of good listening skills. The ability not only to receive all messages sent but also to understand them requires at least two sets of skills. The counselor needs to be able to understand nonverbal communication correctly, as discussed earlier. Additionally, the therapist needs to be able to read between the verbal lines of the client, learning recognition of incongruence and patterns as well as awareness of metaphor and symbolism. Recognition of incongruence will be addressed in the chapter dealing with confrontation. Suffice it to say here that active listening means listening with such alertness and focused attention that contradictions expressed by the client that are subtle and prone to being missed in casual conversation are noticed by the clinician. Such subtle contradictions refer to incongruence between verbal and nonverbal communications, as for example in the client who smiles broadly while talking about a divorce that was very acrimonious. Good active listening would imply awareness on the counselor's part that the smile did not fit with the verbal content of the message. Incongruence can also occur between two nonverbal modalities of expression. For example, a client who speaks about depression may employ congruent paralinguistics in that speech is slowed and volume of voice is low with few inflections or emphases. However, as the client is speaking, kinesics may tell a different story, perhaps one of anger as the hand is pounding the client's leg and crossed legs are kicking the foot of the upper leg. A therapist who listens actively, that is, with full focused attention, notes the inconsistency between speech and kinesics and becomes more fully aware of the client's whole story.

Incongruence can be expressed in many other ways, such as between a client's affect and thought, affect and behaviors, thought and behaviors, or among all three. Again, how to deal with this recognition will be discussed later; for now, the clinician just needs to be concerned with learning to recognize such patterns. Careful active listening also helps the clinician recognize patterns and themes expressed by the client. Patterns refers to repetitive affects or behaviors that the client tends to evidence often or falls back upon in times of stress and challenge. Themes, on the other hand, refers to consistent sets of ideas, beliefs, or notions the client holds about life, self, or others. Such themes or schemas can affect or flavor how a client perceives the world and can help the clinician recognize why and how clients react in certain ways in certain situations. Working with patterns and themes becomes important as the counselor begins to work in the realm of cognitions. Recognizing themes and patterns, however, is a prerequisite of such cognitive intervention and is a direct outgrowth of carefully focused attention and listening.

A final component of active listening is sensitivity to metaphor and symbolism. Human beings think and express themselves in complex and symbolic ways. To understand another person fully, it is important to learn that person's way of using language. Metaphors and symbolism function much like nonverbal communication in that they are unique to each individual and are generally used in an unconscious manner. Deciphering metaphors or understanding symbolic meanings may sound like a daunting task. However, this is not the case. Clinicians usually see clients in a larger context. This context helps give direction about the underlying meaning of a client's symbolic communication. Studying dictionaries of symbolism and metaphor is not generally helpful because even though some general statements can be made, there is no guarantee that an individual client will use a given symbol or metaphor in this general or predictable manner. It is much preferable to learn the symbols and metaphors a client uses and to communicate with the client around these chosen modes of indirect expression. Once a client's metaphorical way of self-expression is understood, listening becomes more accurate and communication becomes quicker and easier. For example, if a client talks about a favorite TV show, this exchange

Skill Development Recommendations

Recommendation 4-3 *For the next week, listen carefully to the conversation styles of others. Attempt to identify their listening pitfalls. Note the consequences of these pitfalls. Do not share your insights as the point of this exercise is not to criticize others, but to begin to gain awareness of how pitfalls manifest. It is easier to begin identification of listening pitfalls in the conversations of others first; then it will be easier to identify them in your own listening.*

Recommendation 4-4 *After having observed others' listening pitfalls, begin to observe yourself in conversations with other people. Try to evaluate honestly how you listen. Pay attention to whether you have any listening pitfalls that get in the way of open and attentive hearing. As you identify your primary pitfalls, make action plans about how to eliminate them.*

Recommendation 4-5 *Practice focused attention to people by practicing with friends and family. Apply all the skills listed in Table 4-6 to your day-to-day conversations with people you know well. Do you notice any changes in responses? Are people aware of what you are doing? How do they feel about it? How do you feel in these conversations? Are you learning more about these people than you used to?*

---

could be perceived as evasiveness or resistance, or the clinician could try to understand the symbolism of the show. This can be done by asking the client questions about what the different characters mean to the client and how the client understands the plot of the show. Thus, much may be learned about the client's beliefs about the world (themes) and about how the client feels and behaves in response (patterns).

Active listening means coming to understand clients through focused attention and concentration with the goal of making them and their communication the most important component of the human exchange that is therapy or counseling. The skills outlined here and a few additional simple (but not simplistic) hints or recommendations that tend to be helpful are summarized in Table 4-6. The application of these skills and their careful and continuous practice will facilitate therapeutic rapport and useful clinical work.

It is important to note that no clinician is always fully focused and aware. All mental-health-care providers have momentary lapses and preoccupations. Humans are incapable of perfection in any area of behavior, and clinicians need to accept that they will fail at times and make mistakes. There is nothing wrong with that as long as the failure is recognized and acknowledged. The novice

TABLE 4-6	HELPFUL HINTS FOR ACCURATE ACTIVE LISTENING

1. Make the client the focal center of attention in the therapeutic exchange
2. Be aware of personal reactions and their implications for, or impact on, the communication process between clinician and client
3. Listen not only to what but also to how something is said, that is, attend to content and paralinguistics
4. Pay focused attention to nonverbal communications such as kinesics, paralinguistics, use of space, timing, and physical appearance
5. Recognize the relationship between the client's verbal and nonverbal expressions (i.e., repetition, contradiction, substitution, complementation, accenting, and regulation)
6. Allow for appropriate silences and pauses, respecting and honoring the client's needs for breaks or bridges in a verbal exchange
7. Instead of interrupting, allow clients to finish their sentences and thoughts, being sensitive to individual differences in length of pauses between words and thoughts
8. Listen to the whole story, paying focused attention to content, affect, behavior, thoughts, context, meaning, and emphasis
9. Avoid all roadblocks to listening (i.e., inadequate listening, evaluative listening, filtered listening, fact-centered listening, rehearsing-while-listening, and sympathetic listening)
10. Learn to read between the lines, becoming familiar with each client's unique use of metaphors and symbolism
11. Listen for themes and patterns in the client's verbal (overt) and nonverbal (latent) communication
12. Develop awareness of incongruence in the client expressions, recognizing incongruence between:

   - Verbal and nonverbal communications
   - One modality of nonverbal communication and another modality of nonverbal expression (e.g., kinesics versus paralinguistics)
   - Thoughts and feelings
   - Thoughts and actions
   - Feelings and actions
   - Feelings, thoughts, and actions

counselor learning these skills can relax in the knowledge that even seasoned clinicians will "screw up" at times. What will distinguish the successful and empathic therapist from the unsuccessful one is the recognition and awareness of mistakes and the willingness to admit to them, explore them, and turn them into learning opportunities.

QUESTIONS TO ENCOURAGE COMMUNICATION

> Effective inquiry increases the likelihood that the
> patient will experience the therapist's comments as an
> invitation to explore rather than take them as a
> challenge to be warded off or as a signal to hide.
> *P. L. Wachtel, 1993, p. 88*

Questions play a large role in therapy and counseling. They are no doubt one of the most used and useful interventions available to clinicians. Questions have a large range of purposes and applications and the following list outlines only the most obvious:

- questions initiate and dominate the intake interview
- questions are used to begin or open individual sessions
- questions are a means of facilitating communication
- questions motivate self-disclosure
- questions can serve to expand the focus of an interaction
- questions can be used to elaborate on a given topic
- questions elicit specifics about given topic areas
- questions enrich the information volunteered by the client
- questions can be used to shift to a new topic area
- questions can serve purposes of assessment
- questions assist with making diagnostic decisions
- questions are useful during crisis management
- questions can help point out patterns
- questions can create meaning and insight in the client
- questions can enhance a client's self-awareness
- questions can be used to guide the client toward problem solving

Despite this diversity of purposes and applications, there are essentially only three types of questions: opening or open-ended questions, systematic inquiry, and clarifying questions. The former two categories of questions are of primary interest in this chapter as they are specifically designed to facilitate communication and client self-disclosure. Clarifying questions, on the other hand, while also enhancing communication and self-disclosure, primarily have the purpose of clarifying meaning or interpreting an event, relationship, behavior, affect, or cognition for the client. They are focused toward the creation of cognitive insight or self-awareness. As such, clarifying questions will be covered in detail in the cognitive chapters. The focus of this chapter will be on opening or open-ended questions and systematic inquiry. However, the many cautions and guidelines provided in this chapter hold true and apply for all three types of questions. To compare and contrast the three types of questions, Table 5-1 reveals their respective purposes and applications.

As is evident from Table 5-1, open-ended questions are used largely to help a client continue on a path of self-disclosure. They essentially pursue the client's agenda, at least initially, by asking for more detail about a topic area originally broached by the client. They reflect a mixture of client and clinician agenda, as the clinician is the person who chooses in which direction to take the questioning, while staying within the content area chosen by the client. Occasionally, clinicians may choose to switch focus, redirecting clients with open-ended questions to the exploration of a new, though related, issue. This exploration of a new topic area is related to the original content and reflects the clinician's decision that a slight shift in focus is therapeutically useful and necessary. This shift, however, imposes a new agenda or goal and reflects the counselor's preference and area of curiosity.

Systematic inquiry is a useful tool for gathering vast amounts of information from a client. In systematic inquiry, the clinician generally chooses the content or topic area, unlike open-ended questions, where the original topic comes from the client. Systematic inquiry is used early on in treatment, when the mental-health-care provider collects data about the client for purposes of assessment, treatment planning, and diagnosis. Systematic inquiry elicits lots of information quickly and systematically, as the label suggests. Often clinicians have a clear sequence in mind, which they pursue in collecting information, making systematic inquiry similar to a structured interview. This comparison, while apt, should not be overly emphasized as structured interviews, being formal and standardized, do not allow a clinician to deviate from the predetermined structure. Systematic inquiry, while having an equally structured agenda, allows the clinician to pursue the agenda flexibly and caringly, with rapport taking priority over data collection. The most common example of a systematic inquiry is the standard intake interview that inquires about a range of client history. Less common examples include questioning for purposes of suicide, violence, child abuse, and other crisis assessments. In all of these instances, the clinician has a certain agenda in mind that dictates the kinds of questions that need to be asked; the structure or order can be abandoned to individualize the interview according to a client's needs. Given the basic or introductory nature

TABLE

5-1

COMPARISON OF THE THREE TYPES OF QUESTIONS

Question	Purpose	Application	Special Notes
Opening or open-ended questions	• Help the client continue on a path of self-disclosure • Facilitate continued communication	• Elaboration and enrichment of a given topic • Expansion of focus beyond a given topic • Direction of the client according to the clinician's agenda	• Can be used any time in the treatment of a client • May even be useful in establishing/supporting rapport • Can reflect clinician's or client's agenda
Systematic inquiry	• Solicit general information about a particular topic area • Solicit specific detail in a given topic area or a new topic area	• Assessment and history taking • Diagnosis • Crisis assessment and management	• Generally reflect the clinician's agenda • Require good rapport and expressed sense of caring by the clinician to increase client cooperation
Clarifying questions	• Create insight and cognitive awareness in the client • Lead the client to a conclusion the clinician has already drawn • Lead the client to problem-solving	• Used widely during the therapeutic phase when the client is focused on recognition of patterns, creation of meaning, problem-solving, and interpretation	• Advance according to a goal/conclusion that the clinician has drawn already • Purposefully work toward a specific outcome • Purposefully seek solutions to problems

of this book, systematic inquiry for the purpose of crisis assessment will not be addressed further. The interested reader is referred to Brems (2000), which deals with these issues in detail, providing outlines and guidelines. Intake inquiry will be dealt with below as it is encountered by all novice clinicians. In fact, this type of systematic inquiry is generally the first task of new clinicians as they have their first contact with their first client.

GENERAL GUIDELINES ABOUT QUESTIONS

Clearly, regardless of type, questions are always somewhat directive. The clinician chooses what to ask and when, and through that action draws implications about what is important. Even open-ended questions, which arise out of a client's agenda and verbalization, tell the client where the clinician places emphasis and what draws the counselor's curiosity. In that sense, no question is truly unbiased. Given this reality, it is critically important that clinicians learn to minimize the level of directiveness and implication in their questions. It would be quite easy to use questions to influence clients unduly, to make hidden suggestions, to convey basic assumptions, or suggest predrawn conclusions.

Pitfalls in the Use of Questions

It is easiest to learn how to use questions correctly by discussing the pitfalls of using (or phrasing) questions the wrong way. There are at least ten types of questions that can be counter-therapeutic.

Suggestive Questions

One type of problematic question to avoid is the suggestive question. Suggestive questions give hidden (or not so hidden) advice disguised as a question. Counselors using suggestive questions may not even be aware that they are giving advice. They may need to listen with a third ear to how a question was phrased to recognize that the client might receive it as advice. Suggestive questions tend to start with stems such as "Don't you think . . . ?," "Could you . . . ?," "Couldn't you . . . ?," "Have you (ever) considered . . . ?," and similar suggestive openers. Although the clinician may think that the question really just motivates the client to consider a point, the client is more likely to hear such a question as suggestive of the very action that follows the stem. Note the following example:

> CLIENT: Well, now you have the whole history of how my husband and I end up in these screaming fits. I still don't know how to get us to change this dance we're doing. I can see it all developing afterwards. But while

I'm in the middle of it I get so caught up in the emotions that it's like I can do nothing to change what I just know is gonna happen. . . . It's not like I haven't tried, but. . . .

Pitfall: Use of Suggestive Question

CLINICIAN: Have you ever tried something like taking a deep breath to slow yourself down while you are fighting?

CLIENT: I guess I could try that again, but I tried it once before and it was a disaster. So I just don't think that works.

Alternative: Use of Well-Phrased Open-Ended Question

CLINICIAN: What kinds of things have you tried?

CLIENT: Oh, I've tried counting to ten—My mother always said that works for her. I've tried just leaving the room, but he follows me and then it just gets worse. A friend of mine said she just takes a deep breath when she gets upset, so I tried that but that was a disaster. . . .

CLINICIAN: How was it a disaster? (*The session continues productively from there.*)

This example shows that a suggestive question can be mistaken as advice by the client even if it was not necessarily intended as such. It can also serve to close the client down. If the suggestion is not well received by the client (for example, is not perceived as a good suggestion), it can undermine the relationship between the client and counselor or may even decrease the therapist's trustworthiness and expertness in the client's eye. An alternatively phrased open-ended question makes the client do the work and suggests no particular solution or course of action.

Assumptive Questions

A similarly problematic type of question is the inquiry that gives the client the impression that the clinician expects a particular answer. Such assumptive questions often start with stems such as "But you have . . . ?," or "But you haven't . . . ?," "You don't really . . . ?," or "Do you really . . . ?" Alternatively, they end with a phrase such as "do you?" or "don't you?"; "have you?" or "haven't you?" In other words, assumptive questions are not questions at all; they are really statements disguised as questions. A convenient "do you?" (or similar phrase) is tacked on to the end of a statement, turning it into a question in an attempt to hide the assumption made by the clinician. Sometimes, assumptive questions are even plain statements turned into a question merely through voice inflection. For instance the counselor may highlight a word or phrase in the middle of the statement and raise the voice questioningly at the end of the sentence, as in "but you *yourself* have never done xyz?" Although occasionally clients may miss the assumption, most commonly they hear it loud and clear.

Clients then have to decide whether to comply with the assumption or to answer honestly. The problem for the therapist then becomes one of knowing whether the answer the client gave was honest or given in a manner as to conform to the expectation detected in the clinician's statement/question. The following example serves to demonstrate this issue.

> CLIENT: He has been a druggie for years. Let's see . . . he's twenty-three now; he moved out when he was sixteen and a half. . . . So yeah, he's been doing one drug or another for at least eight years. I can't say that I like it but I haven't exactly done anything about it, either. You know, in a way he is just following in his mother's footsteps. That was one of the reasons we split up and I got custody.

Pitfall: Use of Assumptive Question
> CLINICIAN: You yourself *haven't* taken drugs now, have you?
> CLIENT: Not really . . . (*looks away*)

Alternative: Use of Well-Phrased Question as Part of a Systematic Intake Inquiry
> CLINICIAN: I guess that brings me to one of my next questions. Have you had personal experience with drugs?
> CLIENT: Well, a little . . .
> CLINICIAN: A little?
> CLIENT: Yeah. I used to drink pretty heavily when . . . (*Session continues from here.*)

This example serves to clarify that assumptive questions can lead clients down a path of unintended dishonesty as they do not want to disappoint the clinician. This is a particular danger during systematic inquiries when the clinician and client are still getting to know each other and when the counselor wants to collect as much reliable information as possible. In the pitfall part of the example, the client is at least giving clues that he may be less than honest in response to the therapist's poorly phrased questions. The use of "Not really . . ." is often a giveaway that a client is skirting the truth. The fact that he also looked away clearly suggests a rupture in the connection between clinician and client. The counselor thus has an opportunity to repair the mistake by following up on the original question with a better-phrased question that makes no assumptions about the client's personal drug use.

Pseudoquestions
Similar to assumptive questions, pseudoquestions are not questions at all. They are actually disguised commands or directives. The pitfall in the use of these

"questions" is that the client may feel manipulated by the pretense of a choice when the reality is that the client is supposed to comply with a directive. It is perfectly acceptable for a counselor to feel the need to direct a client. The problem lies in pretending not to direct the client when this actually *is* the goal. If the therapist, on the other hand, really has no preference and the question came out inadvertently as a command, then perhaps more practice is needed at phrasing questions open-endedly. The first set of examples that follows demonstrates a mental-health-care provider's use of a pseudoquestion, and how the directive could have been phrased more appropriately. The second set of examples rephrases a pseudoquestion into a genuine question to reflect that the clinician actually does not have a preference and was not really giving a directive even though the question sounded like one originally. The third and final set of examples speculates as to what a client may think or feel (overtly or covertly) when the counselor uses pseudoquestions.

EXAMPLE SET ONE: PSEUDOQUESTION TO DIRECTIVE

What the clinician said:	What the clinician meant and could have said:
Do you want to get us started?	Go ahead and start. *OR* Would you please get us started now.
Would you like to start where we left off last week?	Let's start where we left off last week.
Would you like to take a deep breath to calm down?	I'd like you to take a deep breath to calm down a bit.
Do you want to let me help you here?	How about I help you with that?

EXAMPLE SET TWO: PSEUDOQUESTION TO GENUINE QUESTION

What the clinician said:	What the clinician meant and could have said:
Do you want to get us started?	Do *you* want to get us started or do you want *me* to?
Would you like to start where we left off last week?	What do you think about starting where we left off last week? Or is there anything else that you would like to talk about first?
Would you like to take a deep breath to calm down?	You seem very shaken by this. Would you like some help calming down before we go on or are you okay as is?
Do you want to let me help you here?	Would you tell me if you want or need any help with anything?

EXAMPLE SET THREE: PSEUDOQUESTION AND CLIENT REACTION

What the clinician said:	What the client may feel or think but says or does:
Do you want to get us started?	*Thinks:* No! Why do you always pretend like I have a choice. *Says:* I guess so. . . .
Would you like to start where we left off last week?	*Thinks:* As if I have a choice? *Says:* Okay . . .
Would you like to take a deep breath to calm down?	*Feels:* HELP! *Says:* Yes.
Do you want to let me help you here?	*Thinks:* Oh, I guess I'm too stupid to do it alone! *Says:* That's okay. . . . I can do it, can't I?

These examples show that pseudoquestions are not a pitfall because they are commands in disguise. They are pitfalls because they pretend to give a choice when they do not. In some instances in therapeutic work, being directive is important. In the examples, the third occasion in each set is best approached as a directive. The client clearly needs assistance with calming down and a question, whether pseudo or open, is not the best approach. Thus, the important lesson from the pseudoquestions is that if a directive is needed, phrase it as such. If options truly exist, they need to be verbalized. That way the client is not left guessing as to the true meaning or intent of the counselor's question or statement.

Judgmental Questions

Judgmental questions are the reason why questions starting with "why" have fallen into disregard among counselors and therapists. Most judgmental questions begin with "why," and a generalization has occurred that since these are judgmental questions, all "why" questions are judgmental. This is simply not true. Occasional well-phrased and intentioned "why" questions can be quite appropriate, as will be demonstrated below. However, "why" questions that suggest judgment are truly pitfalls in questioning. Such questions put the client on the defensive or create some sense of discomfort in the client. For whatever reason, the clinician phrased a question in a way that sounded judgmental to the client. While some questions will sound judgmental to almost anyone, there are some questions that may be perceived as judgmental by some, but not other, clients. It takes some empathy for and knowledge about each and every client to be able to anticipate whether a certain question will result in defensiveness or discomfort in the client. One prime example of a question that will sound judgmental to almost anyone is the still-often-used "Why did you do that?" It is best to eliminate this question from a counselor's vocabulary as most clients will react defensively. There are many better ways to arrive at the same point. For example, "How did you decide what to do at that point?" will give the therapist the same information without inducing defensiveness in the client. The following example points to some of the pitfalls of and alternatives to judgmental questions.

> CLIENT: Well, my father and I were at it again this week. It doesn't matter that I am hundreds of miles away—we talk on the phone and there we go. He was being a total jerk again, giving me the usual lecture about responsibility and respect and blah blah blah. . . . I really let him have it this time. And I have no regrets—well, I feel a little bad for calling him a shithead . . . and I hung up on him on that note. . . . Yikes.

Pitfall: Use of Judgmental Question

> CLINICIAN: Couldn't you have dealt with that a little differently this time?
> CLIENT: (*defensively*) I don't think so! You should have been there and you would understand! He can be a real jerk. . . .

Alternative: Use of Well-Phrased Open-Ended Question

> CLINICIAN: Now that you're looking back at it, it almost sounds like there may be some things you wish or that you could have done differently? (*picking up on the client's "yikes" as regret*)
> CLIENT: Oh, yeah! (*sounds relieved at being understood*) I have gone through the scenario in lots of different ways since then. I know I tend to overreact. I get so caught up in the moment that I forget that he's only human too. (*smiles*)
> CLINICIAN: What are the different ways you have envisioned? (*Session continues from there.*)

This example demonstrates how doing something that leads clients to become defensive impedes therapeutic work. Clients often come to therapy because they already feel judged by others and judge themselves. What they need from their counselor is unconditional positive regard (yes, Rogers was right!), as well as understanding (Kohut convincingly points this out). When they perceive judgment (that is, lack of understanding and acceptance) from the therapist, clients feel the need to protect themselves, and the only way they likely know how to do this is to become defensive. Defensiveness translates into less-than-genuine disclosure and gets in the way of therapeutic progress. This example also clarifies that the difference in phrasing can be very subtle. The smallest nuance in how a question is worded can make the difference between judgment and genuine exploration.

Attacking Questions

Attacking questions are closely related to judgmental questions. Fortunately, they are more obvious and hence more easily avoided. This type of inquiry is perceived by the client as demeaning or embarrassing. Regardless of the clinician's original intent this type of question serves to shame the client or demonstrates the clinician's power over the client. Attacking questions must be eradicated from a clinician's repertoire of questions. They are harmful and counterproductive to therapeutic work. Developing good self-awareness is the prerequisite for not using attacking questions. Only a counselor or therapist who does not need to feel one-up vis-à-vis a client will be able to avoid attacking questions. Clients make themselves very vulnerable in clinical situations; attacking questions take advantage, however subtle, of this vulnerability by knocking the client down even further. Examples of attacking questions include "Why are you telling me this?"; "What's the point of that story?"; "Aren't you listening to me?"; "Is that supposed to make sense?"; "So?"; "So what?"; "Don't you get it?"; "Can't you understand that simple idea?"; and many others. The following example demonstrates the negative power of attacking questions that were phrased rather subtly.

> CLIENT: My best friend Jim had a big fight with his wife this week. He was really upset—came over at midnight and rang my doorbell. He's never done anything like that before. I was pretty freaked out. I guess he just really needed to talk to someone and had stormed out of his house so he couldn't call. . . . What a night we had. My goodness, the poor guy. They have been struggling for a while, only I didn't know it because he never said anything about it. . . . (*hesitates*)

Pitfall: Use of Attacking Question
> CLINICIAN: So what is your point here?
> CLIENT: (*taken aback; hesitates with answer*) Um, I don't know. . . . (*blushes; shuts down*)

Alternative: Use of Well-Phrased Open-Ended Question
> CLINICIAN: What a powerful experience. What do you make of it? (*empathizes first with the client's emotional state, then inquires as to what the client is driving at*)
> CLIENT: Well, I am shocked he didn't tell me before. We are best friends!
> CLINICIAN: You're surprised . . . (*client interrupts this unnecessary paraphrase*)
> CLIENT: Yes. We have known each other for twelve years! We've been through a lot together. (*Session continues from here.*)

This example shows that attacks lead nowhere. There is really no excuse for using such an intervention. It tends to be driven by therapist insecurity, impatience, and other less-than-therapeutic traits that need to be self-monitored. The alternative shows that with a little empathy a well-phrased open-ended question will open doors and keep disclosure going.

Controlling or Intrusive Questions

This type of question is intrusive in that it ignores the client's agenda and needs, and focuses instead on the desires and wishes of the therapist. There are, of course, times in treatment when a counselor appropriately changes agenda or direction of a session. Such a change is predicated on a genuine need to switch gears for the sake of the client. This may happen, for example, with a client who does not stay on a productive or helpful course. In that situation it is the counselor's responsibility to bring the duo back to a useful topic area. When the therapist switches focus, though, not because it is therapeutic, but for some personal reason, the choice becomes controlling and, at times, intrusive. The counselor may be uncomfortable with the conversation (for example, the client is talking about sex, or values the clinician does not agree with). Sometimes quite the opposite is true, with a clinician who seeks such specific detail that focus essentially shifts away from the client and to a preoccupation of the therapist that may even be voyeuristic (for example, the clinician may ask overly personal and intrusive questions about a client's sexual practices). The pitfall of controlling or intrusive questions is the change of focus from client to clinician, usually for some personal reason of the clinician. Such reasons can clearly be multifold and, if they interfere regularly, suggest that the clinician may not be sufficiently emotionally healthy to be in a counseling or therapeutic role. A listing of some possible reasons for controlling or intrusive questions follows.

Examples of Clinicians' Reasons for Controlling or Intrusive Questions

- idiosyncratic topical preoccupation by the clinician (for example, always shifting conversation to marital issues or financial matters)
- voyeuristic preoccupation with a topic by the clinician (for example, overly personal questions about sexual practices)
- theoretical preoccupations by the clinician (for example, leading questioning regarding how a client's parents may be at fault for current problems)
- preoccupation with concerns related to the clinician's practice specialty (for example, a traumatic-stress therapist always and only focuses on that aspect of a client's case)
- avoidance of certain topics by the clinician because they are deemed unimportant or irrelevant (for example, steering clients away from talking about medical or nutritional issues)
- avoidance due to embarrassment about certain topics in the clinician (for example, clinician who cannot talk about sex)
- avoidance due to countertransference about certain topics in the clinician (for example, the clinician's personal conflict with authority figures)
- redirection of the client because of disagreement (for example, clinician refuses to talk about abortion as a possibility with a newly pregnant client)

- redirection of a client because of fear of a topic (for example, clinician who is unable to follow up on suicidal or violent threats because of fear of what the client may say or do)

Clearly, these examples of reasons demonstrate that control and intrusion arise out of unresolved personal or professional issues of the care provider. The client is pushed to an agenda or to a level of depth of exploration that is undesirable for that individual, but desirable for the clinician. Not surprisingly, controlling or intrusive questions that occur with regularity tend to be indicators of countertransference. The client will feel unheard, misunderstood, and uncared-for at best; invaded and possibly traumatized at worst.

Tangential Questions

On the surface, tangential questions may look similar to controlling or intrusive questions, in that they, too, shift focus. However, where controlling or intrusive questions arise out of a clinician's need to be preoccupied with or to avoid certain topics, tangential questions usually stem from a lack of empathic attunement with the client. These questions are off the mark because of some lack in understanding of the client. Of course, it is possible that lack of empathic attunement and understanding have arisen due to some of the reasons provided under controlling or intrusive questions; however, most of the time this is not the case. If it is the case, what appears tangential will often become more obviously controlling or intrusive as it repeats itself. Tangential questions fail to get at the heart of the client's matter and usually hone in on a nonessential detail in the client's communication. They are not totally out of context or off topic; they are slightly off, not catching the essential message that the client is attempting to explore or communicate. Tangential questions suggest that the clinician needs to enhance empathic skills. If frequent, such questions tend to keep therapy or counseling somewhat aimless and superficial. An occasional tangential question rarely does any harm, especially if the therapist recognizes the misattunement and corrects it (unlike attacking questions, which can destroy a therapeutic relationship in a single application). The following example demonstrates a tangential question along with a nice recovery and reattunement on the part of the clinician.

> CLIENT: Being diagnosed with multiple sclerosis has turned my life upside down. It has just about changed everything—my career path, the way I view my children and my husband, even the way I approach each day. It's all so different now. You know, I thought I was invincible, and when I was feeling tired and draggy before or if my muscles didn't quite cooperate, I dismissed it. Now it has meaning—horrible meaning. My god (*begins to weep*)—then I ask, why me?? You know, I've always taken care of myself, I eat well and exercise. I worked hard all my life. I was there for my children. It's all different now.

CLINICIAN: Your life seems completely changed. . . . (*a paraphrase to let the client know the clinician is listening and present*)

CLIENT: Yes . . . (*nodding; slowly recovering her emotions*) . . . Nothing is the same. I don't know what to do and where to start. Do I focus on my treatment or on my responsibilities, do I quit my job, do I hire a housekeeper, do I just wait and see how things are going to unfold, should I tell my children's teachers? Should I tell my friends and how about acquaintances, do they need to know? Should I see another physician, you know, get a second opinion about all this?

CLINICIAN: Do you want to tell other people about having been diagnosed? (*tangential in that this is not the essence of what the client is concerned with*)

CLIENT: I don't know. (*exasperated*) Don't you see, I don't know. . . . I don't care who knows! I'm just so worried. . . .

CLINICIAN: So is it your job you are worried about? (*tangentially honing in on yet another nonessential detail*)

CLIENT: No. Yes. Well, partly, but that's really not it—it's more the whole thing, you know?

CLINICIAN: You need to figure out *all* the implications, sort of one by one and then for each one figure out what you need to do. Is that it? (*starting to catch on to the whole picture now*)

CLIENT: Yes. You don't really notice how complex your life is until something like this happens and then you realize lots of people depend on you and that you yourself depend on your body being there for you.

CLINICIAN: What has shaken you the most? (*finally a good open-ended question that captures the client's emotional state and need*)

CLIENT: The fact that the very foundation my life rests on is slowly breaking apart. . . .

CLINICIAN: Your body is letting you down?! (*a nice paraphrase, almost a reflection [see Chapter Six]*)

CLIENT: Oh yes. That's it. How can I trust anything now? (*Session goes on from here.*)

This example demonstrates that asking focused and relevant open-ended questions is predicated on understanding the essential aspect of a client's communication. It is very easy to pick up on a detail and ask a specific question about it. It is much more difficult to recognize what the essential question is that the client is asking herself and to help her verbalize that question so that problem solving may begin. The example also shows how sensitive and nondefensive listening to the client after a question can help the clinician recognize when a question was tangential and when a different approach is called for. In the example, it took a few attempts before the clinician recognized the tangentiality of her questions; once recognized, she was able to change tack and reattune to the client. The client acknowledged this reattunement through her heightened responsiveness.

Content-Diverse Multiple Questions

This pitfall occurs when a mental-health-care provider asks several questions all at once and each of the questions addresses a slightly different issue or content. Sometimes, counselors will phrase the same question in two or three different ways and thus will ask multiple questions. That is not what is referred to here, as in essence only one question was asked. When multiple questions get at diverse contents, the client may be left with confusion as to which question to answer. Multiple questions of that type indicate confusion and lack of organization on the clinician's part. Clearly, the therapist does not have the direction of the question well enough formulated to stick with it; one question followed by another one of a different content suggests uncertainty about which way to take the session. It is no wonder that client and clinician sometimes end up feeling confused and floundering with this style of inquiry. In other instances, however, multiple questions do not appear to bother clients much at all. They may merely choose the question they deem most relevant or important and answer it, ignoring the rest. The clinician then only has to decide whether it is important at some point to follow up on the other questions. Following is an example of multiple questions. The first section (pitfall) reflects inappropriate content-diverse multiple questions; the alternative demonstrates multiple questions that are not problematic (though perhaps still not ideal since such multiple questioning is not efficient).

> CLIENT: My sister and I are in total agreement that the family reunion was once again the typical disaster that it always is. Why do we keep going? It sucks every time but somehow both of us keep hoping against hope that something will change and we miraculously will be a happy healthy family. Fat chance, right? My brother was drunk again, of course. You know, the difference was that this time he arrived drunk. I really got on his case about it too because he brought his little girl and if he wants to drive himself around drunk that's one thing. But to drive his kid around like that, now that's child abuse. So I told him I'd report him to the authorities. You should have seen my mother jump on that one. You'd think she'd agree with me on that but *NO*—she was on his side. What is her problem anyway? Maybe she's covering for my father. He is a drunk too. I bet he used to drive us around drunk too. We were just too little to notice. . . . Thank goodness he wasn't there this time. Though nobody knows why. He could be dead for all we know. . . .

Pitfall: Content-Diverse Multiple Questions

> CLINICIAN: So your father drank too? So your mother sided with your brother? Did you end up reporting him? (*inappropriate multiple questions*)

CLIENT: Yeah, I reported him. Turns out they already had a file on him. A neighbor had turned him in. They didn't do anything though. Said he'd never really hurt his kids. . . .

CLINICIAN: Is there anything else you want to do about that situation? (*good open-ended question*)

CLIENT: No. I feel like I did what I could. I know he wouldn't let me take the kid. I've offered before but in some warped way he really loves her. . . .

CLINICIAN: What was it you offered before? (*Session continues from here.*)

Alternative: Content-Repetitive (Appropriate) Multiple Questions

CLINICIAN: Sounds like a lot happened! What has stayed with you the most? You know, what affected you the most?

CLIENT: I guess the thing with my brother and his daughter. I really do worry about her. When I called the child protection guys they said . . . (*Session continues from here.*)

This example demonstrates an instance of multiple questioning that did not appear to bother the client. The client chose to address the question closest to her heart and went on from there without concern about the other questions. For the time being, the therapist followed her lead and dropped pursuit of the other questions. As often occurs in content-diverse multiple questioning, some of the questions were more relevant than others; some were almost tangential in nature. They are often not good open-ended questions as they tend to be focused on specific detail. The alternative in the example demonstrates a much superior approach to an open-ended way of questioning along with a multiple-question format. The two questions got at the same issue. This way of phrasing can have advantages and disadvantages. It is less efficient, but sometimes serves to clarify further what it is the clinician is asking.

Closed Questions

The discussion of multiple questions alluded to the fact that there are certain traits or characteristics of good open-ended questions. This issue will be discussed in detail below. However, another excellent means of deciding whether a question was well-phrased is the differentiation between open-ended and closed questions. Closed questions allow clients to answer with a simple phrase or even to give a yes-no answer. They make it easy for clients to evade issues and do not encourage self-disclosure effectively. The pitfalls are at least threefold. First, clients do not have to provide a lot of information, and the ensuing interaction between therapist and client may not be very rich. Second, counselors who use closed questions end up doing all of the therapeutic work for the client, who merely has to sit and answer yes or no. Finally, closed questions require a lot of verbalization on the part of the clinician, a practice that is not conducive to an active and collaborative way of communicating. This issue is related to shotgunning, the next pitfall to be discussed. Examples of closed questions and open-ended alternatives are provided below.

One other important point needs to be made before delving into examples. Not all uses of closed questions are inappropriate. In fact, when used wisely and purposefully, closed questions can be useful tools in the hands of a skilled clinician. Wise uses of closed questions occur to focus clients during crises, shut or slow down overly talkative clients, pace and organize the thinking and talking of clients whose thoughts are racing, diffuse a client's anxiety by giving them a clear and simple focus, get clear information about a specific issue, or direct a client toward an important point. These purposes are well served with closed questions that force a client to keep answers brief and hone in on the essential issue queried by the clinician. Once the goal has been met and the task accomplished, the clinician will once again switch to open-ended questions. Positive uses of closed questions are outlined in Table 5-2.

Closed Questions	Open-Ended Alternative
Do you like your mother/father/etc.?	How do you feel about your mother/father/etc.?
Did you grow up here?	Where did you grow up?
Did you like school?	What were your years like in high school?
Do you have a best friend?	What can you tell me about your best friend?
Do you like to read?	What are some of your hobbies and what do you enjoy about them?
Is your apartment new?	Tell me about the place where you live.
Do you like the weather here?	How do you adjust to and cope with the different seasons here?
Were you hospitalized after the accident?	How bad were your injuries?
Did you ask him xyz?	What did you say after that?
Do you know how to ski?	What do you do for enjoyment in the winter?

These examples highlight how easy it is for a client to respond with a simple yes or no to closed questions. It is much more difficult to answer with a simple phrase when a good open-ended question is asked. More hints on how to construct good open-ended questions are provided in a later section of this chapter. For now, the examples should serve to demonstrate that closed questions, when not used for a specific reason (as outlined in Table 5-2), are not conducive to facilitating self-disclosure or interactive and collaborative exchanges between client and clinician.

Shotgunning

This final pitfall is related to the use of closed questions. In fact, it will only occur if a clinician overly relies on closed questions. Shotgunning is defined as a series (a *long* series) of closed questions that cover nothing in depth and much

TABLE

5-2

POSITIVE AND PURPOSEFUL USES OF CLOSED QUESTIONS

Situations in Which to Use Closed Questions	Rationale for Use in That Situation	Example of a Closed Question in That Situation
During a crisis situation (e.g., a suicidal threat, a threat of violence, a situational crisis)	• To help the client get focused in on detail • To solicit very specific and detailed information about a given issue	• "You say you want to shoot yourself. Do you have a gun?" • "Do you have a place to stay tonight?"
With a client who is self-disclosing too much too quickly (i.e., too early in the therapeutic relationship)	• To keep the client safe from opening too many wounds at once • To keep the client from feeling too vulnerable vis-à-vis the clinician later	• "Let's go back to your relationship with your father. Did you get along with him?" • "Let's slow down a little. Did you graduate from high school?"
With a client who is self-disclosing when the end of the session is quickly approaching	• To keep the client safe from opening new issues before the end of the session • To pace the client such that a good closure can be achieved	• "Let me stop you there. Did you get the contract?" • "Let's slow down a little. Did you recover your composure then?"
With a client who is excessively nervous, anxious, worried, and self-conscious	• To diffuse anxious emotions • To help the client feel safe • To help the client settle into a new situation without fear and doubt	• "After that you left the room?" • "Did that help?" • "Was that comfortable for you?"
With a client who is scattered or confused	• To help the client get focused • To help the client feel more centered • To help achieve direction and focus	• "Let's start with the housing problem. Is your apartment safe?" • "Let's go to the next issue. Do you have food in the house?"
With a client whose thoughts are racing or who is overly talkative	• To slow the client's thought process • To get the client focused • To slow the client down • To pace the client	• "Let's take it one thing at a time. Your car died in the middle of the street?" • "Did your mother visit you in the hospital?"

in breadth, that is, superficially. The client who is the target of this series of questions is likely to feel bombarded, if not assaulted, by a curious and noncaring therapist who asks endless questions without really allowing the client to self-disclose. Since answers to closed questions are by definition very brief or mere yes-or-no answers, clients end up talking much less than the shotgunning clinician, who reels off one question after another. This clinician will cover a lot of ground, but when looking back at the information, the counselor will notice that there is a dearth of meaning and that the essence or emotional aspects of the client remain hidden. A brief clinician-client interaction based on shotgunning follows.

CLINICIAN: Did you grow up here?

CLIENT: Yes, I grew up in Anchorage.

CLINICIAN: Did you go to school in Anchorage?

CLIENT: Yes.

CLINICIAN: Did you graduate from high school?

CLIENT: Yes.

CLINICIAN: Which one?

CLIENT: East High.

CLINICIAN: When?

CLIENT: 1995.

CLINICIAN: Did you go to the University of Alaska Anchorage after graduation?

CLIENT: Yes.

CLINICIAN: Did you graduate?

CLIENT: No.

CLINICIAN: Did you drop out?

CLIENT: No.

CLINICIAN: What happened? (*the first open-ended question*)

CLIENT: I was kicked out.

CLINICIAN: Did you get a job after that? (*really missing the opportunity for open-ended follow-up here*)

CLIENT: Yes.

CLINICIAN: Where?

CLIENT: At Wal-Mart.

CLINICIAN: Do you still work there?

CLIENT: Yes.

CLINICIAN: So you have worked there how long?

CLIENT: Three years.

CLINICIAN: Do you like your job?

CLIENT: No—it sucks.

CLINICIAN: Are you looking for a different job?

CLIENT: No.

CLINICIAN: Why not? (*adding judgmentalism to shotgunning*)
CLIENT: I don't know (*at this point does not trust the clinician*)

This session could literally go on like that for hours, unless the client got so fed up as to get up and leave—a possibility to be recommended given the skill level of this therapist. This transcript hopefully serves to demonstrate how little real information is obtained through shotgunning. This counselor asked questions about several areas of the client's life, as one would during an intake (that is, a systematic inquiry), but has very little to show for the many questions. The content stays on the surface, is unelaborated, and discloses nothing essential or meaningful about the client. The client no doubt walks away feeling insulted or assaulted and is not likely to feel heard, cared for, or understood.

Additional Thoughts About the Use of Questions

Once aware of the potential pitfalls in the use of questions, the clinician is ready to tackle some of the specifics about how to phrase questions with success. The pointers given here apply to all three types of questions, that is, to open-ended questions, systematic inquiry, and clarifying questions. When humans learn to speak, they also learn to ask. The way they learn to make questions is via a few very specific words that give questions a certain direction. These words of course are what, how, why, when, who, and where. These question stems are useful in therapy as well and will solicit specific information from clients as shown in Table 5-3.

Clearly, in phrasing questions all of these words—what, how, why, when, who, and where—will come in handy to direct a client down a particular path of inquiry. Questions that begin with question words are usually more specific than questions not opened with these words. It is important for clinicians to remember that "why" questions in particular can lead to defensiveness in the client. It is preferable to rephrase a "why" question. There may be times, however, when this is not possible, and then a cautious "why" question may be appropriate. Finally, counselors do not HAVE to ask questions. Much can be accomplished with simple statements. Further, embedding questions in statements that reflect empathy, understanding, caring, and listening is extremely helpful to rapport. Especially in systematic inquiry, when many questions need to be asked, it can be helpful to phrase as many questions as possible in the form of statements instead and to embed as many questions as possible in restatements, paraphrases, and reflections (to be discussed in the next chapter).

OPEN-ENDED QUESTIONS

Everything leading up to this point has hinted at the great importance of open-ended questions in therapy and counseling. Given their importance, it is critical

TABLE 5-3 PURPOSES OF THE "QUESTION WORDS"

Word	Question Example	Purpose
What?	What happened next?	Elicits facts and specific details about a situation
How?	How did that come about? How did you feel at that point?	Elicits process or sequence about a situation; may be used to elicit emotions
Why?	Why do you suppose she chose to do that?	Elicits reasons; may lead to intellectualization, rationalization, or defensiveness
When?	When did it happen?	Elicits specific detail about various time frames
Where?	Where did you go from there?	Elicits specific detail about location(s)
Who?	Who all was part of that?	Elicits specific detail about involved players

that counselors and therapists learn to phrase good open-ended questions and that they understand their applications and purposes. To recapitulate, the primary purposes of open-ended questions are encouragement of self-disclosure and facilitation of collaborative interaction (or communication). How questions are phrased can greatly contribute to or detract from these purposes. Obviously, the pitfalls outlined above need to be avoided. However, there are also a few simple hints about how to phrase good open-ended questions that should help clinicians in training learn how to use this essential skill in their counseling or therapy practice.

It may go without saying that first of all a clinician must have a reason for asking a question. In other words, questions need to be intentional and purposeful. Questions are not asked to kill time or end silences. Once the clinician has decided to ask a question (that is, has identified a need and purpose for a question), timing of the delivery of that question is carefully considered. Clients are best not interrupted while still speaking, just to ask a question. It is not good practice to disrupt a client's concentration in that manner. It is generally more helpful to wait for questioning until an actual break takes place in the client's verbalization. On the other hand, if a clinician has a burning question, it is not a good idea to wait too long to ask it. Waiting too long may result in the client having moved on to another topic, making the question poorly timed or irrelevant.

It is important to be sensitive to the individual needs of each client with regard to the number and speed with which to deliver questions. What may feel like bombardment to one client, may be quite comfortable for another and vice versa. Thus, the number and nature of questions to ask are best adapted specifically to each client's idiosyncratic needs, traits, and characteristics. Knowing a client well enough to make this type of judgment may take some time and may be based in some trial-and-error learning.

It is also important to ask enough questions, that is, a sufficient number of questions to achieve the desired focus and clarity. Not asking too many questions refers to the reality that clients may feel overwhelmed when clinicians ask for too much information all at once. Knowing when to ask follow-up questions and when to let go of an issue or topic is critically important. Clients must never feel harassed by excessive questioning; on the other hand clients should not be allowed to retreat from providing information that is needed for proper treatment planning and diagnosis. If follow-up appears necessary for the sake of appropriate treatment decisions or better understanding of the client, the counselor should ask the question. If, on the other hand, follow-up would add little additional or crucial information and may be perceived by the client as intrusive, the therapist may choose to forego the questioning.

Questions are best phrased in such a manner that they are perceived by the client as supportive and therapeutic, not judgmental or presumptuous. This issue clearly relates to the many pitfalls outlined above. It deserves rementioning if merely to point out that questions often can be asked in a manner that feels supportive to the client rather than challenging or cold (unfeeling). It is often helpful to introduce difficult questions with a gentle lead-in or preface that expresses caring and purpose. An example of such a lead-in may be "I realize this is a difficult issue. However, I feel it's important for me to ask if. . . ." Another possible lead-in may be something like "I have a difficult question for you that you may choose not to answer if it's too painful for you. . . ." Embedding open-ended questions in such a context of understanding and empathy helps clients answer even the most difficult questions. If clients feel understood and cared for they will be much more likely to be willing to disclose very intimate details of their lives than when they feel intruded upon. Relatedly, it is generally best to let open-ended questions arise from the client's choice of agenda and need and not from the therapist's needs. In other words, the area for questioning using open-ended questions is generally chosen by the client, not clinician (very unlike systematic inquiry, where the area of questioning is determined by the therapist).

Once questions have been asked of a client, the individual needs to be given enough time to respond to them. This may seem to be an obvious point, but it is a necessary caution, especially since individual needs for pauses after a question has been asked and before the answer is given are greatly diverse. Clinicians adapt the length of the pause between question and answer to the idiosyncratic needs of the client, a time period that is related to cultural practices and expectations. For reasons of time efficiency and the avoidance of shotgunning, it is good practice for clinicians to reconsider asking any open-ended question to which they already know the answer. Occasionally, in asking clarifying questions that are open-ended in nature, this rule will be broken for a therapeutic reason or purpose. This specific use of questions to which the clinician already knows the answer will be expanded upon in the chapter that deals with clarifying questions in the context of creating cognitive insight.

Finally, it is often, but not always, helpful first to communicate understanding of what the client has just communicated in the form of a paraphrase, reflection, or restatement before asking an open-ended question. This will let the client know that the clinician has heard and understood what the client has disclosed already. Embedded in such a context of caring, clients feel comfortable continuing to disclose and that a truly collaborative effort is made on behalf of their growth or problem solving. In closing this section it is important to reiterate an important point: All open-ended questions need to be phrased in such a manner that the client has many options in how to answer them. Any question that can be responded to with a simple yes or no or a very brief phrase probably does not meet the criteria for an open-ended question. Instead, such a question is likely to have been closed, and if overused may discourage spontaneous self-disclosure.

If clinicians follow these few simple rules about open-ended questions, they should be quite successful in soliciting specific information from their clients and in facilitating self-disclosure. Often a few open-ended questions early in a contact with client will give the client the clear message that the clinician is willing to listen and interested in receiving as much information about the client as possible. This will then motivate the client to self-disclose increasingly spontaneously and will actually reduce the need for questions later in the therapy or counseling process. Although several examples of open-ended questions were provided in the "Pitfalls" section above, a brief sample transcript of an exchange follows that highlights the successful use of open-ended questions.

Sample Transcript of Open-Ended Questions

CLINICIAN: How have you been feeling this week? (*opening session with an open-ended question*)

CLIENT: That is such a hard question, even though you ask it every week. . . .

CLINICIAN: What makes it hard? (*following up with yet another open-ended question*)

CLIENT: Oh, I'm not sure. Probably the fact that I really don't always pay attention to my feelings. But then that's why you ask, isn't it?

CLINICIAN: (*merely smiles and nods*)

CLIENT: Well, how have I been feeling. I guess it's been an okay week— feelings-wise. (*smiles*) Seriously, though, I have felt pretty good. I had no moments of real crisis. . . .

CLINICIAN: How are you feeling right now? (*another open-ended question*)

CLIENT: Oh, nervous, I suppose. Just kind of anxious about not being able to give you a better answer. . . .

CLINICIAN: What does anxious mean to you? (*another open-ended question*)

CLIENT: Well, it means . . . (*Session continues from here.*)

Skill Development Recommendations

Recommendation 5-1   *Turn the following closed questions into open-ended ones:*

- *Did you graduate from high school?*
- *Do you like hiking?*
- *Do you notice a difference?*
- *Do you have any friends in this town?*
- *Do you want to change your mood?*
- *Do you know how to make a nutritious meal?*
- *Do you get along with your mother?*
- *Do you have a car?*
- *Do you have an intimate relationship?*
- *Do you want to make a change?*

Answer each question as it was originally written and as you rewrote it. What do you notice? How does the rephrasing improve each question?

Recommendation 5-2   *Identify the pitfalls in the following questions. Then rephrase each question to turn it into a therapeutic question.*

- *You didn't think that was the best approach, did you?*
- *How did you figure this could possibly work?*
- *Why didn't you ask her to come with you?*
- *Where are you going with this story?*
- *Did you never even consider her feelings?*
- *Did you figure out that this was a poor way to do this?*
- *Was that the right thing to do?*
- *Why did you do that?*
- *How can you possibly justify this action?*
- *You didn't divorce him, did you?*
- *Do you like your father?*
- *You are taking drugs?*
- *Do you really think this will work?*
- *Do you want to end the session now?*
- *Couldn't you have said that differently?*
- *Why would you try that?*
- *Did you hear a word I said?*
- *Would you give me the nitty-gritty details of that sexual encounter?*
- *Did you like the job? And who got you into physics anyway? How old were you when you graduated?*

Look at each question as it was written originally and put yourself in the client's place. How would you feel about each question? Then look at how you have rewritten each question. Does your reaction change? How? To what do you attribute the difference in your reactions to the questions?

Recommendation 5-3 *From now on, as you interact with family members or friends, experiment with open-ended questions, avoiding the pitfalls discussed above. What are the differences you notice in how people respond to you? What are you noticing in terms of changes in your relationships with others as you use this form of interaction?*

SYSTEMATIC INQUIRY

The primary purpose of systematic inquiry is to collect a specific body of data about a client. For the novice clinician, the systematic inquiry of greatest concern is that engaged in during an intake interview. During this initial session with a client, the counselor needs to collect sufficient data to gain a thorough understanding of the client that can be used to arrive at a diagnosis and a treatment plan. Although it is beyond the scope of this book to deal with the intricacies of intake interviewing as a whole, the systematic-inquiry process is outlined briefly. Readers who are interested in learning more about the intake and early-assessment process with a new client are referred to Brems (1999), which outlines this early collaboration with clients in detail.

Systematic inquiry in an intake interview centers around data collection in a number of areas in a client's life. The interview usually begins with an exploration of the presenting concern and from there moves to taking a client's history. Included in the client history are the following topic areas: family history, sexual history, social history, academic and professional history, developmental and health history, substance use history, and nutritional and exercise history. Further, the counselor notes behavioral observations about the client and pays attention to the person's strengths. Within each of these categories very specific information is sought. Regardless of the importance of this information, however, when the counselor recognizes that the client is becoming overwhelmed by the intense questioning, inquiry is interrupted for the sake of rapport. Clinicians use their clinical judgment about when to abandon systematic inquiry during an intake to maintain a good relationship with the client. For example, if very painful contents are discussed, it may be important to slow down and make sure that the client is not overwhelmed with affect or racing thoughts. An empathic listening and questioning style is essential. Of course, it would be asking the impossible of the counselor to develop all components of therapeutic rapport in a single session. A therapeutic relationship develops over a long period of time; however, often the foundation is laid in the very first hour of client contact, while the client's feelings of vulnerability are heightened by the newness of the situation. Nevertheless, the initial session is very structured because the counselor has a clear agenda, namely the systematic inquiry into the client's history and presenting concern. Directiveness and clarity about the focus of the questions is essential and conducive to the purpose of this process.

The content sought in the systematic-inquiry portion of the intake is summarized in Table 5-4. The transcript that follows, a selected portion of an intake interview, demonstrates how a systematic inquiry is accomplished, with its juggling act between data collection and rapport. It points to the importance of embedding systematic-inquiry questions in a context of caring, empathy, and understanding. As is true for open-ended questions, systematic inquiry will be most successful if the questions are prefaced with appropriate restatements, paraphrases, and reflections that let the client feel understood, heard, and listened to. All of the various questioning pitfalls, especially shotgunning, need to be avoided.

Sample Transcript of a Systematic Inquiry

CLINICIAN: Let me shift gears a little bit now. To understand all the circumstance of your depression, I'd like to ask you some questions now about your health and related issues. Sometimes physical things are tied to depressive feelings, and I want to make sure that I am not misunderstanding what is going on with you. Alright?

CLIENT: Sure, I kind of figured as much. . . .

CLINICIAN: Alright then. Let me start by asking about your diet. What's a typical day like for you as far as food intake is concerned?

CLIENT: Well, most of time I eat breakfast, but not every day. I'm usually too busy to eat lunch but I generally make a point of eating a solid dinner every day.

CLINICIAN: Do you snack in between?

CLIENT: Yeah, usually. But I try to eat healthy snacks.

CLINICIAN: That's terrific. What kind of snacks?

CLIENT: Oh, like popcorn or crackers or stuff like that. Sometimes a piece of fruit . . .

CLINICIAN: How many snacks do you eat in a day?

CLIENT: Oh, just one.

CLINICIAN: When do you usually eat that snack?

CLIENT: Usually in the afternoon, since I skip lunch. A lot of times I get hungry around two o'clock or so. That's when I eat my snacks.

CLINICIAN: So tell me, what kind of snack did you have yesterday?

CLIENT: I had a bag of popcorn.

TABLE 5-4	TOPICS FOR SYSTEMATIC INQUIRY IN AN INTAKE INTERVIEW

Inquiry Area	Questions to Be Answered
Presenting Concern	• What is the overriding presenting concern? • What are the circumstances? • When does the problem arise? • Where does the problem arise? • How does the problem arise? • With whom does the problem arise? • How often does the problem arise? • How intense is the problem? • What is the history of the presenting concern? • How long has the problem been occurring? • How has the problem changed over time? • When is the first time the problem was noticed? • When is the last time the problem was not at all present?

Family History— in Family of Origin	• Identification of all family members with whom client interacted childhood
	• Family interactions during childhood and adolescent years
	    interactions with siblings, stepsiblings, half-siblings, etc.
	    interactions with parents, stepparents, foster parents, etc.
	• Structure of family (persons, relationships, communication, etc.)
	    generational boundaries
	    coalitions
	• Family experiences during childhood and adolescent years
	    parenting styles experienced
	    communication styles and patterns
	    memories in the family setting
	    family trauma (history of abuse, witnessing domestic violence)
	• Parental family background
	    parental family trees
	    parental family experiences
	    parental experience of childhood and adolescent trauma
	    parental medical and psychiatric history
	• Current interactions with family of origin
	• Genogram or family genealogy (optional)

Family History— Nuclear Family	• Identification of nuclear-family members in client's adult life
	• Nuclear-family interactions
	    interactions with significant others (SOs) and former SOs
	    interactions with children, stepchildren, foster-children, etc.
	    interactions with family of SOs
	• Structure of family (persons, relationships, communication, etc.)
	    generational boundaries
	    coalitions
	• Nuclear-family experiences
	    parenting styles exercised with own children
	    memories in the family setting
	    family trauma (domestic violence, perpetration of abuse)
	    communication styles and patterns
	• Functionality of the family

Sexuality	• Sexuality in current intimate relationship (quality, frequency, enjoyment, compatibility) • Sexuality in other relationships (quality, frequency, enjoyment, compatibility) • First sexual experience (as a possible lead-in to sexual abuse)

TABLE 5-4 (CONTINUED)

Inquiry Area	Questions to Be Answered

Sexuality (continued)	• Later sexual experiences (quality, frequency, enjoyment, compatibility)
	• Masturbation
	• Sexual abuse (incest, molestation, rape)
	    perpetrator(s)
	    specifics about the abuse (type, form)
	    age, frequency, and duration
	    events surrounding the abuse (e.g., where, when, threats made)
	    presence of a protector/confidant

Social History	• Number and description of close friends (past and current)
	• Acquaintances and colleague relationships (past and current)
	• Interests, hobbies, recreational activities and interests (past and current)
	• Number and level of involvement in community groups (e.g., environmental-protection groups, sports leagues, special-interest groups, clubs, professional associations)
	• Religion and spirituality, including church memberships
	• Sociocultural issues
	    socioeconomic variables
	    cultural background and world views
	    ethnic background and minority status
	    level and context (forced versus voluntary) of acculturation

Professional History	• Description of current employment • Career plans and aspirations • Jobs and/or occupations in the past

Academic History	• Adult academic or vocational preparation background
	    degrees or certificates
	    performance (i.e., grades, level of success)
	    problems (e.g., learning disabilities or physical impediments)
	• School (K to 12) background
	    graduation
	    performance (i.e., grades, level of success)
	    problems (e.g., learning disabilities, peer relationships)

Health History	• Developmental issues
	    mother's pregnancy (i.e., in utero development and exposure)
	    birth information
	    developmental milestones
	• Previous mental-health treatment
	    prior therapy or counseling
	    prior psychological testing or assessment
	    school and vocational assessments
	• Medical trauma (injuries, accidents, head injuries; recent and past for all)
	• Physical health
	    current severe diagnosed illness
	    past acute illness
	    date, circumstances, and findings of last physical examination
	• Name of physician and other health-care providers
	• Hospitalizations, recent and past
	• Current medical treatments other than medications

Substance Use	• Prescription drug use (type, recency, frequency, amount) • Over-counter drug use (type, recency, frequency, amount) • Use of legal drugs, alcohol, tobacco products, caffeine (type, recency, frequency, amount) • Use of illegal substances (e.g., marijuana, cocaine, amphetamines,

Inquiry Area	Questions to Be Answered
	hallucinogens, barbiturates, inhalants) (type, recency, frequency, amount)
	• Family history of substance use
	medications (e.g., prescription and over-the-counter)
	legal drugs (e.g., alcohol, tobacco, caffeine)
	illegal substances (e.g., cocaine, inhalants, marijuana)
	issues related to adult children of substance users
Nutrition	• Daily food intake, exploring timing and quantities for breakfast, lunch, dinner, snacks, and desserts
	• Special diets
	diets for physical illnesses (e.g., for heart or cardiovascular disease)
	vegetarian diets
	macrobiotic diets
	• Daily liquid intake, exploring timing and quantities (water, juices, soft drinks, hot drinks)
	• Daily exercise routine
	• Awareness of nutrition and exercise needs
	• Inappropriate use of food (e.g., under- or overeating; bingeing and purging)
	• Inappropriate use of exercise
	• Family attitudes about foods, liquids, and exercise

CLINICIAN: This may seem picky, but how big was the bag and did you have anything on it, like butter or salt?

CLIENT: It was one of those microwave bags, just a standard portion, and it was buttered, too. I also always add a little bit of Parmesan cheese.

CLINICIAN: Okay, so let me summarize what we have so far. You sometimes eat breakfast, you never eat lunch, you eat a solid dinner every day, and you have a snack in the afternoon. Does that capture it?

CLIENT: Yes.

CLINICIAN: When you say you make sure you eat a solid dinner, what does that mean?

CLIENT: Oh, I mean I eat a big meal. Usually something with a vegetable, meat, and generally I top it off with a nice dessert. I really like food, I just don't have time during the day to eat. So then I really treat myself in the evening.

CLINICIAN: Tell me about a couple of typical dinners that you ate this week. If you don't mind all the detail, I'd like to know exactly everything that you ended up eating, including how much and at what time.

CLIENT: Well, let's see. . . . Yesterday evening I had steamed broccoli, some rice, and a chicken breast. Then for dessert I had a piece of apple pie. I baked it myself the day before. I use pretty good ingredients, like I don't use white sugar, only honey and I use whole wheat flour instead of the white stuff.

CLINICIAN: Can you give me an idea of the size of your servings?

CLIENT: Well, I had a couple of crowns of broccoli and probably a cup of

Skill Development Recommendations

Recommendation 5-4   *Using Table 5-4, answer the structured questions that are generally addressed by an intake interview. What are you learning about yourself from this exercise? What are you learning about the depth and breadth of an intake interview as you do this exercise? How much time may such an interview require? How do you believe clients feel when they are asked to answer these questions? Do any areas appear more difficult to inquire about than others? Do any areas strike you as more difficult to answer?*

Recommendation 5-5   *Choose a topic area of therapeutic interest (for example, childhood abuse, intimate relationships, suicide history). Outline the questions you would want to have answered to feel satisfied that you know everything about a client in this area. Once you have covered all content, try to anticipate the likely order in which the questions may be presented to a client. Evaluate each question for possible pitfalls.*

---

rice. The chicken breast was actually pretty small. I take the skin off and I cut any fat away.

CLINICIAN: And how big was the slice of apple pie?

CLIENT: Well, now, that's a different story. I love sweets. It was actually more than a slice. It was more like half a pie. (*Session continues from here.*)

This transcript shows the importance of not only asking very detailed questions during a systematic inquiry but also asking relevant follow-up questions. In several instances in this exchange, had the clinician not asked follow-up questions, she would have missed important details (such as the size of the apple pie). Despite the level of detail requested from the client, there did not appear to be any defensiveness on the part of the client regarding this difficult topic area. This is perhaps best attributed to the fact that the clinician paid careful attention to maintaining rapport with the client. The introductory statements, the expressions of understanding, and a caring and concerned voice all contributed to a sense of support and caring during this long systematic-inquiry session. In fact, only with this kind of sensitivity will a client tolerate systematic inquiries which otherwise can turn tedious or intrusive.

RESPONSE TYPES

Verbal Communication and Client Disclosure

> Sensitive expression, entailing carefully chosen words spoken from the heart, has the power to move people to tears or laughter—to inspire action that can change the world in ways larger or small.
>
> *Dan Millman, 1993, p. 50*

Once clinicians have mastered the necessary attending and listening skills, are capable of communicating nonverbally, and have learned skillful questioning, they are ready to tackle the next important communication skill that enhances the therapeutic exchange: responding to the client. Although attending, listening, and questioning are necessary for a positive client-clinician interaction, they are not sufficient. Clients also need to receive feedback about their verbalizations, a process that requires caring and accurate responding on the counselor's part. This helps the client feel heard and keeps communication and disclosure going. It serves to explore and clarify content expressed by the client for the clinician. In other words, the responding process serves to further clarify and develop the communication in which the client has already engaged.

The focus of therapeutic responding is not on clarifying meaning *for the client* (that is, on the creation of insight about why a client is feeling, or behaving, or thinking in a particular manner). It is not to be confused with interpretation or confrontation, or any of the other affective and cognitive awareness skills that are concerned with seeking explanations and meaning (or purpose of thought, behavior, and affect). Instead, the basic response types most relevant to communication and disclosure serve their primary purpose by clarifying information *for the clinician*. Additionally, responding skills are designed to help the client feel heard and listened to. This is achieved by feeding back information received from the client, not to clarify or explain underlying meaning, but to allow the client simply to recognize personal affect, thought, and behavior, and to realize that the therapist has been listening attentively and openly. The

155

most important response types for the mental-health-care provider to master include encouraging phrases, restatements and paraphrases, reflections, and summarization. Embedding questions into these interventions can further enhance their utility.

ENCOURAGING PHRASES

Encouragers, or encouraging phrases, are the simplest, and yet perhaps the most important interventions clinicians can use to facilitate the continued communication and disclosure of a client. Encouragers are designed to keep the client talking about a given topic, to explore an issue in a manner that has depth as well as breadth. The clinician using encouragers adds nothing new, suggests nothing new, offers no interpretations, and does not attempt to lead the client. In using encouragers, the mental-health-care provider merely encourages the client to elaborate and explore what is already being talked out. There is no suggestion to the client that a different topic should be broached; instead, encouragers indicate to the client that the clinician is intensely interested in what the client has to say and that the clinician would like to receive more information about the current topic. The power of these simple interventions must not be underestimated. Encouragers are a potent technique to keep the client on a topic and to suggest the importance of its in-depth exploration. Encouragers must be used wisely. Used incorrectly, they may inadvertently serve to reinforce verbalizations that are off the point, rambling, or otherwise irrelevant or nontherapeutic. Thus, clinicians need to learn to use encouragers in a discriminating fashion, applying them when truly interested in additional information about a topic of relevance, and suppressing them when they want to encourage clients to switch topics.

Encouragers, once learned, can become somewhat habitual and reflexive. Using an encourager in a nonthinking, reflexive manner can get in the way when a client is talking about a topic that is less than relevant to the issues at hand. During those times encouragers need to be suppressed to communicate to the client that it is important to move on.

There are four primary categories of encouragers. First, there are nonverbal signs that encourage a client to keep talking. Such nonverbal signs consist of leaning forward, nodding one's head, or raising an eyebrow. Second, simple repetition of a word or phrase the client utters often communicates to the client to keep talking. Third, semiverbal encouragers, which are often combined with nonverbal encouragers, consist of expressions such as "uh-huh," "oh," "aha," and so forth. Fourth, a simple phrase that requests more information is also considered an encourager. Examples of such expressions are "And then . . . ?," "Like what?," or "Tell me more."

Sample Transcripts for Encouragers

Illustration One

CLIENT: I really have a hard time with this relationship. It seems to be overwhelming at times, because I need some freedom that my friend just does not want to grant me. I'm not sure what I would like to do but I know I need to change something.

CLINICIAN: Change something? (*repetition encourager*)

CLIENT: Yes, I have had a sense of wanting to make a change in my life. Maybe it's not even just the relationship. Maybe I'm ready for a major move in my life in general. But I am not really clear about that. . . .

CLINICIAN: Tell me more. (*phrase encourager*)

CLIENT: I guess I feel stagnant and really don't know where to turn with these feelings. Sometimes it's very depressing and it feels as though I have nobody to talk to.

CLINICIAN: (*leans forward*) uh-huh . . . (*semiverbal encourager*)

CLIENT: Yes, I have felt like that at many points in my life; like I have nowhere to turn. I guess I have trouble making decisions about changes in my life. That is true for my relationships and for any other events that are going on.

CLINICIAN: (*nodding*) (*nonverbal encourager*)

CLIENT: There have been so many times in my life that I felt stuck, or stagnant. Somehow I always made it through, though, in the end. I guess what I have to do is just figure out how I did it before.

CLINICIAN: (*now moving beyond encouragers*) So you believe this is not just about your relationships then?

Illustration Two

CLIENT: Sometimes I think that I am going crazy. It's like this thing comes over me—a black cloud or something. And then I'm not myself anymore. . . .

CLINICIAN: Not yourself anymore? (*repetition encourager*)

CLIENT: Yeah. I get so mad I could jump out of my skin, like I want to scream and rant and rave. . . .

CLINICIAN: (*leans forward, nodding her head*) (*nonverbal encourager*)

CLIENT: Well, you know, just jump up and down, throw something and just plain throw a tantrum like a little kid. I used to do that, you know, when I was little. My parents still talk about it—I was a little monster. . . .

CLINICIAN: Really . . . ? (*phrase encourager*)

CLIENT: Yeah, I'd hit my little brother, I'd throw myself on the ground in the grocery store—just would embarrass my poor parents to death. It really seems unreal, doesn't it?

CLINICIAN: Hmm, unreal? (*semiverbal with repetition encourager*)

Skill Development Recommendations

Recommendation 6-1   *Start paying attention to how you encourage people to speak in day-to-day interactions with friends and family members. Once you have a clear idea of how much you are currently in the habit of using encouragers, make it a point to begin to use at least one of each type of encourager in each conversation you have from now on. How does this practice appear to affect your interactions?*

CLIENT: Yeah—like another me takes over.

CLINICIAN: (*moving beyond encouragers now*) Help me understand that "another you"?

These brief client-clinician interactions demonstrate how the use of encouragers can facilitate the exploration of a topic in some depth. Simply through the use of nonverbal signs and the repetition of a few simple phrases, the counselor was able to move the clients to an important conclusion about the topic at hand or to continued disclosure. The use of encouragers in this way is positive, as it allows the client to supply all the content of the conversation. The clinician did not interject any interpretations or suggest any direction in which the client should head. Instead, the counselor was merely curious to find out more about the issue the client was discussing, giving each client the leeway to take the topic to wherever it needed to go from the client's perspective. The choice of encouragers allowed the clients to move through the topic area in a way that was most meaningful to them.

RESTATEMENTS AND PARAPHRASES

Restatements and paraphrases are very similar to each other in structure and purpose. Both are repetitions of content expressed by the client. They are set apart from reflections by the feature of merely feeding back to the client the clinician's perception of content or topic area the client expressed. Reflections, on the other hand, not only repeat content but also attempt to crystallize and feed back underlying affect or hidden meaning the mental-health-care provider derived from the client's communication. Restatements and paraphrases share at least three primary purposes. First, they convey tracking and focusing, along with a sense of hearing what the client is talking about. Second, they serve as a means to double-check or clarify for the therapist that she or he is truly understanding the content and is forming the correct understanding or perception of the client's attempted communication. Third, they can be used for one reason or another to highlight something the client has said. They may highlight an aspect of a client's communication to express its importance, point out its confusing nature, make it more concise, or clarify or crystallize it. Notably, neither restatements nor paraphrases are used to attempt to feed back to the client a client's understanding of underlying affect or possible hidden meanings.

In using restatements and paraphrases, a selective process takes place in that the clinician decides which idea or content to hone in on for repetition. These choices must be made wisely and are best decided upon with the following goals in mind:

- Does the clinician wish to clarify an important point?
- Does the clinician want to reinforce something that was said?
- Does the clinician want to distill out a theme or pattern?
- Does the clinician want to double-check an understanding of an issue?
- Does the clinician want to highlight something of special importance?
- Does the clinician mean to explore any one point in particular in more detail?

Sometimes the choice about what to restate or paraphrase is also made with the opposite goal in mind. Namely, at times a counselor may emphasize one aspect of the communication to help the client shift gears or refocus attention. In other words, the clinician may choose one point over another to extinguish or discourage a certain topic so as not to allow the client to bring in too many things at once or to avoid an important therapeutic issue. Thus used, restatements and paraphrases become powerful tools in steering a conversation. Restatements are also useful if a client's thoughts are racing and the clinician wants to make an intervention that will help the client slow or calm down a bit.

Since the structure of restatements and paraphrases is very similar, they may at times be difficult to differentiate from one another. Both are succinct repetitions of something the client has said. Restatements are similar to encouragers and differ from them primarily in the length of the verbalization expressed by the clinician (being somewhat longer and more thorough than an encourager). Restatements capture the essence of one simple item talked about by the client. Restatements are formulated using the client's words. That is, the client's language is used to feed back the one important content issue derived by the clinician from the client's communication. This feedback is phrased not in the therapist's language, but merely repeats the idea in the client's words. Restatements are sometimes referred to as "parroting." This label serves to point to the potential danger that lurks in the overuse or simplistic use of restatements. The fact that restatements use the client's language may mislead the less-savvy counselor into thinking that exact repetition of a client statement is in order. Such exact repetition can be a hindrance to rapport as the client may feel mocked. It is for that reason that paraphrases are generally preferable to restatements.

Often restatements begin with an innocuous introductory stem such as "What you're saying is . . . " or "What you are telling me is . . . ," followed by the repetition of the most important point gleaned by the counselor. However, restatements can also be phrased with no stem at all, simply feeding back the main point, such as "You're having second thoughts about getting married." A brief restatement can be virtually indistinguishable from a simple phrase encourager. For example, rather than the repetition of the full sentence just demonstrated, the clinician may have chosen to use a simple phrase encourager such as "Second thoughts?" The choice of using a full sentence (a restatement) versus a phrase (an encourager) has more to do with the proximity in time of the repeated phrase or statement to the original verbalization of the client. If the client just finished saying the phrase or statement the clinician wants to highlight through repetition, a simple phrase will usually be indicated. If the phrase or statement was not the last one uttered by the client, that is, if the counselor wants to return to something the client said a little while back, a restatement generally will work better.

The structure of a paraphrase is similar to that of a restatement. A paraphrase contains a clarifier that expresses to the client that the clinician is expressing what she or he thinks was said by the client. This clarifier can take the form of an introductory stem or a closing stem. An introductory stem that expresses that the clinician's perception of what has been said is being reflected back may be as follows:

- "What I'm hearing is . . ."
- "It sounds to me as though . . ."
- "What I hear you saying is . . ."
- "What rang a bell for me . . ."
- "As I see it . . ."
- "My view of this is . . ."
- "The picture I'm getting from what you are saying is . . ."
- "My sense is . . ."
- "I felt . . ."
- "I sense you tried to . . ."

Review of these introductory stems shows that they give the counselor an opportunity to match the client's verbal style by using sensory words that match the client's primary choice of sensory modality. The clinician may choose words in the stem such as "see" or "view" for a client who processes visually, "hear" or "sound" for a client who processes auditorily, or "feel" or "sense" for a client who processes kinesthetically. This choice of words helps the clients perceive that their language has been received and restated by the clinician. A counselor may also choose to use a closing stem instead of an introductory one. Closing stems follow the paraphrasing of the main idea and may be as follows:

- "Am I hearing that correctly?"
- "Does that sound right?"
- "Am I getting the right picture?"
- "Am I seeing things the way you do?"
- "Is that close?"
- "Does that capture it?"
- ". . . ?" (*questioning pause*)

In a paraphrase, the clinician tries to communicate the content that was provided by the client, again focusing on one primary idea, but using the counselor's own language. In other words, in choosing a paraphrase rather than a restatement, the mental-health-care provider runs less of a risk of being perceived as parroting or mocking the client because the client's words are not merely restated. Because of this different word choice, however, it is important to add to the paraphrase the introductory or closing stem that clarifies that the clinician is feeding back information as seen from her or his perspective. This is the primary differentiating factor between a restatement and a paraphrase. A restatement merely repeats what the client has said for clarification purposes. The paraphrase moves one step beyond that by challenging the client to hear and understand the clinician's language. The paraphrase, by virtue of being stated in the counselor's language, is more prone to reflect the counselor's bias in understanding an idea expressed by the client. In that sense, a paraphrase can be viewed as an intermediate step between a restatement and a reflection. The choice of a paraphrase versus a restatement is based on at least two decisions. First, as a general rule paraphrases are preferred because they do not run the risk of mocking the client. Second, paraphrases tend to be preferable if the mental-health-care provider wants to communicate very clearly that the nuance of what the client attempted to communicate was captured. In other words, the clinician has a way of stating the important thought in a manner that enhances, clarifies, highlights, or crystallizes the client's expression. The client feels more deeply understood and heard than with a mere restatement. There are times, however, when the clinician wants to do just the opposite. That is, sometimes a counselor wants to use a client's words to make sure the client hears what they just expressed and how they expressed it. This choice of restatement often represents a challenge to the client and tends to be used later in treatment, after firm rapport has been established. Illustration Three below presents such a purposeful restatement, whereas Illustrations One and Two demonstrate the difference between a restatement and a paraphrase.

Sample Transcripts for Restatements and Paraphrases

Illustration One

CLIENT: What happened then was even more embarrassing. I turned away and she started to scream at the top of her lungs in the middle of the street! Can you believe it?! She just stood there with everybody around and cussed at me. How could I have ever loved someone like that who has no social skills? Am I really that dependent that I would just go out with anyone who says, "Hey, you're cute?" I am really shaken up by this. . . . What does it all mean and what do I do now?

Restatement Response Option

CLINICIAN: You really wonder about being dependent. . . .

CLIENT: Yes! What's wrong with me? This is obviously not the first time I have picked a woman like that. Remember, I told you about. . . .

Paraphrase Response Option

CLINICIAN: What it sounds like to me is that you are really wondering about being emotionally needy right now. (*rephrasing "dependent" into "emotionally needy"*)

CLIENT: Yes, I guess that's it. I feel like I need someone around all the time. I get so lonely when I'm alone that I'd rather be with anyone than no one.

Illustration Two

CLIENT: I am not sure where to start this week. So much has happened that my head is spinning. I can't tell you how much I've been looking forward to this session—I really need it today! But now that I'm here I don't even know where to start. . . .

Restatement Response Option

CLINICIAN: So much happened that it's hard to start today!

CLIENT: Yeah—confusing, isn't it. Oh well, I guess I'll start by telling you about . . .

Paraphrase Response Option

CLINICIAN: You're on overload and that makes it hard to sort out what is the most important thing to deal with first. Is that it? (*rephrasing "head is spinning" into "being on overload" and "what to start with" into "the most important thing to deal with"*)

CLIENT: That's it exactly. I'm on overload! Just too much for one human being to deal with all at once . . .

These examples serve to clarify the minor differences between restatements and paraphrases. Clearly, a paraphrase adds something unique by the clinician. Paraphrases represent more of a belief or leap of faith that the counselor has a clearer way of phrasing what the client is really trying to say. Often, when successful, and as demonstrated in the above examples, a paraphrase will elicit a relieved response from the client. The person feels heard more deeply when the clinician is able to rephrase things just so. However, either response from the clinician helps the client move along and get focused.

Illustration Three

CLIENT: My mother always said that if I don't have anything nice to say I should just keep my mouth shut. But in a strange way that made me wanna do just the opposite. So I find myself saying things a lot that I later regret. Like yesterday, I was mad at Jackie and I told him if you don't like my rules, just move out! And you know what? He did. I can't believe it. He's fifteen and he packed up and moved.

CLINICIAN: Moved where?

CLIENT: To my mother's, of all places!! She thinks I'm a lousy parent so when Jackie called her she told him he could live with her because she knows I'm a loser!

CLINICIAN: She said you're a loser?

CLIENT: Well, no—I'm saying she took him in because I'm a loser. . . .

CLINICIAN: You're a loser. . . . (*purposeful restatement*)

CLIENT: Yes, I am. I've shown that once again, don't you think?

CLINICIAN: *You have once again shown that you are a loser.* . . . (purposeful restatement)

CLIENT: (*wavering*) Well . . . I think I have . . .

CLINICIAN: Listen to yourself—I've shown once again that I am a loser!

CLIENT: When you put it that way, it does sound a little harsh. (*The clinician did not put it that way, the client did; however, this is no time to argue.*)

CLINICIAN: Go with that. (*phrase encourager*)

CLIENT: Well, I did what I had to—I am at the end of my rope with Jackie. After he got caught breaking and entering last month, I've been trying to be a little stricter. It's just so hard, with Mother undermining me like she does.

CLINICIAN: Like she does now?

CLIENT: Yes! . . . (*Session goes on from here.*)

Here a purposeful restatement was chosen to demonstrate to the client how she uses words in a self-defeating manner. This type of restatement clearly has a therapeutic purpose and goes beyond the usual purposes of restatements. It does not just seek to keep communication or disclosure going; it steers the client toward insight. This type of work will generally occur later in treatment after sufficient rapport has been established, but occasionally may be used even early on if the clinician feels the client is able to tolerate this type of intervention. As an aside, this example also demonstrates the targeted use of clarifying questions, a matter that was discussed in detail in the previous chapter.

Finally, it should be noted that oftentimes, clinicians with experience will actually mix restatements and paraphrases in their work with clients. It is a

Skill Development Recommendations

Recommendation 6-2   *Start paying attention to how you respond to people in day-to-day interactions with friends and family members. Once you have a clear idea of how much you are currently in the habit of using restatements or paraphrases, make it a point to begin to use at least one of each in each conversation you have from now on. How does this practice appear to affect your interactions?*

Recommendation 6-3   *For each client statement that follows, write out a restatement and a paraphrase:*

- *I have been incredibly distracted by everything that's going on. It's very confusing to try to figure out what to deal with first.*
- *I don't think I can keep going like this. If something doesn't change in this relationship I'm going to have to get out just to save my son and myself. We can't take this anymore. . . . (weeps)*
- *I am really fed up with you. You are a quack, you know! Did you buy your degree or something?*
- *I don't think I've ever been more scared! It was one of those situations that you have nightmares about and you wake up and think "Oh my God, I'm so glad this wasn't real." And now here it is . . . It's terrifying. . . .*
- *I am lonely . . . all alone in the world. First my husband dies and now my daughter. Mothers are not supposed to survive their children. What am I going to do? It's too much. . . .*
- *I feel like giving up. No one would notice anyway. . . . No one would care. . . . I have nothing, I am nothing. . . .*
- *I am not only happy, I am ecstatic. I have never felt better. That promotion came just at the right time!*

---

good idea for the novice, however, to practice the pure forms first for a while to get a good sense for each form of verbalization. The Skill Development Recommendations above will help with this task.

REFLECTIONS

Reflections are a way in which the clinician can repeat back to clients what was said, while bringing out a metacommunication that was perceived in the communication. Reflections move beyond restatements and paraphrases in that they do not just restate content, either in the client's or the clinician's words, but add an underlying message or feeling that was detected by the counselor even though the client may not have said it directly. For a reflection to be possible, the mental-health-care provider has to listen for such subtle communications, using all the important listening skills outlined previously. Attending to nonverbals is particularly helpful in this regard.

Reflections encourage broader self-exploration by the client and tend to induce a more intense experience, often by connecting verbal and nonverbal communication. They emphasize a focus on affect and help clarify hidden messages that are either consciously known or unknown to the client. The purposes of reflections thus can be summarized as follows:

- help the client feel understood on a deeper level
- deepen the relationship between client and clinician
- encourage freer expression of feelings
- begin to assist the client in managing affect
- make covert context or meaning overt
- uncover hidden messages

To structure a successful reflection, the clinician must first listen attentively and deeply for the hidden affect and/or message the client is conveying. To listen for affect the clinician attends to feeling words, looks at nonverbal expressions of the client, and pays attention to the many emotional subtones during the client's conversation. To find the hidden messages of the client, the clinician must learn to read between the lines. This can often be accomplished in ways similar to listening for affects in that the counselor carefully attends to nonverbals and similarly indirect expressions while the client speaks. Finding affects and hidden messages may sound like an overwhelming task to the beginning counselor; however, it is actually quite an easy feat once a client is well known to the clinician. All clients have ways of expressing the unsayable that become well recognized by the counselor once the client has been seen for awhile. It is not helpful to be so uptight about learning the hidden message that the clinician becomes preoccupied; instead, it is best to just use all the careful attention and listening skills available and then to trust intuition. Clients will not be hurt by the occasional reflection that is off target. Reflections will also be used to express empathy for the client. Thus, the chapter on empathy will help novice clinicians further deepen their reflection skills.

Once the clinician has gleaned an important affect or hidden message, attention needs to be given to how to phrase the reflective statement. First, as for paraphrases, it helps to open or close the reflection with a stem that reflects that the clinician is expressing an impression. The same introductory or closing stems used for paraphrases can be used for that purpose. A questioning pause at the end of a statement may be an appropriate closing stem as well, since it signals to the client some openness on the clinician's part to be corrected if the message was off target. Cautiousness in how the clinician speaks can take the place of a closing or opening stem. How the reflection is delivered can convey the same message as the verbal opening or closing stem. A cautious, caring voice can reflect the same concern and openness to being corrected as a verbal expression of the same through the stem.

Second, the clinician summarizes the affect or hidden message that needs to be fed back to the client. This reflection needs to be succinct, clear, meaningful, and accurate. It is also important to match the affect words chosen in the summary to the actual affective state of the client. In other words, it is not enough to identify the correct affect, but it is best to also evaluate and correctly reflect its intensity. For example, if a client expresses anxiety, the clinician can speak of "unease," "trepidation," "fear," or "panic" (or many others), depending on the level of anxiety expressed. Using the word "panic" when the client is evidencing mild anxiety would be a mismatch; the right affect is identified but at the wrong intensity. Similarly, speaking of "despair" when the client feels discouraged is in the right ballpark, but again at the wrong intensity. The chapter on affective processing will give further guidance about matching affect intensity.

Third, a good reflection adds a context for the affect or hidden message that is reflected back. This context may be as simple as identifying when the affect is occurring (for example, right now, in a certain situation) or what suggested the hidden message to the clinician. Examples of context statements can be as simple as "You were angry *when he did that*" or "You seem angry *right now*, just talking about this"; or the context can be a bit more complex, as in "It sounds to me as though you are getting quite worried *about this impending marriage* [note the complexity of context implied here] and that you are kind of surprised by your own misgivings *right now*." To summarize, a reflection is structured around a stem (introductory or closing), an affect or hidden message, and a context for the affect or message. Despite the fact that these three components are covered, the reflective statement needs to stay as succinct and clear as possible. It can use a combination of the client's words and the clinician's own language, combining elements of restatements and paraphrases.

Sample Transcripts of Reflections

Illustration One

> CLIENT: Every evening we go through the same ritual. I ask her to go to bed; she starts to cry. I am at the end of my rope with that child. She is eight years old and has no respect for my authority. My other kids aren't like that . . . and she's the oldest; oh my goodness, I can't even think of it. . . .
>
> CLINICIAN: I think what I'm hearing are really two worries. Number one, you are overwhelmed with the struggle every night (*reflection of af-*

fect). Number two, you are afraid that Jeannie's behavior may rub off on the little ones. . . . (*reflection of affect and hidden message*)

CLIENT: Yes. They look up to her so much—and they are like her in a lot of ways. Right now they still listen to me but what if I lose control over them too?! What am I supposed to do? I am all alone in this bloody town; first my husband drags me here and then he just gets up and leaves (*getting agitated*); I just don't know what to do. . . . (*starts to sob*)

CLINICIAN: It's just all too much right now—with so many overwhelming feelings and problems you feel paralyzed and powerless. (*reflection of affect*)

CLIENT: (*quietly sobbing*) Yes, and no one there to lean on. . . .

CLINICIAN: (*soft voice*) You feel so alone. . . . (*reflection of affect*)

Illustration Two

CLIENT: (to the clinician) I have had it with you. You just ask and ask and ask and you never give me any answers. I came here because I wanted someone to help me; all you do is bother me with stupid questions! What is your problem?!

CLINICIAN: You are not getting what you hoped for . . . ? (*paraphrase bordering on reflection*)

CLIENT: Hell NO. That's the first smart thing I've heard from you!

CLINICIAN: You sound very frustrated with me. (*reflection of affect; note the nondefensiveness of the clinician*)

CLIENT: Duh! I came here because of my wife and now here you are acting just like her! I guess it's just women. You're all the same—and you make no sense to a normal guy like me.

CLINICIAN: So women are a puzzle to you, is that right? (*reflection of underlying message*)

CLIENT: Oh my—YES. I have no clue how you people think. You are just wired in a whole different way. I think someone left the logic out of you—or maybe women are just there to annoy men; maybe that's it. (*pleased with himself now*) Women are the root of men's problems but then WE get the blame!

CLINICIAN: What I think I'm hearing is that you feel you do what you can, but in the end you get the blame for the trouble between you and your wife? (*reflection of underlying affect*)

CLIENT: Yup! She ends up being the one who cries and then I feel like shit! And then I just run out—I just have to get away from her then.

CLINICIAN: It's like you feel bad for her and then all you know to do is to get out of there. . . . (*reflection of underlying message*)

CLIENT: Yeah—I mean, I'm no monster. I hate it when she cries. And then I wonder what did I do?

Skill Development Recommendations

Recommendation 6-4   *Start paying attention to whether you reflect what people say in day-to-day interactions with friends and family members. Once you have a clear idea of how much you are currently in the habit of using reflections, make it a point to begin to use at least one in each conversation you have from now on. How does this practice appear to affect your interactions?*

CLINICIAN: (*cautiously*) Almost sounds like some guilt . . . (*reflection of affect*)

CLIENT: (*quietly now*) I suppose so. Can you help. . . .

These examples show that simple reflections of affect and recognition of underlying meaning or messages are powerful ways to help clients feel heard, understood, and cared for. In each of these examples the simple act of reflecting led the client to a deeper level of self-understanding and disclosure, moving the counseling in powerful new or more meaningful directions. Reflections move the client away from the surface of issues right into the heart of their experience. Such reflections take skill, good timing, and expressed caring. The tone of voice with which they are delivered can make a big difference in whether the client feels heard, understood, and cared for—or criticized and challenged.

INTERFACING RESPONSE TYPES

The fact that the structure of restatements, paraphrases, and reflections is so similar correctly suggests that these three types of responses to clients are closely related. In fact, it is not too unlikely that some statements counselors make cannot be cleanly classified as one or the other. This is no problem. The main issue for clinicians is to learn all three of these types of responses and then to begin to use them freely and interchangeably. There are some occasions when one type of response may be superior to another. The most important issues are to help clients feel heard and understood, to engage the client in further self-exploration and disclosure, and to let the client know that the clinician is listening attentively, clearly, and in an unbiased way.

A few general guidelines about when to use restatements versus paraphrases versus reflections follow. If clinicians feel comfortable adding an affect or identifying a deeper meaning, a reflection may be used. If the clinician is uncertain where the client is going with a conversation, a restatement or paraphrase may be easiest as the counselor may not yet be clear about the underlying feelings. If a restatement feels too much like mocking or parroting to the client, a paraphrase is the better choice. In fact, as a general rule of thumb, paraphrases, when possible, are preferable to restatements, except in a few very specific situations. Reflections tend to deepen the therapeutic relationship and as such are the most desirable of the three types of responses. It is important to note that encouragers can be used throughout as well, as they can be easily integrated with any use of restatement, paraphrase, or reflection. Whenever the sole purpose of the clinician is to encourage the client to continue talking, disclosing, and exploring, a simple encourager will best serve the purpose. Supplemented with the other response types, such interactions can be profoundly useful and therapeutic.

Guidelines for When Best to Use Which Response Type

- it is best to use a *restatement* over a paraphrase or reflection
  - when it is important to emphasize the specific wording a client chose
  - when it is therapeutic to slow a client down who is talking (too) fast or whose thoughts are racing
- it is best to use a *paraphrase* over a restatement
  - to feed back a simple content when no need exists to highlight specific client word choices
  - when the client is sensitive to being mocked or parroted
  - when the clinician wants to use a particular word instead of the word the client chose
  - when the clinician believes it is an opportune time to begin to reframe a content for the client
- it is best to use a *paraphrase* over a reflection
  - if addressing affect would be premature (for example, because insufficient rapport exists, because the clinician is not yet entirely certain about the specificity or intensity of the affect, or because the client cannot yet handle having the affect made overt)
  - if revealing a hidden message would be premature (for example, because the client is still utterly unaware of it, or because the client cannot yet handle that level of intensity in the session)
  - if revealing the hidden message would be inappropriate (for example, because the client is using the hidden meaning as a means of manipulating the clinician)
  - when content is of greater importance than affect (for example, the content is yet insufficient or unclear, or the content is contradictory)

- when affect tends to be overused by the client (for example, a client who has strong histrionic tendencies and overemphasizes affect in day-to-day life)
- it is best to use a *reflection* over a paraphrase or a restatement
  - any time the clinician has enough information about and rapport with the client to use the reflection accurately and in a therapeutic manner
- it is helpful to use *encouragers*
  - any time the clinician merely wants to keep the client talking, disclosing, or self-exploring
  - interspersed along with all other response types

Sample Transcripts for Interfacing All Response Types

Illustration One

CLIENT: I have been thinking about my work situation a lot since we met last week. I still don't get what's going on. I have really tried my best to please Jennifer but it seems that no matter what I do or say, she gets angry or snaps at me. It's very scary sometimes! Really makes me evaluate everything I want to do before I do it and sometimes I don't say what I want to say because I just know there will be trouble. . . .

CLINICIAN: Sounds like in your confusion you end up walking on eggshells . . . (*paraphrase*)

CLIENT: Yes; every step I take I have to wonder about when she'll explode again. I really can't afford to get fired, you know. I have my family to support since my husband is not due to graduate for another year and a half. . . .

CLINICIAN: So, it's more than just being worried about Jennifer blowing up at you; it's really about being scared of losing your job and leaving your family hanging! (*reflection of affect and paraphrase of content*)

CLIENT: Yes, I guess that's really it. I have worked there for ten years and never had problems with a boss before. She got promoted only four months ago and suddenly I'm in a panic. . . .

CLINICIAN: In a panic? (*simple encourager*)

CLIENT: Yes! I'm in a panic. I didn't realize 'til you said it—but that's really what it is. It's beyond worry. It's not just a job that's on the line; it's my kids, my husband, everything. . . . (*looking terrified now*)

CLINICIAN: Sounds like the problem has taken on a whole new dimension for you?! (*reflection of underlying message*)

CLIENT: Yes. (*beginning to cry now*) I have to be the responsible one in the family right now. I always criticized Greg for not getting along with his boss, always told him he should just shut up and do as he was told. I had no idea . . .

CLINICIAN: It really feels to me that you're not just struggling with your own work situation, but also with some guilt maybe over not having understood Greg better when he was going through something similar? (*bold reflection of affect and hidden message*)

CLIENT: Yes . . . (*sobbing now*)

Illustration Two

CLIENT: I really like the fact that she does not want children. There are very few women that agree with me on that point and so I'm thinking that I need to make sure that this relationship will work out.

CLINICIAN: It's rare for you to meet women that agree with you there . . . (*restatement*)

CLIENT: Yes; in fact several relationships have fallen apart because of that. I am not willing to give on that particular issue. I do not want to have children. The world is not a good place for them and it is overpopulated as it is.

CLINICIAN: Sounds as though you feel unbending about this issue. (*paraphrase*)

CLIENT: You bet.

CLINICIAN: You have let relationships go because of it. (*finally catching on to the most important message and using a restatement to communicate that*)

CLIENT: Yes. Women don't like it, so now that I found one who feels the same way I think, I need to hang on to her.

CLINICIAN: You want to hang on to her but you don't sound very excited about this. (*reflection of underlying affect [or rather lack of affect]*)

CLIENT: Well, I think it's enough to agree on things. I don't have to be excited. . . .

CLINICIAN: You don't have to be excited? (*repetition encourager*)

CLIENT: No. Excitement in relationships is overrated, in my opinion. The main thing is that you agree on basic values. Romance fizzles anyway. . . .

CLINICIAN: Romance fizzles? (*repetition encourager*)

CLIENT: Oh yes. It's just in the movies that people have passion and excitement forever and ever.

CLINICIAN: Am I hearing that in your experience passion and romance don't last? (*reflection of underlying message*)

CLIENT: Yes.

CLINICIAN: Tell me more. (*phrase encourager*)

CLIENT: Well, I guess I have never had a relationship like the ones in movies—You know, where couples swoon over one another or can't wait to grab each other. My relationships tend to be about talking about current events, news, maybe the stock market; they don't really involve much touchy-feely stuff.

CLINICIAN: You don't swoon or touch much . . . (*restatement*)

CLIENT: I've never swooned! And I only touch when I have to. . . .

CLINICIAN: When you have to? (*repetition encourager*)

CLIENT: Yeah—you know, during sex.

CLINICIAN: So touch happens only during sex . . . (*restatement*)

CLIENT: Yes, basically.

CLINICIAN: Tell me more about that. (*phrase encourager*)

CLIENT: Well—I don't know what more you want here. Like, I don't like to hold hands or kiss in public. I don't rub her shoulders or play with her hair. Does anyone do that in real life?

CLINICIAN: (*shrugs shoulders, maintains questioning eye contact*) (*nonverbal encourager*)

CLIENT: Yeah, I guess you're right—I guess they do. I've seen people do it. It always seems so fake though. . . .

CLINICIAN: Fake? (*repetition encourager*)

CLIENT: Oh, you know . . . like they do it because they've seen it done in the movies, not because they really want to or like it . . .

CLINICIAN: You don't like to be touched that way. . . . (*mix of restatement and reflection*)

CLIENT: No—never liked it much. Much to my mother's chagrin. She was a touchy-feely type. Always wanted hugs and kisses and pats on the back and on and on—I hated it.

CLINICIAN: Even when you were a child you didn't like touch very much . . . ? (*paraphrase bordering on reflection of underlying message*)

CLIENT: Right. Maybe it's because she was doing too much of it. . . .

CLINICIAN: She? (*repetition encourager to clarify*)

CLIENT: My mother . . .

CLINICIAN: Tell me how she may have touched too much (*mixture of phrase encourager and restatement*)

CLIENT: Well, I remember when I was really little, she would give me baths a lot, and she took a lot of time with them, just rubbing and doing . . . I just remember feeling strange and wanting to get out of there. But she was so insistent. When I got older she couldn't hold me in there anymore, so then she tried to get her groping in in other ways. . . .

CLINICIAN: Sounds like the kind of touch she used bathing you definitely did not feel right to you? (*reflection of affect*)

CLIENT: No . . . (*embarrassed now; looking away*) I've never told anyone this, but sometimes when she washed my penis, over and over again, I would get erections. I guess I didn't really understand what was happening back then—I just remember feeling strange. . . .

CLINICIAN: (*soft, caring voice*) You say that back then you didn't really understand what was happening. . . . (*restatement*) (*voice softer yet*) Do you understand now?

CLIENT: (*quietly and tentatively, but with eye contact again*) I guess so. . . .

CLINICIAN: (*gently and with caring*) Tell me . . . (*phrase encourager*)

CLIENT: Was it sexual . . . (*looks away again; suddenly overcome with emotion*)

CLINICIAN: (*very quietly and gently*) . . . abuse? (*finishing his thought for him; a nontraditionally phrased reflection of underlying message*)

CLIENT: (*looking up; nodding gently, starting to cry*) (*Session goes on from there.*)

These transcripts show how powerfully encouragers, restatements, paraphrases, and reflections can be combined to help move a client along in counseling. No interpretations were made at all with either client. The clinicians did not draw on much material from prior sessions to understand and respond to their clients, but merely focused on really listening to verbals and nonverbals to glean their clients' state of emotion and underlying context. Then that understanding was simply restated, paraphrased, or reflected back to the clients. The combination of feeling thoroughly understood and feeling supported by preestablished rapport helped the clients open up to a new dimension of experience and understanding of their current situations. The second illustration also serves to show how much more difficult a client can be if she or he does not have a reflective or affective style. Reflections work best with clients who can deal with feelings or at least know how to express emotions. Clients who are cognitive in their style will require more work in terms of getting them to a point where they feel affectively connected to and supported by the clinician. Often more encouragers, restatements, paraphrases, and reflections of underlying messages are needed with such clients before reflections of affect are truly accepted and heard.

Given that the response strategies of encouragers, restatements, paraphrases, and reflections are so commonly used together, it may be helpful to compare and contrast them briefly with regard to their basic purposes, guidelines for use, and general structure. This comparison is provided in very simple form in Table 6-1.

SUMMARIZATION

Summarization is a unique way of combining any or all of the techniques covered so far in this chapter. It is used whenever the clinician wants to feed back more than one idea, content, affect, or hidden message at a time. A summarization can consist of a combination of restatements, paraphrases, and reflections and is less succinct than any one of these strategies alone. Often summarization is used at the end of a session to bring closure to what has been worked on. Occasionally, summarization is used when a client has brought up numerous

TABLE
6-1   **COMPARISON OF THE PRIMARY RESPONSE TYPES**

Response Type	Purpose of Use	Guidelines for Use	Structure
Encouraging statement	• To elicit more content • To encourage further disclosure • To express interest in hearing more	• Few restrictions on when to use	• Nonverbals to express interest or • Repetition of a word or • Semi-verbals or • Repetition of a simple phrase
Restatement	• To restate content • To facilitate disclosure and communication • To demonstrate listening	• When emphasizing a client's word choice • When trying to slow a client down	• Optional introductory stem and • Restatement in client's words
Paraphrase	• To paraphrase content • To facilitate disclosure and communication • To demonstrate understanding	• Can be used freely • Not used if a reflection serves better	• Introductory or closing stem and • Restatement in clinician's words
Reflection	• To demonstrate deep listening • To feed back overt or covert affect • To feed back underlying messages • To deepen rapport and expressed caring	• Response of choice when trying to feed back understanding • Not to be used with insufficient rapport • Not to be used prematurely • Not to be used with insufficient information	• Optional introductory or closing stem and • Expression of underlying affect or hidden meaning or • Expression of affect intensity and • Inclusion of a context

issues all at once at a quick rate, and the clinician wants to make sure that all the important content areas and affects were heard and are fed back to the client. Because of the greater length and complexity of summarization, this response strategy is used with much less frequency than the other response types covered in this chapter.

The structure of summarization varies widely depending on what response types the clinician chooses to combine. Most generally, summarizations will begin with some type of introductory stem or close with a closing stem, much in the same form as discussed above. Then restatements follow for aspects that meet the criteria or guidelines for restatements, paraphrases for feeding back of content that meets the guidelines for paraphrases, and reflections as appropriate given the level of information and rapport. In other words, the summarization follows all the guidelines about restatements, paraphrases, and reflections outlined above and summarized in Table 6-1. It is best to keep even this lengthier statement as succinct and clear as possible. A summarization is not to be mistaken as an opportunity for a speech or monologue. Sometimes, it is a good strategy to break summarizations into component parts, using closing stems between components to give the client a chance to give feedback and input. Such summarizations become an almost collaborative effort between counselor and client while closing a topic, rehashing several content areas, or closing a session. Summarization is perhaps best explained via illustration.

Sample Transcripts of Summarization

Illustration One (End-of-Session Summarization)

CLINICIAN: Well, it is almost time for us to quit. We covered a lot of ground today, and I think I'd like to recap some of the more important points before we leave. I think maybe one important issue was that you are still struggling with how to best deal with your work situation, but you are getting closer to some idea of what to do. Does that capture it? (*reflection of affect and message*)

CLIENT: Yeah, I think I am getting clearer. Maybe next week we can wrap that up. (*smiles*)

CLINICIAN: Sounds great. (*smiling as well*) Then we may want to move on to dealing with your relationship with Jesse because it felt to me today that you had a lot of feelings about that and we only just scratched the surface there . . . right? (*reflection of affect and underlying message*)

CLIENT: Yeah—I don't much like the idea, but you are right—There is a lot happening there, and I do need to look at why I get so angry at her when she does just the least bit to challenge me. . . .

CLINICIAN: And then the last thing that comes to my mind is the fact that we spent some time today looking at your relationships with your parents and your recognition that there are some things you learned from them that maybe aren't helping you in your life right now. We need to look at that some more, what do you think? (*paraphrase and reflection of affect and underlying message*)

CLIENT: Oh, I know we do. You know, I've been avoiding that but you're right. It felt good just doing what we did today. So I imagine it really would help to go back to that. . . . (*smiles*) Boy, I sure am glad we're done for today! (*smiles some more*)

CLINICIAN: I can understand that. Lots of good work! Alright then. I'll see you next week, same time, same place. (*smiles and gets up*) Take care. . . . (*opens door for client*)

CLIENT: Thanks! Bye, see ya. . . . (*walks out*)

Illustration Two (Summarization of Quick Multiple Client Disclosure)

CLIENT: I don't even know where to start. What a week! First, my car broke down—my fault, too. I changed the oil and somehow didn't get the filter back on right, and it leaked and then I blew up the engine. God, I'm an idiot. My wife has even told me before—just take the damn car to the shop—why are you wasting your time on it. And I was trying to save money! Well, so much for that! We're talking a thousand-dollar oil change now. I haven't even told her yet that the damn thing blew up. I can't stand the argument out of that one. Things aren't exactly great between us and this isn't gonna help. You know how she gripes about money all the time. Which, come to think of it, is why I wanted to do the oil change myself to begin with. I thought she'd be pleased. Oh man, there is just no pleasing her, though. I don't know why I keep trying. Maybe if I work some overtime this month I could get the repairs done without even telling her. What do you think? But then again you know how things are with construction in the winter. There may be no overtime to be had. Plus my boss isn't so pleased with me because I was late again three times this week. Like I said—the week from hell. Why was I late? Yeah, I can read your mind—well, I partied a little too hard with Joe. He got divorced last week. Did I tell you that already? They've been separated for a year or so and the paperwork finally got done, so he was in a good mood. He was buying so I went along. You know me—I'm always ready for a party. Met some nice gals, too . . . nicer than the wife. Maybe I shouldn't be telling you this. Man, I feel out of control. . . . And then . . . (*clinician interrupts; client is startled*)

CLINICIAN: (*decides to interrupt as client is becoming increasingly agitated*) Wow, it was a loaded week! (*paraphrase*) No wonder you feel out of control. (*restatement*) Let me see if I got everything. . . . Sounded like the first thing that happened was that you and Ally were fighting about money again and one thing you tried to do was save some money by working on your car yourself, right? (*paraphrase*)

CLIENT: Yeah—I guess that's how it all started. . . .

CLINICIAN: Then the car blew up because of a mistake you made changing the oil, and you're worried about telling Ally because the repairs will cost a lot . . . ? (*paraphrase*)

CLIENT: You got it!

CLINICIAN: Then you thought of a solution, thought about working extra hours to pay for repairs, but realized you haven't exactly pleased your boss recently, so the chances of getting any overtime this month are slim. . . . (*paraphrase and restatement*)

CLIENT: (*nodding*)

CLINICIAN: The reason your boss isn't favorably inclined is because you've been late for work because of partying a bit too freely, and this is also a problem with Ally because you are feeling attracted to other women, right? (*paraphrase bordering on reflection of affect and underlying message*)

CLIENT: Yup.

CLINICIAN: Sounds like it all starts and ends with Ally somehow. You are fighting about money and you are hiding news from her. In the meantime, you are also tempted by other relationships. (*reflection of affect and underlying message*) Does this seem like a good place to start? You know, by looking at what's happening with you and Ally?

CLIENT: Probably. You know, if she was just more reasonable about money the whole thing wouldn't have happened. . . .

CLINICIAN: The whole thing? (*repetition encourager*)

CLIENT: Yeah—you know. The car wouldn't have blown up, and I wouldn't have felt so mad at Ally when I was out partying that I kissed that woman. (*blushes, looks up startled*) Oops—I let that one slip. . . . (*embarrassed now*)

CLINICIAN: So things went a little farther than just meeting some other women? (*moving beyond summarization now*)

CLIENT: I guess soooo. . . .

CLINICIAN: Wanna tell me? (*phrase encourager*)

CLIENT: Well! Joe and I . . . (*Session goes on from there.*)

These summarizations show that the clinician draws on all the other response types in making a summary of either a session or a topic area. They also serve to show how the clinician works with the client by double-checking information and getting affirmation that the counselor is on the right track or that the client agrees with the clinician's understanding of the situation. In both cases, the summarization clarified for both client and clinician where they were or had been in the session. Both affects and contents were restated, paraphrased or reflected to make sure that client and clinician were on the same page. In both cases, summarization was a way to slow down, either to close a session or to organize thoughts sufficiently to know where to take the session. Summarization as a means of slowing down racing thoughts and pressured speech can be quite effective. Allowing clients to ramble with no clear goal or direction generally will only lead them to feel confused. In this case illustration, the client even indicated feeling out of control. Such a statement is an invitation for the clinician to intervene and help organize the flow of thoughts.

A FEW FINAL COMMENTS

This chapter outlined several important response types that clinicians have at their disposal, namely, encouragers, restatements, paraphrases, and summarization, to ensure that clients

- feel heard
- feel listened to

Skill Development Recommendations

Recommendation 6-5   *Practice the response styles presented in this chapter with a group of peers. It is best to work in a group of four, distributing and taking turns with the following roles: a mock client, a mock clinician, an observer of nonverbals, and an observer of verbals. The mock client will role-play a concern presented by a therapy client; the mock clinician will attempt to keep the client talking by using encouragers, restatements, paraphrases, and reflections. Keep the interaction going for about ten minutes. Then stop and give each other feedback about skills with regard to responding. The verbal observer will focus on that realm of interaction; the nonverbal-expression observer will give more detailed feedback about that aspect of the interaction. Discuss and observe how the appropriate use of these strategies facilitates disclosure. Keep feedback to each other constructive and positive at this time.*

- feel understood
- continue to talk freely
- continue to self-explore
- feel comfortable self-disclosing

These response styles are structured and applied in such a way that counselors communicate to their clients that they, as clinicians

- listen attentively
- listen without bias or judgment
- attend to and recognize nonverbal messages
- understand the essence of the client's statements
- understand the feeling tone of the client's communication
- are interested in hearing more
- care about the client
- want to keep the client safe

The most natural way to apply the various response types presented in this chapter is to mix and match them. It is rare that a clinician will rely on one form of encouraging communication or expression of understanding. Instead, clinicians with experience will not only use all of these response types in the course of a session but may also mix and match approaches within a single statement (as was demonstrated in some of the illustrations above). In fact, it is less important to differentiate clearly whether a statement by a counselor was an encourager versus a restatement, or a paraphrase versus a reflection than to have mastered the execution of all of these ways of feeding back understanding to the client. Often clinicians develop their own style of using these important feedback mechanisms, and each counselor's style may result in a unique way of mixing the various strategies. The main thrust in using these techniques is to remember that the work is about encouraging the client to continue to talk, self-explore, and disclose and about helping the client feel heard and understood. If that task is accomplished, it is quite unimportant to define clearly whether it was an encourager or a restatement that did the trick.

MOVING BEYOND SIMPLE COMMUNICATION

The Process of Empathy

> No matter what role we play in life, empathy remains
> the primary tool by which we come to understand and
> communicate effectively with others.
> *C. E. Rowe and D. S. MacIsaac, 1986, p. 21*

Empathy is a therapeutic skill that is difficult to achieve and yet is vital to the counseling process. Empathy requires the sophisticated application of all basic communication skills, as well as a fair amount of insight, in order to help the client achieve the fullest awareness and healing. It can be looked at as a bridge between skills that help facilitate communication and client self-disclosure, and skills that are oriented toward change and growth (both affective and cognitive). Empathy is affectively tinged with regard to clients' experience and clinicians' and clients' language. Empathy is difficult to achieve by the clinician without a combination of affective, cognitive, and behavioral awareness and understanding of the client.

Researchers have long looked at empathy as a composite skill with affective, cognitive, and interpersonal components. For example, Davis (1983) conceptualized empathy as a construct consisting of at least four components: perspective-taking, empathic concern, fantasy, and personal distress. Perspective-taking is the "tendency to adopt the psychological point of view of others" (Davis, 1983, p. 174), and is based on nonegocentric thought, requiring a more advanced level of cognitive and social development. Empathic concern is defined as the "level of other-oriented feelings of sympathy and concern for unfortunate others" (Davis, 1983, p. 174). It is based upon and reflects emotional responsiveness and sensitivity, traits that tend to translate into altruistic helping behavior (Bateson, Duncan, Ackerman, Buckley, and Birch, 1981; Coke, Bateson, and McDavis, 1978; Krebs, 1975; Mehrabien and Epstein, 1971). Fantasy refers to the "tendency to transpose oneself into the feelings and actions of fictitious characters in books, movies, and plays" (Davis, 1983, p. 174), another affective aspect of empathy that is less altruistic and more egocentric

180

or self-focused. Personal distress reflects the level of "self-oriented feelings of personal anxiety and unease in intense interpersonal settings" (Davis, 1983, p. 174), and combines an affective and cognitive approach to empathy that is egocentric in nature. It usually results in anxiety and personal distress, thus being inversely related to the ability to cope effectively and possibly interfering with positive client-clinician relationships.

Successful clinicians will have high levels of perspective-taking and empathic concern, along with low levels of personal distress. Their fantasy may get in the way if the client is perceived like a character with whom the clinician (over-) identifies. Fantasy may be irrelevant in most cases if the client is recognized and related to as a real human being, separate from the self. Clinicians' ability to take perspective hinges upon their cognitive ability to understand the client accurately; empathic concern hinges upon their ability to develop a caring and compassionate relationship with clients. Clinicians' ability to keep personal distress to a minimum requires self-awareness and personal psychological health, that is, presence of the positive traits and absence of the negative traits of mental-health-care providers discussed in Chapter One.

Given these aspects or components of empathy, one question that arises is whether empathy can be learned or is a preexisting trait that merely needs to be honed. It would appear that perhaps the most accurate answer is "both." Empathy is a trait and a skill. Empathy as a trait is the preexisting ability to take perspective, to care for and be concerned about others, to identify with others, and to keep personal distress to a minimum when being confronted with other people's plight. However, these traits need to express themselves in a manner that is therapeutic to be useful in counseling and therapy. In other words, being empathic (that is, having the trait) does not necessarily translate into behaving empathically (that is, using the skill). As Kohut (1984) points out, empathy as a trait implies that the clinician can correctly (and perhaps somewhat intuitively) understand (empathic concern) and explain (perspective-taking) the client's affects, feelings, and behaviors. However, this understanding and insight can be used positively or negatively. Truly understanding another human being can be used negatively if that knowledge is used to manipulate the other person. Truly understanding another person turns into empathic skill when used to help the person grow and improve. The remainder of this chapter will focus on how to maximize the potential of empathic traits by translating them into empathic skills.

EMPATHY—PRELIMINARY ISSUES

Empathy as a therapeutic skill is a highly sophisticated therapeutic technique, and yet is one of the most basic skills mental-health-care providers need to master since it permeates almost all therapeutic work. There is little argument among therapists and counselors of almost all schools of thought that empathy is an essential therapy ingredient. These discussions rarely differentiate between empathy as a trait and empathic skillfulness. It is likely that theorists generally think of both trait and skill when writing or talking about empathy in a generic sense. Although most often associated with Carl Rogers and humanist psychology, empathy has been addressed and researched by many other theorists (for example, Barrett-Lennard, 1981; Brems, 1989; Davis, 1983; Kohut, 1984; Wolf, 1988). Empathy is perceived as a cornerstone of counseling and therapy by behaviorists, existentialists, systems theorists, psychoanalysts, and many other thinkers. Contrary to many students' intuitive beliefs about empathy, some of the most empathic therapists identified through research investigations have actually been behavioral therapists (Ivey, Ivey, and Simek-Morgan, 1997).

Empathy as a trait and empathy as a skill require much of the clinician. They are based on a number of building blocks that need to be in place before empathy can be used successfully or at least optimally as a therapeutic skill by a mental-health-care provider. Some of the traits and skills that are prerequisite for empathic skillfulness are listed below. It is useful to note that empathy as a trait is a prerequisite for empathy as a skill. In other words, a clinician who does not have empathic concern, the ability to take perspective, the ability to keep personal distress to a minimum, and the recognition of clients as human beings with whom the clinician must not overidentify, will also not be able to respond empathically to a client in treatment. More than likely the list of prerequisite skills and traits is inadequate; there are probably many other ingredients that enter the empathic interaction that have not yet been formulated and studied.

Prerequisite Traits and Skills for Optimal Empathic Skillfulness

- empathic concern
- perspective-taking
- absence of overidentification
- low levels of personal distress
- acceptance
- respect
- interpersonal warmth
- genuineness
- congruence
- affirmation skills
- capacity to immerse oneself in another's experience without getting caught up in it
- self-awareness regarding possible countertransferences
- rapport-building skills
- communication-facilitating skills

- ability to understand nonverbal communication
- ability to communicate understanding to clients
- cognitive flexibility
- creativity
- ability to recognize good therapeutic timing
- ability to conceptualize clients' thoughts, affects, and behaviors
- ability to delay insight work

This list will probably resonate with careful readers, who recognize that many of these traits and skills have already been addressed in prior chapters of this text. The ones that have not been dealt with, namely, the last two skills listed, will be addressed in further detail in the chapters dealing with cognitively oriented interventions. The list also shows, as indicated above, that empathy as a trait is a prerequisite for empathy as a skill. To keep the differentiation clear, from here on empathy as a trait will be referred to as trait empathy, and empathy as a skill will be referred to as empathic skillfulness. Whenever the label "empathy" is used by itself, it is employed to reflect the failure to differentiate in existing clinical literature.

Trait empathy needs to be differentiated from similar affective states. Specifically, trait empathy may be confused with sympathy, identification, intuition, co-experience, and so on. Trait empathy reflects caring, clarifies themes, stimulates self-discovery, communicates safety, and provides proof of the expertise of the therapist (Patterson and Welfel, 1993). It helps the client become self-aware and encourages exploration on a deeper emotional level. This is very unlike sympathy, which tends to be designed to squelch feelings by expressing support and the wish for the receiver to get over her or his expressed emotion (Meier and Davis, 1997). Empathy also must be differentiated from the notion that therapists somehow magically intuit their clients' experiences, get caught up in their clients' emotion, provide approval or advice, or attempt to understand how they might feel in the same situation (Rowe and MacIsaac, 1986; Wolf, 1988). Table 7-1 identifies how such traits differ by defining them and pointing out their differences.

EMPATHIC SKILLFULNESS AS A CYCLICAL PROCESS

Empathy, as originally defined by Rogers and expanded upon by modern writers, is the ability to understand the affective experience of others from their perspective. It presumes acceptance of the client, though it does not imply acceptance of a client's specific behavior. Empathy is not used to excuse unacceptable or dangerous behavior, but merely accepts clients and their need to engage in a given behavior (Ivey, Ivey, and Simek-Morgan, 1997). Empathy thus defined most closely resembles trait empathy. Empathy has also been

TABLE
7-1

DIFFERENTIATION OF TRAIT EMPATHY FROM SIMILAR CLINICIAN TRAITS

Similar Trait	Definition	Differentiation
Sympathy	A sympathetic person feels another person's pain and because of that commiseration wishes the other person well. This wish for the other person's wellness arises out of the sympathetic person's sympathetic feeling of pain. Only if the suffering person feels better, does the sympathetic person feel better.	Unlike the sympathetic person, the empathic person, while recognizing the suffering person's pain, does not feel the pain with the other person. Therefore, the empathic person does not have the need for the suffering person to recover quickly. The empathic person can allow the other person to feel or react as necessary for as long as needed and can remain emotionally present and available for the duration.
Identification	The person who identifies makes assumptions about the other person based upon what her or his own personal feelings or perceptions would be like in similar or equal circumstances. The identifying person may assume that the other person has certain reactions because that is how the identifying person would react.	Unlike the identifying person, the empathic person is able to perceive the other person's reaction from that person's perspective. The empathic person does not confuse how the other person feels or responds with how she or he might respond in a similar set of circumstances.
Co-Experience	The co-experiencer becomes so involved in the other person's experience that she or he begins to have the same feelings and gets caught up in the other person's experience. The personal boundaries break down and the two people respond as one. The co-experiencer loses emotional distance and objectivity and sees no way out of the experience.	Unlike the co-experiencer, the empathic person, while accurately understanding the other person's feelings, does not get caught up in them. The empathic person accurately perceives the other's reactions and feelings and cares for the person (expressing warmth) but remains clear about personal boundaries and does not get caught up in the emotion or experience.

Blank Slate

The blank slate is the person who understands the other person and remains untouched by that person's experience or reaction. Although having a cognitive understanding of the person's suffering or reaction, the blank slate remains so neutral as to be uninvolved and emotionally untouched.

Unlike the blank slate, the empathic person has both a cognitive and affective understanding of the other person. While not getting caught up in the other person's reaction or affect, the empathic person has interpersonal warmth and caring for the other person that resonates and feels good to the other person.

Intuition

The intuitive person has a sixth sense about what another individual is feeling. This intuitive sense may or may not be accurate as it is often affected by the perceiver's own personal history and experiences.

The empathic person, while often having a "feel" for the other's experience, bases this perception on a process of vicarious introspection that is not haphazard or instantaneous, but rather based on a prolonged immersion in the other's experience to glean a clear and accurate understanding of that other person's experience.

Warm Fuzzies

Warm fuzzy individuals develop warm and caring feelings for others that often feel soothing and comforting to the receiver of them. The warm fuzzy person does not use the caring feelings for the other person to facilitate their level of self-awareness or insight, or to promote growth and healing, but rather merely using the warm fuzzy feeling to help both individuals feel good in their relationship.

The empathic person also expresses warmth and caring but in a context of healing and encouragement of self-awareness and growth. Although all verbalizations by the empathic individual are delivered with warmth and caring, their importance rests not in making the two people in the relationship feel good about each other, but on helping the other person learn and grow.

conceptualized as a process (Barrett-Lennard, 1981), and in that definition most closely resembles empathic skillfulness. This empathic process has been described as cyclical and consisting of multiple phases or stages (for example, Brems, 1989, 1999; Egan, 1994; Patterson and Welfel, 1993). The cyclical process of empathic skillfulness as defined here has five stages or phases. It begins with Phase One, self-expression by the client (Brems, 1999), and Phase Two, the reception or perception of the client's expressed message. It continues with Phase Three, the clinician's ability to understand and process the message accurately (as affected by theoretical orientation), leading to Phase Four, the clinician's assertiveness to feed the essence of the message back to the client (Egan, 1994). The cycle closes when the client hears the feedback and feels understood and acknowledged (Phase Five). If the cycle closes successfully, the client will be motivated to self-express once again, reinitiating the cycle.

The Phases of the Cycle of Empathic Skillfulness

Figure 7-1 provides a visual representation of this empathic process. The cyclical or process definition of empathic skillfulness sounds somewhat reminiscent of the definition provided earlier for the process of reflection. There is a critical difference, however. A reflection is merely designed to keep the client exploring and talking; an empathic response (although often sounding like a reflection and being structured like a reflection) is designed to enhance the client's self-awareness and to express understanding of the client by the therapist. The statement made in the course of the empathic process is additive; a reflective statement accurately captures the client's expression without adding (or subtracting) information. This issue of the additive nature of the empathic response will be discussed further below. The phases of empathic skillfulness utilize many of the basic communication skills that have been discussed in the context of facilitating client self-disclosure. It is in the context of empathic skillfulness that these basic therapeutic skills truly come to life and are used to their fullest potential. Table 7-2 outlines the essential skills and traits that facilitate each phase of the cycle of empathic skillfulness.

Phase One: Client Expression

Each and every cycle of empathic skillfulness begins with a client disclosure. Much of this text has dealt with how to facilitate self-disclosure. All of the communication skills covered so far (for example, restatements, paraphrases, encouragers, and reflections) serve to help the client share with the clinician those topics that are of importance and concern to the client. Clinicians must not forget that client self-expression is both verbal and nonverbal. Paying attention to what the client does in the therapy or counseling room is as important as hearing what the client says. Facilitating client self-disclosure is not only a generic therapeutic task, but also the necessary first ingredient to initiate the

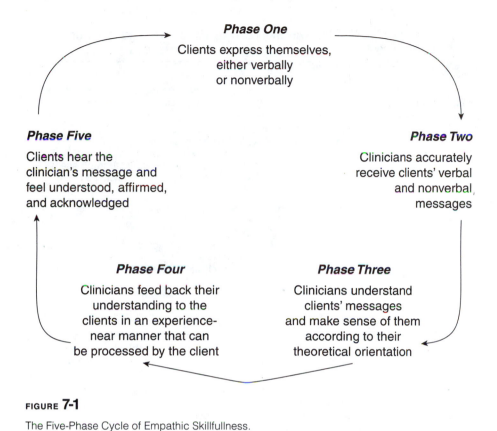

FIGURE 7-1

The Five-Phase Cycle of Empathic Skillfullness.

cycle of empathic skillfulness. Clinicians who talk too much, are judgmental, have prejudices, or subscribe to stereotypes will not encourage or motivate clients to talk. Not surprisingly, these are the very clinicians who are generally not perceived as empathic by their clients and their supervisors.

Phase Two: Clinician Reception

The reception or perception aspect of empathy is greatly dependent upon the therapist's ability to hear, see, and sense what the client is attempting to communicate. It also is dependent upon a counselor's ability to sift through a large set of data to find the essential component or message. The perception of the clinician needs to be unclouded by preconceived notions, and all the cautions provided about the reception process in the chapter about attending skills apply here as well. For example, evaluative, inadequate, filtered, selective, or fact-centered listening in one way or another prevents the clinician from accurately hearing the client. Rehearsing while listening, or getting caught up in the affective content of the client's communication, equally get in the way of receiving the

| TABLE 7-2 | ESSENTIAL TRAITS AND SKILLS THAT FACILITATE THE VARIOUS PHASES IN THE CYCLE OF EMPATHIC SKILLFULNESS |

Phase in the Cycle	Facilitating Trait or Skill of the Clinician
One: **Client** **Expression**	• Facilitation of self-disclosure/client verbalization • Attending skills for client verbal communication • Attending skills for client nonverbal communication • Use of basic communication skills (e.g., encouragers, paraphrases) • Awareness of how personal clinician variables may influence client disclosure
Two: **Clinician** **Reception**	• Physiological functionality and acuity of necessary clinician senses • Good active-listening skills • Avoidance of listening errors • Freedom from or awareness of effects of personal biases, stereotypes, beliefs, prejudices, and expectations • Self-awareness regarding how clinician's personal beliefs can influence hearing accuracy • Personal mental and physical health (to reduce distraction)
Three: **Clinician** **Understanding**	• Ability to make sense of client information according to a theoretical system that explains human behavior • Creation of a larger context for understanding the client (e.g., cultural variables, socioeconomic, religious/spiritual variables) • Vast store of knowledge about the client's past and current circumstances, belief systems, experiences, and values
Four: **Clinician** **Expression**	• Adaptation of verbalization to client's cognitive abilities and preferences • Avoidance of jargon • Expression of warmth, caring, and comfort • Assurance of client's sensed embeddedness in a caring holding environment • Experience-near expression of understanding • Avoidance of experience-distant verbalizations • Emphasis on understanding, not explanation
Five: **Client** **Reception**	• Assessment of the physiological functionality and acuity of client's necessary senses • Facilitation and establishment of the client's attention • Heightening of the client's interest in what the clinician has to say • Timing to support creation of sufficient rapport • Matching of client language

client's message. On the other hand, the active listening skills (see Table 4-6) serve to enhance the clinician's reception.

Beyond being psychologically and emotionally ready to hear the client accurately, reception is also dependent upon the physical readiness of the clinician to hear the client. Clinicians who have hearing impairments need to be responsible enough to wear hearing aids or take other necessary measures to make sure they can literally hear what the client is saying. Similarly, if a clinician did not understand something the client said, perhaps due to distractedness or due to a client's low voice, it is important to ask the client to repeat what was said.

Language differences need to be considered as well. If client and clinician have different native languages, misunderstandings are possible and can derail the reception phase of the empathic process, leaving the cycle incomplete or inaccurate. Clarifying meanings when in doubt is also crucial.

Reception of the client's expression in the context of empathic skillfulness goes beyond the accurate perception and hearing of the client, however. It also includes what Kohut (1977) called prolonged empathic immersion in a client's experience. This immersion refers to the clinician's ability to focus consistently on the experience of the client without clouding that experience with personal reactions or countertransferences. This ability requires that clinicians be self-aware and recognize how their biases, beliefs, values, stereotypes, and expectations may influence their reception of information. Clinicians need to be aware that they may mishear clients if they have preconceived notions about what the client is going to say or how the client may feel. Although client-focus implies that the clinician can recognize what the client experiences, it does not imply that the clinician identifies with the client and gets caught up in the experience. Instead, it implies that mental-health-care providers recognize the depth and intensity of the "moment-to-moment experiences of the [client] but also the continuous flow of these experiences over time. Kohut refers to the attunement to this continuous flow of moment-to-moment experiences as prolonged immersion or as long-term empathic immersion in the psychological field" of the client (Rowe and MacIsaac, 1986, p. 18). Sympathy or overidentification are successfully avoided, leaving the counselor open to perceive the actual experience of the client. Awareness of the client's current experience and its relationship to past experience will help the clinician reach the next phase of the empathic skillfulness cycle, namely, that of correctly understanding the client's experience.

Phase Three: Clinician Understanding

Once the reception phase is mastered successfully and the clinician has accurately (physically and psychologically) received the client's message, it is necessary to process the information in the context of the client's overall history. This processing is not done out loud, but rather takes place (often in the fraction of a second) in the clinician's head. The processing or understanding phase of the empathic cycle requires that the therapist make sense of the client's communications. This aspect of empathy is most susceptible to the therapist's theoretical preferences (Patterson and Welfel, 1993). The affects, thoughts, and behaviors expressed by the client will be understood slightly differently depending on school of thought; cognitive-behaviorists will look for cognitive distortions, irrational beliefs, and automatic thoughts that have been reinforced and developed over a lifetime; humanists will look for evidence that the client is nonauthentic in her or his self-expression, lacking in genuineness and congruence, and will seek to understand how these realities came about; and self-psychological psychodynamicists may look for expressions of specific needs and how their failure to have been met in childhood has affected current relationships and self-perceptions.

It is this phase of the empathic-skillfulness cycle that most closely resembles Kohut's (1982, 1984) definition of empathy as vicarious introspection. As noted above, one aspect of empathy, according to self psychologists, is the prolonged immersion in the client's experience, without getting caught up in it, for the purpose of better understanding clients from their unique perspective. It involves a process of data collection (Phases One and Two) that leads to understanding of the client (Phase Three) (Wolf, 1988) while using the therapist's own affective experience with and reaction to the client as a guide (Mahrer, Boulet, and Fairweather, 1994). The aspect of empathy that is expressed in Phase Three of the empathic-skillfulness cycle is a tool for gaining an understanding of the client that will be used in later phases to help the client gain self-awareness and a sense of being accepted and understood (Kohut, 1982, 1984). Kohut referred to this aspect of empathy (or this phase in the empathic process) as vicarious introspection, emphasizing that this process is a critical element not only in the therapy relationship but also during healthy development. Vicarious introspection helps the clinician know how the client feels in a given situation because of an appreciation of the client's developmental history, relationship history, and larger life context. Parents use vicarious introspection to understand their children; it is a way to gain an appreciation of the other person's experience based on the knowledge about that person's life. Vicarious introspection is useful for parents in knowing how their children feel or predicting how they will react based on their joint experience in life together. Kohut postulated that it is the breakdown in understanding between caretaker and child that is the precursor to psychopathology and hindered development as it makes it impossible for the child to internalize a healthy, cohesive, strong, and orderly self (Kohut and Wolf, 1978; Kohut, 1984). Similarly, clinicians learn to recognize a client's experience or to predict a client's reaction through their joint exploration of the client's life. Therapeutic rapport ruptures (Phase Three of the empathic skillfulness cycle fails) when the mental-health-care provider fails in the attempt to introspect vicariously, that is, when the clinician misunderstands the meaning and nature of the client's experience.

To summarize, understanding, as practiced in Phase Three, considers clients' developmental history, family circumstances, cultural embeddedness, and interpersonal values to make sense of a given self-disclosure or communication. The clinician in Phase Three does not merely grasp the emotional flavor of clients' messages, but understands (explains) them in terms of current levels of functioning, expressed and unexpressed needs, interpersonal adjustment, level of self development, and life circumstances (both past and present). The prerequisites for Phase Three are cognitive in nature. The clinician must possess the cognitive skills to make sense of how the client reacts, feels, thinks, and behaves given the client's life context. These cognitive skills of gaining understanding and forming explanations will be dealt with in the chapter on advanced cognitive skills.

Phase Four: Clinician Expression (or Feedback)

Regardless of the specific content of the understanding gleaned by the therapist (that is, regardless of theoretical orientation), the next phase of the empathic response involves the expression of that understanding in a genuine and warm manner to the client. This response will have a cognitive and an affective component. The cognitive component of the response will have slightly different contents depending on how the mental-health-care provider chooses to derive meaning (that is, according to the clinician's school of thought). However, the affective component of the empathic response is the same across all schools of thought: The communication must be genuine, warm, respectful, and useful to the client. A response that is cliché, gives advice, parrots, or gives sympathy represents an empathic failure (Egan, 1994). Feedback may involve merely expressing understanding and acceptance of an expressed affect or may involve an experience-near interpretation along with the communication of understanding. Phase Four does not consist just of an explanation; it always involves understanding and caring as well (that is what makes it empathic, after all). In other words, in Phase Four understanding is always a necessary ingredient (Strauss, 1996); interpretation or explanation are optional additions, used only in the empathic-skillfulness cycle if they can be delivered in a caring and experience-near manner. The difference between understanding and explanation and between experience-nearness and experience-distance is explained further in the chapter on advanced cognitive interventions.

How clinicians express their understanding of the client is determined not only by their awareness of and insight about a given client's experience, but also by a number of other client factors, such as client cognitive level and complexity, as well as language skills and preferences. For example, the client's cognitive level of processing must not be exceeded lest the clinician's verbalizations make no sense to the client. Adapting clinician verbalizations to the client's abilities and preferences requires paying attention to issues such as

- using the client's native language whenever possible
- using a volume sufficient to be heard
- using the same phrases and vocabulary as the client does (as appropriate; for example, racist language would be avoided even if used by the client)
- adapting to the client's preferred modality (for example, using visual, auditory, or tactile language)
- avoiding jargon
- using simple phrases and easy-to-understand vocabulary
- keeping statements brief and nontechnical

Expression also requires a psychological component that communicates warmth and caring for the client. Often just the content of the clinician's expression in and of itself is comforting and acknowledging, and perceived as caring by the client. However, not all clients can appreciate the content alone. Phase-Four verbalizations will be accepted by the client more easily and will be more useful to the client if delivered with emotional caring and warmth. Communicating empathic acceptance and caring to the client when expressing an understanding requires that clinicians consider the following factors in choosing their verbalizations:

- waiting for appropriate rapport
- waiting for the client to be in an emotional state that is receptive to clinician input
- using a soothing voice or a voice that matches the content to be expressed
- making appropriate eye contact
- achieving appropriate physical proximity
- being congruent in verbal and nonverbal expression
- being genuine in what is being said
- being calm and centered during delivery
- having more concern for the client's well-being than for the clinician's need to be right
- paying careful attention to the client's nonverbal reactions while the clinician is speaking

If the clinician is successful in incorporating both cognitive and affective congruence into the verbalization, the expression of understanding is more likely to be received by the client. Learning to use language appropriately is very important to the success of the empathic-skillfulness cycle.

Phase Five: Client Reception (or Feeling Understood)

The empathic-skillfulness cycle is not complete unless the client receives the clinician's message. Reception refers to both the physical readiness and the psychological readiness of the client to perceive the clinician's expression. In other words, the client must be able to have sufficient cognitive skill to understand what the clinician is saying as well as having the physical ability to hear. The same issues that were discussed with regard to the physical aspects of reception during Phase Two apply here, with the difference being that the clinician must now ensure that the client's physical reception needs are accommodated. Clinicians need to know what if any hearing or perceptual impairments clients may have that may get in the way of pure perception of the clinician's message. More importantly, clinicians need to have an appreciation of how the client tends to react to different modes of expression by others. For example, if the clinician knows that the client tends to shut down and ignore messages if they are delivered in a stern or authoritarian manner, then such delivery would be avoided. Some clients may only pay attention if a message is delivered with authority and confidence, whereas others listen more if a message is disguised in guiding questions. Learning what induces a client to pay attention and to give credence to a verbalization helps the clinician make choices and adaptations in the delivery of a message that optimize client reception.

Most clients have language preferences that help them hear or understand others better if they are matched. For example, some clients may use kinesthetic language (phrases or words such as "I feel . . . ," "I sense . . . ," "my intuition . . . ," "there is a sense that . . ."). Another client may use visual language (phrases and words such as "I see this clearly now . . . ," "I'm having trouble getting a picture of . . . ," "in my mind's eye . . ."), whereas yet another individual may prefer auditory language (phrases and words such as "what I'm hearing . . . ," "that sounds like . . . ," "to my ears that's . . ."). Other clients may choose thought-based vocabulary (including phrases and words such as "I'm thinking . . . ," "I just know . . . ," "what I think is happening . . .") or affect-based vocabulary ("I feel that . . . ," "it really touched me when . . . ," "my skin crawled when . . ."). If clinicians can match the client's modality in expression, they increase their likelihood of being heard by the client. On the other hand, if a clinician speaks in a modality to which the client cannot relate, the client may not receive the clinician's message, although the message itself was very accurate and not threatening to the client.

Another important aspect of delivery that influences client reception is timing. Premature expression of explanations or interpretations in Phase Four will more likely lead to client withdrawal or defensiveness. In the early stages of therapy or counseling, it is best to limit Phase-Four verbalizations to expressions of empathic understanding, rather than explaining. Once firm rapport and caring has been established in the relationship, more-advanced cognitive strategies may be embedded in Phase Four as well. However, if these interventions are used prematurely, they are very likely to decrease a client's receptivity.

Clients who have successfully received the clinician's expression of empathic concern and perspective will feel understood, affirmed, and acknowledged. They will feel profoundly cared for by the clinician who will be perceived as being in tune with the client. Such experiences of being truly heard and accurately understood are rare for many clients in their lives outside of treatment. It is for this reason that empathic skillfulness in and of itself can have "curative" effects. Although there is some debate whether empathy alone suffices to help clients change and grow, there is little argument that empathic skillfulness "may serve a secondary therapeutic function in that it can establish a meaningful supportive bond between" client and mental-health-care provider (Rowe and MacIsaac, 1986, p. 21). If nothing else, client reception of an empathically skillful verbalization by a counselor will motivate the client to self-disclose further.

It will stimulate clients to want to share more of themselves with their clinician and as such is a powerful force in keeping therapy moving and in helping clients explore their lives in increasing depth (Kohut, 1984). Thus, not surprisingly, closure of one empathic-skillfulness cycle often leads directly to the initiation of another (as shown in Figure 7-1).

Sample Transcript of a Cycle of Empathic Skillfulness

Empathic skillfulness affirms, acknowledges, and validates clients, their affects, needs, thoughts, conflicts, relational patterns, and behaviors in a manner that considers the here-and-now, without excusing behaviors or justifying them if they are dangerous or inappropriate (Teyber, 1997). Empathic skillfulness has as its essence "understanding [that] connotes warmth and a feeling of concern for clients" (Teyber, 1997, p. 41) and is the prerequisite for the creation of a therapeutic holding environment wherein the clinician contains clients' distress and need states. Empathy and empathic skillfulness are essential for attachment to occur and, hence, are helpful or perhaps even needed for the establishment of a working alliance that helps clients become motivated for treatment and ongoing self-disclosure. In essence, empathy and empathic skillfulness become the cornerstone of therapy, primary tools through which clinicians come to understand their clients and communicate effectively with them. They are tools without which the process of psychotherapy and counseling may be doomed to failure much as their absence during the developmental phase interferes with healthy self development (Rowe and MacIsaac, 1986; Wolf, 1988). An annotated example of an empathically skillful communication cycle in a client's sixth session follows.

Phase One: Client Expression

The client expresses a concern about being able to tell the clinician about a recent sexual encounter. This has happened before and the clinician has let it go, not wanting to push the client into premature self-disclosure.

CLIENT: I don't really want to talk about it. It's not something I want you to know because I don't want to have to discuss the details and you wouldn't understand anyway.

Phase Two: Clinician Reception

The clinician hears the client's message, which is that he does not want to tell her about his sexual encounter. However, she also hears that this is the first time that he explains why he does not want to talk ("You wouldn't understand anyway"). Thus, the clinician hears the overt verbal message saying the client does not want to talk about it, as well as the hidden message that he fears her judgment. The clinician is aware that the client is making full eye contact this time, whereas on previous occasions he avoided eye contact. She concludes from this behavior that the client may be ready to talk about the sexual encounter if she can give him reassurance about and can explore his fears about her potential judgment (or lack of understanding) of his behavior.

Phase Three: Clinician Understanding

The clinician understands the client's fear of her judgment because she knows that he was raised in a critical environment, by a mother who seldom approved of her son's behavior. The clinician understands that sexuality is the client's way of getting close to people and that he is starved for healthy emotional contacts because of a deprived affective environment (both past and present). She is aware that he has an approach-avoidance conflict regarding emotional relationships, craving them and fearing them at the same time. Superficial sexual relationships are his way of getting closeness for a brief time and walking away from it when it becomes too overwhelming for him.

Phase Four: Clinician Feedback

The clinician chooses to communicate her understanding of the client empathically to encourage further exploration at a deeper level. Her response is cautious and does not add explanation despite the fact that she has insight about the "why" of his behavior. In other words, her empathic response chooses to address his fear of judgment (the "what"), not the reason for it (the "why"). Moving to the "what" still moves beyond the overt message of the client, making the clinician statement empathic (not merely reflective). Moving beyond that understanding to an explanation might have seemed too large of a leap and have been perceived by the client as experience-distant, further affirming for him that emotional contact is painful, increasing his approach-avoidance conflict about getting close to people.

CLINICIAN: I am very touched by how worried you are that I might judge you somehow, that I might like you less somehow because of something you did.

Phase Five: Client Reception

The client listens intensely and is able to hear the clinician's message. He acknowledges feeling heard and then initiates another self-disclosure that begins a new cycle.

CLIENT: Yes. For some reason your opinion is important to me and it would be risky to tell you something you may not approve of. . . .

The client-clinician interaction continues as follows, going through several cycles of empathic skillfulness:

CLINICIAN: It's scary to tell everything about yourself, and you want to be sure you can trust me first. That makes good sense. Is there something I can do to show to you that I will not feel less about you because of something you did?

CLIENT: I'm not sure. . . . I guess, just listen and don't criticize. You know, don't get all moral on me and tell me I shouldn't be doing it. . . .

CLINICIAN: Just listen and keep caring about you; not judge you . . . I can definitely do that.

CLIENT: You can?

CLINICIAN: Yes. But the important thing is that you believe that. That you trust me enough. And that has to be your leap of faith.

CLIENT: I would like to trust you. . . .

CLINICIAN: It sure makes things a lot easier when you can trust. You can be yourself, say what's on your mind and you don't have to worry so much. It would be a relief, wouldn't it?

CLIENT: Yes, it would. It's so hard to hold back, you know. I just want to spill my guts, but I get so scared. (*gets a little teary*)

CLINICIAN: (*nods head*) I know. . . . (*very softly; leans forward slightly*)

CLIENT: A leap of faith, huh?

CLINICIAN: (*just nods and waits*)

CLIENT: Okay. I can do this. . . . (*long pause*)

CLINICIAN: (*continues the silence, empathically allowing the client temporal space to make up his mind*)

CLIENT: (*takes deep breath*) Alright. Well, what happened is . . . (*Session continues from here.*)

This example demonstrates that empathic skillfulness is a process that often, if not always, has its roots in a here-and-now occurrence between client and clinician but must be understood by the clinician as of greater significance in the context of the client's entire life history and development. It is not a warm fuzzy feeling (though conveyed with warmth), but an important tool that encourages self-awareness, self-respect, and self-acceptance. Empathic skillfulness, as demonstrated by this example, is possible if empathy exists as a trait in the mental-health-care provider. Only the clinician who has the empathic capacity to understand the client affectively and cognitively (that is, who can take perspective and has empathic concern without letting personal distress get in the way) will be able to use this understanding to initiate a communication cycle reflective of empathic skillfulness.

The example shows that an empathic (Phase-Four) response purely based on understanding is different from a therapeutic explanation or interpretation. Its purpose is not to explain, despite the fact that understanding and self-awareness are central to its definition. The type of understanding that is referred to in the context of empathic responding has to do with conveying the clinician's recognition and acknowledgement of clients and their essential and powerful emotions and needs (it is, in other words, concerned with *what* the client is experiencing). This is different from conveying an explanation to clients about why these feelings and needs have emerged (this is concerned with explaining *why* the client is having a particular experience). Empathic skillfulness that involves understanding (not explanation) in Phase Four is experience-near; it conveys an important relationship component between client and clinician that often leads clients to accept their own feelings and needs more completely. The self-acceptance and self-awareness of needs and affects is merely that: recognition that these needs and emotions exist within the self (when prior to therapy they most likely were repressed, denied, or otherwise kept hidden from the client's conscious recognition and acceptance). The next step, which is insight (that is, an explanation as to *why* they exist), no longer uses exclusively understanding, but adds explanation, focusing on insight-creating strategies.

THE ADDITIVE NATURE OF EMPATHIC SKILLFULNESS

Two distinctive features of empathic skillfulness are its cyclical and additive nature. The cyclical or process nature of empathic skillfulness has been explored so far. It is now necessary to attend to the additive nature of empathic skillfulness. Unlike in a reflection, in Phase Four when clinicians express an understanding of the client, they not only feed back (or reflect) what the client said or knows, but also add an understanding that has neither been verbalized by the client nor consciously recognized. In making an empathic (Phase-Four) response, the clinician provides an understanding to the client that goes beyond what the client could have expressed or figured out alone. The additive nature of the clinician's response is driven by the clinician's ability to understand the client's expression in the larger life context and history of the client that has been discussed in counseling up to date. The additive component of the clinician's expression derives from an understanding of the circumstances leading to a client's current experience. Theoretical orientation plays some role here in what the clinician perceives as important in having shaped the client's current experience and thus influences the content of what a clinician may add. The fact, however, that an addition is made seems to be accepted among most mental-health-care providers.

Several decades ago, social psychologists began exploring empathic responses and identified the additive nature of the response as the crucial feature that distinguished empathy from other human interactions. Carkhuff (1969) developed a rating system for human responses and verbalizations in interpersonal contexts that looked at the level of addition and attention expressed by a response to another human being. This rating scale has become the basis for looking at level of empathic expressiveness or responsiveness among clinicians and other communication partners (for example, Brems, Fromme, and Johnson, 1992; Hammond, Hepworth, and Smith, 1977). Hammond, Hepworth, and Smith developed an *Empathic Communication Scale* that rates therapists' responsiveness or empathic skillfulness based on the level of subtraction or addition reflected in their verbalizations. They proposed five levels of empathic responsiveness, ranging from responses that subtract from the meaning expressed by the client (that is, that are unempathic) to responses that significantly and accurately add to the meaning expressed by a client (that is, that are empathic). Brief definitions of the five levels follow, quoted from Hammond et al. (pp. 98–99).

Empathic Communication Scale

Level 1.0. The counselor's verbal and behavioral responses are irrelevant, *subtract significantly* in affect and content, and do not attend appropriately to the other's expressions. The counselor communicates no awareness of even the most obvious, expressed surface feelings of the other person. The responses include premature advice-giving, arguing, changing the subject, criticizing, pontificating, and asking questions that shift the focus from the expressions of the client.

Level 1.5. Counselor responses qualify as negligently accurate, and any of the client's feelings that are not distinctly defined tend to be entirely ignored. Counselor responses may mislead or block off the client. The client does not go to a deeper level of self-exploration.

Level 2.0. The counselor responds to at least part of the surface feelings of the other person, but a response *noticeably subtracts affect* or *distorts the level of meaning.* Awareness of the client's expressed feelings is only partially communicated. The counselor may respond to [her or] his own conceptualizations rather than to what the client expressed. Some responses may have diagnostic or psychodynamic accuracy, but not empathic accuracy.

Level 2.5. The counselor wants to understand and makes the effort, but [her or] his responses subtract slightly from the level of feelings the other expresses. Responses that merely parrot expressions of the other person in the same words belong to this level.

Level 3.0. Responses communicate understanding at the level of feeling the client expresses. The counselor's responses are essentially *interchangeable, or reciprocal in affect* with the surface, explicit expressions of the other individual, or they accurately reflect [her or] his state of being. The responses do not add affect or go below the surface feelings, nor do they subtract from the feelings and tone expressed. Factual aspects of the client's message (content), though desirable, are not required; if included, content must be accurate.

When expressed feelings are vague or ill-defined, inquiries used to expand to the expression of feeling or to explore meaning are appropriate. However, if feelings are stated explicitly or are clearly implied, then inquiries alone, without responsiveness to the feelings, are noticeably subtractive (Level 2.0).

Responses at Level 3.0 are minimally facilitative and helpful.

Level 3.5. The counselor's responses reflect not only the feelings but also the reasons for the feelings that the other person expresses—in other words, the counselor's responses complement feelings with content.

Level 4.0. The counselor's responses accurately identify implicit, underlying feelings somewhat beyond the expressions of the client and complement feelings with content that adds deeper meaning.

Level 4.5. Responses exceed Level 4.0 but fall short of Level 5.0.

Level 5.0. The counselor's responses significantly add to the affect and meaning explicitly expressed by the client. Additionally, the counselor's responses accurately communicate the affect, meaning, and intensity of the other person's deeper feelings by word, voice, and intensity of expression.*

Level One and Level Two Responses: Empathic Failure Versus Optimal Empathic Failure

Clearly, responses that meet criteria for Levels One and Two (as well as their sublevels) cannot be considered empathic responses. They are responses by clinicians who are unaware of the client's true affect, unclear about the client's message, and unable to understand the client's current (or past) experience. These clinicians are likely to have poor rapport with clients, especially if Level One and Level Two responses preponderate. All clinicians will, of course, make an occasional Level One or Level Two response, as all humans are fallible. It is only the consistent or predominating presence of responses at Levels One or Two that suggests a problem in the therapeutic relationship that is based on lack of empathy in the clinician. The occasional failure, on the other hand, can even be helpful to the therapeutic process if recognized and handled correctly, paralleling the process that takes place between a child and caretaker during the developmental years. Occasional failure has been labeled an optimal empathic failure (Kohut, 1984; Wolf, 1988). It is an integral aspect of the process of internalization, and has both developmental and therapeutic value. A quick

*Hammond, *Improving Therapeutic Communication,* 1977 John Wiley & Sons, Inc. Adopted by permission of Jossey-Bass, Inc. a subsidiary of John Wiley & Sons, Inc.

overview will be provided here of internalization and how optimal empathic failures may facilitate it; interested readers are referred to Kohut (1984), Rowe and MacIsaac (1986), and Wolf (1988) for thorough discussions of this important process in counseling and therapy.

Internalization is a developmental process that begins at birth and serves to help children develop a cohesive, orderly, and vigorous self through interactions with caretakers and significant others in their environment. Almost from the moment of birth, children observe their environment very curiously and intently (Stern, 1985), learning much of what they will come to know during their lifetime through imitation and modeling after significant others and through internalizing beliefs and experiences that arise in relationships with early caretakers. If the environment is essentially consistent in providing for a child's many needs, it is considered an empathic, or properly attuned, environment. In such an environment, caretakers correctly respond to the child with empathic interactions that reflect an understanding of the child's needs at least at Level Three, but usually at Level Four. Caretakers who are able to understand their children well enough to provide for their needs have an additive understanding of the child, that is, are able to respond at Level Four or Five, because they can recognize from the context of a present occurrence what the child is attempting to communicate. This is true even before children are fully verbal, as is evident from the fact that parents quickly learn to respond empathically to their infants, providing food when the child is hungry, comfort when the child is sick, and support when the child is in need. They do all this based upon their knowledge and understanding of the child's environment, history, and subtle communication. Much in the same way, a clinician learns to understand a client based on knowledge about that client's personal life circumstances and subtle nuances of verbal and nonverbal communication.

If raised in an empathic environment, that is, in an environment with caretakers who are capable of providing Level Four and Level Five responsiveness, children essentially slowly become empathic with themselves, learning to accept themselves in their strengths and weaknesses, and mastering the art of coping with life's challenges (though some need for affirming and strengthening others is never completely outlived; Kohut, 1984; Wolf, 1988). The definition of an empathic environment is not complete unless it also includes a recognition of the reality that even the most perfectly attuned parents will occasionally respond at Level One or Two. Personal preoccupations or needs will no doubt enter the caretaker's life at times in a way that interferes with the ability to respond fully empathically to the child. Although this may appear to be problematic, parents are often relieved to learn that, if handled correctly once hindsight has been achieved, this occasional empathic failure on the caretaker's part is an important component of a child's healthy growth and development. The truly empathic environment, in other words, is fortunately one that includes occasional empathic failures on the part of a child's primary (or secondary) caretakers. This is so because it is the occasional failure of the caretaker that challenges the child to seek strength within the self to bridge the gaps in external empathic availability. Optimal empathic failures or frustrations challenge the child to begin to rely on personal internalized resources to take over the affirming or strengthening response previously provided by the caretaker.

The deciding factor about the usefulness versus harm of empathic failures (that is, responses at Level One or Two) is essentially one of balance. Empathic failures are optimal and allow for internalization of a healthy self if they are occasional and embedded in an overall interpersonal matrix that is adequate and consistent at meeting or gratifying most of the child's needs, that is, in an overall and usually empathic environment. They are optimal if the caretaker (or clinician, in the case of counseling), recognizes the failure at a later time and rectifies the situation, either by once again responding empathically in similar future circumstances, or by openly admitting the shortcoming to the child (or the client). Nonoptimal empathic failures can take many different shapes (see Brems, 1998b; Stern, 1985). Most commonly they manifest as environments that never meet a child's needs. There is a preponderance of Level One and Level Two responses to the child and a chilling absence of the kind of empathic understanding reflected in responses at Levels Four and Five. The absence of Level Four and Five responses leads to an emotional deprivation of the child as she or he is never fully acknowledged, affirmed, appreciated, or supported. No healthy modeling of self-affirmation or self-strengthening has taken place; thus, when yet another unempathic interaction takes place, the child has no cognitive (or inner) model of strength upon which to draw when the caretaker has failed. In such a depriving, unempathic environment the child never internalizes the capacity for self-affirmation and self-soothing because these functions were never provided or modeled to begin with. The same is true for the therapeutic relationship, as will be elaborated below.

An environment also fails to be empathic if it is unrealistically overavailable, that is, if there are never any failures on the part of the caretakers to meet the child's needs for self-affirmation and strengthening. Because caretakers always respond immediately and completely, children in such an environment are never challenged to develop empathy within themselves and to internalize strength to deal with difficult situations. Such children are actually the target of optimal empathic failures as well, as the failure of the caretaker to fail (yes, it sounds strange) deprives the child of opportunities to draw on inner resources and strengths. Such children will for the rest of their lives depend on others to meet their needs. Healthy internalization of self-affirmation and self-soothing depends on the overall embeddedness in an interpersonal matrix that empathically provides for most of children's basic needs while occasionally leaving them to fend for themselves. It is during the occasional empathic failures that children learn to develop skills and to begin to fend for themselves psychologically speaking (Kohut, 1984; Rowe and MacIsaac, 1986; Wolf, 1988).

If it occurs in an overall empathic therapeutic relationship, the occasional empathic failure of the clinician will fulfill the same role in a counseling setting. Therapy and counseling, as real life and human development, rely upon the process of internalization to help clients change. Empathic interactions with mental-health-care providers help clients internalize adequate self-affirming and self-soothing functions, strengthening clients in many ways without the need for insight or explaining. Clients glean self-esteem and strength through empathic and accepting interactions with their clinicians, much in the same way as infants or children in healthy interpersonal environments learn to meet their own needs by modeling after, imitating, and internalizing their parents' responses, values, and behaviors. This process of internalization is more or less incidental to the work with clients as it takes place nonverbally and preverbally, does not rely on cognitive insights, and yet builds the basis for a strong, goal-directed and self-confident self. This type of internalization is neither encouraged nor discouraged by the clinician; it happens as an incidental aspect of the experiential nature of the therapeutic relationship. It is synonymous with similar concepts proposed by social learning theory (Bandura, 1969; Johnson, 1994).

The internalization process that is based on the empathic rupture, or failure, in the clinician-client relationship is an equally unplanned, yet crucial, process between client and mental-health-care provider. As during healthy development, the empathic failure of the clinician is only optimal when it is occasional and embedded in the context of a preexisting empathic relationship that has established an air of acceptance, genuine concern, and caring (Donner, 1991). As stated above, it is completely unavoidable that therapists will occasionally fail their client and will not always adequately understand and reflect their self-expressions during counseling. Just as empathic failures in a child's life can either be helpful or hurtful, empathic ruptures (that is, Level One or Two responses) in the therapeutic relationship can be used to the client's advantage if they occur only occasionally, are embedded in a greater empathic context, and are processed with the client. If clinicians were always empathic and perfectly attuned to every need of their clients (always and infallibly delivering Level Four and Five responses), clients would never have to learn to deal with the negative aspects of human relationships. Clients of clinicians who never fail them could develop the wrong impression that human relationships are about having needs met by external sources, that is, through the constant empathic caretaking by others. The clients may feel better while with the clinician, but often get worse in other relationships, where they will have the same expectations for dependence and caretaking.

The empathic rupture in the therapeutic relationship is an imitation of the developmental process that challenges clients to learn to soothe and care for themselves when people fail them (or when they perceive others as failing them; not all empathic failures are real; some are merely perceived that way by the client). In the therapeutic relationship, clinicians, while not gratifying clients' needs for affirmation and soothing (as a parent would in normal development), usually accept and confirm the existence of given needs in their clients, by responding at Level Four or Five to a client's verbalizations. Consistent empathic responding of that nature (Levels Four and Five) helps clients recognize and accept their needs through the therapeutic relationship. An empathic failure or rupture occurs when clinicians happen to be unaware of an expression of need or fail to accept it and make a Level One or Two response. In such an instance, the client is challenged to take the role usually played by their mental-health-care provider: providing acceptance and understanding for an emerging need alone and without their clinician's help, at least for a while. This is the same challenge that is met and mastered by the child during healthy development. The empathic failure on the part of the clinician challenges clients to internalize (provide for themselves) the self-affirming and self-soothing functions that they did not internalize during childhood (due to the unresponsive environment provided by the caretakers at that time) and to move toward relative independence from the counselor. This internalization ultimately leads the client toward self-acceptance and understanding as well as enhanced self-efficacy with regard to the client's ability to meet personal needs for self-affirmation (mirroring) and self-soothing (idealization) (Kohut, 1984; Wolf, 1988).

To summarize, if clinicians have modeled many Level Four and Five responses during their interactions with a given client, then when they "fail" by making a Level One or Two response, clients will have learned to make Level Four or Five responses for themselves. On the other hand, if all of treatment has consisted of Level One and Level Two responses, the client will never feel valued, affirmed, and acknowledged, and therapeutic rapport will never be established. In that instance the therapeutic relationship recapitulates the same type of negative relationship the client most likely encountered during childhood and no therapeutic growth and development will be possible for the client.

Level Three Responses: Reflection Versus Empathy

Level Three responses are not yet fully empathic responses; however, they are therapeutic responses and tend to be of value when used appropriately and in the correct circumstances. Level Three responses are essentially reflections. Reflections, of course, have already been discussed at length as helpful clinician verbalizations. Reflections keep clients talking by communicating that the clinician hears what the client is saying. They do not include a deeper understanding (as defined by Level Four or Five responses) that adds to the client's communication, but merely reflect content and affect expressed by the client, however nonverbally or hidden. On the surface, reflections may appear to add something because the clinician uses different words than the client; however, upon closer inspection, it becomes clear that nothing the clinician says (reflects) has not already been expressed by the client. Clients are not usually surprised by reflection responses; they already know that they have a given affect or are expressing a particular content. The clinician merely has made overt what the client has implied. Reflections thus perfectly fit the definition of Level Three response as interchangeable or reciprocal.

What makes an empathic response different is its additive nature as defined by Level Four or Five, that is, it deepens meaning and understanding to a level previously elusive to the client. The empathic response can add or deepen meaning and understanding either by further clarifying or refining a client's understanding of an expressed affect or by adding content of which the client was unaware. As such, if focused on affect, an empathic response adds an underlying affect, clarifies a coexisting affect, or highlights a shade of gray (all issues addressed thoroughly in the chapters dealing with affect and emotion). If focused on content, the empathic response adds meaning in the sense of an explanation (as will be discussed thoroughly in the chapters on thoughts and cognition).

Both reflections (Level Three) and empathic responses (Levels Four and Five) have therapeutic application. It is not always better to respond at Level Four or Five; there are times when a reflection is more appropriate than an empathic Level Four or Five response. Reflections are indicated over Level Four or Five responses until therapeutic rapport has been established. Making additive comments about affect prematurely in the relationship may be overwhelming for a client who is not yet ready to look at affect. Similarly, making Level Four or Five content responses prematurely can be quite threatening to clients who are not yet ready to explore the "why" of their behaviors, thoughts, and emotions since they have not even accepted yet that these issues manifest as they do. The many cautions that will be discussed in later chapters about doing affective work on a level commensurate with a client's level of affective self-awareness and expression apply in this regard. Cautions about timing of confrontations, here-and-now process comments, and interpretations also are of relevance. One aspect of demonstrating empathic skillfulness is knowing when to use which level of empathic responding. Being capable of a Level Four or Five response does not always mean choosing to make it. If a client is not ready for that depth of exploration, a simple reflection may be the more therapeutic response.

Level Four and Level Five Responses: Imposing a Viewpoint Versus True Empathic Skillfulness

Once clients have reached a certain level of comfort with their clinician and are beginning to search for the meaning and sources of their affects, thoughts, feelings, needs, and coping choices, Level Four and Five responses can slowly increase in frequency. These responses are theoretically fully empathic in that they are always additive in nature. However, nothing is quite that simple. An additive response may sound like a Level Four or Five response (and even meet the criteria quoted above), but actually be unempathic because rather than bringing out true underlying meanings and understanding, it imposes a clinician's viewpoint. In other words, for a Level Four or Five response to be truly empathic, it not only has to be additive, but also accurate. The issue of accuracy of explanations and affective work is the gist of the work around self-awareness strategies in the chapters that follow.

An additive response always draws upon a clinician's beliefs about what underlies, drives, or creates human behavior. The theoretical orientation or school of thought espoused by mental-health-care providers will enter into their understanding of clients' symptom, behaviors, thoughts, affect, and relationships. They will explain a client's manifestations based upon how they explain human behavior in general. The important issue that will differentiate an empathic theory-bound explanation from an imposing one is its level of accuracy and experience-nearness for a given client. A Level Four or Five response is empathic if it is accurate and idiosyncratic to the client's life circumstances, history, experiences (present and past), and subtle expressions of affect, thought, and behavior. It is imposing if it ignores the client's experience in favor of fitting the client into a framework that is indiscriminately applied to all human beings because of a clinician's belief in a particular school of thought about humans. The latter process has been referred to by Rogers as making every client a nail because the only tool available to the clinician is a hammer. True empathy (at Levels Four and Five) requires that the clinician possess more tools than just a hammer and search for new tools if the existing ones do not fit a particular client's presentation and experience. Each client is treated as unique, and for each client an explanation or meaning is created that fits perfectly for that client and no other. When meaning is specifically and accurately tailored to the client, additive responses become empathic and truly meet Level Four or Five criteria.

Samples of Level One to Level Five Responses

What follows are a few brief client-clinician interactions to demonstrate responses at various levels of the empathic-communication scale. Responses at three possible levels are provided to demonstrate the difference between less-than-empathic (Level One or Two), reflective (Level Three), and accurately empathic (Level Four or Five) responses. An example of an inappropriate additive response is also given to help the readers gain an appreciation of the possible negative effects of imposing viewpoints. Further, the most therapeutic response will be highlighted (note that the most appropriate response is not always the one at the highest level) in a discussion of the scenario.

Scenario One

Over the course of five sessions, client and clinician have been discussing the client's attempts at looking for work. The client has been unemployed for nearly fifteen months and has searched for work on and off during that time. Unlike the client, the clinician has recognized that the attempts have been somewhat half-hearted and that the client has repeatedly sabotaged his chances of actually being chosen for position vacancies that are commensurate with his skills. In the session from which this segment is taken, the client is just beginning to realize his ambivalence about going back to work.

> CLIENT: I guess I could have handled that slightly differently. Just starting the interview with my biggest fears about the job may not have been too smart. . . . (*truly pensive and somewhat startled by this recognition*)

Potential Clinician Responses
Level One: Unempathic Response

> CLINICIAN: Yes, next time you should try to put your best foot forward and talk about your excitement about the job instead. Employers are more likely to hire employees who are self-assured. You certainly have every right to be self-confident—You are a smart man. Don't you believe in yourself?
> CLIENT: Yes, I do! But it's hard to convince others you're good. So many people assume the worst, especially employers. You just can't reason with them. You gotta protect yourself, you know. It's just not that easy!
> CLINICIAN: Well, what can you do differently next time to make sure you have a chance of getting hired?
> CLIENT: I don't know. That's why I'm here.

Level Three: Reflection Response

> CLINICIAN: You are realizing that you may not have made the best choice of behavior. . . .
> CLIENT: Yes. And sadly I think this is not the first time I've done this.
> CLINICIAN: You have hurt your chances before?
> CLIENT: Yes. Oh, I feel foolish. What do you think is going on?
> CLINICIAN: Let's explore that together. What are some possible reasons?
> CLIENT: I didn't feel comfortable in that environment. . . . Something just felt off. . . .
> CLINICIAN: Help me understand what you mean by "off."
> CLIENT: Well, it felt—awkward? No, that's not quite it. I was feeling watched or something. . . .
> CLINICIAN: Scrutinized, maybe?
> CLIENT: Yes! That's it. There were five people in the room and they were all watching me. I was scared to move and since all I felt was scared, that

seemed to be the only thing I could think of to say. So I just started talking about my fears.

CLINICIAN: What are your fears?

Level Four: Accurate Empathic Response

CLINICIAN: You are realizing that you may have been doing things that can get in the way of actually being hired.

CLIENT: I guess so. I didn't think of it that way, but I suppose it's true. Maybe I have . . .

CLINICIAN: Maybe you have . . . ?

CLIENT: Done things that turned employers off.

CLINICIAN: What do you suppose that's all about?

CLIENT: Maybe I'm not ready to go back to work?

CLINICIAN: You have some ambivalence about it, maybe? You've certainly talked about how happy you are with taking care of Sammy and Katie.

CLIENT: Yes, I've really enjoyed being home with the kids. You know, Jennifer took a couple years off when they were little. I didn't have that chance. It's been a lot of fun doing stuff with them during the day. Soon they'll start school and then they'll have a life of their own, just like my older ones. I feel like I might miss something important if I start working again right now.

CLINICIAN: Like you might miss something?

CLIENT: Yeah. You know, with Jean and Tommie I was working through their whole childhood years. Now don't misunderstand. I was a very involved dad as far as time allowed. You know, I never missed a ball game, and I was part of all their important events. But this is different. This is so sweet. I'm there when they feel good, I'm there when they feel bad. They check in with me. . . . I have always loved being a dad and this just is a beautiful way to spend my time. (*gets teary*)

CLINICIAN: You really love your children and enjoy this life. . . .

CLIENT: Yes! If I a were a woman . . .

CLINICIAN: You could just stop looking for work and no one would scrutinize your decision to stay home. It would be okay. . . .

CLIENT: Exactly! (*sighs*)

Level Five: Viewpoint-Imposing (Unempathic) Response

CLINICIAN: It sounds to me as though you are realizing that you are really not ready to go back to work because you have things that you need to do in your private life first.

CLIENT: What do you mean?

CLINICIAN: You missed out on helping raise your older children. Now you have a chance of making that up to your younger children by being home with them before they start school in a couple of years.

CLIENT: I helped raise my older kids. Just because I was working doesn't mean I was an absent dad. I love my kids! And they don't think I was a bad father. (*shuts down*)

Discussion

In this example, the most therapeutic response was the accurate empathic Level Four response. However, the reflection at Level Three was also appropriate and helpful. The client was ready for a Level Four intervention, and it was this readiness that made Level Four most appropriate. If the clinician is uncertain as to whether a client is ready to explore a deeper level, a reflection can begin the process with careful questioning that allows for Level Four intervention if the client evidences insight and willingness to dig deeper. The imposing-viewpoint response demonstrates clearly how inaccurate an additive response of the clinician can be. This clinician imposed a viewpoint based in stereotypic assumptions about family systems (and absent fathers). The assumption was incorrect and led the client to be defensive and to withdraw from the interaction. The Level One response consisted of advice-giving and was somewhat critical. The client certainly perceived the intervention as critical, which is ironic, as he already felt scrutinized and criticized in his circumstances to begin with. Not surprisingly, he became defensive and threatened. The clinician also never managed to get to a true empathic understanding of the client, veering instead in a direction that was irrelevant and counterproductive as it never helped the client get to the point of exploring, accepting, and understanding his ambivalence. The accurate empathic response not only helped the client recognize his ambivalence, it also facilitated an exploration of its deeper cause or meaning. Understanding this deeper meaning helped him accept his conflicted feelings and unearthed his true desire, which was to stay home with his young children for now. It is likely that the reflection would ultimately have led to this recognition, acceptance, understanding, and insight. However, it would have taken slightly longer and hence was a somewhat-less-efficient intervention.

Scenario Two

The client in this scenario has been seen for fourteen months. The clinician has been suspecting a seasonal component to her depression, but the client has been rejecting the notion. Instead, she tends to think that she was "doing something wrong" and that she should be able to "just snap out of it." In this session, the clinician recognizes the cyclical nature of the client's symptoms once again and attempts to help her recognize it through empathic intervention that is designed to move her to this deeper level of understanding about her symptoms. In the transcript that follows, various levels of responses are embedded in a single interaction. The example shows how clinicians move from Level Four or Five empathic responses to reflections and back, and how even occasional failures do not have to interrupt the flow of treatment if they are recognized and acknowledged, as well as embedded in an overall empathic relationship. Response levels are indicated in parentheses for clarification.

CLIENT: Do you realize I've been coming here for over a year now. And I still feel like crap. It's pretty discouraging actually. . . .

CLINICIAN: You had hoped for more progress by now. . . . (*Level 3*)

CLIENT: Uh huh. (*gets teary-eyed*)

CLINICIAN: Feeling badly is becoming very overwhelming. . . . (*Level 3.5*)

CLIENT: (*weeping and nodding*)

CLINICIAN: Can you tell me what you are feeling right now? (*very soft voice so as not to squelch the affect with the question*) (*Level 3 question to move client to a deeper level of experience; preparing client for Level 4 work*)

CLIENT: (*sobs*) Hopeless . . .(*weeps openly now; diverts all eye contact*)

CLINICIAN: Like this will never pass . . . (Level 3)

CLIENT: (*nodding softly; making some eye contact again*)

CLINICIAN: This discouragement, it has happened before, hasn't it? (*Level 4; moving client to a deeper understanding*)

CLIENT: (*looks puzzled*)

CLINICIAN: About a month ago, I remember you started feeling the same way; and I remember a time before that, last year in January or February; like there is a cycle of some sort . . . (*Level 4.5*)

CLIENT: (*looks up with interest now; tears decreasing*)

CLINICIAN: Have you ever noticed anything cyclical about these feelings before? (*Level 4 question to encourage client to explore deeper contents*)

CLIENT: No . . . But something just resonates . . . 'cause I was thinking this morning, it's so dark. . . . If only the sun were back I'd feel better. But I didn't really think about it much. You asked me this before, didn't you, when I was first starting to see you. . . . I dismissed it. . . . (*puzzled*)

CLINICIAN: What are you pondering just now? (*encourager at Level 3, reflecting recognition that client is thinking about something*)

CLIENT: I didn't pay attention. . . . I never pay attention (*starts to cry again*) What's wrong with me? (*sobbing now*)

CLINICIAN: You are feeling so down today that everything you realize somehow makes things worse. . . . You find a way to look at it in a negative way. . . . (*starts with Level 3 reflection and deteriorates to a Level 2 reaction that does not grasp the essence of the client's verbalization*)

CLIENT: You would too if you felt this way. (*looks up; defensive*)

CLINICIAN: You know, that wasn't the best way I could have said what I wanted to express, was it? Sorry for the way that came out. (*repairs empathic rupture to turn the failure into an optimal one*) What I mean is

Skill Development Recommendations

Recommendation 7-1   *In conversations with family and friends, evaluate in hindsight or at the time how you would feel in a given situation and compare it to how they indicate they felt. Try to understand why they feel the way they do, based on their unique history, development, and so forth. Once you reflect on their unique backgrounds and how they have been shaped by them, do their reactions make more sense to you? Do you understand why they may be reacting differently from how you or others may have responded in the same situation?*

Recommendation 7-2   *Listen to the conversations of others (either strangers or friends and family members) and attempt to evaluate what you hear in terms of the levels of empathic responsiveness. At what level of the rating scale do most conversations appear to take place?*

Recommendation 7-3   *Watch a movie or read a novel, choosing from the list below or similar products. Try to take the perspective of a lead character to develop an empathic understanding of that individual. Does consideration of their unique background and history assist you with developing an empathic perspective on their lives? Does increased empathy alter your perception of the individual? How so and why?*

Movies	Novels
Ordinary People	One True Thing
Shoot the Moon	The Accidental Tourist
Birdy	The Glass Bead Game
Good Will Hunting	The Fires of Troy

that some days everything looks bleak and there seems to be nothing you can do about it—no matter how hard you try. (*returns to Level 3*)

CLIENT: Yes! (*weeping again now*) It's like this dark force takes over and grabs hold of me. (*sobs while talking*)

CLINICIAN: Is there anything that you can identify that contributes to this dark force? (*encourages Level 4.5*)

CLIENT: Like what?

CLINICIAN: I'm struck by you calling it a dark force. . . . (*Level 4.5*)

CLIENT: (*thinking*) Of course. It's dark outside . . . again. I love cold weather and snow, but I can't stand to wake up and it's dark; I go to work—it's dark; I go home—it's dark. I miss the sun. . . . (*breaks into sobs again*)

CLINICIAN: It's so hard to feel light when there isn't any. . . . (*Level 3.5; approaching Level 4*)

CLIENT: Exactly! Now what do I do?

CLINICIAN: You just took an important first step. (*caring and soothing voice*) We tied your desperation to something deeper, something outside of you that contributes to it. Having seasonal variations in your mood is an important thing for us to have realized—even if it doesn't help you feel less hopeless right now. . . . (*Level 5*)

CLIENT: In a strange way it does. It's like it's not all my fault. . . .

CLINICIAN: You're not doing anything wrong after all. . . . (*Level 4*)

(*Session goes from here to verbalize the diagnosis of a seasonal-affective-disorder component to the client's affective disturbance and problem solving.*)

Discussion

This transcript clarified that an empathic response is not something that happens once and is finished, but rather, empathic skillfulness permeates therapy and counseling at almost all times. It moves from level to level and creates an interpersonal relationship that is warm, caring, and supportive. Such therapeutic rapport and relating has been called a holding environment. It allows the clinician to begin to work with explanations and interpretations in a way that is accepted by the client and perceived as caring, not intrusive. The creation of this empathic interpersonal matrix and holding environment is an important skill that needs to be in the clinician's bag of techniques before moving on to strategies that help create cognitive or affective self-awareness.

PART three

Skills for Cognitive Awareness in Psychotherapy and Counseling

WORKING
WITH THOUGHT
AND COGNITION

Overview and
Basic Skills

> Man is not disturbed by things, but by his opinion
> about things.
>
> > *Epictetus*

Once communication and empathy have been established with a client, the
therapeutic interchange can deepen to include work around issues of cognition
and affect. Over the course of counseling or therapy, clients need to recognize
their thoughts and feelings to be able to achieve true behavior change and personal growth. There are many ways in which a clinician can assist in this process of self-exploration, deepening understanding, and creation of insight. In
this section of the book, focus is placed on information about and skill development in the area of thoughts and cognitions.

Cognitive work refers to all interventions that focus their attention on clients' opinions, attitudes, thoughts, and cognitions. Some of this work is simple
and straightforward; some of it complex and theoretical. Given the great diversity in level of complexity and intricacy of cognitive work, clinicians need to
keep in mind the level of cognitive development of the client. Just as clinicians
need to assess clients with regard to their affective level, they need to pay attention to clients' cognitive skills. If a client presents with a limited range of
cognitive complexity, advanced techniques of working with thought and cognition may be beyond the reach of the client's cognitive capacity, especially if
phrased in a complicated or complex manner. Although this statement may
sound judgmental, it merely reflects a simple reality that not all human beings
function at the same level of cognitive capacity. It does not mean to imply that
some people will not benefit from counseling or therapy; it merely suggests that
they will benefit more from interventions that are tailored to their cognitive
preferences, style, and abilities.

Level of cognitive complexity is not to be confused with intelligence. Although level of intelligence can indeed be the limiting factor in a client who is
cognitively rigid and unable to think flexibly, there are emotional factors that

215

can contribute to this thinking style. Perhaps it is best to begin with a definition of cognitive complexity versus rigidity. The simplest way to define and differentiate these two concepts is to borrow from Piaget's theory of cognitive development. Piaget conceptualizes cognitive development as progressing from
sensorimotor thought to preoperational thought to concrete operations to formal operations, as defined in Table 8-1. Although Piaget originally conceptualized the cognitive stages of development as discrete stages, modern developmental research clearly shows that these stages are neither concrete nor discrete
at all. Human beings can function at one level of cognitive development with
regard to one type of skill, and at another level with regard to another. It is even
conceivable that they can function at one level in one context, and at another
in a different environment. Most simply put, thought that falls into the first
three categories (sensorimotor thought, preoperational thought, and, most
commonly, concrete operations) is thought that is less than cognitively complex. If evidenced by adults, it tends to be characterized by what other adults
would perceive as rigidity and inflexibility. This is in contrast to thought in the
formal operational stage of development, which has the potential for cognitive
complexity and logic. If clients evidence concrete thought or illogic and inflexibility, it is important to assess whether this pattern is pervasive, that is, characteristic of the client in all settings and contexts, or isolated. Lack of cognitive
complexity overall generally reflects a true limitation in cognitive development;
lack of cognitive complexity or flexibility in select circumstances generally
reflects an emotional or situational component that interferes with cognitive
performance in limited situations. Removal of the emotional interference or
situational circumstance often frees the client to function at a higher cognitive
level, allowing for the use of more-advanced cognitive interventions than the
clinician may have deemed possible.

A Model for Conceptualizing Working
with Thought and Cognition

The progression through Piaget's stages is a normal developmental process.
Children will think in certain ways (that is, sensorimotor, preoperational, concrete, formal) in a developmentally appropriate manner throughout their developmental years. Developmental researchers have observed, however, that
somewhere around the ages of eleven to fifteen a human being should be
developing toward a level of formal operations, and after age fifteen formal
operational thought should be largely in place. Adults who seek counseling
services could theoretically be presumed to function at formal operational
thinking. Formal-operational thinking, in turn, is presumably characterized by
logic, abstracting ability, flexibility, creativity, and deductive reasoning. Most

importantly, formal operations implies that adults can think about objects, events, and relationships without having to perceive or be in these circumstances concretely at that given moment. In other words, formal operational thinkers can take multiple perspectives without being bound by immediate perception about the perspectives they are taking. They can recognize implications of general principles for specific situations or relationships. Clinicians may assume that since their clients have matured beyond age fifteen, they are complex and logical thinkers who have these abstracting skills. Unfortunately, as practicing clinicians can attest, this is not always the case. It is important for clinicians to recognize that adult clients are not always functioning at the same level of cognitive complexity in all situations and circumstances. While they may be remarkably creative and capable of logic and abstracting ability in some areas of their lives, in other areas they may be remarkably concrete. Interestingly, such adults may have high-level professions, college degrees, and much formal or informal education. However, when emotionally challenged or placed in certain situations, they revert to a level of thinking more characteristic of a child of seven to eleven than of an adult.

The Process of Normal Cognitive Development and Implications for Therapy and Counseling

Cognitive development is viewed as proceeding through the development and modification of schemata about the world, a process that consists of organization and adaptation. As children mature cognitively, they begin to form schemata, or patterns of thought about the world. As they continue to have new experiences in their environment, they modify these schemata to make room for new impressions. One way in which this occurs is through organization, wherein the child makes existing schemata increasingly complex, perhaps by combining various basic schemata into one new, single overriding pattern of thought. A second means of modifying existing schemata is through adaptation, which in turn can proceed through assimilation or accommodation. Adaptation of a schema means that the child modifies the schema to adapt it to new environmental demands or uses existing schemata to make sense of new environmental demands. Thus, whereas organization refers to an expansion or reorganization of multiple schemata due to an integration of new learning and new experience, adaptation refers to a revision or alteration of an existing schema or to an understanding of a new environment based on a previously established schema. Organization creates something new; adaptation uses something old to understand something new or modifies something old to fit with new evidence. If adaptation proceeds through understanding a new environmental event by an existing schema, it reflects assimilation; if it proceeds through a revision of an existing schema, it reflects accommodation. Assimilation can go awry if the child uses a preexisting schema for a new environmental event in a manner that is incorrect. For

TABLE
8-1

PIAGET'S STAGES OF COGNITIVE DEVELOPMENT

Type of Thought, Substage, and Age	Characteristics of Thought and Cognition
Sensorimotor Thought (Birth to 2 years)	Preverbal; schemata are largely behavior (i.e., patterns of action); problems are largely solved through action
Reflexive activity (0 to 1 month)	Inherited reflexes are exercised; objects are tracked without reaction to their disappearance; facial expressions are imitated; new objects are assimilated (e.g., sucking reflex is generalized to toys, blankets, fingers)
Primary circular reactions (1 to 4 months)	Repetitious pleasurable bodily actions to practice skills (e.g., kicking legs); repetition of body behavior that was responded to; staring reaction to objects that disappear
Secondary circular reactions (4 to 8 months)	Repetition of actions involving external objects; action is not yet intentional or purposeful although it may appear that way; searching reaction to objects that are partially concealed
Secondary schemata (8 to 12 months)	Coordinates actions to arrive at a new one (simple organization); beginning intentionality; searches for and often finds concealed object but may err about location; makes crude attempts to imitate actions
Tertiary circular reactions (12 to 18 months)	Experiments with new situations to find new outcomes or solutions; searches for and finds concealed objects where they were last seen; increasingly sophisticated imitation of actions; trial-and-error activity expresses curiosity about and exploration of environment
Mental combinations (18 to 24 months)	First evidence of symbolic thought; beginnings of mental problem solving; object concept and permanence are achieved; deferred imitation becomes possible

**Preoperational Thought
(2 to 7 years)**

Language and cognitive development interact; ability to use words and other symbolic thought helps with processing of not only the present but also the past and future; still easily taken in by perception and appearances despite increasingly symbolic and decreasingly perception-bound thought

Preconceptual period
(2 to 4 years)

Inability to consider more than one aspect of a thing, situation, relationship, or person (that is, centration); difficulty with perspective-taking limits ability to take others' point of view and contributes to perceived egocentrism; limited ability to recognize conservation due to lack of reversibility, lack of transformation, and static thought; limited ability to engage in classification

Intuitive period
(4 to 7 years)

Increasing decentration (ability to consider multiple aspects) assisting with increasing the ability to use conservation and classification; increasing perspective-taking leads to decreasing egocentrism; some intuitive impressions of social situations (no longer purely perception-bound)

**Concrete Operational Thought
(7 to 11 years)**

Mastery of conservation (ability to recognize that certain properties of an object do not change with alteration of appearance [e.g., volume, mass, weight number]) and classification (ability to sort objects according to multiple categories and subcategories); recognition of reversibility (ability to reverse an action or process mentally) and transformation (ability to process an object's change in state); movement from largely concrete logic to more sophisticated logic and abstracting ability (e.g., relational logic such as seriation [ability to arrange objects mentally according to particular dimension such as weight, color, size] but without transitivity [ability to recognize relationships among elements in a series]); logic is still bound to concrete perception of objects, events, people, and situations (minimal to no manipulation of purely hypothetical propositions yet)

**Formal Operational Thought
(11 to 15 years)**

Thought no longer bound to concrete perception and time (no longer bound to mental operations on concrete objects, mental operation of ideas is now possible); logic expands to encompass purely hypothetical reasoning and deductive reasoning; mastery of transitivity; increased hypothetical problem-solving ability; blossoming of mental creativity and cognitive flexibility; beginning ability for perspective-taking; can think about relationships of objects, persons, situations, and so forth without actually having to be in them at the moment; thought freed from immediate experience and time example, a child who grew up around large, gentle dogs may have developed a schema that says "furry creatures are cute and cuddly." If this child encounters another furry creature, namely a bear, this schema can lead to problems if the child attempts to function according to the schema "furry creatures are cute and cuddly" and tries to cuddle up to the bear. This is an example where adaptation would proceed more correctly through accommodation, which would lead the child to modify the schema to "the furry creatures in my home are cute and cuddly."

The relevance of the concepts of organization, assimilation, and accommodation to counseling is clear. Not only children come to therapy with certain schemata; adults do as well. The more flexible their thinking, the more skilled they will be in using information from the clinician to form old schemata into new ones (organization) and to accommodate old schemata, rather than to force assimilation where it is not appropriate (successful adaptation). Conversely, the more rigid or inflexible their thinking, the more likely they will be to attempt to explain new information through old schemata, forcing assimilation where accommodation or organization would be more appropriate. Additionally, although not part of Piaget's original thinking, cognitive development is perceived by contemporary researchers as highly influenced by the sociocultural and emotional context in which a child matures or in which an adult currently functions. Interactions with caretakers and other adults and peers will strongly influence the types and styles of coping skills, problem-solving skills, and cognitive patterns or schemata children develop and employ. A child who grew up in an environment that was deprived of successful role models or that was predominated by role models who assimilated inappropriately will be more likely to have stagnated at a concrete operations level of thinking, at least in some realms of cognition. A child, on the other hand, who was challenged by role models to integrate new learning and to take multiple perspectives on new information, is more likely to have achieved formal operational thinking. Guidance and encouragement, focused on providing sensitive instruction that fosters cognitive growth, are critical to healthy cognitive development (Sigelman and Shaffer, 1995). These supportive behaviors are most successful if they are adapted to the child's current level of cognitive development. In other words, the guiding individual encourages the child to stretch beyond existing limits into new realms of cognitive functioning. The level of encouragement needs to be such as to be comprehensible at the child's current cognitive level while suggesting movement to a new level of cognitive capacity. Guidance that is provided at a level of cognitive capacity that is beyond the grasp of the child will not be successful as it overchallenges the child and may lead the child to give up in frustration.

Language is the primary mode through which encouragement and guidance take place. Thus, even language has to be adapted to a level that results in understanding in the child. Adults generally spontaneously adapt their vocabulary when they interact with children, eliminating professional jargon or so-

TABLE 8-2	**A HIERARCHY OF COGNITIVE STRATEGIES AND INTERVENTIONS**	
Strategy	**Brief Definition**	**Primary Purpose**
Imparting information	Providing objective knowledge or understanding the client did not previously have	Alter a client's reaction or interpretation in response to a given situation
Pointing out patterns	Pointing out and tying together multiple similar contents or messages given by the client over time	Help the client recognize relational patterns, core affects, or core beliefs that have become habitual or maladaptive to create the motivation to change
Asking clarifying questions	Planfully or purposefully questioning to lead the client to an insight or understanding the clinician already has	Facilitate self-discovery, understanding, and insight in the client
Confrontation	Pointing out inconsistencies, discrepancies, and mixed messages in the client's communication	Help the client recognize incongruence and help the client increase awareness and a new way of looking at old information
Here-and-now process	Pointing out interactions with the clinician that mirror interactions, behaviors, attitudes, or reactions also expressed with others	Help the client gain insight about reactions, attitudes, and behaviors that occur predictably and perhaps inappropriately in multiple contexts
Interpretation	Providing explanations based on knowledge of the client about the origins of a client's reactions, behaviors, interactions, and so forth	Help the client understand the reason behind the reactions, attitudes, behaviors, and so forth that manifest frequently, predictably, or inappropriately

phisticated words from their conversation. Although guidance and prodding are most important in childhood, they remain of great value in adulthood. And this is, of course, the link to psychotherapy and counseling. The cognitive interventions that will be discussed in this and the following chapter are conceptualized as cognitive guidance and encouragement. They are designed to be used as a means of facilitating clients' cognitive growth to a more complex, abstract, logical, informed, and flexible level of functioning. This goal can only be achieved if the clinician can adapt language and intervention to the client's current level of cognition. Mental-health-care providers adapt their interventions and language to a different level of cognitive complexity when they work with children; they need to do the same in their work with adults. As clinicians use the cognitive strategies that follow (and that are outlined in Table 8-2), they need to keep the following points in mind:

- clinicians need to assess or appreciate clients' cognitive capacity and style, carefully differentiating optimal cognitive functioning from situational impairment

- choice and style of implementation of cognitive strategies are adapted to clients' level of cognitive capacity in a given situation, and thus may differ depending on situational impairment versus optimal functioning
- clinicians need to be attuned to the identification of forced assimilation on the part of the client
- clinicians facilitate accommodation and organization through guidance and encouragement, challenging the client toward cognitive growth
- interventions need to be phrased in a manner commensurate with clients' cognitive capacity and language skills, optimal and situational, as appropriate
- statements have to be formulated as clearly and succinctly as possible
- information may need to be given at multiple cognitive levels to ensure clients' understanding
- statements are best formulated more concretely than complexly when a choice is possible
- conversation optimally will be in clients' native tongue
- language is best adapted to the preferences of clients (this does NOT include the use of offensive or prejudicial language)
- language is best free of jargon
- if jargon is unavoidable, it needs to be clearly and simply defined

A Hierarchy of Interventions and Strategies for Working with Thought and Cognition

The strategies for working with thought and cognition that are outlined in Table 8-2 and discussed in this and the subsequent chapter offer a new way of looking at the issues presented by a given client. All suggest a shift in clients' perceptions or cognitive interpretations of an issue or situation at hand. All strategies require cognitive skills on the part of the client, most importantly requiring clients to organize new schemata and to accommodate where necessary. Clearly, some amount of cognitive flexibility and creativity on the part of the client will greatly facilitate success with these interventions. Guidance and encouragement, as explained above, may be necessary to help clients make therapeutic use of these interventions. The strategies will be presented hierarchically, not only according to the level of cognitive complexity they require of the client, but also according to a number of other therapeutically relevant issues. Specifically, the strategies, as ordered in this text (and in Table 8-2)

- require increasing levels of cognitive complexity and flexibility on the part of the client
- require increasing levels of cognitive complexity and flexibility on the part of the clinician

- create increasing levels of depth in the cognitive shift or insight that will be achieved through their use
- require increasing levels of understanding and knowledge of a given client by the clinician
- require increasingly stable rapport and sustaining attachment between client and clinician
- will be increasingly reflective of the clinician's theoretical orientation

Given their characteristics presented in this listing, it is not surprising that the strategies described earlier will be used earlier on in treatment and less and less so later in therapy or counseling (though they may be used to some extent throughout treatment with a given client). The strategies presented later, especially the strategies presented in the advanced-cognitive-skills chapter, will be used later in treatment with a given client, as they require more stable rapport and more insight on the part of the mental-health-care provider about the client. The strategies, as they grow increasingly complex, require more and more complexity and insight on the part of the clinician. This is truly an area where a clinician's own personal cognitive limitations may get in the way of therapy and counseling. Advanced cognitive strategies, such as interpretation and here-and-now processing, require that clinicians understand underlying dynamics that are manifested in the client's symptoms and behaviors. Only then can they help clients recognize inappropriate or irrelevant assimilations and the need for shifts in existing schemata.

Increasingly, cognitive strategies will reflect clinicians' personal theoretical orientation. For example, although interpretation as a strategy in and of itself is theory-free, the content placed in the interpretation will vary given the clinician's own personal theoretical beliefs about what has motivated a given client's behavior, opinion, reaction, or attitude. Thus, a Rogerian may interpret a given reaction of a client as evidence of personal incongruence, whereas an existentialist may understand it as a manifestation of existential angst; whereas a cognitive behaviorist may see it as evidence of automatic thinking that has become maladaptive; and so on. Clearly, the use of higher-level cognitive strategies requires clinicians to be aware of their biases and values and how these may enter treatment. This issue will be addressed again as it becomes relevant to each strategy under discussion.

Dealing with Clients' Cognition-Related Crises in Session

The clinician needs to be prepared for a few contingencies in working with thoughts and cognitions. Just as mental-health-care providers have to be prepared to deal with out-of-control emotions while working on helping clients gain awareness of affect, so do they have to be prepared to deal with thoughts that may spin out of control. The most common manifestations of problems revolve around racing thoughts (usually associated with and recognized by pressured speech) and dealing with psychotic symptoms, most commonly and relevantly, delusions, but also hallucinations. A few guidelines are provided here to help beginning clinicians deal with these situations. However, these interventions are much less clear-cut than suggestions that are possible for out-of-control affects. Mental-health-care providers may find themselves making modifications as client needs arise and as client idiosyncrasies manifest. Reading the material on dealing with out-of-control emotions in the affective-awareness chapter will help clarify some of the suggestions below.

Dealing with Thought Racing and Pressured Speech

If the primary problem appears to be that the client's thoughts are racing and resulting in pressured speech, the mental-health-care provider intervenes with calming strategies. The clinician begins by asking the client to stop talking altogether and to begin breathing and relaxing. The clinician asks the client to pattern her or his breathing after the therapist's. (For example: "Let's get your breathing back to normal. Follow my lead. Slowly breathe in ... [*clinician takes a long, calm breath*] and out ... [*clinician releases the breath forcefully*]; in ... and out ...) This joint rhythm of breathing is maintained until the client becomes notably calmer. The client is asked to model breathing according to the therapist's example and not to talk during this exercise. The simple breathing can be kept up for some time if the clinician believes that it is sufficient in slowing down the client's thought process. If the client's thoughts appear to continue to race (as perhaps suggested by a difficulty in slowing down the breathing or fidgety psychomotor behavior), a focal-point exercise can be added. The client is asked to find a focal point and to place her or his total attention on it. Once the client has established eye contact with the focal point (for example, a picture in the therapy room), the client is asked to describe it. (For example: "I need you to look at ... right there across from you. Okay, now tell me what you see. Describe it in detail.") This simple task serves to distract the client's focus of attention away from the racing thoughts. The client may need some assistance, as thoughts may be highly preoccupied. If this is so, the counselor may need to do some modeling of description. (For example: "Okay—what do you see? I see a brown picture frame—do you see it? Okay ... What shape does it have? ... Yes, that's how I see it; it's almost square. ... What else?" and so on.) Overall the focus is on helping the client stop thinking about the obsessive thoughts to slow cognitive processing and to model calmness and relaxation through calm breathing, controlled body language, low and slow voice, and firm directives about what the client needs to do next. The focal-attention exercise is generally very successful with these clients.

Dealing with Delusions and Hallucinations

The key to successful intervention with a client who is experiencing a psychotic break is to reestablish psychological contact with the person. Counselors frequently and calmly use clients' names to get their attention. Clinicians respond with calmness to clients' hallucinations or delusions to make psychological contact and do not get caught up in the psychotic content of the delusions or hallucinations the client is describing. It is best to respond to delusions and hallucinations by listening and expressing caring and concern without encouraging or validating the psychotic content. In other words, delusions are neither challenged nor argued with; instead, the clinician focuses on giving the client a sense of being heard and understood. It is very likely that the client is used to being the target of ridicule, challenge, and harassment when voicing delusional thinking or while talking about specific hallucinations; it is important to provide an alternative experience. An understanding and accepting attitude by the clinician is very useful in these instances and greatly facilitates psychological contact.

The second goal is to reestablish contact with reality. This is accomplished not by challenging the delusional content of the client's verbalizations or by challenging the reality of the perceptions, but rather by redirecting the client toward a here-and-now concern. (For example: "I understand what you are saying. Tell me, how did you deal with your son when you heard this voice telling you to kill yourself?" And then "And what do you do to get your son to daycare on time when this happens?" and similar interventions to get the client refocused on a real but related problem.) It is also important to explore and then allay any fears stemming from the hallucination or delusion by asserting the clinician's awareness of reality. (For example: "I understand your fear, but please let me assure you that I can guarantee you that Satan is not in this room with us.") If there is a kernel of truth to a client's delusion (and there usually is), it is important to find it and to respond to it. (For example: "I believe that you have been followed, especially that one time you told me about when . . . Can you tell me more about THAT incident?")

While reestablishing psychological contact and some degree of touch with reality, counselors remain calm and focused themselves, being careful not to become frightened of the client and not to be persuaded to reinforce the client's delusions. It is quite possible to express understanding as to why the client may have certain thoughts or beliefs without suggesting that the counselor shares them. It is also quite possible to acknowledge that the client is hearing or seeing things and that this is distressing, while remaining clear that others do not hear or see these same things. It is important to maintain an empathic stance that provides understanding and guidance. In other words, it is not enough to keep the client happy by giving emotional support; it also important to set firm limits on the client's behavior to ensure the client's and the clinician's safety. (For example: "I need you to do xyz before we can go on," or "I understand you feel . . . ; however, right now we need to do . . . to keep you safe.") A final note is necessary here: Despite their portrayal in the media to the contrary, psychotic individuals are no more dangerous and no more aggressive than the general population. They certainly can be aggressive (especially if their delusions involve paranoia or if clients experience a need to defend themselves from a threat). However, more often than not, aggression is not something the clinician has to fear from the psychotic client. As a rule of thumb, it is more important to get the client reoriented than to worry about physical safety. Obviously, if the client cannot be reoriented, the in-session intervention may need to end with the institutionalization of the client. A client is typically not allowed to leave the clinician's office alone and without a follow-up plan while flagrantly psychotic (see Brems, 2000, for more detail).

BASIC STRATEGIES FOR WORKING
WITH THOUGHT AND COGNITION

The common thread that ties together the basic strategies theoretically is their straightforward and nonchallenging nature. These strategies require less cognitive complexity on the part of the client than confrontation, here-and-now processing, or interpretation. All are focused, at least to some extent, on increasing the client's fund of information, either about life in general (as in *Imparting Information*) or about the client in particular. The patterns that are pointed out or the questions that are asked are clear and sufficiently straightforward that the client does not have to have enormous abstracting ability to understand what the clinician is driving at. Minimal effort is usually required on the part of the clinician to help the client recognize the point the clinician can already see. These strategies are also rarely perceived by the client as a challenge or a criticism, a danger that lurks in the use of the more advanced techniques. These strategies not infrequently lead to an increase in the client fund of information or a shift in the client's way of understanding a situation that in and of itself is sufficient to alter the client's attitude about or opinion of a given issue. The three categories of strategies that meet this description most accurately are those of *Imparting Information, Pointing Out Patterns*, and *Asking Clarifying Questions*. This is not to say that these strategies will always be basic; at times, clinicians may make very complex points by merely pointing out a pattern or asking a few clarifying questions. The fact is, however, that all of these strategies *can be* used in a straightforward manner (they just do not always *have to be* used that way).

Imparting Information

Many clinicians may not even consider imparting information as a therapeutic strategy, viewing it instead as an educational intervention. In either case, most do end up using this strategy at one point or another. Whether it is therapeutic or educational is somewhat irrelevant; clinicians need to know how and when to use it, and perhaps even more important, when not to use it. Although imparting information is the first cognitive strategy presented, it is not used very often in counseling and therapy. It is merely first because of its low level of complexity. If the hierarchy had been arranged with regard to how often strategies are likely to be used, imparting information would have ranked last, behind all other cognitive strategies.

Potential pitfalls of imparting information are many and need to be considered before (over)using this simple intervention. Imparting of information is most appropriate when a client appears to be operating under a set of factual information that is faulty, inadequate, or incomplete. The emphasis of this definition is on factual. The information in question is not a set of values or opinions; it is truly a set of facts that can either be verified or disproven. The decision to correct a client's factual set of information by imparting new, different, or additional information is a difficult one. Not all sets of factual information that meet one of the criteria (that is, are incomplete, inadequate, or incorrect) need to be addressed. If they are irrelevant to the issue at hand, are not part of why the client seeks treatment, or seem to play no role in the client's presenting concern, the clinician may not feel obliged to correct the client. However, if the imparting of information may lead to a revision, updating, expansion, or completion of a factual set of information for the client, which in turn may lead the client to have a different response to a situation that is related to or relevant for the presenting concern, such an intervention may not only be appropriate but necessary.

In using this strategy, counselors need to be careful to not come across as condescending or arrogant. Sharing information is a joyful and helpful process, not a means of demonstrating superior knowledge or greater value or skill. However, because clients may perceive the imparting of information as something that demonstrates that they are less educated or "smart" than their therapist, it is used sparingly and when used is done matter-of-factly and carefully.

Before imparting information it is always useful to be certain about what the client does and does not know. Sometimes clients may appear to know less than they do. Then imparting information would be ill advised because the client actually knows but just does not disclose. Therefore, imparting information is best done in manner that looks like a joint exploration of a subject to which both client and clinician contribute what they know. This way the discussion is balanced and the clinician is not perceived as merely "preaching" or "lecturing" to the client.

TABLE
8-3

IMPARTING INFORMATION: PSYCHOEDUCATION, NORMALIZATION, AND RELABELING

Issue	Psychoeducation	Normalization	Relabeling
Clinician action	Impart knowledge the client did not previously have	Impart knowledge that shows that the client's reactions, feelings, and so forth, fall within the range of what would normally be expected in a similar situation	Provide an alternative label or viewpoint for data presented by the client to provide a new wisdom that frames the problem or issue in a new way
Desired outcome or purpose	Alter the client's perception or interpretations of, or reaction or behavior to, a given situation or issue	Help the client accept own reaction to and decrease concern over a given situation or reaction to an event	Give the client a new perspective to create a cognitive shift in the perception or interpretation of a given situation
Cautions or shortcomings	Knowledge may not suffice for the client to change behavior or perception	Client may refuse to classify self with others with the same experience and hence may not alter perception or reaction	Client may not be open to or may reject the new label or frame due to limited cognitive complexity or emotional readiness
Potential pitfalls	Clinician may be perceived as arrogant, condescending, judgmental, blaming, or lecturing	Clinician may be perceived as belittling the client's concern or as nonempathic to the client's pain	Clinician may be perceived as judgmental, nonempathic, or misunderstanding
Helpful hints for implementation	• Matter-of-fact presentation • Well-timed and sequenced presentation • Brief presentation • Respectful attitude • No "one-upping" • Placed in a larger therapeutic context • Collaborative work	• Use sparingly • Never be dishonest • Never mislead client into believing something is normal that is not • Do not overuse lest credibility is lost • Use only in a larger therapeutic context • Fact, not opinion	• Keep as concrete as possible • Never argue with a client who refuses to accept the new frame or label • Try to get the client to come up with a new label or frame through questioning • Stay as objective and factual as possible

Imparting information can take at least three forms. These three forms can occur separately or may co-occur in a single intervention. A comparison and overview is provided in Table 8-3.

Psychoeducation

First, imparting information can focus on providing information the client does not (yet) have about a psychological or development process, a strategy often referred to as psychoeducation. Psychoeducation is often a strategy of choice for group therapy interventions, and is the process that occurs in groups advertising parenting education, anger management, stress reduction, and so forth. Psychoeducation can occur in individual treatment whenever the clinician deems it important to give the client information about a particular topic, be that parenting, developmental milestones of children, facts about sexuality, or resources about relevant workshops in a community. The commonality of all psychoeducation rests in the fact that the clinician merely imparts objective information and does not make value judgments or give opinions, but merely informs the client about a topic area of relevance or concern. For example, a clinician working with an adolescent who is becoming sexually active may take the responsibility to talk with the client about contraception, sexually transmitted disease, and so forth. It is possible for psychoeducation to lead to a discussion of values. Hardly any topic of relevance is going to be free of values. However, the focus of the information imparting is strictly on objective facts of which the clinician is aware and the client appears not to be. Once the client has the facts, therapeutic work can be done around the behavior and whether the client wants to choose to engage in it. That is a separate issue and would no longer be considered imparting of information. Teasing out fact from opinion can be difficult at times. The best rule of thumb is that if information is based in knowledge gleaned from scientific sources (professional journals, professional conferences, textbooks), it can be considered more or less factual and objective; if it is based on popular sources (television, magazines, newspapers), it may better be considered opinion. If it appears to be opinion, the clinician should first do some reading in scientific sources before using imparting information as a strategy. Psychoeducation is never the only therapeutic strategy employed by a counselor. It is best kept brief and embedded in a larger therapeutic context.

Normalization

The second form of imparting information provides information about the universal or normal nature of a client reaction to a situation others have encountered as well, a strategy often referred to as normalization or universalization. This strategy can be used successfully when a client questions a reaction in the self that the clinician recognizes to be appropriate, perhaps even healthy. A common example of this form of imparting information is the educating of a rape victim about the normal stress response that follows the assault. Many women, in the aftermath of a rape or similar traumatic occurrence, question their adjustment, especially when others in their environment minimize the enormity of the experience. Helping a woman recognize that her reactions are completely within the norm of what other women in similar situations experience can be healing and calming. If more information is given about what to expect and how to prevent additional problems in the future, psychoeducation is being added to normalization.

The label of what clinicians are doing is less important than the recognition that they are imparting information and hence need to remain objective, factual, and as free of values as possible. Once the information has been shared, processing may occur that deals with the value-laden and decision-making (that is, truly therapeutic) aspects of the situation at hand.

One important caution is indicated here. A therapist must never normalize or universalize a client response that is not healthy, adaptive, or common, even if the client desperately wants the clinician to do so. If a client's reaction falls out of the norm of what counselors might expect, they must not be tempted into saying that the reaction is normal because the client is asking for such feedback. Normalization is used sparingly, never used dishonestly, and not used in isolation but only contextually.

Relabeling

Third, imparting information can consist of providing an alternative label or viewpoint for a situation with which the client is struggling, a process that is often called relabeling, reframing, or refocusing. An example of the use of this strategy may be to relabel as "protective" a parent whom the client labeled as "nosey." Similarly, reframing may consist of the clinician labeling the client who refers to the self as "cowardly" as "careful" or "cautious." The new label changes the perspective, basically giving the client a new way to look at old data. In that sense it imparts information, information about how to look at the same situation through a different filter. It could be argued that this strategy goes somewhat beyond imparting of information as it may not be entirely factual, but may begin to introduce some subjective reinterpretation of a situation by the clinician. It is not important to settle this argument. What is important is to understand that the strategy should stay as objective and factual as possible. If the client truly was "cowardly," the clinician would not have chosen to reframe; the new label of "cautious" would only be suggested if the clinician truly believed it to be a more accurate description of reality. In other words, reframing or relabeling needs to be so clear-cut that consensus would likely exist across practitioners as to its appropriateness. If the clinician wonders whether the reframing or relabeling reflects personal values or may be inaccurate, it may be better not to use it. On the other hand, some subjectivity may enter all of these strategies and thus it is difficult to tease out when relabeling stops being a strategy of imparting information. Perhaps one of the most important issues is to make sure that the reframing process is presented in such a way that the client can understand what the clinician understands, both cognitively and emotionally. That is, the suggestion of a different label or of a different way of looking at a situation must resonate with the client to be effective. If the client cannot understand what the clinician is trying to do because the counselor presents the new label in a way that exceeds the client's cognitive capacity, then the strategy will obviously fail. Similarly, a client may not be emotionally ready to let go of a particular way of labeling or viewing a situation. In such a situation, the strategy will not lead to the desired outcome. At each step the clinician is advised not to argue with a client who rejects an attempt at relabeling or reframing.

Sample Transcript of Imparting Information

The sample transcript that follows shows how a clinician uses imparting information to arrive at a therapeutic aim. The sample shows how mental-health-care providers frequently mix psychoeducation, normalization, and relabeling in imparting information. It also demonstrates a collaborative way of imparting information in that both client and clinician share what knowledge they have. This approach reduces the risk of the client feeling "dumb" or lectured to. As each form of imparting information is used, it is identified in parentheses to help the reader follow what is happening. The sample also includes a few inappropriate uses of imparting information (also clearly labeled as such) to show how easy it is to misuse these strategies. The reader is encouraged to review Table 8-3 one more time, with particular attention to the cautions and potential pitfalls of each of these strategies.

> CLIENT: I am just not ready to do that, but my husband is really pushing me to do it. It's actually pretty scary, you know.
> CLINICIAN: Tell me more. . . .
> CLIENT: Well, this is how it is. He thinks that the best way to go is to have a mammogram every six months. But I'm really afraid of the radiation exposure. I guess we have always had a different approach about that kind of thing.
> CLINICIAN: You have?
> CLIENT: Yes. I don't really believe in just using traditional medicine for anything, but he obviously does. I mean he is a surgeon after all. I guess I should be glad that he doesn't just want me to go ahead and have a preventive mastectomy.
> CLINICIAN: Was that an option you discussed?

CLIENT: Yes, but even he seemed disinclined. . . . Just because of a benign lump—That would be pretty radical.

CLINICIAN: Why the mammograms?

CLIENT: Well, he thinks that because my mother died from breast cancer and now I had this lump removed I'm at pretty high risk. . . .

CLINICIAN: What do you think your risk is? (*exploring whether the client has sufficient information or if she needs more*)

CLIENT: Oh, I know he is right. I am high risk. There's my mother, my history of lumps. . . .

CLINICIAN: Anything else? (*following up on the need for education here*)

CLIENT: Well, it's kind of embarrassing, but I don't really know what other risk factors he's talking about. He just says to believe him. I guess I ought to be looking into that a bit. . . .

CLINICIAN: That's a great idea. It always helps to learn about things you have to make decisions about. Would you like me to run through some of the risk factors with you?

CLIENT: Oh, do you know them? That would be great.

CLINICIAN: Well, I know a few more that we can talk about. But I still think it would be a good idea for you to check out more, regardless of what we come up with, okay? You know I'm not a physician. . . .

CLIENT: I know. . . . What are some other risks?

CLINICIAN: Well, let's see. There is diet. What kind of diet do you have?

CLIENT: (*explains her diet in detail; clinician follows up with a number of questions*)

CLINICIAN: (*explains which aspects of the client's diet appear to be associated with higher risk and which appear helpful*) (*psychoeducation*)

CLIENT: Anything else besides diet?

CLINICIAN: Well, there is risk associated with how many years a woman actively ovulates. So we could look at when you started menstruating, how many pregnancies you had, and things like that

CLIENT: (*provides information in detail; clinician follows up with a few additional questions*)

CLINICIAN: (*responds with what the client's information may mean*) (*psychoeducation*)

CLIENT: Wow, this is a lot of information. Is there more?

CLINICIAN: There can be environmental factors. Like exposure to certain chemicals, pollution, radiation exposure . . .

CLIENT: Yes, I know that! Well, you know, I guess I know more than I realized. I have been worried about radiation exposure. In fact, that's what the whole mammogram argument is about.

CLINICIAN: (*realizing her mistake of not catching this nuance sooner*) Of course. I should have picked up on that. You did mention that you worried about radiation exposure. Just X-rays, or other kinds, too?

CLIENT: Mainly X-rays. See, when I was a little girl I had breathing problems. Back then they didn't worry much about X-rays so I had lots of them. Of my lungs. Well, you can see my concern because when they X-ray your lungs, your whole chest is exposed.

CLINICIAN: Of course. So how many X-rays do you think you had?

CLIENT: Oh, at least two a year for several years there. I've lost track. I'd really have to think about it. Maybe there weren't really all that many. So I guess you must think I'm nuts for worrying so much about X-rays. My husband does. I guess maybe I'm a little extreme. But it really scares me!

CLINICIAN: It seems to me that you are not excessively scared. Your concerns seem very reasonable and realistic to me. (*Normalization*)

CLIENT: They do?! (*relieved*) So do you think I should have the mammograms?

CLINICIAN: That's not a decision anyone can make for you. It's your body and you'll have to decide that for yourself. What do you think you need to do? It's your decision. . . .

CLIENT: Well, my husband doesn't think so. He thinks he should make the decision for me because he is the physician and he knows better. You know, he is smarter about these things than I and so I should listen to him. . . .

CLINICIAN: Is that what you want?

CLIENT: Well, not really. But I know he's just worried about me. He just wants to help me make this decision. . . .

CLINICIAN: He wants to control your decision. (*an inappropriate relabeling that reflects a value judgment on the clinician's part*)

CLIENT: Oh . . . Oh my . . . Do you think so? He can be controlling, you know. It comes with his job. (*a little defensive*)

CLINICIAN: My apologies. That was a little judgmental on my part. Do you perceive it as controlling? (*apologizes but realizes she cannot take the judgment back, so tries to work with it*)

CLIENT: Well, I never thought of it as controlling.

CLINICIAN: Okay, then it probably isn't—my mistake. So your husband may be trying to be helpful in the best way he can, and he thinks you should have the mammogram. What would you like to do? (*getting back to the issue at hand*)

CLIENT: I don't want it! I am scared of it! My sister is refusing them. My husband calls her extreme.

CLINICIAN: Do you think that's a fair label? (*tries to get client to relabel on her own*)

CLIENT: No. I think she is being smart and cautious! (*client does the job*)

CLINICIAN: That does seem to be a better perspective on her behavior. . . .

CLIENT: Yeah; she knows what she's talking about. She gave me some studies to read that show that mammograms can create problems because of the radiation and that they can spread existing disease.

CLINICIAN: It's good for you to realize that you have information already. Earlier you seemed to imply that you didn't. . . .

CLIENT: Oh, I forget sometimes. You know, my sister and I, we read a lot about mammograms after Mom died because we were trying to figure out what we should do. Being high risk and all.

CLINICIAN: Back then what did you decide?

CLIENT: That it wasn't worth it. In other countries they don't recommend annual mammograms anymore. I forget why. I wish I could remember details like that better. . . .

CLINICIAN: Because they don't really extend life span. They may detect disease earlier, but they do not extend lifespans, and they can increase risk due to radiation. *(psychoeducation that may or may not have been appropriate because the client may have been able to retrieve the information from her memory with a bit of prodding)*

CLIENT: That's it. Now I remember. They also detect a certain kind of cancer that may not ever even do anything to the woman.

CLINICIAN: CIS, carcinoma in situ. Cancers that are well encapsulated and may never spread and grow.

CLIENT: Right, the kind they used to find in autopsies of women who died of old age or other things but not because of cancer.

CLINICIAN: Right. And so the theory is that these kind of cancers are now overdetected and overoperated on. *(psychoeducation that was unnecessary and may have been perceived as trying to sway the client in a certain direction in her decision making)*

CLIENT: Yes, I remember these things now. I'm glad you are helping me fill in the gaps. I really think I'm going to just keep doing what I've been doing. No mammograms, just monthly self-exams.

CLINICIAN: That is how you found this recent lump, isn't it?

CLIENT: Yes. I hate doing them, you know. . . .

CLINICIAN: The monthly self-exams?

CLIENT: Yeah. I am always terrified of what I might find. Crazy, isn't it?

CLINICIAN: Seems pretty understandable to me. *(Normalization)*

CLIENT: Really? Do other women go through this agony every month?

CLINICIAN: Many women with your history probably do. *(repeats the normalization)*

CLIENT: Well, that's it then. I'll keep doing the BSE [breast self-exam] and I won't do the mammograms. I think that's a good course of action. What do you think?

CLINICIAN: Does it feel right to you?

CLIENT: Yes, though I have to say I wish there were other things I could do.

CLINICIAN: Well, there might be. There are other methods of detection. They are not all perceived as acceptable by traditional physicians but many women swear by them, as do some alternative physicians and a number of researchers.

CLIENT: Wow. I haven't heard that. What else is there?

CLINICIAN: Well, for one thing there are ultrasounds. They are safe and can be quite effective in detecting certain types of lumps. There are also devices that you can use to make your BSE more sensitive. *(adds more psychoeducation about nontraditional methods of early detection)*

CLIENT: Wow. I will check some of these things out.

CLINICIAN: Do that. You will have to make your own choices, but it helps to be fully informed.

(Session continues from there.)

This transcript shows how imparting information can be done in a back-and-forth manner so that it does not feel like a lecture to the client. Therapist and client collaboratively help the client fill in knowledge gaps that may be important to her decision making. The transcript also demonstrates that imparting information is obviously only possible if the clinician is informed and has information to share. A clinician who knows nothing about breast cancer or mammograms could not have helped the client in the same way as this counselor. She would have had to encourage the client to seek out information on her own and then would have had to do some reading herself. It is very dangerous to impart information that is opinion-based rather than based on fact. Many clinicians might have fallen into the trap of agreeing with the husband's recommendation based on popular opinion and media exposure. Luckily for this client, her clinician was informed and thus able to lead the client to make her own decision. The transcript also demonstrates the fine line between fact and opinion. Much of what clinicians perceive as fact is actually opinion, often based on information shared by the popular media. Since the popular media are not always accurate in their representation of scientific fact, clinicians need to be aware that when they impart information they need to have a source for that information other than television, newspapers, and magazines.

Pointing Out Patterns

Pointing out patterns is about raising client's awareness to the reality that there are certain habitual ways of relating or responding that have developed over time in the person's life and that may or may not be adaptive and useful. For clinicians to be able to use this very effective strategy, they obviously have to be attuned to the fact that clients manifest such patterns to begin with. It is helpful to explore where, why, and how patterns tend to emerge.

Clients may manifest at least four types of repetitive themes or patterns in their lives (cf., Teyber, 1997). The first kind of pattern that may be noticed is *relational patterns*. Relational patterns are interpersonal scenarios that the client plays out over and over again with a variety of people in a variety of contexts. For example, a clinician has identified a relational pattern if noticing that a client reacts with hostility to all authority figures, or that a client becomes anxious around all people of the opposite gender. These are examples of very simple interpersonal patterns that are often easily recognized. At times, interpersonal patterns can be subtler. For example, an interpersonal or relational pattern is present if a client tells multiple stories of having been used by friends. The clinician may recognize after a few of these stories that the client appears overly sensitive to being taken advantage of and may actually misinterpret friends' actions or intent. Relational patterns are some of the more easily recognized patterns, especially since they may even be detected or played out in the relationship with the clinician.

A second type of pattern that clients can manifest is one that consists of *rigid cognitive beliefs*. These core beliefs underlie and maintain a repetitive pattern of reactions that may include behaviors or emotions and that reflect selective and repetitive bias in cognitive processing. These patterns may only become clear as cognitive patterns after the clinician has recognized that a variety of apparently diverse behaviors, reactions, and affects are actually all traceable to the same basic underlying cognitive belief or distortion. The clinician may not recognize the common thread that ties these diverse events together until suddenly the connection becomes clear. For example, a client may have told the clinician of feeling enraged after a certain event in her life. The next session, the same client may report having overslept several times that week. Finally, she may relate having experienced a severe lapse in self-confidence after a particular work incident. The clinician may not recognize until some thorough exploration of the events and the client's reaction to them that the same cognitive pattern explains all of the client's reactions: her anger, her oversleeping, and her lapse in self-confidence. Specifically, the clinician may recognize that during or after each event, the client (inappropriately or irrationally) took all blame for the occurrence on her own shoulders, reinforcing her belief that she is not performing up to her own standards for herself. One reaction to her self-blame may be rage or anger about perceived slights in the other person involved in the event, a not-uncommon way in which clients externalize (or project) self-blame; another may be excessive concern about future work performance which leads her to oversleep as a means of avoiding work altogether; another and most obvious tie can be made to the client's fading self-esteem. Thus, there are three apparently different responses, but one underlying cognitive theme of self-blame and over-assumption of responsibility.

A third type of pattern that can emerge is related to *core affects.* Core affects are long-standing and recurring, reflecting an affective style that is maintained by the client across situations and contexts, regardless of circumstances. Such a client may respond with depression to all different types of situations, even those that are actually joyous or at least neutral. Core affects can also be called default affects and are described in the affect-related chapters. Core affects are generally easily recognizable as the client will manifest the affect in session with the clinician. They may be somewhat more subtle if the client is not aware of the affect but still has some outward expressions of it.

A final pattern is recognized in *habitual behavior.* Habitual behavior is basically similar in nature to core beliefs or default affects in that the client has a certain behavior pattern to which she or he resorts in any and all relational, cognitive, and affective contexts. No matter what the external event, the client responds with the same behavior. These patterns lead to almost-automatic responses that leave the client trapped in behaviors that have long outlived their adaptiveness and usefulness. For example, a client who yells when he is happy, yells when he is sad, or when things go wrong at work, or yells when he disagrees with his wife manifests a behavioral pattern. Clearly, behavioral patterns tend to be easily recognized as they will usually show up in session as well. The client in the example will sooner or later yell at the clinician, and the clinician will have a firsthand experience of how the client's behavioral pattern plays out in interpersonal contexts.

Although it is generally easy for clinicians to pick up on a client's patterns, it is surprisingly difficult for clients to recognize them. They often fail to realize that they react to certain people in the same way over and over again (relational pattern); they fail to be aware that the same thoughts tend to run through their minds in all different types of situations and with all different types of people (cognitive patterns); they do not recognize that they behave identically with many different people and in many contexts (behavioral patterns); in fact, they may not even be fully aware that they react with the same emotion to situations that do not elicit such an affective response in others (affective patterns).

Clients tend to develop patterns for a reason. Patterns usually served an adaptive function at their inception, which is often traceable to childhood learning or learning that was salient in adulthood. Patterns are reactions that are predictable and habitual and generally maladaptive. But they did not start out that way. They often started out as the client's best effort at self-protection and at dealing with difficult circumstances. Because of this history, patterns are difficult to break. The purpose of pointing out patterns is not their discontinuation. Instead, pointing out patterns has the primary purpose of helping clients become self-aware so that they can begin to recognize the patterns and to identify the habitual responding (whether affective, relational, cognitive, or behavioral) as it occurs. Once clients have become aware of how certain patterns repeat themselves in their lives and how they manifest either behaviorally, cognitively, affectively, or interpersonally, they will often become curious about why the pattern developed in the first place. This curiosity in turn often leads to explorations of the origins of the patterns and an explanation (or interpretation) of the purposes they once served. Once the client has recognized the original purpose as well as the outdatedness of that purpose, the pattern can usually disappear on it own. However, the simple strategy of pointing out patterns does not concern itself with this exploration, which is actually in the realm of confrontation, here-and-now processing, or interpretation.

The pointing out of patterns as a basic cognitive therapeutic technique simply consists of a therapist's repeating events, reactions, or contents the client has communicated over time to identify a common thread (relational, affective, cognitive, or behavioral) that ties all of them together. This common thread is pointed out to clients to help them recognize that apparently disconnected events or reactions are actually reflections of a single process or symptoms of a single problem. Once the pattern is pointed out, the client is encouraged to look for it on a day-to-day basis. If the client is open to it, this work will proceed quickly both in and outside of sessions. While in sessions, the clinician will continue to point out patterns that have now been identified to the client. This needs to be done respectfully and caringly so that the client does not feel judged or made fun of. As clients improve their detection skills they often begin to recognize patterns independently and then begin to recognize that they have response choices of which they were not previously aware. Thus, although the primary and initial goal of this basic strategy is merely awareness raising, the ultimate outcome is often insight and behavior change.

What follows is an example of a simple process of pointing out a pattern to a client who has a habitual way of relating to others. The example demonstrates the ease with which this strategy can be implemented. However, not all incidences of pointing out patterns are this straightforward. In fact, the next section (clarifying questions) will provide an example that uses careful questioning to point out a more subtle and less straightforward pattern in the same client.

> CLIENT: Well, that's pretty much all that happened. Dorothy hung up the phone. I haven't heard from her since.
> CLINICIAN: That's all? You disagreed about whether to go see a movie and she hung up on you?
> CLIENT: That about wraps it up.
> CLINICIAN: Nothing else happened?
> CLIENT: Nope.
> CLINICIAN: So, that's pretty similar to what happened with your mother last month, right? You were talking on the phone, and then suddenly she says she's done talking to you.

CLIENT: Yup. Said she didn't need to listen to me that way and hung up. . . .

CLINICIAN: Listen to you what way?

CLIENT: I don't know what she was talking about. . . .

CLINICIAN: You don't?

CLIENT: Nope.

CLINICIAN: Seems to me this has happened to you a few other times. I recall you said that your ex-wife used to storm out when you had arguments.

CLIENT: Yeah, she did. She just didn't like to argue, I think. You know, I think she just couldn't handle it when we disagreed. So her way of getting out of it was to just walk out.

CLINICIAN: And nothing you did made a difference?

CLIENT: I don't think so . . . but that was a few years ago, you know.

CLINICIAN: Have other people cut conversations short with you?

CLIENT: I'm not sure . . . at work maybe. Sometimes my boss says that she won't tolerate my talking to her like that and that we'll finish talking when I calm down.

CLINICIAN: When you calm down? What does she mean by that?

CLIENT: I guess I get a little worked up when I talk with her at times.

CLINICIAN: And what does that look like?

CLIENT: When I get worked up?

CLINICIAN: Uh huh . . .

CLIENT: Oh, I guess I get emphatic.

CLINICIAN: As in loud?

CLIENT: I guess so. . . . *(grins sheepishly)*

CLINICIAN: Isn't that what Dorothy said, too, the other day?

CLIENT: Yeah . . .

CLINICIAN: She said something about yelling, right?

CLIENT: I guess . . .

CLINICIAN: And I seem to recall that when we talked last time about the phone call with your mother, you said she said something like she didn't need to listen to you yell at her. . . . Am I remembering that right?

CLIENT: I suppose so. I guess I kinda forgot about that. . . .

CLINICIAN: So do you notice a pattern here? Do people really just stop talking to you randomly, or is there something else going on at the time?

CLIENT: A pattern? *(not wanting to admit to it)*

CLINICIAN: Yes, a pattern . . .

CLIENT: Like what?

CLINICIAN: Like you yelling and people deciding they don't want to be yelled at.

CLIENT: Yeah. Oh man, it was easier to think that they just quit talking to me because of no reason at all.

CLINICIAN: But I guess they have a reason, at least from their perspective, huh?

CLIENT: I suppose they do. No one likes a yeller.

CLINICIAN: No, not really. Could you see why they might want to quit talking to you when you yell?

CLIENT: Well, I do get pretty loud. . . .

CLINICIAN: And you are not exactly small. . . .

CLIENT: Do I intimidate?

CLINICIAN: What do you think?

CLIENT: Oh my god. You know, I do this with my kids, too. They just can't walk away from me because I don't let them.

CLINICIAN: Tell me more about that. *(Session continues from here.)*

This example shows how the clinician slowly helps the client recognize his own relational pattern. She had become aware of his tendency to raise his voice from interactions in session, as well as many different stories about relationships that had been problematic. However, she chose to point out the pattern cautiously and step by step, almost allowing the client to arrive at the recognition of the pattern on his own. When he showed himself disinclined to open his awareness to the fact that he yells a lot, she became increasingly direct about her observations and recollections. Finally, the client had to own the pattern and did so. The clinician could just have pointed the pattern out directly but believed that this lengthier and more indirect route of helping the client notice it on his own would be more impactful and effective. It is usually preferable to allow clients to recognize their patterns by pointing them out piece by piece as was done in this example, rather than to just hit them over the head with an observation. Clients are always more open to understandings, awarenesses, and insights that they actively help shape and unearth.

Asking Clarifying Questions

It is a somewhat arbitrary decision to call clarifying questions a strategy in their own right. Clarifying questions can essentially be used for any type of cognitive strategy, all the way from the most basic reframing (see example under *Imparting Information* above) to the most sophisticated interpretation (see interpretation sample in the next chapter). Since they can also be used in a way that may not be covered by the other techniques, it appeared best to include them as a separate strategy. Again, semantics are not important; the important issue is that the new mental-health-care provider knows how to use questions to work with thoughts and cognitions.

It may be best to start by briefly recalling how clarifying questions differ from open-ended questions and systematic inquiries. Open-ended questions have as their primary purpose to keep communication going between client and clinician. The clinician pursues areas of inquiry without having a clear goal or path in mind. Systematic inquiry is used to explore a certain topic area and is focused on collecting data or increasing the fund of information the clinician has about the client. As was true for open-ended questions, the clinician has no preconceived notion about where the questioning will lead and is not trying to lead the client down a particular path or toward a particular insight. Clarifying questions, on the other hand, are planfully and purposefully asked to lead the client to a recognition, insight, conceptualization, or understanding that the clinician has already developed about the client's thoughts, affects, behaviors, or relationships. The clinician uses clarifying questions to prod the client toward an understanding the clinician has gained about the client that the client does not yet have but seems capable of deducing with some help. When using clarifying questions, the therapist has a goal in mind; the counselor is leading the client down a predetermined path of self-discovery. Clarifying questions are the essential therapeutic strategy that is used to allow clients to come up with their own insights and to own their own discoveries in treatment. It is through the use of clarifying questions that clinicians invite clients to make discoveries about themselves that were really already present in their mind but had not yet been verbalized or consciously formulated. It is the ultimate strategy for allowing clients to own their own progress and to take credit for their own discoveries, awareness, insights, and progress. Sometimes clients will recognize that the clinician led them to an insight through questioning; often, however, they will not be aware that they were coached to a discovery. The latter situation is preferable as it will lead to the truest ownership of the understanding or insight achieved by the client. If the client does recognize that the clinician led through questioning, it will be helpful to downplay the counselor's role in leading the client to the insight and to encourage the client to take credit for the discovery.

It is, of course, the very fact that clarifying questions allow the client to take credit for a therapeutic understanding or insight that makes these kinds of questions so useful in the realm of cognitive work and that makes them the primary means of implementing most other cognitive strategies. Thus, although the primary purpose of clarifying questions can be defined as a strategy that leads the client to an insight or understanding at which the clinician had already arrived, clarifying questions can also be used for many other purposes. Specifically, they can lead to the same desired outcomes and meet the same goals as strategies that

- educate
- reframe
- normalize
- point out patterns

- problem-solve
- generate solutions
- reveal contradictions
- uncover incongruence
- result in insights about habitual patterns of relating
- reveal transferences
- explain behaviors, thoughts, affects, and interactions
- create understanding and self-awareness
- create insight about causes for behaviors, thoughts, affect, and interactions

In other words, clarifying questions can be used for psychoeducation, relabeling, universalization, pointing out patterns, confrontation, here-and-now process, and interpretations. As such, they can be very basic techniques for working with cognition and thought, or they can be highly advanced techniques. They are truly the bridge between the less and more complex cognitive strategies. There is nothing magical about how clarifying questions are phrased. All of the cautions mentioned in the chapter about questions in general apply here; thus, it may be useful for the reader to reread Chapter Five at this time. Perhaps the most important rule of thumb, and the only one that will be reiterated here, is the rule about avoiding "why" questions whenever possible. There may be times when a "why" question is appropriate. For the most part, however, clients will be less defensive and less likely to feel judged if alternative phrasing is chosen. Beyond that, clarifying questions can take just about any form as long as they avoid the pitfalls mentioned in Chapter Five (suggestive, assumptive, pseudo, judgmental, attacking, controlling, intrusive, tangential, content-diverse multiple, and shotgun questions).

The example that follows uses clarifying questions to build upon the example provided in the *Pointing Out Patterns* section above. The continuation of the transcript, from a later session with the same client, will show how careful, clarifying questioning can be used to help clients recognize that patterns often coexist. For example, a habitual way of relating may actually be accompanied by a core belief about people. What may initially have looked like a single pattern thus evolves into a complex fabric of patterns that interrelate and maintain each other. As clients become aware of one, they often become more conscious of the others. Similarly, as one pattern is abandoned, others will drop away as well. The example shows that clients may be aware of certain patterns within themselves without understanding why they occur. Careful questioning can guide the client toward recognizing some of the contributing factors. Sometimes when they are helped to realize through questions that there is a second, perhaps more subtle and underlying, pattern, they suddenly understand the more obvious one (that is, gain some insight, not just awareness) and begin to move toward behavior change.

CLIENT: So it happened again this week. I screamed at my boss again. Now, she had told me if this happened one more time I'd be fired. But she didn't do it. God, I'm glad she forgot she said that!

CLINICIAN: How did it come about?

CLIENT: I don't know. Before I knew it, I was yelling. I do that a lot and I really cannot for the life of me figure out why it happens. It's like something snaps and there I go. I really have been trying to figure it out. You know, you and I have talked about this yelling thing so many times now. Ever since you pointed it out to me I have been noticing it more and more. You were absolutely right—I yell all the time. I yell at my kids, I yell at people when I'm driving, I yell at my ex-wife—of course that one's normal, isn't it? *(grins at his own joke)* So what's it all about, doc?

CLINICIAN: My guess is you don't always yell. So how about we start by looking at when you do and when you don't?

CLIENT: I yell with my kids, I yell with my boss, I yell with everyone. I do always yell. . . .

CLINICIAN: You're not yelling now. . . .

CLIENT: Oh . . .

CLINICIAN: What else can you tell me about when you yelled at your boss this time?

CLIENT: Well, we were working on a project that's due next Monday and she got a phone call. She took a long time and I just kept working. Then she came back and somehow we got into it. It just happened just like that.

CLINICIAN: Okay now. Here is a question. I remember you telling me about yelling at Terry last week. Can you remind me. . . .

CLIENT: *(client interrupts)* Yeah, he had come into my room while I was working on the cabinet I'm making for my parents for their anniversary next month. I'm kind of behind on the work. Anyway, Terry came in and wanted me to take him to the movie theater. Now I had told him earlier in the day that there was no extra time in my day and that he needed to get one of his friend's parents to take them. Well, anyway it just all came out in a big screaming match.

CLINICIAN: And the time you told me about when you yelled at Jamie . . .

CLIENT: *(client interrupts)* Oh, two weeks ago? Well, she was supposed to pick up the kids at three, like every Saturday. Well, she showed up at four, and I was pissed because I was supposed to be at work, the other job, you know, by four. So she made me late again! That's just her irresponsibility. She was like that when we were married so why would I think it would be any different now?

CLINICIAN: *(not allowing the derailment)* Now I also remember some kind of shouting match recently with your mother?

CLIENT: Uh huh. Boy, that's a while ago now. I don't remember much of

the specifics. I just know that I was really pressed for time because . . .
(stops suddenly) Oh shit!

CLINICIAN: Yes?

CLIENT: I just got it. Did you know all along?

CLINICIAN: No, I only just put it together today too. . . .

CLIENT: *(client interrupts)* I don't yell all the time. I yell when I'm
stressed out.

CLINICIAN: When your mind tells you you don't have time . . .

CLIENT: Right!

CLINICIAN: So the pattern is really about you telling yourself you don't
have time . . .

CLIENT: Well, but then I really don't . . .

CLINICIAN: Let's look at that, I guess. Do you ever feel like you don't
have time and don't yell?

CLIENT: Yeah. I feel pressed for time right now. You know, I got lots of
stuff to finish up today and being here makes me short of time.

CLINICIAN: But you're not yelling . . .

CLIENT: No because I figure somehow it'll all get done. It always does.

CLINICIAN: So what's different, between right now and those times when
you do yell? *(moving into using clarifying [that is, has some idea where
this might lead] or open-ended [that is, is not entirely certain of the path]
questions for here-and-now processing)*

CLIENT: I'm not sure. I guess that's the million-dollar question. *(grins)*
For some reason right now I can tell myself "yes, it will all get done," but
the other times I just can't seem to do that.

CLINICIAN: So what makes the difference? What are you aware of right
now, that helps you say "it will get done"? *(using open-ended questions
now to explore here-and-now process; that is, no longer is sure about
where the client's answers will lead) (Session continues from there.)*

This example shows how clients can be led to recognize their own patterns
through skillful questioning. It also demonstrates that to recognize patterns,
especially patterns within patterns, clinicians have to have a good memory for
detail. It was only because the clinician suddenly remembered that all examples of yelling also contained some form of time pressure that she could
guide the client in the right direction. The pattern that ultimately became the
focus of the session was that of time pressure. In the prior session, it had been
the pattern of yelling, a more obvious and perhaps destructive pattern. The
recognition that a cognitive pattern underlay the behavioral patterns led to an
exploration of the cognitive pattern. Once the client recognized the meaning
of the self-imposed time pressures and other cognitive patterns that went along
with it, he became increasingly self-aware and ultimately able to change his
overt behavior.

Skill Development Recommendations

Recommendation 8-1 *Pick a topic area that you think will be likely to come up with the clientele with which you anticipate working (for example, sexually transmitted disease or birth control if working with adolescents, or disease prevention if working with aging adults). Check the popular media and the scientific literature about this topic and write down what you learned from each. What did you learn that was new? What did you learn that surprised you? Was the information derived from scientific sources different from that in the media? Was the information you had about the topic before you did this search fact-based or opinion-based?*

Recommendation 8-2 *Pick a possible new label (as you would in reframing) for the following adjectives that are commonly used by clients. Your new label needs to represent a shift in perspective that would be derived from new facts or new ways of looking at old data.*

Examples:	meddling	concerned
	intrusive	protective
	passive	laid-back
Reframe:	uninvolved	_____
	controlling	_____
	interfering	_____
	rigid	_____
	unprincipled	_____
	overemotional	_____
	cold	_____
	unfeeling	_____
	angry	_____
	careless	_____
	scattered	_____
	thoughtless	_____
	heartless	_____
	distant	_____

Recommendation 8-3 *To train yourself to detect patterns, begin to look for patterns in yourself, your friends, and your family members. Pay attention to patterns in behavior, thought, affect, and relationships. As you detect patterns, attempt to determine how and why they may have developed, what function they used to serve, and how they are working right now.*

Just to reiterate, although this example focused on pointing out a pattern, clarifying questions can be used not only to point out patterns. They also can be used to help clients arrive at virtually any conclusion or point the clinician had already reached. Thus, clarifying questions are often also used in conjunction with more advanced cognitive techniques. The alert reader will find many clarifying questions in the examples in the next chapter. It might be useful (though somewhat nitpicky) to note that sometimes the mental-health-care provider will not know exactly where the client will end up in exploring a particular contradiction, here-and-now event, or potential explanation of behavior, affect, thought, or interaction. In such cases, questions that are asked may better be labeled open-ended rather than clarifying.

WORKING WITH THOUGHT AND COGNITION

Advanced Interventions

> Interpretation is dependent upon the circumstances in which it occurs. . . . A strategy for finding a context may be essential to all interpretation as a condition for the very possibility of interpretation.
>
> *D. Hoy, 1978, pp. 69, 76*

The strategies presented in this chapter, namely confrontation, here-and-now process, and interpretation, are perhaps some of the most difficult interventions clinicians will use with clients. They are best not overused and certainly always need to be used in a larger context of thorough understanding, solid rapport, and profound caring. Since these strategies can be perceived by clients as more confrontational than the interventions presented thus far, they need to be used with skill and presented with caring. Establishing a context is critical for the optimal use of these strategies, especially for interpretation, but also for here-and-now process and confrontation. Of the three strategies, confrontation is easiest to learn and apply. Here-and-now process is the one most frequently used and most powerfully effective (at least usually). Interpretation tends to be one of the most overused strategies. It can be profoundly helpful when properly timed, and profoundly ineffective, even hurtful, if poorly timed or forced onto a client. When in doubt about the usefulness or timing of an interpretation, it is best not to use it.

The establishment of a context is the most difficult aspect of the use of these three advanced strategies. The application or implementation of the strategies proper is easy. The mechanics are simple and straightforward and not much different from those for other, simpler strategies. The establishment of a context is largely dependent upon a clinician's theoretical framework for conceptualizing clients' lives and presenting concerns. Any advanced cognitive intervention will reflect the clinician's preferred way of thinking about human behavior. Two hypothetical clinicians, working with the same hypothetical client, may both decide to intervene with the same strategy (for example, both may decide an

247

interpretation is in order). They will use the same or similar mechanics, but the content of what they are ultimately going to communicate to the client will differ according to their chosen theoretical orientation. For example, a cognitive behaviorist will use interpretations just as much or as often as a psychodynamically-oriented therapist (although the common perception is that interpretation is largely used by those who adhere to psychodynamic or psychoanalytic schools of thought). However, the two mental-health-care providers will differ in what they express in their interpretation. The cognitive behaviorist will focus the interpretation on learning histories, distorted thought processes, and similar concepts tied to the conceptualization chosen; the psychodynamic thinker will focus instead on childhood experience, relationships with parents, and resulting current transferences or projections. Neither clinician is wrong; neither is exclusively right. The reality is that there are many ways in which to interpret and understand human behavior. The most important issue ultimately is whether the clinician is consistent across time, has tailored the understanding to the client, does not force a perception on the client, and arrives at an understanding and explanation that resonates with and rings true to the client.

ESTABLISHMENT OF A CONTEXT FOR ADVANCED COGNITIVE INTERVENTION

Clinicians of any school of thought will be able to use confrontations, here-and-now process, and interpretations as long as they take the time to establish a proper context and to create an empathically correct understanding of the client. The nuances of whether cognitive behavioral, humanistic, existential, psychodynamic, or other jargon is used is much less critical than the issue of whether the client's understanding is correct and relevant to current experience. A responsible clinician will learn about as many conceptualization options as possible to arrive at a system of understanding clients that will encourage careful intake and conceptualization procedures. Regardless of the conceptualization underlying a cognitive intervention, it is best to communicate with the client without jargon. It is best to translate understandings into everyday language that is accessible for the client and does not dehumanize the client by being presented in mechanical language. A relatively nontheoretical framework for thorough assessment and conceptualization work is presented in Brems (1999) and Cormier and Cormier (1998); an exceptionally detailed and complex metatheoretical framework has been presented by Wilber (1993). A few brief guidelines will be suggested here, sufficient for the beginning clinician to understand what is involved and what still needs to be learned, and to begin to practice advanced cognitive strategies (that is, confrontation, here-and-now process, and interpretation), and perhaps to experiment with a variety of theoretical conceptualizations.

Most simply put, understanding a client is based on at least four steps or competencies.

1. First, the mental-health-care provider needs to learn as much about human nature and different ways of understanding it as possible.
2. Second, the therapist needs to develop a clinical procedure for establishing a detailed fund of information and knowledge about each client.
3. Third, the counselor uses the fund of information established about the client and the familiarity with numerous schools of thought about human behavior to arrive at a careful conceptualization that is tailored to and recognizes all of the client's specific circumstances.
4. Fourth, the clinician keeps the conceptualization of each individual client in mind during all work with that person and uses all strategies within the context of that understanding to keep interventions experience-near for the client.

Step One Toward Building Context

The first step toward competency minimally requires that clinicians become familiar with the most commonly used theoretical schools of thought. Mental-health-care providers need to read about and gain a thorough understanding of the basic underlying principles and conceptualizations espoused by psychodynamic/psychoanalytic theory, humanism, existentialism, cognitive behavioral theory, rational emotive theory, behaviorism, learning theory/social-learning theory and modeling, systems theory, and perhaps transpersonal psychology. Suggested resources for this process follow.

Primary References:
- *Analytical psychology: Its theory and practice.* (Jung, 1968)
- *Casebook of multimodal therapy.* (Lazarus, 1985)
- *Cognitive therapy: Basics and beyond.* (Beck, 1995)
- *Ericksonian methods: The essence of the story.* (Zeig, 1994)
- *Family therapy techniques.* (Minuchin and Fishman, 1981)
- *Flash of insight: Metaphor and narrative in therapy.* (Pearce, 1996)
- *Focusing.* (Gendlin, 1981)
- *Gestalt therapy integrated.* (Polster and Polster, 1973)
- *Gestalt therapy verbatim.* (Perls, 1969)
- *How does analysis cure?* (Kohut, 1984)
- *International handbook of behavior modification and therapy.* (Bellak, Herson, and Kazdin, 1990)
- *Interpersonal process in psychotherapy: A relational approach.* (Teyber, 1997)

- *On becoming a person.* (Rogers, 1961)
- *Paradoxical psychotherapy.* (Weeks and L'Abate, 1982)
- *Process experiential psychotherapy.* (Greenberg, 1994)
- *Psychosynthesis.* (Assaglioli, 1965)
- *The practice and theory of individual psychology.* (Adler, 1969)
- *The practice of multimodal therapy.* (Lazarus, 1981)
- *The practice of rational-emotive therapy (RET).* (Ellis and Dryden, 1987)
- *The structure of magic (Volumes I and II).* (Bandler and Grinder, 1975)
- *The will to meaning: Foundations and applications of logotherapy.* (Frankl, 1969)
- *Treating the self: Elements of clinical self psychology.* (Wolf, 1988)
- *Toward a psychology of being.* (Maslow, 1968)
- *Zen and the heart of psychotherapy.* (Rosenbaum, 1999)

Secondary References:
- *Counseling psychology.* (Gelso and Fretz, 1992)
- *Current psychotherapies.* (Corsini and Wedding, 1997)
- *Foundations of clinical and counseling psychology.* (Todd and Bohart, 1994).
- *Introduction to therapeutic counseling.* (Kottler and Brown, 1992)
- *Personality theory and psychopathology.* (Rychlak, 1984)

Although most clinicians will ultimately develop a preference for one or two schools of thought over the others, it is important to recognize that it is the client and the client's presentation that should determine the conceptualization of the case. Thus, for some clients the clinician's usually preferred school of thought may fall short; the responsible counselor will seek alternative explanations and understandings. Learning about different schools of thought does not mean committing to one and then forcing all clients to fit into that mold. It means learning to understand which school of thought and which strategies fit best for which client and then working out of that model consistently and empathically with that particular client. Thus, knowing many ways of conceptualizing client behavior is crucial to responsible mental-health work as it will prevent forcing clients into a mold. Rogers' adage that "if the clinician only has a hammer, all problems will look like a nail" has perfect applicability here. The clinician needs as many tools as possible to respond flexibly and adaptively to the unique presentation and development of each and every client. The ability to apply a particular way of thinking about human behavior and to recognize which understanding is most appropriate for a given client requires cognitive flexibility on the part of the clinician as well as creative thought, the ability to think outside of a box, and sufficient information about the client to work with confidence and clarity.

Step Two Toward Building Context

Not surprisingly then, the second step toward establishing competency in creating a proper context for advanced cognitive work minimally requires the development of a thorough intake procedure based on systematic inquiry to build an adequate data base about the client. Optimally, the intake interview would be supplemented as needed by additional special assessments centered around special issues such as substance use, medical interface, mental status, complex psychological symptomatology, and crisis issues (for example, suicide or violence). This thoroughness in data collection will ascertain that the mental-health-care provider has collected sufficient information to understand the client's workings and to conceptualize the client's life and presenting concern as accurately as possible. Review of Table 5-4—data to be collected in an intake interview—in this new context may help counselors absorb the information in a new light. The intake is not just a tedious process imposed on the client for an arbitrary purpose, but is actually the basic building block of all therapeutic work that is to follow. If therapists do not collect thorough intake data, their conceptualizations will likely reflect their personal beliefs about how humans develop and behave in general, rather than reflecting the specific realities and circumstances of that particular client. It is when intake data are incomplete that the clinician works only with a "hammer" and every client becomes a "nail." The more data the clinician has available about the given client, the more likely that the client will be recognized and appreciated as a complex human being with a complex and detailed history that makes the client much more than a simple nail that can be fixed by a simple stroke of a hammer. The clinician will make use of a much larger toolbox, selecting the specific tool that is appropriate to the client's specific concern and its etiology or background.

For example, two clients may present with the same symptoms of depression; both have difficulty sleeping, decreased experience of pleasure in activities they used to enjoy, loss of appetite and weight, difficulty rousing themselves in the morning, and a tendency toward withdrawal from social interaction. It would be easy for clinicians to look at the two clients and to decide that they will benefit from the same treatment plan given their very similar presentation of pathology. However, thorough data collection may reveal that these two clients have very different life circumstances, both current and past, and actually have two very different types of depression despite their similar symptoms. One client may come from a deprived childhood home that never facilitated the development of a healthy, vigorous self upon which the client could draw during times of stress. This client has always been vulnerable to depression and has a personality style that reflects a basic insecurity and fragmentation that derives from the uncertainty experienced by the client in the family of origin during the client's shaping early years. The other client, however, may come from a psychologically nurturing home and may experience a depression that is not tied to a basic vulnerability in self development but to an existential recognition of life's finality and personal mortality. Perhaps this client was recently confronted with life-and-death issues due to a close family member's death or due to a personal medical crisis. The same symptoms may be presented but for a vastly different reason and superimposed on a vastly different personality structure. Only sufficient data collection will help the clinician recognize the profound differences in the meaning of the client's symptoms and the nature of the depression. Had the clients' childhoods not been explored, the clinician would not have been able to discern that one client has a vulnerable self while the other has a healthy self; had the clients' current life circumstances not been explored, the clinician would not have been able to discern that for one client existential issues play a role while for the other client much more basic issue were the crux of the presentation. Only thorough data collection prevents the clinician from making generalizations about symptoms and their development.

Thoroughness in intake interviewing sometimes goes even beyond the data suggested for collection in Table 5-4. Occasionally clients will present with special circumstances that beg for more information. Such circumstances include presentations that suggest the involvement of substance use, medical issues, violence, suicide, and similar crisis states. Assessment will have to be expanded accordingly and often exponentially to achieve a complete and accurate picture of such clients. Assessments necessary for special challenges are detailed in Brems (2000). Their discussion is beyond the scope of this book. An example, however, will suffice to point to their importance. It is possible that a third client will present with yet again the same depressive symptoms outlined above. In this case the therapist recognizes the need for questions regarding medical and substance use involvement. This additional data collection leads to the discovery that the client may actually suffer from hypothyroidism, a physical disorder that often presents with depressive symptomatology. Although psychotherapy or counseling may be profoundly helpful for the client for many reasons, the depression would never be resolved without the recognition of the physical involvement and appropriate medical treatment. The use of the most profound and well-meaning affective and cognitive strategies would fall short of helping this client combat a depression that is physiologically-based. A skilled counselor will have asked enough additional questions to have recognized the need for a medical referral and, thus, will have laid the groundwork for the next step in this process of establishing a context, namely, accurate and relevant conceptualization and treatment planning.

Step Three Toward Building Context

The third step toward competency is that of accurate conceptualization and treatment planning. Clearly, this step is impossible without the second step, that is, without the collection of unbiased and detailed data about the client.

Once the data have been collected, they are collated in a manner that can be used to arrive at an understanding of the client based upon the client's unique life experience, biology, culture, and all other data points at hand. Such a conceptualization pays careful attention to the possible predisposing, precipitating, and perpetuating factors that are functioning in the client's life and that contribute to or explain the client's current presentation. It outlines the dynamics of the case, detailing intrapsychic factors, interpersonal matrix, and family-related dynamics that appear to relate to the client's presenting concern and way of being in the world. The conceptualization is not complete until it accounts for most if not all problems, behaviors, cognitions, and affects presented by the client (Weiss, 1993). It considers the context for each presenting problem, integrating all apparently separate parts of the client into one cohesive and holistic network of events and experiences that can explain even apparent inconsistencies or contradictions (Karoly, 1993). A good conceptualization is free of biases or stereotypes, keeping all attributions logical and rational (Olson, Jackson, and Nelson, 1997). In the words of Basch (1980), "A therapist should not make a [conceptualization] simply on the basis of the main complaint, nor should he [*sic*] center on a patient's symptom. The therapist should consider the context in which the complaint is made or in which the symptom occurs, for it is the context that often leads to an understanding of what is going on with the patient and of what needs to be done for him" (Basch, 1980, p. 121).

Dealing with case conceptualization in detail is beyond the scope of this book. The complexity of this issue is underscored by the fact that whole books have been written about this very topic (for example, Berman, 1997; Eells, 1997). However, understanding the purpose of a conceptualization will greatly enhance the clinician's ability to develop one. Hence, some of the preliminary and core questions that need to be answered through the conceptualization are offered here. If the clinician can answer most or all of these questions, therapy or counseling is possible and the use of advanced cognitive strategies is indicated and potentially successful.

Preliminary Questions to Be Answered
by a Case Conceptualization

- How did the client's thoughts, expectations, beliefs, affects, behaviors, and relationship patterns develop over the life span?
- What is the purpose served by the client's thoughts, expectations, beliefs, affects, behaviors, and relationship patterns in different situations, circumstances, and relationships?
- How do the client's thoughts, expectations, beliefs, affects, behaviors, and relationship patterns manifest in current relationships?
- How did the client's thoughts, expectations, beliefs, affects, behaviors, and relationship patterns manifest and solidify in past relationships?

- What is or was the potential or past adaptive value of the client's thoughts, expectations, beliefs, affects, behaviors, and relationship patterns?
- What benefits in general does the client derive from her or his thoughts, expectations, beliefs, affects, behaviors, and relationship patterns?
- What benefits does the client derive from her or his thoughts, expectations, beliefs, affects, behaviors, and relationship patterns in particular situations, circumstances, or relationships?
- What are the negative consequences in general of the client's thoughts, expectations, beliefs, affects, behaviors, and relationship patterns?
- What are the negative consequences in particular situations, circumstances, or relationships of the client's thoughts, expectations, beliefs, affects, behaviors, and relationship patterns?
- What are the coping patterns or styles that result from the client's thoughts, expectations, beliefs, affects, behaviors, and relationship patterns?
- What are the coping failures that result from the client's thoughts, expectations, beliefs, affects, behaviors, and relationship patterns?
- What types of expressed and unexpressed needs result from the client's thoughts, expectations, beliefs, affects, behaviors, and relationship patterns?
- What kinds of conflicts (both intrapsychic and interpersonal) have resulted or may result from the client's thoughts, expectations, beliefs, affects, behaviors, and relationship patterns?

Core Questions to Be Answered by a Case Conceptualization
- Given the answers to the preliminary questions, how are the client's presenting concerns best understood in terms of their development, purpose, and past and current manifestation?
- Given the answers to the preliminary questions, how are the client's other symptoms (not presented by the client as problematic but identified by the clinician) best understood in terms of their development, purpose, and manifestation?
- Given the answers to the preliminary questions, what has predisposed the client for her or his presenting concerns and other symptoms?
- Given the answers to the preliminary questions, what has precipitated the development of the client's presenting concerns and other symptoms?
- Given the answers to the preliminary questions, what factors in the client's life are perpetuating the existence of the client's presenting concerns and other symptoms?

A conceptualization that can answer most, if not all, of these preliminary and core questions provides a more-than-adequate foundation from which to begin therapeutic work with a client. A conceptualization of this nature must be clearly differentiated from a diagnosis; the terms diagnosis and conceptualization must not be used interchangeably, though many writers unfortunately continue to do so. A conceptualization is much broader than a diagnosis. A diagnosis looks at a client's symptoms and then arrives at a label that will be used to classify the client's behavior within a particular diagnostic category, using some form of diagnostic categorization (such as the DSM-IV [American Psychiatric Association, 1994]). A conceptualization, on the other hand, looks at why, when, with whom, and how a client's presenting concern developed and manifests and is not concerned with how best to label the client (also see Brems, 1999). Diagnosis does not lead to treatment planning; conceptualization does. Conceptualization is a necessary prerequisite for the determination of an individual treatment plan. The development of a treatment plan is a process, not a single static decision, and it is highly contextual and flexible. It results in choices regarding desirable treatment goals and outcomes, as well as decisions about how to achieve these end states. This how-to translates into choices of strategies and interventions and is directly related to and relevant for the next step in context development.

Step Four Toward Building Context

The fourth step in competent therapeutic work requires translating the correct understanding of the client into content that permeates the strategies that will be chosen from here on out. In other words, once clinicians have arrived at a detailed and accurate conceptualization of a client's presentation, they are ready to begin treatment, using interventions that move beyond simple communication-facilitating work. All their interventions, but especially advanced cognitive interventions, will reflect the clinician's understanding of the client's thoughts, affects, behaviors, relationships, and presenting concerns. Thus, if the conceptualization was inadequate (if the client is viewed as a nail because the clinician only brought a hammer), even the most skilled application of confrontation, here-and-now process, and interpretation will fail because it will be perceived by the client as unempathic, off-target, and experience-distant. This lack of resonance and perceived acceptance will lead the client to feel misunderstood and may result in premature termination or dissatisfaction (rightly so) with the counselor or therapist. All strategies have to be used for a reason and the reason has to be based in an accurate understanding (conceptualization) of the client. Inaccuracy in the clinician's understanding of the client will be most harmfully evident in the application of advanced cognitive strategies, as these strategies are aimed toward helping clients gain an understanding of their symptoms and lives. If the counselor's conceptualization is incorrect, this misunderstanding will be communicated to (or even forced upon) the client through interpretations or here-and-now process comments. Because the interventions reflect misunderstandings, they will fail to resonate with the client, and at best will be rejected, at worst will be used by the client as evidence that truly no one, not even the therapist, can understand. Correct, well-timed conceptualization, on the other hand, will lead to interpretations and process comments that will resonate with the client and can lead to self-acceptance, insight, and perhaps even attitude or behavior change.

In summary, the establishment of a context is critical for all therapeutic work but most importantly so for the application of advanced cognitive strategies. Interpretations and process comments will be accepted and usefully applied by the client if they are based in accurate understanding or conceptualization of the client's life and presenting concerns; they will be perceived as intrusive and unempathic if they are based in stereotypes, prejudgments, and inaccurate conclusions about insufficient data. Context cannot be ignored in advanced cognitive work; in fact, context is everything. Without accurate context, advanced cognitive work can literally hinder therapeutic progress regardless of how well-meaning and caring the clinician who applies it. Not surprisingly, advanced cognitive strategies are not often used early in treatment; they are reserved for later points in treatment when the mental-health-care provider has developed sufficient data (context) to understand (conceptualize) the client accurately. If used late and sparingly, they can be profoundly effective; if used early and often, they can engender defensiveness and rejection by the client.

CONFRONTATION

Confrontation is a strategy, or rather a process, that is used purposefully to point out an incongruence, discrepancy, inconsistency, or mixed message of a client that the clinician understands to have a meaning, impact, or purpose in the client's life. The purpose of this pointing out is not to attack, humiliate, or challenge the client, but to increase self-awareness and understanding, and consequently motivation for change. Despite the label and colloquial understanding of the term, confrontation does not imply a harsh challenge or attack on the client. Its purpose is not to move against or provoke the client, but rather to clarify something about the client that seems to be contradictory or incongruous. Confrontations are neither aggressive nor hostile but are actually delivered in a gentle and caring manner (Ivey, Ivey, and Simek-Morgan, 1997). Clearly, a therapist has to be able to identify incongruence, discrepancy, inconsistency, and mixed messages to use this strategy effectively. It is best to learn to be aware of issues ripe for confrontation by paying attention to consistencies (or lack thereof) in clients' behaviors, attitudes, emotions, relationships, and

TABLE 9-1	CATEGORIES AND EXAMPLES OF CLIENT INCONSISTENCIES AND DISCREPANCIES

Category	Example
Behavior versus feeling	Client claims not to be frightened of peers but evidences behavioral signs, such as nervous tics or fidgeting, when talking about or exposed to them
Behavior versus thought/attitude	Client talks about the importance of respecting and valuing a spouse and not believing in divorce, but engages in domestic violence
Actual behavior versus talked-about behavior	Client claims to be a patient and tolerant parent, but when observed with children reacts with annoyance, anger, and impatience
Behavior in one setting versus behavior in another setting	Client behaves withdrawn and shy in social settings with strangers, but outgoing and exuberant in a small circle of close friends
Behavior with one individual versus behavior with another individual	Client is subservient and passive with authority figures but aggressive and demanding with people in equal or subordinate positions
Feeling versus thought/attitude	Client is tearful and despondent about the loss of a relationship but claims an attitude of indifference about the person who left
Actual feeling versus talked-about feeling	Client talks about feeling frightened and upset about trouble at work, but outward signs of emotion convey aggression, rage, and anger
Feeling in one setting versus feeling in another setting	Client is anxious and panicky when home alone, but feels confident, safe, and strong while at work
Feeling with one individual versus feeling with another individual	Client evidences symptoms of depression with spouse, but is happy and relaxed around friends
Thought/attitude in one setting versus thought/attitude in another setting	Client expresses optimism and goal-directed thought at work, but has black-or-white thinking and a skeptical attitude in intimate relationships
Thought/attitude with one individual versus thought/attitude with another individual	Client jumps to conclusions and makes prejudgments when with parents, but is open-minded and flexible when with friends

verbalizations across settings and modalities. Some examples of possible incongruence are shown in Table 9-1. The list is no doubt woefully incomplete, but should give the reader an idea of what to look for. Most simply put, discrepancies and inconsistencies can occur across thoughts, behaviors or relational patterns, and feelings; in terms of what is expressed (nonverbal) versus claimed (verbal), in terms of what occurs in one setting versus another, and in terms of what occurs with one set of individuals versus another.

Basic Mechanics of How to Use Confrontation

One very common inconsistency, expressed by almost all clients, is that they come to therapy or counseling asking for assistance with behavior, attitudinal, or affective change but then evidence strong resistance to new ways of being, feeling, or thinking. This apparent contradiction has many explanations. Often symptoms developed for a specific reason and at least at one time in the client's life served a particular purpose or function. Giving up the symptom therefore means relinquishing its function and finding a new behavior, thought, or emotion to replace it. This is a very difficult process, as the client in the meantime will feel vulnerable and unprotected. Understanding symptoms as self-protective mechanisms and not focusing treatment solely on the letting-go of symptoms can help the clinician be more empathic and the client more open to change. The same process tends to be true for all inconsistencies and discrepancies. Some reason or purpose exists for the discrepancy. How the clinician understands that reason or purpose will be guided by the theoretical orientation to which the mental-health-care provider subscribes. However, the commonality across all schools of thought is the importance of understanding discrepancies before pointing them out. In this way, the confrontation will not be delivered as a challenge, but in a context of empathic understanding and caring. When engaging in the confrontation the clinician will not address its purpose, but will merely help the client recognize the inconsistency. Once the inconsistency is noted and accepted as real by the client, an exploration can begin of how it developed or came about. This exploration will lead the client toward recognition of the role or purpose of the discrepancy, an insight-creating process that needs to precede change. Thus, confrontation as conceptualized here has four steps.

Step One: The clinician points out a discrepancy of the client in a caring and empathic manner, being straightforward and not challenging the client.

Step Two: The client and clinician explore the discrepancy together, helping the client recognize and accept the reality of the discrepancy or incongruence.

Step Three: The clinician then helps the client explore how the incongruence or inconsistency developed, what purpose it served at the time of its development, and the impact it has on the client's current life.

Step Four: The client recognizes the meaning and impact of the inconsistency and makes a conscious choice about whether the purpose or impact of the inconsistency has an importance or consequences that justify maintaining the incongruence in the client's life. If the decision is yes, there will be no change; if the decision is no, change (in behavior, thought, or affect) will ensue.

Some practitioners consider a confrontation complete after the first step of this four-step process, perceiving a confrontation as a strategy, not a process. Such clinicians view confrontation as the task of pointing out an inconsistency or discrepancy without using this as a step toward a larger goal, namely, the goal of creating understanding and change. This use of confrontation as a single-step strategy appears incomplete and unfortunate, as the client may never glean the full potential benefits of the process of confrontation as defined here. It must be noted, however, that the four steps outlined above may not always occur immediately or at once. A confrontation may begin in one session with one or two steps and then may continue to be explored and addressed in subsequent sessions until all four steps are complete. A complete confrontation is not a quick and easy process, but a long intervention that requires patience and the ability to track progress on the part of the clinician. Once a confrontation has been initiated, the mental-health-care provider must ensure that it is processed to its logical end (that is, to Step Four), even if it takes several sessions to do so. Just engaging in the first step (that is, pointing out the inconsistency) and then never following up on it seems less than helpful. It is important to finish what is started (unless, of course, clinicians recognize that they made an error and that there was no need for even the first step; this would then be acknowledged to the client and the matter would be dropped).

Guidelines for the Use of Confrontation

In addition to paying attention to implementing all four steps of a confrontation, the clinician has a few other concerns that need to be kept in mind when using this strategy. Following are a few general guidelines of which to be aware when using confrontation:

- begin confrontations only after understanding their purpose, meaning, or origin (that is, have a context for them)
- do not confuse therapeutic confrontation with social confrontation; therapeutic confrontation is used to enlighten, not to challenge
- render confrontations (especially the first step) gently and with caring, within an environment of empathy and concern
- initiate the process of confrontation only when necessary and therapeutically indicated
- time confrontation well within sessions (do not initiate the first step at the end of the session when insufficient time is left to process it and repair any damage to rapport it may have precipitated)
- time confrontation well over the course of therapy or counseling (do not initiate the process prematurely, but rather pace it according to rapport)
- use specifics that are as detailed as possible when presenting the first step of a confrontation, as opposed to being vague and indirect

- initiate the process of confrontation only when certain that the client can tolerate it psychologically and emotionally
- do not turn the first step of a confrontation into an attack, accusation, or judgment
- do not present the first step of confrontation with anger or hostility, or out of defensiveness or personal offense
- do not overuse the process of confrontation; in fact, use it sparingly
- consider embedding the confrontation into Phase Four of the empathic-skillfulness cycle

Sample Transcript of Confrontation

Following is a transcript of a complete confrontation, that is, a process of confrontation that proceeded through all four stages in a single session (each clearly marked). This process occurred quickly and easily as the client was already well-advanced in treatment and had both an inkling of the presence of the inconsistency and a curiosity about its reality. Completion of a confrontation in a single session is common with a simple incongruence or with discrepancies the client has slowly become aware of and was ready to deal with (as in the example). Also, the closer a client is to termination (that is, the more insight the client already has achieved), the more likely it is that confrontations can be completed in a single session. Early in counseling, it is much more likely that the process of confrontation will be spread over multiple sessions.

> CLIENT: When Tracy said that, I just got flustered, I didn't know what to say and so I said nothing. Somehow that seems to happen to me with her. I'm not sure why. . . .
>
> CLINICIAN: You mentioned that it seems to happen with Tracy. . . . Does that mean you realize that this is somehow unusual and that it doesn't happen with others? (*Step One in clarifying-question format*)
>
> CLIENT: Exactly. I realized that just now. I get flustered with her but that never happens to me in other relationships with women.
>
> CLINICIAN: Does it happen in other relationships, like in relationships with men?
>
> CLIENT: I don't know why I said it that way. . . . Hmm . . . (*thinking out loud now*) Does it happen with anyone else? I don't remember feeling that way with anyone else. . . .
>
> CLINICIAN: Ever?
>
> CLIENT: Ever! It's only with Tracy. Hmm . . .
>
> CLINICIAN: You said it somehow seems to happen only with her. But has it always happened with her? (*continues Step One and begins Step Two to determine if it is an inconsistency strictly in feeling and associated behavior with Tracy versus other persons or across situations*)

CLIENT: Oh, that's a tough one. It's been happening for a while now—but has it always . . . Hmm . . . I tend to think, yes, it has. But . . .

CLINICIAN: But?

CLIENT: Well, maybe really early on when I knew her it didn't . . .

CLINICIAN: Really early on?

CLIENT: Yeah, before we, before I got really serious . . . *(long pause; client clearly thinking deeply)*

CLINICIAN: Help me understand.

CLIENT: Well. About six months ago, I had this dream, remember, we talked about it in here, where Tracy and I were married, and we were babysitting our grandchildren?

CLINICIAN: Yes, I remember. That was the day when you realized you really loved her . . .

CLIENT: *(interrupts)* Yes. Really love her, you know, not like I ever loved anyone else. Love her like in a way that makes me scared to lose her . . . So I think that's when it started . . .

CLINICIAN: That's when you started getting flustered when she said things like that?

CLIENT: Yeah, I think so. . . . I don't remember ever running out of words or being speechless before. It's like freezing up with fear or something. . . . Definitely, that's it; that's when it started.

CLINICIAN: And it never happened with anyone else before? *(being thorough about Step Two)*

CLIENT: Right. This is new.

CLINICIAN: So we have two kinds of inconsistencies, or changes. . . . First, you react differently with Tracy when she says unpleasant things as compared to when others do. Right?

CLIENT: Right. With other people I can blow it off or it makes me mad and I get mean. With her I freeze up. . . .

CLINICIAN: And the other thing is that with Tracy it has changed. When you felt less emotionally close to her, it was easier to react to her like you do with other people. Right again?

CLIENT: Right. *(Step Two is now complete; the discrepancies are established, agreed upon, and accepted by the client.)*

CLINICIAN: So what, would you say, made the difference? *(beginning Step Three, exploration of meaning, purpose, or impact)*

CLIENT: I guess my own level of feelings about her . . . You know? I was never that in love before. I always felt like I would be okay if something happened. Never thought about marriage . . . Didn't worry about being without her . . .

CLINICIAN: So some shift happened in you, and it created a change in how you relate to Tracy versus other people you've cared for. . . .

CLIENT: Exactly. She became important to me in a real basic way, like to my survival almost. Does that sound corny?

CLINICIAN: Not at all. Does it sound that way to you?

CLIENT: A little . . . *(blushes a little)*

CLINICIAN: To me it sounds more like a change in your level of commitment. . . . Would you say that's corny?

CLIENT: Hmm, I didn't think of it that way. But that's it, isn't it. I want to commit to her somehow. You know, I bet that's why people get married, isn't it? Because they wanna make sure they can have the other person around for the rest of their lives . . . Kind of selfish in a way . . . *(long pause)*

CLINICIAN: What are you pondering?

CLIENT: I'm a little shocked by this recognition of feeling committed and how it's affecting me. . . . how it's changing me . . . *(another long pause)*

CLINICIAN: How it makes you feel different, or react different *(catching her mistake of shifting from action to feeling)* . . . *(choosing for now to explore the discrepancy, not pursuing the selfishness issue)*

CLIENT: Yes. It's like I'm someone else with her. I guess it's like I'm so afraid to lose her that I can't be myself anymore, like if I'm myself she won't like me anymore.

CLINICIAN: And being yourself would mean doing what?

CLIENT: Doing what I do with others who say or do something that annoys me—say something, maybe even get nasty, scream, defend myself somehow, take a stand, for goodness sakes . . .

CLINICIAN: And you're afraid if you do that with Tracy, she'll disappear. . . .

CLIENT: Exactly. And that horrifies me. . . .

CLINICIAN: It's more horrifying to think of losing her than to think of not being yourself.

CLIENT: Huh?

CLINICIAN: You'd rather not be yourself than face the possibility of losing her?

CLIENT: That's kind of what I'm saying, isn't it. Sounds terrible when you put it that way, though . . .

CLINICIAN: What sounds terrible about it?

CLIENT: Well, some day, maybe I'll be myself by mistake, you know, out of habit, and then it'll be such a big change for her that it really scares her off . . . or . . .

CLINICIAN: Or?

CLIENT: Or maybe some day I'll get tired of being flustered and swallowing my anger . . . Wow!

CLINICIAN: Good point. What about that?

CLIENT: Well, I guess that would really be a shame. How can I think about, dream about marriage and kids and grandkids *(grins)* if I don't feel like I'm me when I'm with her. . . . oh boy . . .

CLINICIAN: So it's in a way a decision you might need to make now. *(moving to Step Four, considering behavior change given the consequences of the discrepancy)* Do you keep up the discrepancy between who you really are and how you react, and risk losing her now . . .

CLIENT: *(interrupts)* Or do I start being myself now and see what happens before we have grandkids!

CLINICIAN: That about sums it up!

CLIENT: What a dilemma. There are potential costs either way. It's like a cost-benefit analysis, isn't it? Well, I should be able to do this. It's what I do at work everyday.

CLINICIAN: Uh huh . . . ? *(nonverbal encourager to go on)*

CLIENT: It seems pretty clear though, in a way. I mean, how happy will I be in the long run if I keep feeling flustered and say nothing and later get pissed off. I mean that's why I told you about it, right, because I was upset that I did what I did, or didn't do. . . .

CLINICIAN: *(nods; nonverbal encourager to go on)*

CLIENT: It's only a matter of time before I'd explode. And that would be bad news. Also, she might see me around other people and realize that I treat her differently, too. That may be weird. Like she'd see a side of me that she didn't know before. And she may get disappointed. If I just react that way I always do now, maybe I won't overreact . . . and I'll see how she responds to a little bit of back talk. I mean we're not talking about me screaming or yelling. Okay, sometimes I do, but I don't think I would. . . . Well, I guess I sort of have my answer, don't I? *(client worked through Step Four independently)*

CLINICIAN: Sounds like it to me . . . *(affirms that Step Four is complete)*

CLIENT: Well, I guess I'd better try it next time. . . . Scary, though . . .

CLINICIAN: Oh, I bet it feels scary. And if you don't do it next time, you'll have other chances. The main thing is you've realized something and now it's just a matter of figuring out how to make a change happen. One step at a time . . .

CLIENT: True. I'll probably have lots of opportunities to practice. *(grins)* *(Session continues from here.)*

This transcript demonstrates how all four steps may be accomplished in a single session with an insightful client who was ready for the confrontation. It also clearly shows that a confrontation is not an attack or challenge but an opportunity to help clients recognize relational, behavioral, attitudinal, or affective patterns or manifestations that are unusual, different, or discrepant in some way. This can be done gently and caringly, as the transcript shows. The example

Skill Development Recommendations

Recommendation 9-1   *Explore inconsistencies in your own life through journaling or talking to a trusted friend who will give you honest feedback. Pick one of these inconsistencies and try to figure out its meaning and purpose. Given its purpose, do you want to change? If so, how might you want to go about that?*

Recommendation 9-2   *Begin to learn how to recognize and identify inconsistencies by starting to look for them in others with whom you interact. Do not do this with close friends or family members (to avoid conflicts).*

---

also serves to highlight that some conceptual notions will enter the confrontational process, that is, that context will become important and will emerge in a manner that may differ slightly from clinician to clinician. Not every clinician, for example, may have framed the client's behavior in terms of level of commitment. Some counselors may have focused on exploring whether the client observed a similar pattern in others (for example, parents), or may have focused on the client's fears of loss. The basic confrontational process, however, stays the same. All four steps are covered, usually in the order given above, though sometimes with two steps being worked on simultaneously.

HERE-AND-NOW COGNITIVE PROCESSING

The importance of a thorough and clear conceptualization multiplies as increasingly depth-oriented, or insight-oriented, advanced cognitive strategies are being used. Once the utilization of here-and-now process is being considered, therapists need to be very clear about how they conceptualize their clients. Counselors at this point will work with clients' general and developmental relational, affective, behavioral, and cognitive patterns as they manifest in the current (here-and-now) relationship with the clinician. Using here-and-now processing requires the therapist to understand most, if not all, of the clients' patterns, developments, and manifestations of presenting concerns and symptoms.

The clinician's awareness of how the client behaves, feels, thinks, and relates and how these functions have developed and play themselves out in terms of coping ability and need states in the client's current life precedes the client's own enhanced understanding of these issues. It is not the function of the mental-health-care provider to meet a client's expressed relational, behavioral, cognitive, and affective needs; it is merely important to recognize, understand, and accept them. Once this is accomplished, it becomes the task of the clinician to acknowledge the client's needs empathically to help the client achieve the same recognition, understanding, and acceptance. There are many ways in which this therapeutic function can be accomplished (including all cognitive strategies and the higher-level affective strategies); however, one primary means is the use of here-and-now cognitive processing, or process comments. Here-and-now process means using the immediate relationship between client and clinician to help the client recognize (gain awareness of), understand, and accept needs, coping styles, symptoms, and expressive patterns.

There are many ways through which the client's behavioral, affective, cognitive, and relational patterns (and hence the client's needs, conflicts, coping style, and so forth) express themselves in the therapeutic relationship. Process comments are excellent techniques to use whenever such here-and-now manifestation occurs. What are these ways in which clients' patterns manifest in the current relationship with the counselor? Most simply put, here-and-now process is appropriately used whenever an obvious transference or client-specific countertransference process has occurred or is occurring between client and clinician. Both transference and countertransference can manifest in as many ways as there are client and counselor behaviors, thoughts, and feelings. There is no single way or content that defines all possible here-and-now process situations. Clinicians need to be able to recognize transference and countertransference to be able to use here-and-now process.

Transference and countertransference are concepts that, although originally derived from psychoanalytic theory, have been accepted as real interactions that occur between clients and their mental-health-care providers by clinicians of almost all schools of thought. They are processes that acknowledge that neither clinician nor client react and relate in a vacuum, but rather that both will relate with the other from a way of relating that was developed over the lifespan through some form of learning process. Clients rarely just talk about their problems or concerns when they see a therapist; they also tend to act them out in the therapeutic relationship. They display and express the same behaviors, relational patterns, cognitive styles, interpretations, affective reactions, source feelings, and need states with their clinicians that they display or use with other human beings and that they learned through interpersonal interactions over the course of their life span (cf., Brems, 1999; Strupp, 1992; Teyber, 1997). Counselors are as much a target of ingrained patterns, behaviors, cognitions, and affective responses as anyone else in a client's environment. Similarly, mental-health-care providers are not the blank screen or neutral person traditional psychoanalysts had hoped for. Such neutrality is impossible given the reality that clinicians are as human as their clients and hence are reactive in relationships as well. If clinicians accept the ubiquity of a client's transference, they must also accept the ubiquity of their own countertransference (Wolf, 1988). The key to success is to use transference and countertransference productively and not to allow them to get in the way of an empathic therapeutic relationship. This interpersonal cycle of client expression and therapist reaction essentially captures the definition of a transference-countertransference cycle, or transference relationship, between client and clinician.

A definition of transference as understood here is in order. Given the intense experiential and relational nature of the therapeutic relationship, it is very likely that the current here-and-now relationship between client and therapist becomes a stage for ingrained feelings and needs related to the client's past and current relationships. The recapitulation of the client's behaviors, affects, emotions, and relational patterns in the relationship with the mental-health-care provider is the essence of transference. This transference relationship, however, is not independent of what the clinician brings to treatment, a definition of transference that deviates somewhat from traditional psychoanalytic models. Instead, the current definition of transference asserts that the here-and-now relationship between client and clinician is always affected by both the client's transference and the therapist's countertransference. This definition of transference is entirely compatible with Gill's (1982) conceptualization of transference as the patient's experience of the relationship with the therapist, and Wolf's (1988) definition of countertransference as the therapist's experience of the relationship with the client. Both experiences are subjective and flavored by each individual's history, background, and current affective and need states. The client-therapist relationship is an intersubjective relationship that reflects both the client's and the therapist's reality (cf., Atwood and Stolorow, 1984; Natterson, 1991). It is through this relationship to which both client and therapist contribute knowledge and wisdom that they arrive jointly at a higher and more accurate understanding of the client (who despite this definition always remains the sole focus of therapy).

Clients contribute to the transference relationship with the clinician because they have grown up in a unique environment with individualized interpersonal relationships that influenced their self-development in a manner that defines how they react emotionally, cognitively, behaviorally, and relationally. These patterns are not only relied upon in day-to-day relationships, but are also stimulated and expressed in the here-and-now context of psychotherapy. Skilled clinicians can facilitate the activation and expression of clients' needs and reactions without altering them, in the sense of producing needs or affects that would not otherwise have been expressed by the client. Skilled counselors recognize when clients' affects and needs, however grounded in past relationships, are stimulated in the here-and-now therapeutic relationship. It is the inspection of the transference relationship that transpires between client and therapist at that moment that is the purpose of here-and-now processing. Process comments thus used increase understanding and insight into the client's development, environment, needs, and directions for change.

Several forms of countertransference were already defined in Chapter One. Only client-specific countertransference is of issue in this context and will be briefly revisited. Client-specific countertransference refers to any feeling or reaction in the clinician that is unique to the work with a particular client. For example, if a clinician becomes impatient with a client and does not usually feel this way with other clients, a potential client-specific countertransference exists. If the client complains that others tend to react impatiently to the client, the likelihood of a client-specific countertransference has increased significantly. The clinician can then use this reaction as a springboard for here-and-now process; a reaction has taken place between client and clinician that reflects a more generic process that the client tends to encounter in life outside of the therapy room. Process comments thus used become excellent facilitators of insight and motivators for change and self-recognition (Teyber, 1997).

Basic Mechanics of Here-and-Now Process Comments

Given their basis in a here-and-now transference or countertransference, here-and-now processing is most commonly initiated through questions or comments that direct clients' attention to their reactions in this moment. These questions or comments draw the client's attention to a feeling, thought, behavior, need, conflict, or coping response expressed in the relationship with the clinician right here and right now. They request that the client pay attention to a reaction that occurred in the therapeutic relationship. Most often, early in therapy or counseling, clients are unaware of how they replay patterns in the therapeutic relationship. As therapy progresses, clients will become increasingly aware of how they react to the clinician and how this reaction may be representative of their general interpersonal style. As clients become more attuned to here-and-now process, they will be more and more open to answering here-and-now process questions and to responding to here-and-now process comments. Regardless of the client's initial reluctance about here-and-now processing, it is a useful strategy that can be used often and liberally, as long as it is delivered with caring and acceptance. If an initial here-and-now process comment or question (samples follow) is rejected by a client, it is best to let the issue drop, especially if rapport is still tenuous. Later in treatment, as rapport has deepened and the client has made a commitment to counseling, the issue may be pursued further with follow-up questions as long as the clinician believes that the exploration of a here-and-now event will lead to increased understanding or insight in the client.

Examples of Initial Process Comments or Questions
- "What are you thinking right now?"
- "What thought just went through your mind?"
- "What were you just thinking but decided not to say out loud?"
- "Have you had these thoughts in our relationship as well?"
- "Is that what you are thinking right now, too?"
- "How are you feeling right now?"
- "How are you feeling about me right now?"
- "What was that feeling that peeked through just then?"
- "What's that feeling you are having at the moment?"
- "Have you felt that way with me?"
- "Is that what you are feeling right now, as well?"
- "What did you want to do just then?"
- "What did that movement mean just now?"
- "What's your body doing right now?"
- "What is your body telling you right now?"
- "Have you wanted to do that in here with me?"
- "What is happening with you right now?"
- "What's going on with you at this very moment?"
- "What's going on between us right now?"
- "Is that what's going on in our relationship right now?"
- "What would you like to say to me right now, but aren't?"
- "How was our work for you today?"

If questioning is not sufficient to draw out a client's immediate reaction or response, the mental-health-care provider may move toward simply pointing out the observed reaction of the client. Such pointing out of observation may take many different shapes. A few examples follow. These statements are most useful when rapport is sufficient to allow the clinician to pursue a here-and-now exploration even when the client initially rejected a request to do so or failed to respond to a process comment or question.

Examples of Follow-Up Process Comments or Questions
- "I noticed that you turned away from me. What do you think that's all about?"
- "I noticed a flash of feeling in you just then, and you don't seem to want to become aware of it."
- "Your body is saying something to you and you seem not to want to pay attention."
- "I heard hesitation in your voice. What might that be about?"
- "I have noticed that reaction in here with me as well. Have you?"
- "There seemed to be some feeling in your voice and then it disappeared. What happened?"

- "Your eyes became teary when I said that. Can we talk about that?"
- "Your tight fists suggest that you are holding something back. What do you suppose is going on?"
- "You reacted when I said that. Help me understand what went through you."
- "You became very quiet after I asked that question. Can you help me understand what happened?"
- "I noticed you stopped looking at me at that point. What do you think that may be about?"
- "I can see that you want to say something but instead you seem to try to keep it in."

All of these comments and questions focus the client on the present and on the current relationship or immediate interaction with the clinician. This immediacy can have a tremendous emotional impact on the client and is a most powerful therapeutic tool. It draws the client's attention to an occurrence in the here-and-now which the clinician believes is of importance in the client's life outside of the therapy room. This understanding of here-and-now processing can accommodate various theoretical frameworks, as it neither implies the specific content of the client's expressions, nor the therapist's means of understanding or interpreting (explaining) them. For example, a cognitive behaviorist may focus on clients' cognitions (content) and will try to understand their current manifestation through inspecting their experience in the here-and-now relationship (understanding) as well as gleaning insight into the development through learning histories in clients' lives (interpretation or explanation). Humanist clinicians will focus on the client's feelings and self-expressions (content) and will look for meaning in the here-and-now relationship (understanding) while also searching for the origins of feelings and self-expressions in the family environment and the varying levels of acceptance, genuineness, warmth, and empathy (interpretation) to be found there. Family systems theorists will explore relational patterns and behaviors (content) and will attempt to recognize their activation or stimulation in the here-and-now relationship (understanding), as well as tracing their origins to family interactions, paying attention to issues such as inappropriate boundaries, triangulation, and so forth (interpretation).

As was true of confrontations, here-and-now processing does not involve the implementation of a simple strategy, but rather represents a series of interventions. Process comments are a multistep process, not a unidirectional, simple event. They can be part of an empathic-skillfulness cycle (that is, would be used during Phase Four) or can be presented in their own right. If used outside of an empathic-skillfulness cycle, their steps are as outlined roughly below. Their order may not always be the same, and several steps may overlap or be accomplished simultaneously. The final steps, involving exploration of the development of a pattern and the creation of change, may not always be accomplished right away but may be therapeutic goals that will be reached at a much later time. Thus, not all here-and-now comments will lead client and clinician through all of these steps; the clinician, however, has all of these steps in mind when initiating here-and-now processing. In that sense, the steps are a kind of flowchart of what may occur in the mental-health-care provider's mind rather than a rigid structure imposed upon the client.

An Outline for Processing Here-and-Now Events

- clinicians recognize that a here-and-now event has transpired that reflects a transference relationship between them and their client; that is, they recognize an event as representative of how the client reacts with others outside of therapy
- clinicians gain an understanding of the here-and-now event (or transference expression) in terms of what it communicates about the client's needs, affects, cognitions, behaviors, and relational patterns in general
- clinicians conceptualize the here-and-now event in terms of what it communicates about the development of the client's affects, cognitions, behaviors, and relational patterns
- clinicians gain an understanding of what activated or motivated the client's here-and-now expression and experience of transferential needs, affects, cognitions, behaviors, and relational patterns
- clinicians tease out their own countertransferences related to the here-and-now event and recognize when their response is idiosyncratic to themselves, as opposed to client-specific
- clinicians make a process comment or ask a process question to assess whether the client is aware of the here-and-now event and the pattern it may represent
- clinicians help the client recognize the here-and-now event (whether reflecting emotions, needs, thoughts, behaviors and relational patterns) as it manifests in the therapeutic relationship
- clinicians help clients recognize how they respond similarly with others in their environment outside of therapy or counseling
- clinicians may help clients recognize how the pattern played out in the here-and-now event developed and what purpose it once may have served, that is, clinicians may help clients understand the here-and-now event and underlying pattern
- clinicians avoid getting drawn into the emotional valence of the here-and-now event and thus become able to provide an accepting response that is different from what the client expects in the here-and-now and/or has experienced in the past

- clinicians avoid recapitulating the client's conflicts or patterns through an unaware (perhaps countertransferential) response and by accepting the client's here-and-now response
- clinicians help the client accept the pattern underlying the here-and-now event while instilling the motivation for change
- clinicians assist the client with the exploration of alternate responses to current relationships to break the pattern of response reflected in the here-and-now event

Recognizing and Utilizing Opportunities for the Use of Here-and-Now Process Comments

For here-and-now processing to take place, the clinician has to recognize that a here-and-now event has occurred. If the clinician fails to recognize that a client has responded to the clinician in a way that is representative of reactions that manifest in other relationships, it is likely that the interchange will simply recapitulate a pattern. Recapitulation of patterns usually means that the clinician responds exactly in the same way to the client as the client expected and has experienced in other relationships. This often means the recapitulation of destructive, unhealthy, or negative patterns. For example, a slightly suspicious, passive-aggressive client may elicit a countertransference in the clinician that involves anger and impatience. If the clinician is unaware of this emotional response as stemming from the client's behavioral or relational style, she or he may respond impatiently or angrily, an affect that will be easily recognized by the client, as this is the very response the client tends to receive from others outside the therapy room, and hence expects. The interaction between clinician and client becomes similar to any other human interaction the client has experienced and serves to strengthen this client's belief in a hostile world. If, on the other hand, the clinician can recognize that her or his impatience and anger is a client-specific countertransference, she or he may be able to respond with acceptance and understanding. The client will have a different experience in the therapeutic relationship than in relationships outside of the therapy room and may recognize that not all human exchanges must involve hostility.

Some clinicians may recognize a here-and-now event, but hesitate to use it therapeutically. Although they recognize that the client is reenacting with the clinician a general pattern that emerges in all relationships, this counselor fails to address the here-and-now event through a process comment. This failure may occur when a clinician feels uncomfortable with the client's pattern or with the therapist's own countertransferential response. For example, a given female client may have a highly sexualized way of responding to men. A male clinician who is uncomfortable with the topic of sexuality may be well aware of how the client's sexualized pattern of relating is played out in the therapeutic relationship, but may never address this issue in a here-and-now process comment.

Leaving the client's mode of relating unexplored will hinder therapeutic progress in this regard as she may not be aware that this is how she comes across in male-female relationships.

Given the potential negative consequences of not seeing here-and-now patterns or not responding to them if they are recognized, it is important to explore factors that may contribute to such blind spots among clinicians. Inability to recognize or reluctance to address process issues or events can arise for a number of reasons. First, clinicians may have a personal issue (a countertransference based on a trait, issue, or stimulus) that prevents them from recognizing the pattern expressed by the client in the therapeutic relationship. For example, clinicians may fail to recognize patterns that are similar to their own or that elicit a response in the client's communication partner that is similar or identical to a response style exhibited routinely by the clinician. In either situation, the clinician is so involved in the pattern that it becomes invisible or unrecognizable. Such a countertransference scenario usually is only resolved when a supervisor or consultant recognizes how client and clinician encourage each other in a certain interpersonal style.

Second, clinicians may feel that making process comments is too personal or emotionally charged. They are reluctant to point out clients' feelings in the here-and-now because this process will involve the clinician-client relationship very directly. The clinician and client will need to work at a level that is usually highly experience-near for both individuals. Clinicians who have difficulty tolerating affect, interpersonal closeness, or conflict will shrink back from such therapeutic exchanges and therefore will prefer not to work on the process dimension.

A third possibility is the clinician's inexperience with the level of intimate and open communication involved in here-and-now process. Process comments are highly unlike anything humans usually do when they communicate with each other. It makes the unspoken overt and challenges both communication partners to acknowledge reactions in relation to each other that often remain unspoken. This completely different way of communicating may feel intrusive to the clinician, not only vis-à-vis the client, but even the self. Clinicians may hesitate to point out here-and-now events they have recognized because they perceive the intervention as too personal or too unusual compared to their usual communication style. Relatedly, they may choose not to use a process comment because they perceive it as potentially offensive or confrontational for the very reason that it does represent a different mode or level of communication.

A fourth factor that may interfere is clinicians' fear about not knowing what to do once the process comment has been made. Especially novice clinicians worry about what to do once the client acknowledges a feeling or thought about the clinician. For example, clinicians may be reluctant to point out that a client experiences anger toward the clinician for fear of unleashing rage against the self and not knowing how to stop it. Others may not address sexual overtones in the relationship because of the discomfort this topic may bring and because of a lack of knowledge about how to deal with this type of transference once it has been pointed out. Process comments often lead to powerful therapeutic interactions, and clinicians may be afraid of not knowing how to manage the emerging intensity that develops in the relationship with the client. Rather than unleashing this amount of potential affect or impact, they decide not to intervene at all.

Occasionally, clinicians may hesitate to make a process comment because they are not certain if the observation about the here-and-now event is based in a true transference or client-specific countertransference. In such instances, reluctance may be appropriate until the clinician has determined whether the here-and-now event is truly client-related or rather clinician-related. If a here-and-now event is based on the clinician's trait-, stimulus-, or issue-specific countertransference, it is clinician-related and does not warrant a process comment. In fact, a process comment would be inappropriate as treatment is about the client, not the clinician. If such a here-and-now event occurs, the clinician needs to explore outside of therapy or counseling why it occurred, what it means, and how it is best dealt with. Supervision or consultation may be invaluable in such circumstances.

Sample Transcript of Here-and-Now Process Comments

A generic (theory-free) example of a therapeutic exchange involving here-and-now processing follows. This transcript will demonstrate a straightforward process comment that was pursued with an insightful client and that managed to move through several of the steps outlined above. It is worth repeating that not all here-and-now processing will accomplish everything from identification of the event to its manifestation in other relationships, development, acceptance, and change. Clinicians have already accomplished a lot if they can help the client recognize here-and-now events within the therapeutic relationship. Helping clients recognize patterns of any sort in the here-and-now will be highly useful and can be built upon in future sessions even if the client does not advance through all the steps that clinician can foresee.

> CLIENT: I am thinking about breaking up with Mike again. The relationship is just so complicated and I don't have the energy to deal with it. He's so intense emotionally—I can't cope with that. He overwhelms me, really, with all his talk about feelings and getting in touch with feelings, and expressing emotions, and on and on. It's just too much. . . . I can't handle that much affect. You know, it wears me out. Feel, feel, feel, feel. Isn't it okay sometimes just to do something and not analyze how I feel about it. My god, even when we go see a movie, we then have to talk

about how we felt about the different characters. He even cries in movies. I've never cried in a movie. It's not real, so what's the point. *(getting somewhat worked up now)* Anyway, I'm thinking about getting out before he drives me crazy. *(calms down)*

CLINICIAN: It wears you out to talk about feelings?

CLIENT: Oh yeah. Absolutely. It's a real chore.

CLINICIAN: What about it is so hard?

CLIENT: It takes a lot of energy, you know. It's easier to just talk and have fun.

CLINICIAN: What kind of energy?

CLIENT: Oh, emotional energy. You know, energy that draws from my very inner resources. It's like it demands something from me I don't want to give . . . something very personal . . .

CLINICIAN: Such as?

CLIENT: Well, personal parts of me that I don't want to talk about—how I really am, who I really am. My innermost self or something. It's scary. . . . *(long pause)*

CLINICIAN: Your innermost self . . .

CLIENT: Yeah, personal stuff, stuff I don't want to talk about . . . with anyone!

CLINICIAN: Not with anybody?

CLIENT: No! *(relinquishes eye contact)*

CLINICIAN: What's going on with you right now? *(process question)*

CLIENT: I don't know. . . . *(withdraws)*

CLINICIAN: I can't help but realize that we talk about feelings a lot, about that very innermost part of you. . . . *(follow-up process comment, leaving the question unspoken for now)*

CLIENT: I know . . . *(does not volunteer more)*

CLINICIAN: Help me understand what's going on with you right now. . . . *(process comment that acknowledges the client's emotion/reaction into the here-and-now)*

CLIENT: I feel annoyed. Like I wanna break up with you too . . .

CLINICIAN: Just like with Mike. We're getting too close. . . . *(process comment that ties here-and-now to other relationships)*

CLIENT: Yes. It's like you know everything about me and it scares me.

CLINICIAN: It's scary right now?

CLIENT: Yes. It's scary because what if you don't like my feelings. . . . *(long pause)*

CLINICIAN: What if I don't like your innermost self?

CLIENT: Exactly. Then what?

CLINICIAN: What's your fear of what I might do?

CLIENT: You won't like me. You'll kick me out. . . . *(looks up a little)*

CLINICIAN: You're feeling very vulnerable that if I know your innermost self and don't like it, I'll leave . . . or make you leave somehow. . . . *(reflection)*

CLIENT: Yes. *(weepy now)*

CLINICIAN: And you're afraid that will happen with Mike? *(moving the here-and-now insight to the larger context of other relationships now)*

CLIENT: *(cries now)* Yes. And then I'll be alone again. I don't wanna lose you. I don't wanna lose Mike.

CLINICIAN: You'd rather quit therapy or break up with Mike first.

CLIENT: At least then I won't look so pathetic. . . . *(still crying)*

CLINICIAN: You said you'd be alone again.

CLIENT: Yes. I always end up alone. All my life people have disappeared. . . . You know all that. . . . We've talked about my parents, my husband. . . .

CLINICIAN: You've lost a lot of people. . . .

CLIENT: Yes . . . *(weeping again)*

CLINICIAN: And you don't want to lose any more. . . . You don't want Mike to leave, you don't want to lose me. . . .

CLIENT: *(nods vehemently, still crying)* I couldn't take it if he left me. . . .

CLINICIAN: You'd rather break up with him first?

CLIENT: *(looks up startled)* Yes . . . *(hesitates)* Yes. I guess so . . . *(stops weeping)*

CLINICIAN: And you've done that before. . . .

CLIENT: Yes. Yes, I have . . . with Jack . . . and George, I guess . . .

CLINICIAN: And Susan and Janet *(prior therapists)* . . .

CLIENT: Oh my . . . You're right. It's a real pattern, isn't it?

CLINICIAN: *(simply nods)*

CLIENT: I came here today planning to tell you this was my last session. . . .

CLINICIAN: I thought you might have. . . .

CLIENT: *(smiles sheepishly)*

CLINICIAN: We're getting very close. I know a lot about you; you've been very open with me, and last week we covered some pretty difficult ground. . . . Scary, huh?

CLIENT: Yes.

CLINICIAN: How are you feeling right now? *(simple process question)*

CLIENT: Strangely relieved. Like, whew, now I can stay because we got this out in the open. . . .

CLINICIAN: This?

CLIENT: This scary feeling . . .

CLINICIAN: This vulnerable feeling of being so exposed and then maybe rejected . . . abandoned . . .

CLIENT: Yes. You know, because it happened.

CLINICIAN: Yes, it did, or it felt like it did when your parents left you behind.

CLIENT: How could they do that? *(starts crying again)* What did I do?

CLINICIAN: Could you have done anything? You were three. . . . *(Session continues from here.)*

This transcript shows how subtle a here-and-now event can be. The clinician immediately realized that the client's complaints about her lover had clear implications and possible manifestation in the therapeutic relationship, as many of the noted features were identical (talking about feelings, revealing her innermost self, escaping from emotional closeness). Thus, the clinician knew immediately to listen for here-and-now manifestations of the client's relational pattern of leaving before being abandoned. Once the client gave an opening, the clinician pursued it and then tied the here-and-now event back to the originally discussed relationship as well as further back to the relationships in which or from which the client's pattern developed. The next step of the process will entail helping the client accept that this is how she has learned to respond and that she now has control over changing her behavior to arrive at a new, more satisfying relational pattern or style. Much here-and-now processing starts the way this example starts: The client makes comments about others that also apply in the therapy setting. This is often a way for clients to communicate difficult feelings in the therapeutic relationship without having to confront the clinician directly. It is important that clinicians learn to pick up these hidden here-and-now events and to make a process comment that brings them into the open so that they may be dealt with directly and openly.

INTERPRETATION

Interpretation is the next, and final, logical step in advanced cognitive processing. As has been noted, it can be part of confrontations and here-and-now process comments, but it is also a strategy in its own right. Interpretation must be embedded not only in the context of an overall conceptualization, as emphasized for all cognitive strategies, but also in a context of profound caring, rapport, and empathy. Interpretations are best delivered in a context of Phase Four of the empathic-skillfulness cycle. Interpretations have many potential shortcomings and pitfalls and are best used sparingly. They can feel experience-distant to clients, if delivered abruptly, out of context, intellectually, or quickly. Interpretation is the cognitive strategy that has the most depth, requires the most cognitive flexibility of both client and clinician, necessitates the highest level of rapport and understanding before being used, and is most likely to reflect the clinician's theoretical orientation. Interpretations establish a meaning for a cli-

Skill Development Recommendations

Recommendation 9-3   *Take a mental time-out in groups and one-on-one relationships to step back and observe the process. Do this by asking what is happening right now, trying to analyze the process dimension of a given interaction.*

---

ent by rendering explanations for presenting symptoms, conflicts, needs, coping strategies, defenses, affects, thoughts, behaviors, and relational patterns based on the client's past relationships or experiences. They help clients understand what has shaped and maintains their current self-experience and reactions by making meaningful links between current relational patterns and responses to formative relationships and significant experiences in the past.

Assumptions Underlying the Use of Interpretations

Meaning is established based upon the clinician's way of interpreting or understanding human behavior. Two different clinicians may explain the same client behavior in slightly different ways, depending on how they tend to conceptualize human behavior. The difference in the content of their respective interpretations does not imply that one is right and the other is wrong. In fact, once one looks beyond the jargon of two clinicians, who claim adherence to two different schools of thought, one often finds remarkable consistency in meaning. On the surface, however, as far as content and language are concerned, the same client may receive different explanations for the same behavior. A behaviorist may explain a client's experience by pointing out reinforcement histories and cause-and-effect relationships. A cognitive behaviorist will attempt to help the client recognize and understand the origins of irrational beliefs or automatic thoughts. A self psychologist will attempt to help the client recognize that empathic failures on the part of caretakers in the past resulted in certain vulnerabilities in the client's self development that have resulted in behavioral patterns and responses designed to protect these vulnerabilities. Beyond this content, however, all of these clinicians use interpretations in the same way, often look back in the client's life to establish meaning, and share three basic assumptions about interpretations:

1. Current reactions and experiences do not occur unpredictably and co-incidentally, but rather are tied to past and/or present experiences, relationships, and (social) learning histories that continue to influence and shape a given client's development, reactions, experiences, or adjustment.

2. Clarification of the developmental history, deeper meaning, and explanation of past, current, and here-and-now relationships or reactions (affects, behaviors, thoughts, needs, conflicts, symptoms, and so on) facilitates and motivates change and growth.
3. Explanations to create meaning and clarification of developmental history are useful only if they are individualized for each client and do not follow a patent formula that is forced upon all clients.

The first assumption is truly common to all schools of thought. It would appear that there is consensus among psychologists, counselors, social workers, and other mental-health-care providers that human behavior is shaped in an interpersonal context during the developmental years and beyond. How clients were raised and how they grew up in a smaller and larger interpersonal matrix (ranging from the nuclear family to the extended family to the community, the social setting, the culture) can often help explain why they behave, feel, and think the way they do. This knowledge helps clinicians understand why the client developed certain relational patterns, symptoms, needs, conflicts, and coping styles and the purposes each served for the client over the life span. Emphases may vary across schools of thought with regard to the level of importance of distant-versus-not-so-distant past. But most if not all theorists look at clients in a temporal context that goes beyond the here-and-now.

The second assumption must be common to all clinicians who use interpretations, lest the act of choosing interpretations be useless or nonsensical. Why use a strategy if it does not lead to change or growth? Resultant client self-knowledge is a motivator for change through the enhancement of self-awareness, self-understanding, and self-acceptance (Cormier and Cormier, 1991; Teyber, 1997). Interpretations are an excellent means of helping clients achieve insight into their reactions and relationships and serve a multitude of purposes. Weiss (1993) and other writers point out that through well-delivered and well-timed interpretations,

- clients tend to become more self-aware, recognizing automatic reactions or habitual ways of relating as they occur;
- clients learn to see themselves more accurately and positively, recognizing how their needs, conflicts, coping styles, and defenses manifest in a variety of settings and circumstances;
- clients begin to understand their here-and-now affects, cognitions, behaviors, and relationships in a broader context that ties them to past experiences and events;
- clients come to accept their current responses and experiences because they can begin to understand how they developed;
- clients feel reduced anxiety about themselves and their reactions because interpretations (or more accurately, explanations contained within them) provide answers to pressing questions;

- clients feel reduced shame because they begin to understand how certain responses developed and that they served adaptive purposes;
- clients can begin to let go of pathological beliefs because they can recognize their roots and original self-protective meaning, as well as the reality that these beliefs are no longer warranted or needed;
- clients feel reduced helplessness because by showing how reactions developed, interpretations imply that these same reactions can be changed and are under the client's control.

The third assumption underlying the use of interpretations is one that is occasionally violated by therapists or counselors. It is rather tempting to develop a way of interpreting human behavior and then to fit every single client into that mold. It is extremely important to make sure that every given client is seen as unique and that the specific circumstances of the client's life and development are considered when developing explanations and understanding. Interpretations work only if they have been individualized for the client and express the essence of the entire client. Interpretations are not formulas that can be used equally for all clients (Nichols, 1987); they should not be phrased to fit people in general; they cannot press people into a single mold; and they must not be based on stereotypes, prejudices, or easy assumptions about what "causes" certain behaviors (Ivey, Ivey, and Simek-Morgan, 1997). Instead, interpretations must fit the unique and highly personal, idiosyncratic history and experience of each client. This issue was addressed above and will not be reiterated further here except to once again emphasize its importance. There are several other cautions that must be considered before a clinician delves into the use of interpretations. It is very tempting for clinicians to share their insights about clients' behaviors as soon as they have occurred to the counselor or therapist. However, clinicians are usually far ahead of their clients in terms of understanding what motivates clients' reactions and relationships. If the explanation is rendered as soon as it occurs to the clinician, clients are often offended, overwhelmed, startled, or shocked by the clinician's revelation. Not surprisingly, such poorly timed interpretations tend to be the very ones clients will reject. Good timing and empathic delivery are the crucial components that define a good interpretation. They will be achieved only if the clinician follows a number of safety guidelines that help increase the likelihood of an interpretation's success. These guidelines will now be explored as factors to consider when using interpretations.

Factors to Consider When Using Interpretations

Because interpretations involve explaining currently manifested affects, thoughts, behaviors, and relationships through past experiences or learning, they can feel overwhelming, cold, imposed, or otherwise negative to the client if they are rendered without preparation or outside of the context of a stable and trusting therapeutic relationship. If an interpretation is verbalized prematurely or without preparation, the discrepancy between where clients are with regard to understanding their problem and how clinicians explain the problem may be too large for clients to tolerate or accept (Cormier and Cormier, 1998). An interpretation thus delivered will be perceived by the client as experience-distant and will not have as much impact as an interpretation that is experience-near and understandable by the client (cf., Kohut, 1984). Experience-distance refers to a client's perception of an intervention by the clinician as incongruent with the client's current way of thinking, feeling, or understanding. The client perceives the counselor's statement or action as sudden, unempathic, or confrontational because it does not correspond to the client's current experience or understanding. When experience-distance occurs in the therapeutic relationship, clients tend to withdraw, react with anger, or experience an intensification of symptoms. They perceive the relationship with the counselor as similar to other conflictual relationships outside of the relationship and experience a decrease in rapport and motivation for therapeutic work. Experience-distance can get in the way of clients accepting a perfectly good interpretation and reduces the chance for creating change and growth.

Experience-nearness, on the other hand, implies that the intervention chosen by the therapist resonates with the client in some way. The client feels profoundly understood, cared for, or connected with the counselor. When an intervention is experience-near for the client, the insight conveyed by the clinician makes sense to the client because it will feel right, corresponding to the client's current experience or perception of the issue at hand. Experience-nearness implies that the intervention was well-timed and more or less accurate. It is respectful of the client and the client's current needs and puts the client's speed or pace in therapeutic work ahead of the clinician's needs for sharing brilliant insights. Achieving experience-nearness and good timing is one of the more difficult skills for novice clinicians. Often, when clinicians have achieved an understanding of the client's concerns, they want to share this insight and the corresponding excitement. However, if this insight is perceived by the client as not related or relevant to what is being discussed, the ensuing sense of disconnection with the therapist is experience-distant. It is crucial to make sure that the client is ready to hear an insight achieved by the counselor before it is delivered. A context for the explanation must have been created; the client must have been prepared (often carefully and slowly) for the explanation so that it is not perceived as coming out of left field. If experience-nearness is achieved in interpretation, the client is more likely to accept the interpretation (if it is accurate) and through this acceptance will change and grow.

It is helpful with regard to timing of interpretations to appreciate the difference between understanding and explanation. A client always needs to feel that a clinician understands a reaction (or need, or conflict, and so on) before explaining it. Understanding, or rather the expression of understanding, consists of clinicians communicating that

- they have empathically heard the client
- they can accurately understand what the client is trying to convey
- they understand that it is logical and important for clients to react the way they did given their current personality structure
- they do not judge the client

The expression of understanding is the verbalization of empathic concern and acceptance. It implies that the clinician understands that the client feels no choice about current affects, thoughts, behaviors, reactions, needs, conflicts, coping choices, and relational patterns since all of these reactions are reflections of who the client is at this moment in time. Understanding does not try to explain why the client is that way. It merely expresses understanding of the fact that the client's current personality (or self) leads to the client's current reactions, seemingly outside of the client's control. Once clients have repeatedly felt understood and not judged by a counselor, they are more open to hearing a feeling not only acknowledged, but also explained. An explanation focuses on helping clients realize how they developed the personality style or self that leads to the outward behaviors, affect, thoughts, and so forth. Understanding accepts and acknowledges that clients' personalities or selves lead to particular reactions; explanation seeks to look at why the personality style or self developed to begin with. Interpretations deliver explanations.

For example, a therapist working with a client who feels interpersonally fearful and shy may right away have the insight that this behavior developed at least partly due to the client's learning history. Whenever the client expressed interpersonal exuberance or engaged in behavior that was outgoing, her mother chastised her and criticized her for wanting to be the center of attention. Over time the client learned that she should not be outgoing and became shy and withdrawn to avoid upsetting her mother and being criticized by her. Although the clinician knows this explanation, it is best not to share it right away. The client would perceive the explanation as experience-distant, and it may even recapitulate the relationship with her mother. The clinician instead empathizes with the client's shyness and communicates to the client an understanding of how difficult it is for the client to be outgoing and exuberant in social settings. He expresses understanding whenever the client becomes self-critical about her inability to be outgoing and sociable, verbalizing (reflecting) the client's need to stay on the fringe for now and to withdraw. The counselor consistently supports the client in her choices and does not try to change the client's behavior in any way (yet). Once the client feels supported and accepted in her relationship with the clinician, he can move toward an exploration of how long the behavior has been in place, the circumstances in which it occurs, and so forth. Once both counselor and client have gained a level of comfort in dealing with the issue on such a cognitive, exploratory level, an explanation (interpretation) becomes possible. Sometimes this process of setting the stage for an explanation via a period of understanding takes a few minutes; sometimes it may take months. The experience of the client in relationship to the clinician will determine when the clinician moves from understanding to explaining. When it is possible to move toward interpretation in the context of the client's current experience in the therapy room, that is, when the explanation can be received by the client in a way that feels experience-near, the counselor can deliver it. Given the importance of good timing and careful delivery of interpretations, a few guidelines are best followed that are designed to increase the likelihood that the explanation is perceived as experience-near by the client, and the chance for growth and change is enhanced.

Guidelines for Using Interpretations

- It is best not to begin the interpretive process in therapy until a firm therapeutic alliance has been established wherein the client has experienced ample understanding by the therapist.
- It is best not to use interpretations until after some of the more basic cognitive strategies (outlined above and in the previous chapter) have been used successfully on several occasions.
- Interpretations need to be phrased respectfully and gently; they should never imply that the clinician is right and the client is wrong or that the clinician has some special knowledge with which the client has to agree.
- Interpretations must not be used to blame, attack, humiliate, or deride the client; careless phrasing of interpretations can make them sound more confrontational or derisive than intended, thus, careful phrasing is important.
- Interpretations need to be phrased to minimize defensiveness and guardedness on the part of the client; they need to be worded so that the client can perceive them as helpful and positive, not dogmatic or absolutely true.
- Interpretations must be idiosyncratically tailored to the client, never making assumptions that what may explain a behavior or reaction for one person will also explain it for another.
- Interpretations need to be relevant to and respectful of the entire personhood of the client and should never make clients feel only partially responded to by addressing (explaining) only selected parts of them while ignoring others.
- Partial interpretations are to be avoided as clients may wonder whether the therapist only accepts and understands a part of who they are rather than understanding them wholly and completely.

- Interpretations must be free of jargon; they must be phrased in common language that is cognitively easy for the client to understand.
- Interpretations need to be phrased so that they are relatively concrete and straightforward or must otherwise match the cognitive flexibility and level of abstraction of the client.
- If a client does not have the requisite cognitive flexibility and level of objectivity and abstraction, interpretations may not be the best strategy for that client (for example, with children or developmentally challenged individuals, interpretations should be used sparingly if at all).

If clinicians follow these guidelines, subsequent use of interpretations is likely to be helpful and growth-promoting. Novice clinicians may need to wait to use interpretations until they have learned to read clients well enough to know when a statement will be perceived as experience-near versus experience-distant. Interpretations are best not delivered as a monologue but rather given piece by piece, perhaps even leading the client to verbalizing the insight through guiding questions. The clinician can lead the client to the insight through clarifying questions, without ever having to state it for the client. The client makes the interpretation; the counselor merely paves the road for it. A client who can arrive at an explanation through a process of clarifying questions never perceives an interpretation as experience-distant because the client delivers the explanation out of the current experience with the clinician. If a clinician is ever uncertain as to whether clients are ready for a given explanation, it may be best to use clarifying questions first, to see if they can arrive there themselves. To repeat an important point, when in doubt, clinicians should not use interpretations. Much excellent therapeutic work can be accomplished without this (perhaps somewhat overrated) counseling strategy. When the time is right for an explanation, clients will accept it, in fact, they may verbalize it first. Counselors need to learn patience and constraint in using this very advanced and difficult strategy.

In terms of the actual mechanics of how to deliver or phrase an interpretation, there is no single way in which an interpretation is accomplished. There are as many ways of phrasing an explanation as there are clinicians, clients, and problems. It is impossible to provide a formula. Only practice will lead to mastery of this technique.

Sample Transcript of Interpretation

Following is an example of an interpretation. This interpretive process could have occurred in many different ways and still have met the criteria or guidelines outlined above. The transcript demonstrates how the counselor first acknowledges and accepts the client (that is, conveys understanding). Then he moves toward exploring why the client developed the type of personality structure or self that would result in the specific behaviors and needs. This exploration through clarifying questions leads the client toward an understanding and explanation of his self or personality structure in a meaningful and experience-near manner. The example demonstrates how questions and simple statements can be combined to lead a client toward making an interpretation independently.

CLIENT: I just don't know if I'll ever be able to trust any woman enough to ask her to live with me. It's my experience that as soon as people move in together, they forget they ever loved each other. . . .

CLINICIAN: You just don't trust that love can survive the daily ups and down of life. . . .

CLIENT: Exactly. You know, how much can you love someone when your stomach is cramping or the phone is ringing off the hook or you have to clean toilets. There's just nothing romantic about cleaning and working and taking care of physical needs. . . . You know, how can you love someone if he farts in bed? *(grins)*

CLINICIAN: Love can only survive your best behavior. . . . *(also smiles)*

CLIENT: Something like that. So, there, now you know. I've really not enjoyed being alone but it's the only safe thing.

CLINICIAN: And to you it's important to be safe! *(understanding)*

CLIENT: Yes. I'm not much of a risk taker.

CLINICIAN: I understand that. It's your way of being in the world. If you don't take risks, you don't get hurt. *(understanding)*

CLIENT: Yes. You know, lots of people can't accept that, though. I get made fun of a lot for not being more daring. Being a guy, I guess it's even worse. I could see a woman getting by with my personality. . . . But somehow guys are expected to be bold and daring. You know, go all the way on everything.

CLINICIAN: It's hard to get people to accept and understand that that's just who you are and that you're okay with that. . . . *(understanding)*

CLIENT: Exactly. You understand, though. . . . You've never pushed me to take risks. . . . I always thought counselors made you face your fears. I was actually worried about that before I started seeing you, you know. . . .

CLINICIAN: Would it make sense for me to push you into stuff that feels risky?

CLIENT: No way—I wouldn't come back. . . .

CLINICIAN: Yeah, exactly. And what good would that be?

CLIENT: But I'm still alone. . . .

CLINICIAN: Right. So maybe rather than us pushing you to ask someone to move in with you, *(grins)* we could look at what experiences in your life you've had that may have made it important to be safe, not to get hurt, not to take risks. We may find there is a reason for why you are the way you are. . . . *(setting the stage for seeking explanations)*

CLIENT: That makes sense. . . . But how do we do that? *(puzzled)*

CLINICIAN: Well, we could start by looking at some events in your life when you felt unsafe, maybe even hurt, or scared. . . . We've talked about some of those already. . . . What do you think?

CLIENT: Oh, there are plenty to choose from, I guess. You know, given my father's temper . . .

CLINICIAN: Yeah, I kind of figured . . .

CLIENT: So were do I start?

CLINICIAN: Maybe at the beginning? Like with the first time that you can remember when you were in a situation that felt unsafe . . . or hurtful . . .

CLIENT: The first time. Hmm . . .

CLINICIAN: *(nods encouragingly; allows for a long pause)*

CLIENT: Well, it may not have been the first time but I remember one time after we had moved into our new house when I was a little kid . . . before my sister was born. My parents were fighting. . . . *(hesitates; tears up a little; then controls his emotions)*

CLINICIAN: Uh huh? *(semi-verbal encourager for client to go on)*

CLIENT: Well, I remember I woke up in the middle of the night because of a loud crash. It was pitch-dark outside—It must have been pretty late. I didn't know what was going on, so I got out of bed to check it out. *(hesitates)*

CLINICIAN: What did you find out?

CLIENT: Well, the crash was my mother's head smashing through the window. She and my father were fighting again, something they were doing a lot. She didn't fall out the window. She came back at my father, looking all bloody. He started screaming at her to get away from him. But she kept coming. Then I saw her grabbing the fireplace poker and she started chasing him through the living room. He was screaming at the top of his lungs. But she was just quiet. She didn't say a word, she just kept chasing him. Finally, she swung at him. And cracked his shoulder. I think he didn't really think that she would do it. Otherwise, maybe he would have left the room or something.

CLINICIAN: And where were you while all of this was happening?

CLIENT: I was standing there watching.

CLINICIAN: Standing where?

CLIENT: In the living-room door.

CLINICIAN: Did they realize you were there?

CLIENT: I'm not sure. I didn't make a sound. They never said anything to me. I finally went back to bed and hid under the covers.

CLINICIAN: How long do you think you stood there?

CLIENT: Well, at the time it seemed like an eternity, I'm sure. But it must have only been a few seconds. They kept screaming at each other after I went back to bed. At some point I heard my father leaving the house. The next day he came home and he had his arm in a sling. I think she broke his shoulder. He had his arm in a sling for a long long time.

CLINICIAN: Go back to that living-room door, would you?

CLIENT: Okay . . .

CLINICIAN: How old were you?

CLIENT: I was about five.

CLINICIAN: What do you suppose went through your mind as you were standing there, watching your parents chase each other?

CLIENT: Probably not much. They did this a lot. I saw them fighting many, many times, and I suppose I just kind of got used to it.

CLINICIAN: You got used to it?

CLIENT: Uh huh . . .

CLINICIAN: You're saying it didn't affect you?

CLIENT: No, I don't think so.

CLINICIAN: And yet somehow this is the event you thought of when you were looking for something in your early life that made you feel unsafe or that hurt you. . . . *(mild confrontation)*

CLIENT: Yeah . . . Well, I mean I must have been scared, I suppose. You know, to see your parents going at it like that . . .

CLINICIAN: (nods)

CLIENT: My sister, you know, she is just like me. Scared, alone, doesn't trust anyone. But she wasn't even born when this happened.

CLINICIAN: But you said it happened all the time. Did it happen after she was born too?

CLIENT: Yeah. I guess so. Yeah. I should be honest with you. . . . It happened even more after she was born. My dad didn't want another baby. So he got meaner after she was born. Started hitting me, too. For anything. If I made noise, if I was quiet; if I played, if I just sat around. He picked on her, too. . . .

CLINICIAN: On your sister?

CLIENT: Yeah. And my mother . . . My mother stopped hitting him, though. Or maybe I should say she stopped defending herself. She would sit there for hours, staring at the wall. My sister, when she still was a baby, would scream and scream, and my mother did nothing. It would scare me to death. I was worried she would die and my mother wouldn't notice. It was like they had forgotten about us. You know, life was so . . . It felt like you couldn't count on anything. Not even your next meal. And all because life got too complicated for my father. . . . You know, like when he had to face the daily chores of having a wife and kids, he fell out of love with all of us. . . . *(looks profoundly surprised)* Oh . . .

CLINICIAN: Oh!

CLIENT: There it is, isn't it?

CLINICIAN: Tell me . . . *(wants the client to give the interpretation)*

Skill Development Recommendations

Recommendation 9-4   *Recall the movie or novel you chose in Chapter Seven for the empathy exercise. For the lead characters, identify how you would express understanding (of what they are doing, feeling, thinking, and so on) and how you would explain (why they are doing, feeling, thinking, and so on, as they are). In the novel or movie, how and when did understanding emerge? When did explanations become clear? Was the sequence leading to the understanding and explanation optimal from a therapeutic perspective? Why and how?*

CLIENT: I learned this attitude from my father. . . .

CLINICIAN: Or at least you interpreted his behavior to reflect that attitude . . . And you felt firsthand how unsafe things were when you felt like the love was gone. . . .

CLIENT: Yes! I learned to play it safe after that. I was a mousy kid. Took no risks because the less I was noticed, the less I got hit. The fewer risks I took, the safer I felt!

CLINICIAN: (nods encouraging client to go on)

CLIENT: So now I keep doing it. I try not to get into the situation my father was in by not letting daily life into my relationships. And I play it safe in everything to keep from ever feeling that unsafe and scared again. No wonder I'm still living alone. I guess it's a miracle that I have dated at all! *(Session continues from there.)*

This example demonstrates how a client can be guided toward profound insights without much obvious explaining or interpreting by the clinician. The counselor merely had to have the insight first, and then led the client with questions to a place where he could realize the connections on his own. An interpretation made in that manner is an outgrowth of the client's current experience and hence is experience-near and of great impact. Had the clinician moved directly into the interpretation after identifying the client's personality style, the client might have rejected the interpretation. This is particularly likely as he initially claimed that the fighting between his parents did not affect him. He could not recognize the impact of the parental relationship until he was ready for it, until he himself arrived at a memory and experience that created a feeling within him in the here-and-now. It is within the context of a here-and-now experience that recapitulates a past experience that experience-nearness is most easily and commonly achieved, setting a perfect stage for interpretation.

The example also demonstrated the working together of many therapeutic strategies in a single exchange with a client. In a textbook, strategies may be dealt with separately, but real life (or real counseling or therapy) does not work like that. A clinician does not set out to use a single strategy; counselors use all strategies they have at their disposal as they are needed, often many simultaneously. In fact, skilled clinicians will not *set out* to use any strategy. They will have all strategies ready in their bag of tricks and will pull out whichever strategy or intervention appears most appropriate when the context for it arises. It is impossible to plan which strategy mental-health-care providers will use with a given client. They will need to have the flexibility to use any strategy, depending on the needs of the client, any time.

four

Skills for Affective Awareness in Psychotherapy and Counseling

WORKING WITH AFFECT AND EMOTION

Overview and Basic Skills

> If we really want to live a full life, both the ancient tradition of Buddhism and the modern one of psychotherapy tell us that we must recover the capacity to feel. Avoiding emotions will only wall us off from our true selves—in fact, there can be no wholeness without an integration of feelings.
>
> *Mark Epstein*

That this book first dealt with issues of cognition is not to imply that work with affect is secondary to or occurs after work with thoughts. Most commonly, mental-health-care providers work with clients on many issues simultaneously. They may be using affective strategies to help clients gain affective awareness, while at the same time also dealing with clients' thoughts and cognitions. Both thoughts and affects need to be addressed, through the use not only of specific cognitive and affective strategies, but also the many communication and questioning skills that were presented as the basis of all therapeutic work in earlier chapters.

Perhaps no aspect of humanity is more complex than that of feelings, that is, emotional awareness, experience, and expression. Emotional awareness refers to a person's ability to recognize that feelings are present and a willingness to accept that emotions are an important and genuine aspect of human experience. Awareness, that is, the willingness to acknowledge that emotions exist and play a role in the human experience, immediately precedes and is the foundation for the recognition of emotional experience. Emotional experience refers to the ability to recognize subtle physical changes and to interpret them correctly. Emotional awareness requires the individual to be able to take stock of simple physical changes that occur when a certain affect is present and to learn to label these emotions according to some agreed-upon semantic system. Awareness and experience help clients differentiate subtle differences between and within emotions. They are intimately tied at every step of the process of gaining affective self-understanding. A certain level of affective self-understanding has to be gained before affective expression can be explored and altered. Affective expression refers to the outer expression of the internal experience, which is based on awareness that there is an internal experience. The three aspects of emotionality, awareness, experience, and expression are closely tied; nevertheless, it is important to recognize their separateness as well, as this has implications for how to proceed with treatment.

Often clinicians fail to differentiate the three aspects of emotionality (awareness, experience, expression), for example, working with a client on emotional expression without realizing that the client does not yet have clarity about inner emotional experience or even awareness. There must be a progression of work with regard to affect. First, clients have to be aware that affect exists and accept that it has legitimacy; then they can begin to explore how they experience it to achieve full and conscious affective awareness in the moment. Only after they have both awareness and internal experience can they turn toward healthy and conscious outer expression. It is true of course that clients may react emotionally (that is, engage in emotional expression) without awareness of this reality. They may deny vehemently that they are expressing an affective state. Such emotional expression is neither conscious nor healthy as it is based on a lack of awareness and is not consciously (internally) experienced by the client before or while being expressed. If a clinician were to attempt to alter such a client's emotional expression, for example from anger to compassion, failure would be very likely. The client would have no understanding of what it is the clinician is getting at because the basic premise that affect is involved would not be shared. Unconscious or automatic emotional expression is dealt with by helping clients gain awareness of and accept their emotional self, followed by an exploration of how affect is experienced internally. Only then can treatment progress to working with altering emotional expression. The models of working with affect that follow are based on this very premise. The first model will concern itself with the creation of awareness and exploration of inner experience, as these two aspects of emotionality are intimately tied to each other and cannot be explained or understood in separation. Once this model has been clarified, a model for affective expression will be added. Since working with affect requires a certain comfort level of the clinician, the chapter concludes with helpful hints about how to facilitate and deal with emotional expression when it occurs in session, either in a planned or spontaneous manner. It is imperative that mental-health-care providers who invite clients to begin to experience and express affect know how to manage emerging affects in session. The clinician's ease and comfort with tolerating affect influences how safe (and successful) the client is in allowing affect to emerge. Throughout the work with affect, clinicians keep the strategies for managing affect in the forefront of their minds.

A MODEL FOR AFFECTIVE AWARENESS AND INNER EXPERIENCE

Although it may oversimplify matters somewhat, it is useful to think of affective awareness and inner experience as consisting of a continuum that ranges from absence of any emotional awareness whatsoever (including absence of any conscious inner experience) to presence of awareness accompanied by clear inner experience coupled with deep understanding. Many steps connect this continuum, as will be outlined below and shown in Figure 10-1. Given this conceptualization of affective awareness and experience, a model for working with affect emerges that proceeds from helping clients gain awareness to recognizing, accepting, and understanding their inner experience with clarity. The clinician first has to establish the client's current level of affective consciousness and then proceed to help deepen affective awareness and understanding, beginning intervention at the appropriate level. What follows is a discussion of the conceptual model of assessment and of level of intervention. Actual strategies that can be used at each level of affective awareness and inner experience are outlined in detail in the next chapter.

It should be noted that while the model is presented and proceeds in a linear fashion, clients might not always present in this linear form. Especially at the higher affective levels, some overlap may occur in the different levels of experience. For example, acceptance of affect, dealt with below as Level Eight, may begin to play a role in a client's affective experience as early as Level Six, which deals with conflicted and mixed emotions. However, for ease of discussion these two experience levels are presented separately. As the reader moves through the levels, it is important to remember that overlap across stages is possible, in fact, likely, and that work always needs to proceed in a fashion that is tailored to the individual client. Also, the reader will note that various exercises that work with affect will be recommended at more than one level of affective experience. When the same exercise can be used at different levels, this implies that the exercise *mechanics* are the same, or similar, across purposes. In other words, the mental-health-care provider may choose the same process to go through with a client, but will do so for different reasons and with different expectations about outcome. The purpose of the exercise will dictate the level of depth that is pursued and the types, number, and nuances of affects to be worked with and explored. The next chapter, which will detail the mechanics of the exercises, will present examples at different affective experience levels (where applicable) in the attempt to clarify how the same process (or exercise) can be used for different purposes, to meet the client's therapeutic needs arising at different levels. The model for affective awareness and inner experience that follows is loosely based on research that has explored and defined normal affective development (for example, Lane and Schwartz, 1986; Stern, 1987).

Level One: Basic Awareness of Affect

The first step in this model of working with affect is the assessment of whether a client is aware of affect. Many clients come to counseling or therapy with painful affects and emotions but are not actually aware that this is so. Some express affects outwardly without any inner recognition of this fact. For example, a client may come across as hostile and angry and when queried about affect may deny any awareness of angry emotions. Such a client enters treatment at the most basic level of affective awareness and inner experience, unaware of affect within the self. This is not to say that this client does not talk about feelings. However, any discussion of feelings is just that: a cognitive treatise without true inner experience. Often talk about affect will involve the emotions of other people or will recapture what others have claimed about the feelings of the client, without the client having conscious experience of this affect personally. For example, many obsessive-compulsive clients have learned to talk about feelings, without making any inner connection to the words they are using. They will indicate that someone else (often an intimate partner or parent) has referred them for treatment because that person perceives the client as depressed. The client will be able to detail what the referral source describes as signs of depression. However, when asked how that depression feels to the client, the client will be unable to answer: Awareness and inner experience of the affect is lacking. Clients who present at this point on the affective continuum need to be worked with at a very basic affective level. Strategies focus on opening the client up to a very basic awareness of inner physiological experiences that may later be correlated to feelings. Examples of such strategies are the *Breathing Exercise, Bodily Awareness Exercise,* and the *Basic Bodily Experience Exercise* (see the next chapter). Trying to force the client at this level to explore feelings on a more advanced level will lead to frustration for the client and the clinician. Instead, intervention will need to focus on slowly developing physiological awareness in the client. The client will first have to learn how to listen to the body in general; sometimes this may start as simply as exploring with the client what it physiologically feels like to be hungry. Clients at this level of affective awareness are so detached from their body that such basic explorations can be difficult and challenging in and of themselves. Only when some physiological awareness of physical feelings (hunger, thirst, sexual arousal, aches and pains) has been gained will a progression to physiological exploration of affects be in order and possible.

Is the client aware of the presence of affect?

   ↓   ↓   →   Intervention begins at this level:
 Yes   No   Basic strategies that facilitate basic
   ↓   awareness

Can the client identify an inner (physiological) experience of the affect?

   ↓   ↓   →   Intervention begins at this level:
 Yes   No   Advanced strategies to facilitate
   ↓   basic awareness

Does the client know how to attach a basic label to the inner experience of the affect?

   ↓   ↓   →   Intervention begins at this level:
 Yes   No   Strategies to identify basic range of
   ↓   affects; experience in here-and-now

Has the client avoided the development of this affect as a default affect?

   ↓   ↓   →   Intervention begins at this level:
 Yes   No   Strategies to identify basic range and
   ↓   expand repertoire of affects

Does the client recognize levels of intensity (shades of gray) within a given affect?

   ↓   ↓   →   Intervention begins at this level:
 Yes   No   Strategies to identify levels of intensity
   ↓   within any given category of affect

Does the client recognize mixed or conflicted affects?

   ↓   ↓   →   Intervention begins at this level:
 Yes   No   Strategies to explore affect overlap and
   ↓   coexistence (even incongruent ones)

Does the client know how to differentiate screen and underlying or base affect?

   ↓   ↓   →   Intervention begins at this level:
 Yes   No   Strategies to expose screen affects
   ↓   and explore underlying affects

Does the client fully accept experienced affect(s)?

   ↓   ↓   →   Intervention begins at this level:
 Yes   No   Strategies to enhance acceptance
   ↓   of affects

Does the client understand the origin and role of experienced affect(s)?

   ↓   ↓   →   Intervention begins at this level:
 Yes   No   Strategies to explore sources of affect
   ↓   and to show that knowledge of "why"
                                     can be used to alter "how" and "when"

Client has achieved full affective awareness and inner experience

          └──────────→   Move to exploration of Affective
                                Expression (see Figure 10-2)

FIGURE 10-1

A Flowchart for Assessment of Level of Affective Awareness and Inner Experience

Level Two: Basic Inner Experience of Affect

If a client has basic awareness of physiological arousal and affect, the next level of affective experience can be explored. The critical question at this level is whether the client can identify the inner experience that goes along with some kind, any kind, of emotionality. Some clients come to treatment complaining that something "feels off," that they "don't feel right," or that they are somehow "out of kilter" (that is, there is affective awareness), but they are unable to explain further. They have neither a label for nor an understanding of what that feeling may represent. It is important to explore whether such a client can identify the inner experience, or physiological state of being, that is associated with this diffuse feeling of something not being quite right emotionally.

A client at this second level of affective awareness and experience will be unable to identify or connect with a physiological response spontaneously. This client may not even recognize that an "off feeling" has a physiological aspect to it (that is, is experienced in the body). Thus, intervention has to begin by linking the diffuse feeling(s) the client reports (but cannot identify!) to an internal state of being. This can be done through interventions that help the client recognize that mental states have bodily correlates that can be identified. Such clients can be helped to recognize, for example, that when they say they feel out of kilter, their stomach hurts or their neck is stiff. Linking such basic physiological reactions to the "off feeling" will help clients gain inner experience of affects of which they are aware only in a very rudimentary form. Strategies that are helpful with clients at this level include the *Body Attunement Exercise* and the *Basic- and Advanced-Bodily-Experience Exercises* (see the next chapter). Some clients at this level may have vague emotional awareness of some feelings but are completely cut off from awareness of other affects. Although these clients will label no affects yet with certainty, they may express more understanding and may have more physiological awareness and experience for some emotions than for others. For example, some clients may be able to connect with feelings in the body that to the clinician may signal anxiety, but they may not be able to identify an inner experience when their presentation appears more depressed to the clinician. Clients may be at Level One with regard to some feelings (in this example, depression) and at Level Two with regard to others (in the example, anxiety).

Level Three: Labeling of Basic Affect

Clients may be aware of feelings that manifest physically within their body but they have not necessarily labeled the feelings yet. In this instance the clinician will need to ask the critical question that identifies the next, or third, level of affective awareness and experience, namely, whether the client has a label for that feeling and physiological state. It is not uncommon for clients to have a diffuse feeling, to be able to explain where and how they feel it in their body, but not to know what to call the emotion. Such clients may complain that they "haven't been feeling right" and may connect this emotional state to a physiological one, recognizing that when they feel poorly their head hurts, or they feel fatigued, or they may have a tendency toward stomachaches. Even if such clients do not verbalize the physiological correlate at first, they are readily able to do so with some questioning. They may be able to recognize that they "have butterflies in their stomach" or that their "heart aches." If clients have this level of awareness and recognition of inner experience, the next step involves finding out whether they can accurately and reliably label this emotion. Can the client differentiate whether this feeling is depression, anxiety, or anger? Often clients are not able to do this. If clients lack labels for their emotions and their inner experience, intervention needs to focus on helping them develop a basic vocabulary for a basic range of feelings. No great sophistication is sought here. The client merely receives help in figuring out how to differentiate very broad human emotions such as anger, anxiety or fear, sadness, happiness or joy, and similar large categories of human affective experience. The labeling process is easiest if the client has learned to relate different physiological reactions to certain types of (yet unlabeled) experiential feeling states. The client who can identify that feeling "off kilter" involves butterflies in the stomach and trembling hands, whereas feeling "out of it" involves a headache, increased sleep, and lack of pleasure, will progress faster toward labeling than the clients who have not yet succeeded in identifying different physiological states.

Once Level-Two work has helped clients identify a number of experience states, labeling (Level-Three work) can begin. This is achieved by building on clients' inner (physiological) experience in the here-and-now. The *Here-and-Now Affect Exploration Exercise* in a later chapter outlines the basic process for such work, mainly by example. If a clinician recognizes, for example, that a client has arrived in a sad mood, this can be used as an opportunity to help the client learn the label for this current state of being by identifying, with the client, the inner experience (essentially Level-Two work) and then attaching a label to it. This is much the same process that occurs developmentally with young children, when a parent provides a label for an affect that is clearly experienced by a child. Who has not heard a parent say something to the effect of "Yes, that was really, really sad, wasn't it? Those tears show just how sad you feel, don't they?" The same thing, perhaps in more sophisticated language, but perhaps not, will occur in counseling and therapy with clients who are struggling to advance to this level of affective experience. They need to learn basic labels for their inner experience so that they can become more effective and efficient at recognizing and communicating their feelings both in and out of treatment. Labeling of feelings is only useful if the client clearly has identified the corresponding physiological or inner emotional state. Providing labels to a client without tying the labels to experience will help the client talk about feelings without any better awareness of what the feelings are really about. Caution is necessary not to jump to labeling without experience work first (experience first, label later). It is better for a client to recognize a physiological process that signifies a feeling and not to know the label for the emotion than to pick a convenient label without truly knowing the physiological or inner manifestation of the word.

Level Four: Identification of Default Affect

As the client develops a basic repertoire of feeling labels, it is paramount to ascertain that the client does not just conveniently use the same label for all affects or respond to all experiences with the same affect. Sometimes, once clients have learned to identify a particular affect, they generalize this label to all emotional experiences. Such a generalization of labels can be called a default affect; no matter what the client experiences, the label is always the same. It is helpful for the clinician to sort out whether an affective label has become a default or whether it is used genuinely. A clear indication that a label has become a default is when it is used exclusively. The counselor will note that the client is applying the same label in all situations, to all bodily experiences. If this happens, it is necessary to help the client recognize the singularity of the affective-label choice. Once this recognition takes hold, the same interventions are used as at the prior affective awareness and experience level. Work is done to help the client expand the repertoire of experienced affects and their commensurate labels. This can be done by assisting clients in recognizing that a range of affects are possible in any given situation and to differentiate labels connected with different inner experiences. In some ways this level of assessment is a mere double-checking that the client has learned how to label a range of affects, not just a single one, and may be viewed as an extension of the second and third levels. Interventions chosen at this level are therefore basically identical to those used at Level Three.

Level Five: Identification of Affect Intensity

Once it has been established that clients correctly label their inner affective experience in terms of broad strokes of basic feelings, the next level of affective awareness and experience can be explored. At this level, differentiation with regard to the intensity of a particular affect is assessed. Often clients who have not quite reached this level, but who know how to identify and label basic affect, are unaware that there are shades of gray within each category of basic affects. They may not recognize that there are many intensities of anger, depression, fear, joy, and so forth, focusing only on the broad category. If clients are unaware of nuances of feelings within a broad category, intervention needs to begin at this level. It focuses on helping clients identify the different levels of intensity within each category of emotion, helping them develop labels for the different shades of gray. Exact labeling may vary from client to client. The important point is not to come up with an exact continuum or classification of words, but a continuum of affective nuances within a category of affect *for a particular client*. For example, for one client, anger may be broken down into four sublevels of intensity, ranging from irritation to frustration to anger to rage. Another client may feel more subtle differences and may end up identifying six sublevels of intensity, perhaps ranging from irritation to exasperation to aggravation to annoyance to anger to fury. The point of intervention at this level is to help clients recognize that feelings have subtle nuances and vary in intensity across situations. Being able to differentiate subtle shades of feeling often helps clients feel more in control of their affect as they do not have to feel that the entire spectrum of affect is unleashed all at once all the time. For example, often clients who are first learning to identify sadness become fearful of being overwhelmed by depression and morbidity. They are afraid that just by labeling a feeling as sadness, they will be utterly depressed. For such a client, sadness has only one intensity: overwhelming depression. It is helpful for such an all-or-none client to recognize that sadness comes in many levels of intensity and as such can be handled successfully. A client may recognize that having the blues is a mild form of sadness that can easily be overcome with a simple strategy such as exercise. Differentiating the blues from despondency and despair is helpful for this client. The exploration of intensity of affect can of course be accomplished in many ways. A later chapter outlines the *Affect Continuum Exercise* as a concrete example of the basic process that needs to take place with a client at this level of affective awareness and inner experience. The *Basic and Advanced Bodily Awareness Exercises* and the *Here-and-Now Affect Exploration Exercise* can be modified to render them helpful in letting clients experience the subtle differences in physiological response at the different levels of intensity of the same basic affect.

Level Six: Identification of Mixed and Conflicted Affect

Once clients can differentiate levels of intensity within a given category of affect, they are ready to be assessed for the next level of affective awareness and experience, which deals with the recognition of mixed and conflicting feelings. From a developmental perspective, the ability to hold conflicting or even just differing affects at the same moment develops rather late. Children move through affective development in a manner that progresses very similarly to the levels outlined here. Most clients enter treatment at about this level of affective awareness and inner experience. They are not yet aware or cannot yet accept that they can react with two completely different emotions to the same event; for example, they may not be able to integrate feeling sad and angry about the same thing at the same time. The experience of affect is viewed by clients who have not yet achieved the identification of mixed and conflicted feelings as something that is unitary, or confined to one type of emotion. Clients at this level will be confused and unable to identify what they are feeling when more than one affect emerges in a given context. Intervention is targeted to helping clients recognize that affective experience is rarely unitary, but often quite complex. Not only does a single affect have various levels of intensity (as established at the prior level), but it is often accompanied by other affects, which are also experienced at various levels of intensity.

Lack of recognition of mixed feelings often has to do with having a second (or additional) emotion that may be perceived as inappropriate or unpredictable. For example, clients may experience both relief and anger at being fired from a job that was very stressful. It is very likely that this client would feel rather confused by the jumble of emotions that emerges after the event. Such a client may come to counseling indicating confusion about the reaction to the event, perhaps not being able to recognize or admit the sense of relief that was experienced. While anger may be a predictable and acceptable emotion in response to being fired, the client may not perceive relief as a feeling that should emerge. Confusion may arise from either an inability to recognize that emotions can blend, or from an unwillingness to accept some versus other emotions in certain circumstances. The focus of this level is less on those clients who are unable to sort out what they are feeling because of not accepting a certain affect (acceptance of affects being the focus of Level Eight). Rather, this level is more concerned with assessing whether clients are able at all to experience more than one emotion at the same time. Intervention at this level focuses on helping clients recognize when more than one affect emerges at the same time, when affects overlap and maybe even conflict with one another, and when affects mix to blend into a new and unique affective experience that may be quite difficult to label with a single word. The complexity of human emotions is quite clear to the client achieving this level of self-awareness. Exploring affect in the here-and-now will be one of the best ways to help clients become aware of their own emotional reaction and complexity as it will serve to help them explore and experience when a blend of emotions occurs as it occurs. The *Here-and-Now Affect Exploration Exercise* used for various purposes since Level Three will be helpful again here, as will the *Basic- and Advanced-Bodily-Experience Exercises* (all detailed in a later chapter).

Level Seven: Identification of Underlying Affect

Once clients can experience both nuances of single and mixed emotions, they are ready to explore whether they have achieved the next level of affective awareness and experience. At this level, the basic question has to do with the client's ability to differentiate screen affects from underlying affects. Clients who have reached the affective sophistication to gain awareness of mixed and conflicted feelings are ready to explore when an affect they appear to experience is the truly important and primary affect, and when it serves to cover a deeper or more profound (often more painful) affect. Not all immediately identified affects are at the base of the client's experience. Often clients can become aware of some affects and not of others. Affects that tend to emerge more readily and that tend to fill in for or cover up more painful or underlying affects can be called screen affects. Screen affects are the affects clients tend to be able to identify easily and tolerate readily. They are affects clients have experienced often and are familiar with. Clients generally have the resources to deal with these affects and accept them freely and easily. However, the readily and easily experienced affect may not reflect the client's true reaction to a situation. Instead it may serve to cover up a more painful or subtle emotional experience of which the client is unaware. This underlying affect may also be called the base or primary affect. At this level (Level Seven), the client is assessed for the ability to differentiate base and screen affects. This is accomplished via strategies that help the client look deeper into their emotional experience and is often motivated by an intuition on the part of the clinician that the affect (screen) that is being explored is not all there is to the client's true experience. Clinicians often recognize an affect as a screen before the client does and then through careful questioning and here-and-now work with affective experience help the client recognize a deeper and subtler affective response. Underlying affects are often recognized first not as primary affects, but as mixed emotions. The client begins to get an inkling that there is another emotion that is perceived in a given situation and, since having achieved Level Six, may perceive it as equal to the other affect that was already identified. What differentiates an underlying affect from mixed emotions is that the screen affect often disappears once the underlying affect is recognized. This is not true for mixed emotions. Here, each emotion already identified previously continues to be felt even as additional emotions emerge in the client's awareness. Primary or underlying affects are often more painful and subtle, and the client often has reasons for not being aware of them. They may represent affects that appear overwhelming, too painful, or too profound. The type of work that is done with the client is very similar, however, to that done at Level Six and the same exercises can be used and modified for the specific purpose of exploring primary affects. The modifications have to do with the clinician being more persistent in getting the client to explore physiological states of being and being more forceful about here-and-now explorations of emotional reactions.

Often in looking for underlying affects it is helpful to search for affects that appear to be the very opposite of the affect already identified by the client. As such, if the client identifies depression, it may be useful to search for anger; if the client experiences anxiety, there may actually be excitement; exuberance may cover sadness; fear may be a screen for aggression. Underlying affects are often affects that have been projected and declared as alien by the client for some reason or another. The client has disavowed the underlying affect, but has attributed it to others in the environment. For example, a client may have strong aggressive impulses. These, however, were not deemed appropriate in the client's home and the client learned quickly to disavow this affect in the self. However, because the aggressive affect remained, the client learned to attribute it to an external source. Thus, the client came to view others as aggressive and consequently developed fear (of the aggressive impulses projected onto others). Fear becomes the screen affect; aggression is the underlying affect. By pushing past the fear, the client will recognize the underlying aggression and the fear will resolve. Work then focuses on helping the client accept the underlying affect (that is, aggression), leading to Level-Eight work. As clinician and client begin to work on underlying affects, both need to be prepared for painful work. Clearly, this reality is yet another excellent example of why affective work proceeds according to a careful model based on levels, in which intervention is tailored to the client's affective awareness and inner experience. That way, the clinician does not push the client into therapeutic work for which the client is not yet emotionally prepared. It is also at this level that the clinician's preparedness becomes paramount. The in-session management of difficult emotions becomes important as clients explore new and painful emotional landscapes.

Level Eight: Acceptance of Affect

Identification of affects (especially of differing intensities, mixed emotions, and underlying affects), no matter how profound and insightful, does not guarantee that a client will also accept the affect that is experienced. Level Eight is concerned with exploring with the client whether affects that emerge (whether they be mixed, conflicted, screen, or primary) are truly accepted by the client as an important and valued aspect of the client's self-experience. For many clients, acceptance is not a black-or-white issue. They are able and willing to accept some affects, but reject others. Often clients can accept that they may feel afraid or anxious, but reject the notion that they may respond in anger. Similarly, clients may accept their own sadness, but for whatever reason, cannot accept their own pleasure or joy. Assessment of acceptance proceeds slowly and cautiously, exploring the degree of a client's acceptance of each affect as it emerges. Awareness of certain mixed emotions or underlying affects (work at Levels Six and Seven) may be thwarted by lack of acceptance of those particular affects. Thus, clients working at Level Six who are beginning to be able to identify mixed and conflicted emotions may not be able to recognize or label their feelings in some instances, because they have not accepted one of the affects involved. In such cases, work at Level Six and Level Eight would have to alternate. For example, the client might have to gain awareness of a certain affect by itself, gain acceptance of it, and then learn to recognize it in a blend of emotions.

In exploring acceptance the clinician needs to be sensitive to partial acceptance or selective acceptance. There are many reasons why a client may not accept a given affect. Possibilities include the following:

- the client is frightened of the affect
- the client is overwhelmed by the experience of the affect
- the client was not allowed expression of this affect during the developmental years
- the client is threatened by an affect

Understanding the reasons underlying lack of acceptance often has to precede acceptance of any affects the client does not already value and accept. Much of this work will have to be rather cognitive in nature and hence the strategies covered in working with cognition and thought apply here. If lack of acceptance derives largely from a sense of being overwhelmed by affect, relaxation strategies can be helpful. For example, if a client has severe anxiety, that person may be greatly assisted by learning how to calm the body and mind so as to achieve greater equanimity even during normally stressful situations. Two types of relaxation exercises, *Progressive Muscle Relaxation* and *Focusing Relaxation,* are detailed in a later chapter. *Breathing Exercises* can be helpful as well, both in and of themselves and as an integral part of the relaxation exercises. Additional helpful techniques that can be applied during interactions with clients to facilitate affective acceptance include

- the mental-health-care provider's communicated acceptance of the client's affect(s)
- the dispelling of myths about a particular affect
- the teaching of strategies for managing affects by which the client feels overwhelmed
- normalization of the experience of affects the client perceives as unacceptable or inappropriate
- reshaping of learning about certain affects during prior life experiences
- focus on here-and-now experience to desensitize the client to the affect and to make it manageable and agreeable

Level Nine: Understanding of Affect

Acceptance of affects often is closely tied to understanding where and how a particular affect developed or emerged. Thus, work at Level Eight and Level Nine is often done simultaneously and without clear differentiation. Both levels heavily involve cognitive work, and although the levels are included here because they are part of the affective awareness and inner-experience model, the work involved in terms of intervention is actually cognitive in nature, alternating with affective work. One set of more strictly affectively-focused exercises that can be used as well, however, is that of guided imageries. There are endless variations of guided imageries; a skilled clinician can also use guided imagery for earlier levels of inner awareness. However, it is recommended that mental-health-care providers who want to apply guided imagery receive specialized training with this powerful set of techniques.

Understanding of affect refers to helping the client become aware of how and where certain affective response styles developed over the life span. It is a process of helping clients recognize that there are at least two possible sources for affects: the here-and-now occurrence, and past experiences that continue to influence how the client responds in certain situations. The client is given assistance in differentiating when affects are truly an expression of a reaction to a particular here-and-now event and when they are reactions that are ingrained, learned in the past, and carried forward into the present. Often as clients recognize why they have the affective experience they have, they begin to feel more control over their emotional reactions.

If a certain affect, for example, was learned in the past and continues to emerge in the present regardless of appropriateness, learning this may assist the client in beginning to curb the affect in situations that do not really call for it. For example, a client may have grown up in an environment that was highly critical and learned that any performance presented to a parent was judged harshly and deemed inadequate. The client slowly learned to associate feelings of depression and self-loathing with having to present work. This client may now be an excellent employee in a large firm who has responsibility for monthly presentations of work done. Because of the strong association learned early in life, the client may not be able to engage in these presentations without feelings of depression and despair. This may be despite the fact that the client's employer is very pleased with and praising of the work. The old experience and ongoing expectation of criticism, however, overrides the current experience and profoundly affects how the client experiences the situation. Clients who learn of such connections (that is, gain understanding about their affects) often feel profound relief and can then slowly begin to learn to alter their affective responses.

A MODEL FOR AFFECTIVE EXPRESSION

Just as affective awareness and inner experience need to be thoroughly assessed to determine how to proceed with intervention, affective expression also needs to be closely explored. Affective expression is explored in terms of how it relates to the underlying inner affects experienced by the client, and cannot be separated from affective inner experience and awareness. Thus, it is best dealt with after the mental-health-care provider understands where the client functions with regard to affective experience.

The main issues to be explored in the context of affective expression have to do with how consciously and congruently the client expresses emotions to the outside world. The suggested flow of questioning is shown in Figure 10-2. One important note is necessary in the context of outward expression. There is a great deal of individual variation with regard to how people express themselves affectively. The same intensity of emotion may lead to two completely different levels of intensity with regard to their outward expression. This difference is largely mediated by personality style and emotional maturity. Introverts will be less expressive than extroverts; emotionally mature individuals are less likely to overreact outwardly and may show a more tempered expression of a like feeling. One example of this variation in expression may be that of many practicing Buddhists who, despite heightened inner awareness, have very well-modulated outer expressiveness. Their low expressiveness is not at all pathological or problematic, but rather healthily mediated by their spiritual beliefs.

Step One: Conscious Outward Expression

The first step is to ask whether the client evidences any outward expression of affect, and if so, whether it is conscious. If there is no outward expression, the first step will be to explore why this is so. If the client evidences no outward signs of emotion because of a lack of awareness of affect, that is, because of no recognition of inner experience, the clinician needs to backtrack to the exploration of inner experience. Clearly, if a good assessment was done regarding awareness and inner experience, this would not have to happen as the clinician would already know that the client has no inner experience and would have begun intervention at that level. Occasionally, clients may have no outer expression despite having some level of inner experience. There is a multitude of possible reasons that can be explored for such a behavioral pattern. The client may be intellectualizing or sublimating emotionality, expressing affect that is experienced inwardly in outer ways that are out of the ordinary and not recognized as affective expression. Such a client may work very hard when feeling anxiety, may exercise when feeling annoyed, or may sleep longer hours when feeling sad. Alternatively, the client may talk about the emotions rather than expressing them openly and emotionally. This client may have intellectually stimulating conversations about affects without ever letting on that this talk hides a profound inner experience of that very emotion. The mental-health-care provider will know if this is the case since questioning regarding inner experience would have provided enough information about the client's inner awareness to let the clinician know that the lack of outer expression is not congruent with the level of inner experience. If

Does the client engage in outward expression of affect?

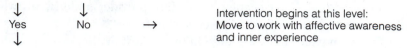

			Intervention begins at this level:
Yes	No	→	Move to work with affective awareness
			and inner experience

Is the client aware of this outward expression of affect?

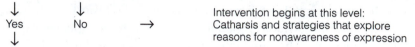

			Intervention begins at this level:
Yes	No	→	Catharsis and strategies that explore
			reasons for nonawareness of expression

Has the client avoided a ritualized (default) style of affective expression?

			Intervention begins at this level:
Yes	No	→	Strategies that explore patterns and
			increase repertoire of expression;
			facilitation of catharsis

Is the client's affective expression congruent in intensity with inner affective experience?

			Intervention begins at this level:
Yes	No	→	Strategies that explore reasons for
			incongruence and create congruence

Is the client's affective expression congruent in type or quality with inner affective experience?

			Intervention begins at this level:
Yes	No	→	Strategies that explore reasons for
			incongruence and create congruence;
			facilitation of catharsis

Client has achieved healthy and conscious affective expression, congruent with inner experience and awareness

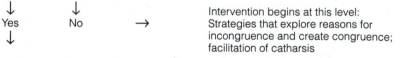

	Move to the exploration of other possible
└────────→	reasons for seeking treatment at this
	time (if assessed at intake) or consider
	termination of treatment

FIGURE 10-2

A Flowchart of Questions for Assessment of All Aspects of Affective Expression

---

there is no outer expression although client and clinician have been working on and have succeeded in establishing inner experience, then strategies will need to be employed that facilitate outer expression. Most importantly, catharsis needs to be encouraged. How to do this will be covered later.

Some clients will show outer expression of affect but upon query the mental-health-care provider recognizes that the client is not aware of this expression. The client is visibly exuding emotionality to others, but denies recognition of this outer expression. If such unaware outer expression is accompanied by lack of inner experience and awareness, the clinician will backtrack to work on inner experience first. Occasionally, however, a client may have achieved some level of inner experience without having recognized how this affect is evidenced outwardly. It will be helpful to intervene by assisting the client in recognizing how certain behaviors and actions suggest affect to the observer. This process will help the client build interpersonal as well as individual self-awareness. For example, a client may appear clearly angry to the clinician. It may help the client to hear what affect this demeanor suggests to the clinician. The clinician may gently point out an intensely pitched voice, clenched fists, harsh vocabulary, furrowed brow, and other physical signs of anger or hostility. Similarly, some clients may be unaware of how their depression manifests outwardly. These clients may benefit from being helped to recognize their slowed speech, low voice, stooped shoulders, unkempt appearance, and similar physical signs. The mental-health-care provider makes good use of knowledge about nonverbal communication to work with this client who unconsciously expresses what is felt inwardly. The clinician uses empathic statements to reflect back the client's reality, applying knowledge gained with regard to strategies for facilitating communication.

Step Two: Ritualized Outward Expression

The clinician also explores whether the affect that is being expressed is always the same. Just as in inner experience, the mental-health-care provider has to establish that the client does not default to the same affect in all situations. In the case of outer experience, the clinician needs to assess how the client expresses affect outwardly. Is the expression the same regardless of the inner experience? For example, does the client react with an angry, high-pitched voice and clenched fists regardless of inner experience and outer situation? Do depression, joy, anxiety, and anger all look the same on the outside? If such ritualized expression of affect occurs, the client needs assistance in recognizing how the outer expression comes across to those with whom interactions take place. This is done in some manner of feedback, as discussed for Step One, using good communication skills, knowledge about nonverbal information, and cognitive-awareness skills. Occasionally, clients have ritualized outer expression not because they express all inner experiences the same way, but because they are stuck with an inner experience of a default emotion, that is, they are stuck at Level Four of the inner-experience hierarchy. If this is the case, intervention has to be targeted there. Once the client is unstuck with regard to inner experience, outer expression should change automatically.

Step Three: Congruence with Level of Intensity

It is also important to check whether an emotion that appears to be expressed outwardly matches the intensity of the emotion as felt inwardly. It is not uncommon for clients to show affect with either significantly more or less intensity outwardly than inwardly. This incongruence will result in miscommunication as observers will either over- or underestimate the client's given affect. For example, some clients may express sadness with crying, slumped shoulders, a sad face, and slowed movements, regardless of the level of intensity with which they experience it inwardly. The client may verbalize that on a given day the intensity of sadness is at mild upset or at despair with regard to inner experience. However, outer expression does not change. Another client may have the same way of expressing an inner sense of anger regardless of intensity. Such a client may be perceived as enraged even when the person's inner experience is one of mild annoyance. The outer expression is intense regardless of inner experience. Such incongruence with intensity needs to be explored first with regard to the reasons for it. One possibility includes the absence of inner awareness about subtle shades of gray in the experience of emotions. This lack of inner awareness has left the client at a lower level of inner experience (Level Three or Four) and has made correct identification of the subtle nuances of affect difficult if not impossible for the client. If this is the reason for the client's incongruence, intervention needs to be targeted to the appropriate inner-experience level. Once the clinician has clarified that the client has subtle and nuanced inner experience, outer incongruence is addressed. For some clients, it may be necessary to engage in cognitive strategies that actually teach modulation of affective expression. An example may be a client who reacts with severe outer aggression at the slightest hint of inner experience of anger. This client may have inadequate controls over behavior and may benefit from anger management techniques, a psychoeducational approach to helping the client gain control over this particular affect's expression.

Step Four: Congruence with Type of Emotion

The final aspect of outer expression that is explored is that of congruence in expression with mixed emotions or conflicted feelings. Some clients with conflicted feelings express outwardly only one of the many feelings they may have. For example, the client who has just been fired and experiences relief and anger may only show hostility. The client does not express the full range of experiences that are perceived internally, leaving a whole aspect of self unexpressed and creating the opportunity for miscommunication with others. Exploration of this style of incongruence is identical to that in Step Three. First, the clinician has to assess whether the lack of differentiated outer expression is due to lack of inner differentiation or recognition of conflicted and mixed emotions. If this is the case, intervention takes place at that level of inner experience. If inner experience is clear about the mélange of affects involved but does not translate into outer expression, intervention takes place at the expressive level. It may be important to determine whether the choice of which of the many experienced affects to express is driven by a ritualized outer expression of affect. Similarly, the clinician may want to double-check on the possibility of a screen affect receiving outer expression and the underlying affect not being expressed even though it is experienced. Working back and forth between inner experience and outer expression is critical in this step to make sure that intervention is targeted to the correct cause of the incongruence. Once the clinician is clear that the problem rests with outer expression, not inner experience, intervention can be focused on facilitating the expression of affects involved internally. This is best accomplished by assisting the client with appropriate catharsis.

FACILITATING CLIENTS' AFFECTIVE EXPERIENCE AND EXPRESSION IN SESSION

The affective model, as discussed earlier, presented the clinician's need to be able to draw out a client's inner experience and outer expression of affect. Drawing clients out emotionally is particularly helpful to intervention at the affective-expression level but actually also supports the work done to create inner experience. This is so because the facilitation of emotion—that is, catharsis—is not only about outer expression of affect, but also inner awareness of how emotions manifest in physiological reactions. Even though catharsis may be typically thought of as facilitating an outer show of emotions, it is actually a process of helping the client get in touch with feelings, both as they are experienced inwardly and as they are expressed outwardly. Thus, the process of facilitating catharsis is one that is applicable at all levels of affective work and is a valuable standard tool for the mental-health-care provider. The same can be said about empathic responding. It too is a therapeutic strategy that has ubiquitous applicability in working with affect, as the careful reader has already noted.

The client's experience of catharsis is dependent upon the mental-health-care provider's ability to help the client experience and ventilate feelings and needs. The mere experience and subsequent release and expression of emotion is highly therapeutic for many clients despite the fact that it necessarily leads neither to internalization of change nor to insight and growth (Young and Bemark, 1996). Catharsis can be said to have a number of related benefits:

- catharsis is useful in helping clients gain recognition of the intensity and type of affect that was formerly held in, repressed, or otherwise kept from being experienced

- catharsis is useful in helping clients express emotions according to the intensity and type of affect that is felt and previously was not outwardly demonstrated
- catharsis represents a recognition by the client that a strong inner affective response exists and must be acknowledged through conscious inner experience
- catharsis represents an acknowledgment by the client that a strong inner affect is experienced that must find expression
- through the conscious inner experience of affect, the client raises inner self-awareness and may increase affective acceptance
- through the outer expression of the affect, the client takes ownership of and thus responsibility for the affect
- inner experience and outer expression of affect may facilitate a new self-perception and may lead to insight regarding the self in relationships

For catharsis, or ventilation (Corsini and Wedding, 1997), to take place, a client has to feel safe in the therapeutic environment and accepted by the mental-health-care provider. Clients are well aware that catharsis does not necessarily result in the ventilation or release of only positive, but also of negative affects, affects that may appear quite frightening and overwhelming to the client. Being in a safe place and with a person whom the client can trust is not surprisingly an important ingredient in actually allowing for inner experience and outer expression to occur. Because catharsis can lead to sudden and perhaps painful or overwhelming experience of affect, there are some clients with presenting problems or diagnostic presentations for whom catharsis may not be the best course of action or experience early on in the therapeutic relationship. For example, clients with post-traumatic stress disorders may best not be encouraged to become affectively aroused early in treatment as their level of arousal may become too intense to be easily tolerated and helpful (Young and Bemark, 1996). Histrionic clients may already be overemotional; encouragement of catharsis with such clients may be counter-therapeutic in that it encourages a means of expression that is already overused. Encouragement of catharsis must be a conscious choice by the clinician that is carefully tailored to the specific needs of each client.

There are a number of variables that can either hinder or help with the process of catharsis (see Table 10-1 for an overview). As already mentioned, the client needs to perceive the therapeutic environment as safe and supportive. Additionally, the clinician needs to be able to communicate acceptance of the client regardless of what affects may emerge. The client must feel perfectly secure in the assumption that the clinician will not be turned off by angry, hostile, demeaning, or otherwise negatively flavored affects that may reach the client's awareness or that may be expressed. Additionally, the mental-health-care provider must be clear about giving permission for the experience and expression of all affects. The expression has to be safe, of course, and it is the clinician's responsibility to let clients know that they are capable of assuring such safety. The ability to communicate permissiveness and safety about affective experience and expression also rests on the clinician's personal willingness to participate in a cathartic process and to allow it without being personally frightened or overwhelmed by it. Knowing how to manage affect is of particular importance in this regard. If mental-health-care providers feel secure in their own ability to help the client modulate expressed affect when this is necessary, or retreat from overwhelming inner experience if this should be the requirement, then they will be able to communicate this trust and security to the client. In turn, the client will feel less frightened and more open to experimentation, knowing that the clinician will set appropriate safety limits and will keep the client safe. Allowing clients uninhibited expression of affect is not easy, especially for novice counselors who may not be sure yet whether they will indeed be able to contain a client's affect once it is experienced and expressed. Not surprisingly, newer clinicians may inadvertently and unintentionally inhibit a client's affective experience or emotional expression because of their own uncertainty about what to do once a strong affect emerges. The process of catharsis can further be hindered by clients' tendencies to want to avoid affective arousal. Only a therapist who is able to help the client maintain arousal safely and to express it productively will be able to make the cathartic process therapeutic and helpful (Young and Bemark, 1996). For these reasons, facilitation of catharsis can be considered a quite-advanced therapeutic skill that requires careful self-awareness about possible stumbling blocks on the part of the clinician (Brems, 1999).

DEALING WITH CLIENTS' AFFECT IN SESSION

As indicated above, if clinicians attempt to apply counseling skills that facilitate affective experience and expression in clients, they also must know how to deal with emotions when emotions do burst forth. In fact, even clinicians who are not particularly keen on allowing for emotional catharsis do not really have a choice about this matter. Most clients enter counseling because they are in an emotional crisis; their propensity toward affective expression, whether conscious and healthy or unconscious and unhealthy, is high. Mental-health-care providers need to be prepared to deal with the emotions clients bring to sessions and need to have a certain comfort and confidence in realizing that they can handle anything a client has to offer. Dealing with client affect is not all that difficult as long as the clinician is prepared for it and has a template for how to deal with feelings when they do emerge and appear to overwhelm the client. Following are a few guidelines that can be useful. They clearly do not represent

TABLE 10-1   **FACTORS TO CONSIDER IN FACILITATING CATHARSIS**

Variables That Encourage Catharsis	Variables That Encourage Affective Experience or Expression	Variables That Squelch Affective Experience or Expression
• Safe environment	• Clinician's lowered voice	• Clinician's fear of clients' affect in general
• Private, confidential environment	• Clinician's slowed body language	• Clinician's fear of certain affects
• Environment that does not allow for interruptions	• Clinician's ability to tolerate affect	• Clinician taking premature measures to regulate affect
• Environment conducive to emotional experience and expression (e.g., lighting, comfort)	• Clinician's encouragement of the client to stay with affective experience	• Clinician asking questions about content while client is in an affective state
• Clinician's conveyed willingness to allow affective experience	• Clinician's encouragement of the client to stay with affective expression	• Clinician becoming focused on cognitive issues
• Clinician's conveyed willingness to allow affective expression	• Clinician's ability to draw the client's attention to hints of affective experience	• Clinician intellectualizing
• Clinician's openness to affective arousal in self and others	• Clinician's ability to point to outward signs of affect	• Clinician giving advice
• Clinician's knowledge about how to deal with affective experience and arousal	• Clinician's ability to express empathic concern	• Clinician providing premature or false reassurance
• Clinician's ability to set safety limits by helping regulate affect and expression	• Clinician's ability to stay with the client and communicate understanding throughout the affective experience	• Clinician becoming noticeably upset
• Clinician's ability to let client know that affect can be contained if needed	• Clinician's expression of caring without shutting the client down	• Clinician becoming fearful of client's emotion
• Clinician's ability to communicate safety		• Clinician overidentifying with client
		• Clinician providing sympathy instead of empathy

the only ways in which feelings can be safely contained, but they give the novice mental-health-care provider a starting point from which to expand. This discussion is based on Brems (2000), where the reader can find additional detail.

Dealing with Loss of Control Over Emotion

Even the most out-of-control affect cannot last forever; in fact, it usually cannot even sustain itself for a whole session. Consequently, depending on the amount of time left in a session, the first approach to apparent loss of emotional control is to let it play out as long as it is not destructive to the client. The catharsis that comes from allowing the emotion to flow freely for a while is often quite helpful for the client as long as the affect is not accompanied by seriously uncomfortable physical feelings or dangerous behaviors. For example, out-of-control anger may need to be reined in if the client appears to be on the verge of violent action; a panic attack is always controlled to prevent the client from hyperventilating or experiencing other severe physical consequences.

If the emotion is one for which catharsis is appropriate (for example, depression or sadness, frustration, or anxiety that is not of panic proportions), this is the first choice. The intensity displayed by the client will decrease on its own once the affect has been given free rein for a while. If the length of time elapsed becomes too long (either because the session is almost over or because either client or therapist becomes too uncomfortable), the clinician can calmly begin to take steps to deal with the affect. This is started by asking the client to begin to focus on the counselor. (For example: "I need you to: look at me; look up; catch my eyes; look at my hand; . . .") Next, any behavior connected to the affect is talked about and stopped. (For example: "I want you to stop pacing now; please sit back down" or "I need for you to stop bouncing your leg and picking on your hair" or "Please stop wringing your hands.") In so doing, clinicians lower their voice significantly and speak much more slowly than usual, but with emphasis. Once clients have stopped the associated behavior and have begun to focus on the clinician, the clinician can ask clients to pattern their breathing after the therapist's. (For example: "Let's get your breathing back to normal. Follow my lead. Slowly breathe in. . . . [*clinician takes a long, calm breath*] and out . . . [*clinician releases the breath forcefully*]; in . . . and out. . . .) This joint rhythm of breathing is maintained until the client becomes notably calmer. All along, the counselor remains keenly aware of her or his own personal body language, which is most effective if it expresses confidence, calmness, and collectedness. This is one time when the mental-health-care provider definitely does not want to mirror the client's body language. All demeanors on the clinician's part exude relaxation and calm. For clients who lose control over their affects on a regular basis, it may be useful to develop a structured and predictable sequence of interventions for dealing with this situation. Not only will this help clients begin to be aware of how to regain control over affect with the therapist's help in session, but they are also able to begin to use the same, regularly rehearsed, strategies outside of the session.

Dealing with Uncontrollable Crying

If uncontrollable affect includes uncontrollable crying and this crying needs to be stopped (again, if feasible, catharsis is the first choice as it may be sufficient to stop the crying in and of itself), a few additional strategies are available. First, handing clients a box of tissues is usually a nonverbal signal that it is time for them to pull themselves together. Once clients have been given this nonverbal message to alter their behavior, clinicians ask them to look directly into their eyes while talking calmly to the clients. (For example: "I am going to help you stop crying now so that we have enough time to talk about what happened before you have to leave today. I need you to look into my eyes—look directly into my eyes.") Once clients are able to maintain firm eye contact, the same breathing exercise mentioned above can be initiated. The clinician encourages clients to blow their nose to clear their head. The reason for the insistence on firm eye contact is simple: It is physiologically difficult to cry and focus one's vision at the same time. Thus, if the client is asked to focus on the clinician's eyes, crying will automatically stop in most cases. Occasionally clients will respond to increased eye contact with more intense experience of affect. If a clinician encounters such a client, eye contact may not be the best method to stop the client from crying. However, in most cases eye contact is incompatible with crying. Clients can be taught this trick for home use as well—they can simply look at and focus on their own eyes in a mirror and get crying under some control. If the breathing exercise can be added in such independent practice, calming will almost always be assured.

Dealing with Strong Anxiety Reactions and Panic

A strong anxiety reaction or panic attack requires intervention much sooner than the type of emotion referred to above because it often is self-perpetuating and can be physically dangerous. Highly anxious or panicked clients have physiological responses that further frighten them and often serve to increase the panic. The actual intervention is not very different from that outlined above. However, it is even more important that the clinician appear calm, in control, and capable of setting firm limits. (For example: "I have to stop you from . . . NOW" or "You need to stop talking about . . . now" or "We need to move on NOW to think about how to get you ready to leave today.") The practitioner uses voice and body language to underline the command nature of the directives, providing verbal and physical structure (for example, handing the client a tissue box; taking away the pillow the client may be beating, stopping the client from twirling hair, perhaps by physically moving and then holding on to the hand). The clinician's voice must be firm but caring, as well as calm and controlled. Once the structure has been set, the client is asked to find a focal point and to place total attention on it. Once the client has established eye contact with the focal point (for example, a picture in the therapy room), the client is asked to describe it. (For example: "I need you to look at . . . right there across from you. Okay, now tell me what you see. Describe it in detail.") This simple task serves to shift the client's focus of attention away from the distressing thoughts that fuel the anxiety or panic. All the while, the clinician also needs to pay attention to the client's breathing. If the client is hyperventilating, intervention in this arena is imminently important. This can be accomplished through the same breathing exercise outlined above, in which the client is asked to model breathing frequency and intensity after that of the therapist. In extreme cases, the counselor may need to ask the client to breathe into a paper bag or through a straw (or to engage in any similar strategy that prevents overbreathing). As was explained with regard to intervening with other out-of-control affects, it is important to slow all interactions with the client to a calm level. This is accomplished through lower and slower voice. All along, the clinician gives reassurance about the safety of the room and setting, doing so with calming firmness. If the client is still panicking, it is often helpful to ask the person to pick up a pillow and hug it tightly to the body. This action helps reestablish some body boundaries and may help with any beginning symptoms of depersonalization.

Any and all of these strategies can be combined in any order depending on what the clinician believes most likely to work. If the client is hyperventilating, the first step of intervention would be the breathing exercise; if the client appears to have a sense of loss of boundaries and self, the pillow intervention is best (if no pillow is available in the room, clients can hug a purse or bag; or as a last resort, can hug themselves firmly around the torso). If the client appears extremely cognitively preoccupied, the focal-point exercise is best. Combining strategies can be easily accomplished as well, in that the client can hug a pillow, do slow breathing, and focus on a specified object (including the clinician's eyes) all at the same time, while the clinician calmly talks about the safety of the room and the setting. Certainly, whenever anxiety is high, the client may need special help with transitions of any sort, including beginning and ending sessions or changing topics within sessions. Specific instructions, more time, clear directions, and similar structuring events may assist clients in moving more successfully through the treatment process even while highly anxious or agitated.

Dealing with Anger and Hostility

If the counselor or therapist is faced with an angry, agitated, or hostile client, the primary concerns become the diffusion of the affect and maintenance of behavioral safety for client and therapist. It is best not to challenge the accuracy or truthfulness of an agitatedly angry client, and this is increasingly true as the levels of anger and agitation rise. Rather than challenging, counselors are best advised to acknowledge the client's feeling and validate it. (For example: "I certainly understand that you are very angry right now. And I can certainly see why. After all, what happened to you when . . . was very upsetting.") It is important to remain calm and not to get defensive, even if the client's affect and behavior become a personal attack against the clinician ("And it's all your fault. If you were a better therapist you would have helped me by now"). In other words, it is very important not to get caught up in the client's affect. If, for example, clients accuse clinicians of various transgressions or misdeeds, clinicians are advised not to defend themselves but rather to acknowledge the client's experience. NOT: "I think you are wrong there. I really have been doing my best, but you have not been following the advice or recommendations I have made." And NOT: "If you had listened you would know that that is not what I said. What I really said was. . . ." Instead, say "I understand that you feel as though I have let you down. Please tell me what I could have done differently to help you better." Or "I really appreciate that you are disappointed in therapy. We have not progressed as much as you wanted. . . ." or "I am sorry that you heard me as so critical of you. How could I have said things differently that would not have been so hard for you to hear?"

While acknowledging clients' affects and validating their right to them, therapists insist on basic safety rules. In other words, clients are allowed to get angry, but they do not have permission to act out this anger physically in aggressive or hostile ways. Behavioral boundaries on clients' actions have to be very clear. (For example, yelling is fine, so is hitting a pillow; but acting out physically against the counselor or breaking therapy-room furniture is not). The mental-health-care provider may choose to avoid too much direct eye contact if the client escalates, and should generally not touch the agitated client. Providing extra interpersonal space can also be helpful. Especially when dealing with angry affect that appears to have the potential to be acted out, clinicians are advised to remember the caution never to be a hero. If a client becomes too agitated or openly aggressive, it may be time to end the session or call for help. It is generally clear to a therapist when a situation reaches a danger zone of potential physical aggression. The clinician will begin to feel unsafe and will sense a loss of control on the client's part that involves not merely affective but behavioral control. The strength of a client's voice in and of itself is generally not the best predictor. Better predictors are a client's eyes and physical movements. Specific physical symptoms that signal increasingly angry affect include muscle twitching or restlessness, getting up and pacing, pantomiming aggression (such as pounding, choking someone, beating), staring or lack of eye contact, shallow breathing, quivering or loud voice, clenched fists, and angry words. When counselors begin to notice these symptoms, quick diffusion of the affect is important or the session may need to be discontinued. This resolve is communicated to the client directly as it may often serve to diffuse the behavioral reaction. (For example: "Unless you can calm down a little bit, we will not be able to keep working today.") Similarly, if the clinician feels the need to end the session or call in a helper, an explanation is given. (For example: "I believe we are no longer safe in this room because I am sensing that you are about to blow up. Let's stop for today and continue our work next. . . ." or "Let's stop for a moment and call in one of my colleagues to get her or his perspective on this issue.")

If the clinician is working with a client who regularly and predictably becomes uncontrollably angry, it is a good idea to plan ahead and have supervision and consultation available. If the mental-health-care provider is lucky enough to have videotaping facilities or one-way mirrors, it is best to have a colleague watching the session from the other room. Thus, if the clinician misjudges the intensity of the client's affect and behavior, help is immediately available. If this route is chosen, the clinician needs to make sure that the observer does not overreact. It is best for the clinician and the observer to agree on a (nonverbal) sign that tells the observer when to intervene. If nothing else, knowing that backup is available will help the therapist feel less nervous and concerned, and thus more emotionally accessible and available to the client.

Even with the knowledge about how to handle in-session affective crises, it must be noted that it never pays for a counselor to be heroic and that it is important to know when it is time to seek assistance (Bellak and Siegel, 1983). If clients are imminently dangerous due to out-of-control anger and hostility, clinicians need to get help; if therapists are anxious and unsure about their ability to manage a crisis, they need to seek input and immediate consultation or supervision. If mental-health-care providers anticipate working with dangerous clients on a regular basis (for example, due to a caseload of court-referred clients), it is best to be prepared in terms of special equipment as well. Such clinicians may consider having an alarm system in place, as well as a backup support system of staff who are present in the clinic when (certain) clients are being seen. If a client is extremely dangerous, but the counselor would like to attempt to manage the crisis on an outpatient and immediate basis, confidentiality may have to be weighed against safety. In that instance the clinician may want to consider having someone else monitor the session through video or one-way mirrors.

Dealing with Depersonalization and Dissociation

During an episode of depersonalization, a client loses a clear sense of self and feels detached from the self. Sometimes this manifests by perceptions of being out of the body, being an automaton, or otherwise being a spectator of the self as opposed to being in control of the self. Reactions of depersonalization are often closely tied to anxiety and a loss of sense of personal boundaries. Not surprisingly, the same techniques that have been outlined so far (for emotional control, for anxiety and panic, and for racing thoughts and pressured speech) all are useful to some extent. The breathing exercise may be the most important and effective exercise as depersonalization can be due to overbreathing (Bellak and Siegel, 1983) or underbreathing, where clients breathe so minimally that they fall into a trance state (Linda Olson-Webber, 14 August 1997, personal communication). In severe cases of overbreathing, asking the client to breathe into a paper bag or through a straw may be helpful. The pillow-hugging exercise is very useful in that it provides the client with some definite body boundaries that can be experienced very concretely. If the hugging is not enough in and of itself, the clinician may ask the client to explain what it feels like to hug the pillow, focusing on establishing a clear perception of body boundaries. (For example: "Tell me how the pillow feels. Is it soft? hard?" and "On which parts of your body can you feel the pillow? your arms? where else?" and "Tell me how your stomach feels with the pillow pressing on it" or "Squeeze the pillow a little tighter. What changes can you feel? Where can you feel the additional pressure in your body? in your arm muscles? on your stomach?") Using the client's name can be helpful in getting the client's attention. Beginning all verbalizations by repeating the client's name is good routine practice.

For clients prone to dissociation—that is, clients traumatized as children or adults by events such as chronic and inconsistent abuse, combat, natural disasters, and so forth (Pope and Brown, 1996)—the therapist must learn to pace sessions carefully and must prepare signals (explained below) for the client to become alertly oriented to the present and to return to the safety of an unaltered state of consciousness. Dissociation-prone clients need help in learning to recognize the feelings and thoughts they have that might signal the onset of a dissociative experience so that they may learn to prevent the episode from occurring both in and out of sessions (Sanderson, 1996). Careful pacing of clinical material is critical to avoid retrieval of painful memories that is too quick and painful and triggers a dissociative episode. As explained by Gil (1988), it is most helpful to determine when dissociation occurs (in what setting or under what circumstances), its precipitants (the specific events that lead to the flight response), and emotions associated with it. Further, the client is helped to understand dissociation as an adaptive strategy developed for purposes of psychic or emotional survival. Once clients have gained this understanding, they can be taught alternative strategies of coping or defense under circumstances that usually would trigger a dissociative response (relaxation exercises, activities for purposes of distraction, conversations with supportive others, and so forth). If dissociation occurs during a session, the clinician needs to be prepared to assist the client in regaining a normal, alert state of consciousness. This eventuality is best prepared for by developing a bridge between the dissociative or trauma-related state of consciousness and the present or nondissociative state of consciousness (Dolan, 1991). One such bridge is called "symbol for the present," wherein the client is asked to identify an item in the client's possession that can be used as a reminder of the here-and-now. Should a dissociative event threaten or occur, the symbol of the present can be used by client and clinician to bring the client back to a normal alert state (Dolan, 1996). A similar bridge, also recommended by Dolan (1996), is called "the first-session formula task" in which the client is asked to make a list of events or activities that are currently ongoing in the client's life to which the person has a strong positive commitment. The list is then used during dissociative periods to remind the client of current resources that were not available at a time in life when the dissociative defense was developed. A third bridging or grounding technique developed by Dolan (1991, 1996) is called "the older, wiser self." This technique involves seeking advise from an older, wiser version of the client's self during stressful periods that can be invoked to prevent a dissociative episode. This older, wiser self is described to the client as follows:

Skill Development Recommendations

Recommendation 10-1   *Since clinicians cannot help clients grow beyond the level of affective awareness that they themselves have attained, self-evaluation about affect is important. Using the information in this chapter, take an honest inventory of your own level of affective awareness, experience, and expression. Talk to a trusted friend for additional insights. If this exercise proves inconclusive or overly difficult, this will be a good time to seek personal therapy or counseling.*

> Imagine that you have grown to be a healthy, wise, nurturing, old woman (or man) and you are looking back in this time in your life in which you were integrating, processing, and overcoming the effects of the past experience of sexual abuse [or other traumatic event]. What do you think this wonderful, old, nurturing, wiser you would suggest to you to help you get through this current phase of your life? What would she/he tell you to remember? What would she/he suggest that would be most helpful in helping you heal from the past? What would she/he say to comfort you? And does she/he have any advice about how therapy could be most helpful and useful? (Dolan, 1996, p. 406)

All of these centering or grounding techniques can be used to return the client to the here-and-now. More explicit techniques that involve imagery have also been described (for example, Sanderson, 1996). These grounding techniques encourage clients to imagine themselves as a tree with a strong root system that is anchored in a safe setting and is indestructible even by the most powerful forces. Such visualization exercises can help the client regain equilibrium after a dissociative episode, as well as being useful in preventing dissociation during stressful periods (Sanderson, 1996).

WORKING WITH AFFECT AND EMOTION

Focus on the Body

> I have repeatedly stressed how afraid people are to feel their bodies. On some level they are aware that the body is a repository of their repressed feelings, and while they would very much like to know about these repressed feelings, they are loathe [*sic*] to encounter them in the flesh. Yet in their desperate search for an identity, they must eventually confront the state of their bodies.
>
> *Alexander Lowen, 1967*
> *(quoted in K. Wilber, 1993, p. 241)*

Once mental-health-care providers have a clear idea about the conceptual underpinnings of working with affect, that is, understand how to appreciate a client's awareness, inner experience, and outer expression, they are ready to plan and use affective strategies for intervention. As detailed in the previous chapter, levels of inner experience and outer expression have clear implications for how to intervene around affective issues. A variety of affective strategies can be used to assist clients in achieving awareness and gaining clarity about inner experience. This then will translate into congruence with outer expression. Several of these exercises can be used at multiple levels of inner experience and therefore for multiple purposes. Their basic mechanics remain the same regardless of level, but their purpose and content of implementation will vary slightly. Table 11-1 provides an overview of affective strategies along with level of intervention with regard to inner experience, and the specific purposes for which the exercise is useful at a given level. The exercises covered in this chapter all share a common focus on and use of the body (or of select parts of the body or processes) as a means of helping clients achieve affective awareness or gain a deeper understanding of their affects at higher levels of affective experience and expression. The exercises in the next chapter will be focused more directly on affect itself, with bodily explorations being secondary.

320

All throughout this and the next chapter, words that are spoken by the mental-health-care provider directly to the client are placed in quotation marks and blocked format. These words need to be spoken in a well-paced manner. It is better to go too slow than too fast. Some practice may be required to get the pacing just right. Ellipses, that is, three periods (. . .), indicate places where the clinician is to pause for a moment before moving on. The length of the pause is idiosyncratic to the client and will need to be adjusted as the clinician becomes familiar with a given client's needs. Actions the clinician takes while practicing a particular exercise with the client are printed in *italics*. Basic comments and instructions to the mental-health-care provider are printed in regular typeface. Any directions that need to be tailored to insert a client's particular affect or body area are placed in [brackets]. The content in the brackets will consist either of an example or a directive as to what to fill in the brackets. None of the instructions (including introductions and debriefings) has to be used verbatim. All transcripts are simply examples and reflect the content that needs to be covered; how this is accomplished will be up to each individual mental-health-care provider. In fact, it is best not to work from a transcript while with the client, even during exercises for which clients close their eyes. The rustling of paper can be distracting, and the pacing is often not as attuned as when the clinician speaks from memory. Although this may seem overwhelming at first, none of the scripts is actually very difficult. Memorizing the gist of each is usually pretty easy and just takes little bit of practice.

FOCUS ON THE BREATH

Breathing exercises have their greatest applicability at Levels One and Eight of affective inner awareness. However, they are an integral part of many of the affective exercises, being used in abbreviated form at the beginning of the *Bodily-Awareness Exercise*, the *Basic-Bodily-Experience Exercise*, the *Body Attunement Exercise*, and the *Relaxation Exercises*. They can be useful in helping clients begin to explore inner sensations of their body, helping them gain awareness of physiological processes. They are often the first and best way to introduce clients to working with their body to reach the goal of increasing affective awareness and experience. Some clients feel less threatened by listening to the physiological processes of their body than by talking about affect directly. For these clients, breathing exercises are an excellent way to start. Breathing exercises facilitate relaxation and calming; they can be a relaxation strategy in and of themselves or can become an integral part of other, more formal relaxation exercises, such as the ones to be covered in the next chapter. Some information about breathing was already provided in the chapter on self-care. Review of this material should be helpful here as that knowledge may be shared with clients as well. To reiterate a few of the important points about and benefits of breathing:

TABLE
11-1

INNER AFFECTIVE-EXPERIENCE EXERCISES: APPLICATION AND PURPOSE

Exercise	Application	Purpose
Breathing Exercises	Level One	Assist the client in feeling the basic physical body motions of a simple and automatic bodily function
	Level Eight	Assist the client in gaining mastery over a given affect or to become ready for and open to relaxation strategies
Bodily-Awareness Exercise	Level One	Assist the client in becoming aware that the physical body has sensations
Body Attunement Exercise	Level Two	Assist the client in becoming spontaneously aware of sensations in the body to increase clarity in the experience of physiological processes
Basic Bodily-Experience Exercise	Level One	Assist the client in becoming aware that the physical body has sensations and building rudimentary awareness of differences and changes in sensations
	Level Two	Assist the client in becoming aware that the physical body has sensations and building rudimentary awareness of how outer events may influence these sensations
	Level Five	Assist the client in becoming aware of subtle nuances in the sensations of the physical body and tying them to different meanings with regard to level of intensity of a given affect
	Level Six	Assist the client in becoming aware of confusing and subtle nuances in the sensations of the physical body and tying them to multiple coexisting affects
	Level Seven	Assist the client in becoming aware of subtle nuances in the sensations of the physical body and tying them to an underlying primary affect
Advanced Bodily-Experience Exercise	Level Two	Assist the client in becoming aware that sensations and movements in the physical body may be tied to outer events or inner processes
	Level Five	Assist the client in becoming aware of nuances in sensations or movements of the physical body and tying these to varying levels of intensity in a given affect
	Level Six	Assist the client in becoming aware of confusing and subtle nuances in sensations or movements of the physical body and tying these to multiple coexisting affects
	Level Seven	Assist the client in becoming aware of subtle nuances in sensations or movements of the physical body and tying these to an underlying primary affect

Intervention	Level	Description
Here-and-Now Affect Exploration Exercise	Level Three	Teach the client how to identify and label possible affects that may be reflected by certain inner sensations and movements
	Level Four	Help the client expand the repertoire of labels available for different inner sensations and movements
	Level Five	Teach the client how to identify and label levels of intensity of a given affect that are reflected by subtle nuances and differences in inner sensations and movements
	Level Six	Teach the client how to recognize multiple coexisting affects reflected in subtle or confusing nuances and differences in inner sensations and movements
	Level Seven	Teach the client to recognize an underlying primary affect reflected in subtle nuances and differences in inner sensations and movements
Affect Continuum Exercise	Level Five	Assist the client in learning to tie subtle nuances in sensation to subtle variations in intensity of the same basic affect by developing a repertoire of labels
Progressive-Muscle-Relaxation Exercise	Level Eight	Assist the client in gaining a sense of control over and thus acceptance of seemingly overwhelming or painful affects previously perceived as unacceptable
Focused-Relaxation Exercise	Level Eight	Assist the client in gaining a sense of control over and thus acceptance of seemingly overwhelming or painful affects previously perceived as unacceptable
Guided-Imagery Exercises	Level Eight	Assist the client in exploring possible reasons for the lack of acceptance of certain affects
	Level Nine	Assist the client in exploring possibilities with regard to where and how an affect developed and what it may represent in a given situation
Cognitive Strategies (e.g., clarification, confrontation, interpretation)	Level Eight	Assist the client in exploring possible reasons for the lack of acceptance of certain affects
	Level Nine	Assist the client in exploring possibilities with regard to where and how an affect developed and what it may represent in a given situation

- breathing is helpful in that it draws attention to an important physiological process that can be felt in the body
- focus on breathing can assist with relaxation and calming
- paying attention to the breath can help clients slow down their responses and can be helpful in delaying automatic behaviors and reactions
- many people hold their breath when stressed, a process that only further increases the tension in the body
- deep breaths can be refreshing and rejuvenating
- learning to pay attention to the breath can help clients gain control over affect

Basic Breathing Exercise at Level One of Inner Experience

The simple breathing exercises that are practiced with clients at the basic-awareness level are focused on helping the client explore the breathing process as an example of a bodily sensation. As the client at this level has not paid a lot of attention to the body, much of the instruction for the exercise focuses on helping clients listen their body. Modeling is helpful in the sense that the clinician will breathe in the same rhythm and pattern as is requested of the client. Such breathing is done audibly so that clients can follow what the clinician is talking about. What follows is an example of an introduction, a transcript, and a debriefing for a simple breathing-awareness exercise. The introduction only has to be given the first time a breathing exercise is used with a client or if a client appears to have forgotten the basic premises of the exercise. The instructions are used whenever a breathing exercise is used with the client. The debriefing will be longest the first time a breathing exercise is used. Then it will be applied in abbreviated form upon subsequent application.

Introduction to Basic Breathing Exercise

"One thing that people often find helpful in learning more about their body and their feelings is to begin to pay attention to their breath. There are many good reasons why we need to learn to pay attention to our breath. For one thing, a lot of times when we are in difficult situations, we actually hold our breath. That, of course, is not a good thing because it tenses the body and reduces the amount of oxygen that is available to the brain. So learning to take nice deep breaths can be very refreshing and very calming. Learning to pay attention to the breath also has the advantage that it teaches us a lot about our bodies. Learning to pay attention to where we feel the breath, as it enters and leaves the body, often helps us figure out how our bodies work and has the positive side effect of getting us more in tune with the workings of our body. This is often a first step in learning more about feelings and emotions that we might have. So, what I would like for you to do at this point is to sit or lie back and make yourself as comfortable as possible."

The clinician also settles back and models a comfortable seated position. If the client decides to lie down, that is acceptable. However, the clinician remains seated.

"You might want to go ahead and place one of your hands on your stomach. This will help you follow your breath on the outside of your body with your hand as well as on the inside of your body with your mind. However, if putting a hand on your belly is not comfortable, you can also rest your hands on your sides or in your lap or wherever they feel comfortable."

For modeling purposes, the clinician places and leaves one hand on the abdomen during the whole exercise.

"One thing we will focus on as we breathe is diaphragmatic breathing. This way of breathing is automatic for babies, but as adults we tend to have forgotten how to do it. The trick babies know is to use their diaphragm as a means of pulling the air more fully into the lungs. Most people breathe using only their chest muscles."

Here, the clinician points to the intercostal muscles between the ribs.

"That's actually a pretty inefficient way of breathing. If you breathe that way, the abdomen doesn't move when you inhale. Only the chest expands. In diaphragmatic breathing, you will actually focus on observing the rise and fall of your abdomen. When you breathe in, you will try to make sure that your abdomen extends; when you breathe out, it pulls back in."

Here the clinician models a full diaphragmatic breath, allowing the abdomen to swell on inhalation and to retract on exhalation, while also demonstrating the correlated expansion and contraction of the chest.

"The reason that movement happens is that in diaphragmatic breathing, we use the diaphragm to help gather in as much air as we can. The diaphragm is the big muscle right here between the abdomen and the chest."

Here the clinician points to the general area of the diaphragm, that is, to the large muscle between the thoracic and abdominal cavities.

"When you breathe in, the diaphragm flattens or expands downward."

Here the clinician makes a hand motion to show the movement of the diaphragm by sweeping down from below the chest cavity to the abdominal cavity.

"That motion of the diaphragm pushes the abdomen out to make space for the lungs to expand with air in your chest."

Here the clinician points to the abdominal and thoracic cavities and models the extensions of an inhalation.

"When you breathe out, the diaphragm shrinks back, making room for the abdomen to flatten."

Here the clinician models a full diaphragmatic breath, making sure to extend and retract the abdomen and chest as appropriate; exaggeration of the movement may be helpful to make the point of using the diaphragm.

"Does that make sense to you?"

The clinician now answers any questions the client might have about diaphragmatic breathing.

"I will be doing the breathing exercise with you. So you can also pay attention to my breathing sounds and maybe pattern your own breathing rhythm after mine. Keep your eyes closed, though, and your attention focused on your own breathing. If you find that my rhythm is too fast or too slow for you, feel free to breathe at a rate that is most comfortable to you."

The clinician will watch the client's breathing during the exercise and will attempt to find a rate and rhythm that works for the client. Thus, it should be rare that the client will have to find a rate or rhythm different from that modeled by the clinician.

Instructions for Basic Breathing Exercise

"Now that you are seated comfortably, go ahead and close your eyes. This will draw your attention to the inside of your body. Try to consciously focus your mind inside your body and then follow my instructions. Start by taking a deep breath in through your nose and then out through your mouth. Follow my example."

Here the clinician takes in a deep audible breath through the nose and then blows the breath out through the mouth. This may be done a couple of times.

"And now breathe in"

Clinician inhales audibly.

". . . and out through your nose."

Clinician exhales audibly through the nose.

"And in . . . and out . . . and in . . . and out."

Clinician establishes a comfortable audible breathing rhythm. This should be done without speaking for about twenty to thirty seconds, or whatever period of time is comfortable for the client.

"Now as you breathe, begin to pay attention to where you can feel the breath in your body. . . . For example, notice how the breath feels as it enters your nose; . . . feel the coolness of the air in your nose . . . and notice the movement of the small hairs inside your nose. Keep breathing in . . . and out . . . at a comfortable rate."

Clinician inhales and exhales audibly.

"And in . . . and out."

Clinician inhales and exhales audibly.

"And in . . . and out.

"Now notice how the breath feels . . . as it approaches your lungs . . . through your throat. Notice the cool air . . . entering your body through your throat . . . and pay attention to how your stomach rises . . . as the air . . . enters your lungs. As you breathe in, . . . allow your belly to expand comfortably; . . . allow your abdomen to extend . . . to make room for your lungs . . . to take in as much air as possible. Keep breathing in . . . and out . . . at a comfortable rhythm."

Clinician inhales and exhales audibly.

"And in . . . and out."

Clinician inhales and exhales audibly.

"And in . . . and out.

"Often when we breathe we don't allow our stomach to inflate; . . . instead we just expand our chest. We can't take in nearly as much air this way as when we allow our stomachs to expand. So, with your next inhalation, be sure to allow your belly to rise, . . . and then draw the breath into your lungs. . . . Take a few nice deep breaths, in . . . and out, . . . at a gentle rhythm, and notice the sensations of your body as it takes in air; . . . draw your attention to your nose, . . . your throat, . . . your stomach, . . . and your lungs."

Clinician inhales and exhales audibly.

"And in . . . and out."

Clinician inhales and exhales audibly.

"And in . . . and out.

"Now notice the sensations as your breath leaves your body. . . . Notice how your stomach flattens when your diaphragm begins to pull

back. . . . Feel your lungs expelling old stale air through your throat. . . .
Notice how much warmer the air is that leaves your body . . . as it moves
through your throat . . . up into your nose . . . and out through your nos-
trils. Now keep breathing comfortably, . . . either following my rhythm . . .
or establishing your own, . . . paying close attention to all of the different sensations you experience . . . as the breath enters . . . and leaves
your body."

Clinician inhales and exhales audibly.

"And in . . . and out."

Clinician inhales and exhales audibly.

"And in . . . and out."

*The clinician continues the exercise for a few minutes, observing the client's vis-
ible physical movements. After a comfortable amount of time, the clinician asks
the client to end the breathing exercise as follows:*

"Now that you have observed the movements and feelings in your body
as you breathe in and out, I'd like you to bring back your awareness to
this room. . . . Slowly begin to focus your attention away from your body . . .
and to the outer world. . . . Do that by beginning to notice any sounds
that you may hear and when you're ready go ahead and open your eyes."

Debriefing of Basic Breathing Exercise
After each use, but most importantly after the first use of a basic breathing exercise, the clinician debriefs the experience with the client. Attention is paid in
particular to any sensations of which the client was aware during the exercise.
It may be necessary to ask the client specific and detailed questions, since the
issue for clients at this level of affective awareness is that they are not consciously
aware of what goes on in the body. The clinician asks about sensations in each
involved body part, as well as overall questions. The more often the exercise
has been repeated, the less intense the querying during the debriefing needs
to be. Also, if clients spontaneously offer a lot of sensory information, clinicians
have to do less probing. The hope for the debriefing is that it facilitates greater
awareness in clients not only as relevant to the current event, but also with regard to what they will attend to during the next time that the exercise is practiced. All clients can be encouraged to practice the exercise on their own. This
encouragement is best given as a suggestion, not as a directive. The debriefing
also needs to explore whether the client had any negative impact from the experience. This is unlikely, as the exercise is a fairly innocuous and pleasant one.
It is best to check nevertheless, to modify the exercise accordingly the next time
it is used.

Advanced Breathing Exercise at Level Eight of Inner Experience

At this level of inner experience, the client is already highly self-aware. Thus, breathing exercises at this level have a different purpose. They are used to give clients a strategy to calm or center themselves, either through calming breathing by itself or in combination with relaxation exercises. The focus here is on using breathing as a strategy that can stand alone. The use of breathing in combination with a relaxation exercise is similar; the main difference lies in its abbreviation. The introduction to the breathing exercise is very similar to that at Level One; it serves to introduce the client to diaphragmatic breathing. If the clinician has been using Level One exercises with a client, a lengthy new introduction is not necessary. The client is merely told that the original breathing exercise will be used again, but this time with a different purpose. The purpose is then quickly explained and should make sense given the current issue at hand in session. The clinician can then delve directly into the basic instructions. What follows are the instructions for the advanced breathing exercise for a client who has practice with the basic exercise. Only brief new directions are given in the introduction as these are essentially the same, and both mental-health-care provider and client are familiar with the basic mechanics. For a client with whom breathing exercises have never been used, the introduction will be a mixture of the basic and advanced introduction and the client needs to learn some basic diaphragmatic breathing before focusing on calming. Debriefing is identical in mechanics and differs only in purpose. As a reminder, all directions in brackets indicate that the mental-health-care provider should fill in the text appropriate to the client.

Introduction to Advanced Breathing Exercise

"Do you remember the breathing exercises we used to do? Well, they have another application. They can also be very helpful when you try to calm yourself down. When you use the breathing exercise for this reason, you focus on slightly different things than you focused on before. Yes, you still use your diaphragm, and you still pay attention to using your abdomen and your lungs correctly. But primarily you use the breathing exercise now to give yourself a sense of calmness and centeredness. You can use the exercise anytime and anywhere. No one will be aware of what you are doing. So whenever you feel . . . [insert the client's problem affect here], just use a variation on the exercise we will practice in a minute to calm yourself down and to slow down your reaction. Would you like to try this?"

The clinician now gives the client a chance to ask questions and may or may not explain further how the client can apply the exercise alone during stressful situations.

Instructions for Advanced Breathing Exercise

"Seat yourself comfortably and close your eyes. Draw your attention to the inside of your body. Try to consciously focus your mind inside your body and then follow my instructions. As always, let's start by taking a deep breath in through the nose . . . and then out through the mouth."

Here the clinician takes in a deep audible breath through the nose and then blows out the breath through the mouth. This may be done a couple of times.

"Breathe in . . . "

Clinician inhales audibly.

". . . and out . . . through your nose."

Clinician exhales audibly through the nose.

"And in . . . and out . . . and in . . . and out."

Clinician establishes a comfortable audible breathing rhythm. This should be done without speaking for about twenty to thirty seconds, or whatever period of time is comfortable for the client.

"Now as you breathe, . . . begin to pay attention to where you can feel your [problem affect] . . . in your body. For example, notice how the feeling may affect your [head, . . . or neck, . . . or stomach]. All the while, . . . keep breathing in . . . and out . . . at a comfortable rate."

Clinician inhales and exhales audibly.

"And in . . . and out."

Clinician inhales and exhales audibly.

"And in . . . and out."
"Now allow your breath to bring in a calming, . . . centering energy with each inhalation . . . and to expel all [negative affects] with each exhalation."

Clinician inhales and exhales audibly.

"And breathe in calmness . . . and breathe out [your anxiety]."

Clinician inhales and exhales audibly.

"And in with tranquility . . . and out with [negativity]."
"With each inhalation, . . . become more aware of the calm . . . warm . . . energy that begins to permeate through your body. . . . Notice how each in-breath helps relax . . . your [neck, . . . head] and how it spreads a quiet peacefulness through your body. . . . Draw that calmness

in . . . through your nose, . . . down your throat, . . . and deep into your lungs."

Clinician inhales and exhales audibly.

"And breathe in calm . . . and breathe out [any anxiety]."

Clinician inhales and exhales audibly.

"And in with warmth . . . and out with [depression]."
   "Now allow each out-breath to take with it the [negative feelings] you tend to have. . . . Allow the [anxiety] to leave your body with each exhalation."

Clinician inhales and exhales audibly.

"And breathe in restfulness . . . and breathe out [upsetness]."

Clinician inhales and exhales audibly.

"And in with peacefulness . . . and out with [agitation]."

The clinician continues the exercise for a few minutes, observing the client's visible physical movements, repeating the instructions for inhalation and exhalation occasionally, but not on each breath.

"And breathe in calm . . . and breathe out [anxiety]."

Clinician inhales and exhales audibly.

"And in with warmth . . . and out with [sadness, depression].
   "Now allow each out-breath to take with it the [negative feelings] you tend to have. Allow the [anxiety] to leave your body with each exhalation."

Clinician inhales and exhales audibly.

"And breathe in restfulness . . . and breathe out [hurt, pain, discomfort]."

Clinician inhales and exhales audibly.

"And in with peacefulness . . . and out with [agitation]."

After a comfortable amount of time, and when the client has visibly calmed, the clinician asks the client to end the breathing exercise as follows:

"Now that you have welcomed calmness . . . and peacefulness . . . and expelled all [negative emotions], I'd like you to bring back your awareness to this room. . . . Slowly begin to focus your attention away from your body . . . and back to the outer world. Do that by beginning to notice any sounds that you may hear. I will slowly count back from five to one and with each number you will become more and more alert. When

I get to one, you will be fully alert. Then take what time you need, and when you're ready open your eyes."

Clinician slowly counts back from five to one and then allows the client to pace her or his own return by opening the eyes.

Debriefing of Advanced Breathing Exercise

The mechanics of the debriefing are identical to those for the basic exercise. However, the purpose is not to find out what sensations the client was able to identify in the body, but rather on assessing how successful the client was in calming and centering. Questions are focused on exploring where the client could feel calmness and relaxation and where the client was successful in eliminating negative emotions and sensations. Some processing about why some areas of the body may have relaxed whereas others did not may be necessary. The more often the exercise has been repeated, the less intense the querying during the debriefing will be. If a client spontaneously offers information, the clinician probes less. Clients can be encouraged to practice breathing on their own during situations that are triggers for negative affect. As recommended above, encouragement is given as a suggestion, not as a directive. The debriefing also explores whether the client had any negative impact from the experience. Sometimes a client may not be successful in expelling the negative affect and may get into an inner struggle between tranquility and negativity. If this happens clients may feel as though they failed the exercise. The clinician needs to be careful to point out that a first attempt does not guarantee success and may need to help clients find some small indication by which an improvement in emotional state occurred. This small change can then be the definition of success and can become the springboard for better results next time. All clients should be given more than one or two opportunities to try this exercise if it seemed to fail the first time. Asking clarifying questions about what worked and did not work for the client is particularly important in instances when success was low to moderate. Appropriate alterations can then be made during the next application with the same client.

FOCUS ON THE BODY

Several exercises fall into the category of focusing on or gaining awareness of the body. Of course, strictly speaking even the breathing exercises fall into this category as they focus the attention on the breath and the parts of the body affected by it. The exercises included in this section focus on the experience of the whole body, or at least major parts. Each exercise can be shortened if needed to hone in on certain parts of the body; however, all transcripts are written to explore the whole body. These exercises are not yet concerned with identifying

Skill Development Recommendations

Recommendation 11-1   *To become familiar with what may be asked of clients in the future, begin to practice the breathing exercise as described for Level One. Do this at a set time every day. Many people find it helpful to do this type of breathing either first thing in the morning upon awakening, or as the last thing of the day, before going to sleep. Choose a routine that fits best into your day to make it more likely that you will stick with the practice.*

---

affects; they are strictly geared toward guiding clients to begin to recognize that the body has physiological sensations at all times. On the surface, these exercises are quite similar. However, there are profound subtle differences that need to be noted. For example, the *Bodily-Awareness Exercise* and *Body Attunement Exercise* cover the same parts of the body, and the introductions to them are very similar. However, there is one profound and planful difference: The awareness exercise assumes that the client is not yet capable of independent bodily awareness and hence incorporates movements of body parts to catch and direct the client's attention. The movement inherent in this exercise is planful in that it is not large, deep, or painful movement, but merely motion to give the client a hook for awareness. In the attunement exercise, the client has gained some ability to listen to the body. Movement may detract from feeling the body. Thus, the client now is directed to draw attention to the same body part, noting only what is already there. Once the client is attuned to the body, the clinician moves to the next step, the *Basic-Bodily-Experience Exercise*, wherein more emotional and feeling words are used (hence its categorization as a bridge exercise). No attempt is made initially (that is, at lower levels of affective experience) to label bodily experiences as signaling a specific affect; only the concept is introduced that feelings and physiological responses coexist in the body.

Bodily-Awareness Exercise

This exercise is a natural extension of the breathing exercise in that it challenges clients to get to know even more about the sensations in their bodies. It guides the client through the exploration of various parts of the body to gain familiarity with internal physiological reactions. The exercise directs the client to pay attention to particular parts of the body and then to move these parts in certain ways, paying attention to what each movement feels like. This process helps the client identify and recognize internal bodily sensations. The exercise can be modified for individual clients. With some clients, the mental-health-care provider may cover all parts of the body, spending as much as twenty minutes in the exercise. With other clients, the clinician may begin with only a few parts of the body, making the exercise shorter and more targeted. For some clients shorter exercises may be appropriate if there are parts of the body the clinician does not want to include the first few times this exercise is used. For example, clients with a history of sexual abuse may be threatened by the focus on particular parts of the body that are normally included in this exercise (for example, the buttocks or the chest). The genitalia are not included in this awareness exercise as they may be difficult to deal with for too many clients. What follows is an example of a general introduction to this type of exercise, and a transcript for an entire body awareness focus (that is, all parts of the body are included). The transcript is written for a client who is seated. Minor adjustments will be necessary if the transcript is used with a client who is lying down. The script is written to ask the client to attend to and move the body bilaterally (that is, both feet, hands, arms, legs, and so on at the same time). With some clients such a dual focus may not be possible and the mental-health-care provider may alter the transcript first to work a given body part on the right side and then on the left side (right foot to left foot, right calf to left calf, and so on). Clinicians may also want to adjust this transcript to adapt it to the needs of a given client, both in terms of time available to complete the exercise and in terms of presenting symptoms. The amount of time spent on breathing can be shortened or lengthened as needed. If a client is already familiar with and adept at the breathing exercise, less verbal instruction may be necessary than with a client who still struggles with breath focus. The transcript is followed by comments about debriefing.

Introduction to Bodily-Awareness Exercise

"You know the breathing exercises we have been doing? Today I'd like to introduce you to an exercise that is similar in the sense that it also gets you to focus on what is going on in your body. But it's different in that this time the focus will be on many parts of your body and you will have do certain movements to learn to be aware of what your body feels like in certain situations. We'll start the exercise with the same kind of breathing that we have been doing and then I'll ask that you just follow my instructions. I will ask you to pay attention to different parts of the body at different times and will ask you to move them in certain ways. Then I'll ask you to pay attention to what it is that you are sensing in that body part. Does that sound acceptable to you?"

The clinician now gives the client a chance to object or ask more questions. Then the following points need to be made if they were not already covered by the client's questions:

"If at any point something feels uncomfortable or you don't want to do something that I asked you to do, just don't do it. I'll notice and I won't push you into doing it. If I don't notice, just lift one of your hands to let me know to back away from a certain body part or a certain way of moving it. You can do this exercise sitting comfortably or lying down, just like with the breathing exercise. Is there anything I need to know about before we start? For example, do you have pain in any body part that I should be aware of?"

This represents another opportunity for the client to ask questions. Once all questions are answered, the clinician moves on to the basic instructions.

Instructions for Bodily-Awareness Exercise

"Seat yourself comfortably and close your eyes. Draw your attention to the inside of your body. Consciously focus your mind inside your body and then just follow my instructions. . . . Remember, you have to do nothing that does not feel right. . . . If you need to signal me to stop something I'm asking you to do, just raise one of your hands. As always, let's start by taking a deep breath in . . . through the nose . . . and then out . . . through the mouth."

Here the clinician takes in a deep audible breath through the nose and then blows out the breath through the mouth. This may be done a couple of times.

"Breathe in . . . "

Clinician inhales audibly.

". . . and out through your nose."

Clinician exhales audibly through the nose.

"And in . . . and out . . . and in . . . and out."

Clinician establishes a comfortable audible breathing rhythm. This should be done without speaking for about twenty to thirty seconds, or whatever period of time is comfortable for the client. When the client has established a good rhythm and appears at ease, the clinician moves on to the next set of instructions.

"As you continue to breathe calmly and in this comfortable way, draw your attention to your feet. See if you notice any sensations in your feet. . . . Now slowly and gently wiggle your toes . . . Pay attention to what sensations that movement creates in your feet. . . . Notice which muscles move . . . as you wiggle your toes . . . and notice where in the feet you can perceive the motion in the toes. . . . All the while, keep breathing . . . gently and calmly, enjoying your focus on your body. . . . When you are ready, stop wiggling your toes and note the difference in the sensations in your feet as they once again are still."

Clinician gives a slightly longer pause here in anticipation of moving to the next body part. The clinician might want to breathe in and out audibly for a few breaths to remind the client to do the same.

"Now draw your attention up the leg and into your calf. See if you notice any sensations in your calves . . . your lower legs. . . . Now slowly and gently flex your feet, keeping your heels on the ground and raising the toes . . . Pay attention to what sensations that movement creates in your calves. . . . Notice which muscles move . . . as you flex your feet, toes up, heels down . . . and notice where in the lower legs you can perceive the motion of your feet. . . . All the while, keep breathing . . . gently and calmly, enjoying this focus on your body. . . . When you are ready, stop flexing your feet and note the difference in the sensations in your calves as they once again are still."

Clinician gives a slightly longer pause here in anticipation of moving to the next body part. The clinician might want to breathe in and out audibly for a few breaths to remind the client to do the same.

"Now draw your attention further up the legs and into your knees and thighs. See if you notice any sensations in your knees and thighs . . . your upper legs. . . . Now slowly and gently flex your knees, keeping your thighs on the chair and swinging the lower half of your legs up as high as is comfortable. . . . Pay attention to what sensations that movement creates in your knees, . . . your thighs. . . . Notice which muscles move . . . as you flex your knees, thighs on the chair, calves and feet in the air . . . and notice where in the upper legs you can perceive the motion of your lower legs. . . . All the while, keep breathing . . . gently and calmly, enjoying this focus on your body. . . . When you are ready, lower your feet and calves and note the difference in the sensations in your knees and thighs as they once again are still."

Clinician gives a slightly longer pause here in anticipation of moving to the next body part. The clinician might want to breathe in and out audibly for a few breaths to remind the client to do the same.

"Now draw your attention even further up the legs and into your buttocks. See if you notice any sensations in your buttocks . . . your bottom. . . . Now slowly and gently flex your thighs and buttocks, squeezing the buttocks closer toward each other, . . . raising your body a bit with the power of your muscles in the backs of your thighs. . . . Pay attention to what sensations that movement creates in your buttocks. . . . Notice which muscles move . . . as you flex your thighs, and squeeze your buttocks together. . . . Notice now where in your bottom you can perceive the motion of your thighs. . . . All the while, keep breathing . . . gently and calmly, enjoying this focus on your body. . . . When you are ready, stop flexing your thighs and bottom and note the difference in the sensations in your buttocks as they once again are resting in the chair."

Clinician gives a slightly longer pause here in anticipation of moving to the next body part. The clinician might want to breathe in and out audibly for a few breaths to remind the client to do the same.

"Now draw your attention to your arms and into your hands. See if you notice any sensations in your hands . . . your fingers. . . . Now slowly and gently flex your fingers by making a soft fist . . . don't clench too hard . . . just curl your fingers toward the palm of your hands. . . . Pay attention to what sensations that movement creates in your hands and lower arms. . . . Notice which muscles move . . . as you flex your fingers inward . . . toward your palm . . . and notice where in the hands and lower arms you can perceive the motion of your fingers. . . . All the while, keep breathing . . . gently and calmly, enjoying this focus on your body. . . . When you are ready, open your fist and note the difference in the sensations in your hands and lower arms as they once again are relaxed."

Clinician gives a slightly longer pause here in anticipation of moving to the next body part. The clinician might want to breathe in and out audibly for a few breaths to remind the client to do the same.

"Now draw your attention up the arm and into your upper arm and shoulder. See if you notice any sensations in your biceps . . . your shoulders. . . . Now slowly and gently raise your arms overhead, lift your whole arm straight up in the air. . . . Pay attention to what sensations that movement creates in your upper arms and shoulders. . . . Notice which muscles move . . . as you hold up your arm, high in the air above your head . . . and notice where in the arms and shoulders you can perceive the motion of your arms. . . . All the while, keep breathing . . . gently and calmly, enjoying this focus on your body. . . . When you are ready, lower your arms and note the difference in the sensations in your upper arms and shoulders as they once again are resting comfortably at your side."

Clinician gives a slightly longer pause here in anticipation of moving to the next body part. The clinician might want to breathe in and out audibly for a few breaths to remind the client to do the same.

"Now draw your attention further up the body into your neck and throat. See if you notice any sensations in the small of your neck . . . your throat. . . . Now slowly and gently turn your head to the right, only as far as feels good. . . . Chin toward right shoulder. . . . Pay attention to what sensations that motion creates in your neck and throat. . . . Notice which muscles move . . . as you hold your head to the right, chin above the right shoulder. . . . Notice where in the neck and throat you can perceive the turn of your head. . . . Now slowly and gently turn your head to the left, only as far as feels good . . . chin toward left shoulder. . . . Pay attention to what sensations that motion creates in your neck and throat. . . . Notice which muscles move . . . as you hold your head to the left, chin above the left shoulder. . . . Notice where in the neck and throat you can perceive the turn of your head. . . . All the while, keep breathing . . . gently and calmly, enjoying this focus on your body. . . . When you are ready, turn your head back to its normal position and note the difference in the sensations in your neck and throat as they once again return to their usual place."

Clinician gives a slightly longer pause here in anticipation of moving to the next body part. The clinician might want to breathe in and out audibly for a few breaths to remind the client to do the same.

"Now draw your attention up the neck and to your scalp and forehead. See if you notice any sensations in your scalp . . . your forehead. . . . Now slowly and gently raise your eyebrows without opening your eyes. . . . Pay attention to what sensations that movement creates in your forehead and scalp. . . . Notice which muscles move. . . . Now drop your eyebrows back down to their usual position . . . and raise them . . . and lower them, repeating this motion a few times, doing it slowly and gently, . . . each time noticing where in the forehead and scalp you can perceive the motion of your eyebrows. . . . All the while, keep breathing . . . gently and calmly, enjoying this focus on your body. . . . When you are ready, stop moving your eyebrows and note the difference in the sensations in your forehead and scalp as they once again are at rest."

Clinician gives a slightly longer pause here in anticipation of moving to the next body part. The clinician might want to breathe in and out audibly for a few breaths to remind the client to do the same.

"Now draw your attention across the scalp and forehead into your face. See if you notice any sensations in your eyes . . . your cheeks . . . your chin. . . . Now slowly and gently open your mouth wide, . . . then slowly close it, . . . and open it, . . . continuing to open wide and close at a comfortable pace. . . . Pay attention to what sensations that movement creates in your face. . . . Notice which muscles move . . . as you open and close your mouth slowly and gently. . . . Notice where in the cheeks, . . . eyes, and chin you can perceive the motion of your mouth. . . . All the while, keep breathing . . . gently and calmly, enjoying this focus on your body. . . . When you are ready, close your mouth and note the difference in the sensations in your face and all its features as they once again are at rest."

Clinician gives a slightly longer pause here in anticipation of moving to the next body part. The clinician might want to breathe in and out audibly for a few breaths to remind the client to do the same.

"Now draw your attention down past your chin and throat to your chest and abdomen. See if you notice any sensations in your chest . . . your stomach. . . . Now slowly and gently take a deep breath, inhale and exhale . . . deeply . . . slowly, expanding your rib cage as much as you can. . . . Pay attention to what sensations this deep, . . . deep . . . breath creates in your abdomen . . . your chest. . . . Notice which muscles move . . . as you inhale . . . and exhale . . . deeply . . . slowly . . . gently. . . . Notice where in the chest and abdomen you can perceive the rhythm of your breath, . . . the motion of the air . . . circulating through you. . . . Keep breathing . . . deeply . . . gently . . . calmly, enjoying this focus on your body. . . . When you are ready, return to your normal breathing rhythm and note the sensations in your chest and stomach as they continue to move . . . gently now . . . up and down."

Clinician gives a slightly longer pause here in anticipation of moving to the next body part. The clinician might want to breathe in and out audibly for a few breaths to remind the client to do the same.

"Now draw your attention to your breath. Take a few moments to observe the movements and sensations in your body as you breathe . . . in . . . and out. Enjoying each breath . . . enjoying the clean air it brings to your body. In . . . and out, . . . in . . . and out."

Clinician inhales and exhales audibly.

"And in . . . and out."

Clinician inhales and exhales audibly.

"And in . . . and out."

"Now that you have observed the movements and sensations in your body, I'd like you to bring your awareness back to this room. . . . Slowly begin to focus your attention away from your body . . . away from your breath . . . and to the outer world. . . . Do that by beginning to notice any sounds that you may hear and when you're ready go ahead and open your eyes. Take all the time you need."

Debriefing of Bodily-Awareness Exercise

The mechanics of the debriefing are virtually the same as those for the basic breathing exercise. The purpose is merely expanded to include not just the parts of the body affected by the breath, but also to find out what sensations the client was able to identify in the entire body. The clinician may want to ask general questions at first, and then hone in on specific body parts as needed. The more often the exercise has been repeated, the less intense the querying during the debriefing will become. The more information a client offers spontaneously, the less probing the clinician will have to do. Clients can be encouraged to practice the body awareness exercise on their own at home. If possible, the mental-health-care provider makes a tape of the exercise as it was conducted in session for the client to take home to use for that purpose. In making tapes for clients, it is best to make tapes the third or fourth time a given exercise was practiced in session. That way the clinician can make needed modifications after the first few debriefings. The taped session would then be one that has been altered according to the client's specifications and that felt comfortable and acceptable to the client. As recommended above, this encouragement to practice at home is given as a suggestion, not as a directive.

As implied already, one important aspect of the debriefing is the exploration as to whether the client had any negative impact from the body awareness experience. The clinician needs to be careful to point out that a first attempt does not guarantee success. The clinician and client may need to collaborate to modify the exercise in a way that is comfortable for the client. For example, if the client perceived a particular movement as painful, a different motion may need to be substituted; if the client objects to exploring a particular body part, a different portion of the body could be covered or the exercise could be shortened. Such small changes can make a tremendous difference with regard to the perception of the experience by the client and will increase the likelihood that the client may practice at home. All clients should be given more than one or two opportunities to try this exercise if they did not appear to benefit from it the first time. Asking clarifying questions about what worked and did not work for the client is particularly important in instances when success was low to moderate. Appropriate alterations can be made until the client is satisfied and benefits from the experience.

Body Attunement Exercise

This exercise is geared toward more independent recognition of physiological processes in the client's body. Whereas in the preceding exercise the client was given help in recognizing what the body feels like by putting it in motion, the client is now challenged to learn to listen to the body in its natural state. Attention is drawn to various parts of the body and the client is directed to listen for, watch for, and sense for different sensations that may arise. This exercise is much more difficult than the awareness exercise, and clients need to have successfully repeated the awareness exercise before they are introduced to the attunement exercise. If a client has extreme difficulty with this exercise, the clinician can return spontaneously to the awareness exercise. Following are the introduction for the attunement exercise, detailed instructions, and debriefing directions. Instructions are once again based on a seated client. All cautions and comments outlined for the *Bodily-Awareness Exercise* apply to this exercise as well.

Introduction to Body Attunement Exercise

"You know the bodily-awareness exercises we have been doing? Today I'd like to change that a little bit. Rather than telling you to move the different parts of the body we've been paying attention to, I just want you to observe what they feel like as they are. In other words, listen, watch, or use whatever sense you can to attend to the parts of the body I'll mention. If you feel nothing, that's fine; there's no need to panic. Just keep trying as we move on to the next part of the body. Does that make sense?"

The clinician now gives the client a chance to object or ask questions.

"As always, we'll start the exercise with the same kind of breathing that we have been doing and then I'll ask that you just follow my instructions. I will ask you to pay attention to different parts of the body at different times and then I'll ask you to pay attention to what it is that you are sensing in that body part. Does that sound okay?"

The clinician gives the client a chance to ask more questions. Then the following points need to be made if they were not already covered by the client's questions:

"If at any point something feels uncomfortable, just lift one of your hands to let me know to back away from a certain body part and I'll move on. You can do this exercise sitting comfortably or lying down, just like with the other body exercise. Is there anything I need to know about before we start?"

This represents yet another opportunity for the client to ask questions. Once all questions are answered, the clinician moves on to the basic instructions.

Instructions for Body Attunement Exercise

"Seat yourself comfortably and close your eyes. Draw your attention to the inside of your body. Consciously focus your mind inside your body and then just follow my instructions. . . . Remember, you don't have to endure anything that does not feel right. . . . If you need to signal me to move on to the next body part, just raise your hand. As always, let's start by taking a deep breath in . . . through the nose . . . and then out . . . through the mouth."

Here the clinician takes in a deep audible breath through the nose and then blows out the breath through the mouth. This may be done a couple of times.

"Breathe in . . . "

Clinician inhales audibly.

"... and out through your nose."

Clinician exhales audibly through the nose.

"And in ... and out ... and in ... and out."

Clinician establishes a comfortable audible breathing rhythm. This should be done without speaking for about twenty to thirty seconds, or whatever period of time is comfortable for the client. When the client has established a good rhythm and appears at ease, the clinician moves on to the next set of instructions.

"As you continue to breathe calmly and in this comfortable way, draw your attention to your feet. . . . Just pay attention to your feet and toes. . . . See if you notice any sensations in your feet. . . . Slowly and gently pay attention . . . to all parts of your feet . . . from your heels . . . to your toes . . . Pay attention to any sensations you might have in your feet. . . Maybe they are cold, . . . maybe the toes are touching, . . . maybe there seems to be nothing at all . . . Just notice your feet, . . . Notice what they experience, . . . right now . . . in this moment, . . . not trying to change anything, . . . just being aware of what's there. . . . All the while, keep breathing . . . gently and calmly, enjoying this focus on that very unique and special part of your body. . . ."

Clinician gives a slightly longer pause here in anticipation of moving to the next body part. The clinician might want to breathe in and out audibly for a few breaths to remind the client to do the same.

"As you continue to breathe calmly and in this comfortable way, draw your attention to your lower legs. . . . Just pay attention to your calves and ankles. . . . See if you notice any sensations in your lower legs. . . . Slowly and gently pay attention . . . to all parts of your lower legs . . . from your ankles . . . to your knees . . . Pay attention to any sensations you might have in your lower legs. . . . Maybe they are stiff, . . . maybe there's an ache, . . . maybe there seems to be nothing at all. . . . Just notice your lower legs, . . . notice what they experience, . . . right now . . . in this moment, . . . not trying to change anything, . . . just being aware of what's there. . . . All the while, keep breathing . . . gently and calmly, enjoying this focus on that very unique and important part of your body. . . ."

Clinician gives a slightly longer pause here in anticipation of moving to the next part of the body. The clinician might want to breathe in and out audibly for a few breaths to remind the client to do the same.

"As you continue to breathe calmly and in this comfortable way, draw your attention to your upper legs. . . . Just pay attention to your knees and thighs. . . . See if you notice any sensations in your upper legs. . . .

Slowly and gently pay attention . . . to all parts of your upper legs . . . from your knees . . . to your thighs. . . . Pay attention to any sensations you might have in your upper legs. . . . Maybe they are resting comfortably on the cushion, . . . maybe there's a tightness, . . . maybe there seems to be nothing at all. . . . Just notice your upper legs, . . . notice what they experience, . . . notice what they feel like to you . . . right now . . . in this moment. . . . All the while, keep breathing . . . gently and calmly, enjoying your focus on this very important and special part of your body. . . ."

Clinician gives a slightly longer pause here in anticipation of moving to the next body part. The clinician might want to breathe in and out audibly for a few breaths to remind the client to do the same.

"As you continue to breathe calmly and in this comfortable way, draw your attention to your buttocks and hips. . . . Just pay attention to your pelvic area. . . . See if you notice any sensations in your buttocks. . . . Slowly and gently pay attention . . . to all parts of your pelvis . . . from your buttocks . . . to your hips. . . . Pay attention to any sensations you might have in your buttocks or hips. . . . Maybe they are aching, . . . maybe there's a sense of ease, . . . maybe there seems to be nothing at all. . . . Just notice your buttocks, your hips, . . . notice what they experience, . . . right now . . . in this moment, . . . not trying to change anything, . . . just being aware of what's there. . . . All the while, keep breathing . . . gently and calmly, enjoying your focus on this very distinct and useful part of your body. . . ."

Clinician gives a slightly longer pause here in anticipation of moving to the next body part. The clinician might want to breathe in and out audibly for a few breaths to remind the client to do the same.

"As you continue to breathe calmly and in this comfortable way, draw your attention to your hands. . . . Just pay attention to your fingers and palms. . . . See if you notice any sensations in your hands. . . . Slowly and gently pay attention . . . to all parts of your hands . . . from the tips of your fingers . . . to the palms . . . to the connection with your wrists. . . . Pay attention to any sensations you might have in your hands. . . . Maybe they are warm, . . . maybe some fingers are trembling, . . . maybe there seems to be nothing at all. . . . Just notice your hands, . . . notice what they experience, . . . right now . . . in this moment, . . . not trying to change anything, . . . just being aware of what's there. . . . All the while, keep breathing . . . gently and calmly, enjoying your focus on this very important and amazing part of your body. . . ."

Clinician gives a slightly longer pause here in anticipation of moving to the next body part. The clinician might want to breathe in and out audibly for a few breaths to remind the client to do the same.

"As you continue to breathe calmly and in this comfortable way, draw your attention to your arms. . . . Just pay attention to your wrists, . . . your lower arms, . . . your elbows, . . . your biceps. . . . See if you notice any sensations in your arms. . . . Slowly and gently pay attention . . . to all parts of your arms . . . from your wrists . . . to your elbows . . . to your upper arm. . . . Pay attention to any sensations you might have in your arms. . . . Maybe they are touching your upper body, . . . maybe there's a tightness in the joints, . . . maybe there seems to be nothing at all. . . . Just notice your arms, . . . notice what they experience, . . . right now . . . in this moment, . . . not trying to change anything, . . . just being aware of what's there. . . . All the while, keep breathing . . . gently and calmly, enjoying your focus on this very miraculous and special part of your body. . . ."

Clinician gives a slightly longer pause here in anticipation of moving to the next body part. The clinician might want to breathe in and out audibly for a few breaths to remind the client to do the same.

"As you continue to breathe calmly and in this comfortable way, draw your attention to your shoulders and back. . . . Just pay attention to your shoulders and upper back. . . . See if you notice any sensations in your upper back. . . . Slowly and gently pay attention . . . to all parts of your shoulders and upper back . . . from the outside . . . to the inside . . . from top . . . to bottom. . . . Pay attention to any sensations you might have in your shoulders and upper back. . . . Maybe they are tight, . . . maybe they are slumping, . . . maybe there seems to be nothing at all. . . . Just notice your shoulders, . . . notice what they experience, . . . right now . . . in this moment, . . . not trying to change anything, . . . just being aware of what's there. . . . All the while, keep breathing . . . gently and calmly, enjoying your focus on this very unique and important part of your body. . . ."

Clinician gives a slightly longer pause here in anticipation of moving to the next body part. The clinician might want to breathe in and out audibly for a few breaths to remind the client to do the same.

"As you continue to breathe calmly and in this comfortable way, draw your attention to your throat. . . . Just pay attention to your neck and throat. . . . See if you notice any sensations in your neck. . . . Slowly and gently pay attention . . . to all parts of your neck . . . from front . . . to back . . . inside . . . and outside. . . . Pay attention to any sensations you might have in your throat and neck. . . . Maybe there's a lump in your throat, . . . maybe there's soreness, . . . maybe there seems to be nothing at all. . . . Just notice your neck, . . . your throat, . . . notice what they experience, . . . right now . . . in this moment, . . . not trying to change anything, . . . just being aware of what's there. . . . All the while, keep breathing . . . gently and calmly, enjoying your focus on this very distinct and special part of your body. . . ."

Clinician gives a slightly longer pause here in anticipation of moving to the next body part. The clinician might want to breathe in and out audibly for a few breaths to remind the client to do the same.

"As you continue to breathe calmly and in this comfortable way, draw your attention to your scalp. . . . Just pay attention to your forehead and the skin covering your head. . . . See if you notice any sensations in your scalp. . . . Slowly and gently pay attention . . . to all parts of your scalp and forehead . . . from the nape of your neck . . . to right above your nose. . . . Pay attention to any sensations you might have in your scalp and forehead. . . . Maybe there's tightness, . . . maybe an itch, . . . maybe there seems to be nothing at all. . . . Just notice your scalp and forehead, . . . Notice what they experience, . . . right now . . . in this moment, . . . not trying to change anything, . . . just being aware of what's there. . . . All the while, keep breathing . . . gently and calmly, enjoying your focus on this very unique and special part of your body. . . ."

Clinician gives a slightly longer pause here in anticipation of moving to the next body part. The clinician might want to breathe in and out audibly for a few breaths to remind the client to do the same.

"As you continue to breathe calmly and in this comfortable way, draw your attention to your face. . . . Just pay attention to your eyes, . . . nose, . . . mouth, . . . and chin. . . . See if you notice any sensations in your face. . . . Slowly and gently pay attention . . . to all parts of your face . . . from your eyes, . . . your nose . . . to your cheeks . . . your mouth . . . and your chin. . . . Pay attention to any sensations you might have in your face. . . . Maybe the nose hairs are tickling, . . . maybe there's a trembling, . . . maybe there seems to be nothing at all. . . . Just notice your face, . . . notice what all the parts experience, . . . right now . . . in this moment, . . . not trying to change anything, . . . just being aware of what's there. . . . All the while, keep breathing . . . gently and calmly, enjoying your focus on this very important and wondrous part of your body. . . ."

Clinician gives a slightly longer pause here in anticipation of moving to the next body part. The clinician might want to breathe in and out audibly for a few breaths to remind the client to do the same.

"As you continue to breathe calmly and in this comfortable way, draw your attention to your chest and abdomen. . . . Just pay attention to your chest area and stomach. . . . See if you notice any sensations in your torso. . . . Slowly and gently pay attention . . . to all parts of your torso . . .

from your chest . . . through your diaphragm . . . to your abdomen. . . . Pay attention to any sensations you might have in your chest and stomach. . . . Maybe they are warm, . . . there's a movement, . . . up and down, . . . maybe there seems to be nothing of note at all. . . . Just notice all the parts of your torso, . . . notice what they experience, . . . right now . . . in this moment, . . . not trying to change anything, . . . just being aware of what's there. . . . All the while, keep breathing . . . gently and calmly, enjoying your focus on this very crucial and life-giving part of your body. . . ."

Clinician gives a slightly longer pause here in anticipation of moving to the next body part. The clinician might want to breathe in and out audibly for a few breaths to remind the client to do the same.

"Keeping your attention on your chest and abdomen, . . . slowly and gently take a deep breath, inhale and exhale . . . deeply . . . slowly, expanding your rib cage as much as you can. . . . Pay attention to the sensations of this deep, . . . deep . . . breath in your abdomen . . . your chest. . . . Notice all the sensations as muscles move . . . when you inhale . . . and exhale . . . deeply . . . slowly . . . gently . . . notice the rhythm of your breath in your chest and abdomen, . . . the motion of the air . . . circulating through you. . . . Breathing . . . deeply . . . gently . . . calmly, enjoying your focus on this part of your body. . . . When you are ready, return to your normal breathing rhythm and note the sensations in your chest and stomach as they continue to move . . . gently now . . . up and down."

Clinician gives a slightly longer pause here in anticipation of moving to the next body part. The clinician might want to breathe in and out audibly for a few breaths to remind the client to do the same.

"Now draw your attention to your breath. Take a few moments to observe the movements and feelings in your body as you breathe . . . in . . . and out. Enjoying each breath . . . enjoying the clean air it brings to your body. In . . . and out, . . . in . . . and out."

Clinician inhales and exhales audibly.

"And in . . . and out."

Clinician inhales and exhales audibly.

"And in . . . and out.
    "Now that you have observed the sensations in your body, I'd like you to bring your awareness back to this room. . . . Slowly begin to focus your attention away from your body . . . away from your breath . . . and to the

outer world. . . . Do that by beginning to notice any sounds that you may hear, and when you're ready go ahead and open your eyes. Take all the time you need."

Debriefing of Body Attunement Exercise

The mechanics of the debriefing are virtually the same as those for the *Bodily-Awareness Exercise*. The focal point is merely shifted to sensations that arose spontaneously for the client while attending to the various body parts. The clinician may want to ask general questions at first, and then hone in on specific body parts. Each body part is addressed during the first debriefing of sensations that arose spontaneously. The exercise is the first one that gives the clinician information about the client's usual physiological state, not a state induced either through focus on the breath or focus on bodily movements. The more often the exercise has been repeated, the less intense the querying during the debriefing will become as the client will spontaneously disclose which body parts felt something (and what) and which did not. The more information a client offers spontaneously, the less probing the clinician has to do; but the clinician should keep track to make sure all body parts were covered. Clients can be encouraged to practice body attunement on their own at home. If possible, the mental-health-care provider makes a tape of the exercise as it was conducted in session for the client to take home to use for that purpose, applying the same cautions provided above. As recommended above, encouragement to practice at home is given as a suggestion, not as a directive.

The debriefing of this exercise is the most important aspect of the experience for the edification of the clinician and the consolidation of inner experience for the client. This may be the first time that the client has ever listened to inner sensations as they arise spontaneously. Often clients are amazed by what they notice through listening to and watching their bodies. Perhaps for the first time, they consciously recognize their bodies as vital, sensing, feeling, and pulsing with life and experience. Clients can be profoundly shaken by this experience. Other clients may not be affected at all. They may not have been able to get in touch with many sensations and may not yet perceive the usefulness of the exercise. Persistence is important with such clients, along with encouragement that success is not only likely but imminent. Success may need to be redefined for such a client as the identification of one single experience in one body part. The next time the exercise is used, perhaps that will be the first body part that will be explored, to prime the client for experience. Regardless of the client's reaction, it is important that the clinician help the client frame the experience in a positive light and that the clinician can convey optimism and belief in the power of the exercise in the future. This is true, of course, for all therapeutic interventions.

Skill Development Recommendations

Recommendation 11-2   *Practice the* Bodily-Awareness *or* Body Attunement *exercise with a friend or family member. You may want to start by reading from the script, and then try it from memory. Pick a friend who is willing to give feedback about your technique. Practice with this person until they report enjoying the exercise and deriving benefit from it. Then try it with another friend or family member before using the exercise with a client.*

Recommendation 11-3   *Make a tape of the exercise for your own use. Practice the exercise a few times until you get an appreciation of what it feels like for the client. If you have a friend or peer who can guide you through the exercise, that may be an acceptable substitute to making a tape. The main idea is for you to experience the exercise so that you can identify with what your future clients will go through.*

FOCUS ON THE BRIDGE BETWEEN BODY AND AFFECT

This group of exercises moves the client beyond pure and simple awareness of physiological sensations and of the body as a whole to a rudimentary integration of bodily reactions with emotions. The exercises in this category begin to tie language used for the expression of emotion to bodily sensations in a subtle attempt to help clients recognize the connection between physiological sensation and emotional experience. These exercises are not yet concerned with specific labeling of feelings; their main thrust is awareness-raising with regard to the connection between body and affect. The specifics of affect will be addressed once the rudimentary understanding has been developed that affect is carried and reflected in the body. Once that recognition exists, the clinician will move the client toward an exploration of how different affective experiences in the body can be differentiated using a variety of feeling labels.

Basic-Bodily-Experience Exercise

As mentioned previously, this exercise looks surprisingly similar, at least on the surface, to the *Body Attunement Exercise.* The critical difference is that the mental-health-care provider now uses openly emotionally tinged language to help the client explore the body. At Level Two no attempt is made to tie a particular affect to a specific set of sensations in the body. However, if this exercise is used for higher-level work, this may occur spontaneously and will alter the focus of the debriefing used in the exercise. In fact, the debriefing more than anything differentiates work at different levels. The *Basic-Bodily-Experience Exercise* can be used to explore the entire body or can be used in a targeted manner to single out parts of the body the clinician believes are most relevant to the client's affective state. The clinician may initially choose to do a whole body exploration only to hone in on specific smaller parts of the body after an initial debriefing has suggested that they are most relevant or affected. What follows are two sample introductions. First, an introduction is given for a client at Level One who is being exposed to this exercise for the first time. Similarities to the *Body Attunement Exercise* can be noted. If the exercise is used with a client at a higher level, minor modifications are necessary. The main difference rests not in the introduction and instructions, but in the debriefing. The only difference in the introduction is the description of the purpose adapted to level of work. A sample of a Level Seven introduction is provided to highlight how this is accomplished. Then instructions are provided for a full-body exploration of experience. It should be noted that if only a smaller part of the body is explored (for example, if the clinician notes that the most affected part of the body is from the shoulders up), much more detailed focus on smaller and smaller muscle groups can be chosen. The overall-body exercise can be expanded by adding smaller muscle groups or can be shortened by collapsing some of the parts of the body into larger groupings. For example, to shorten the exercise, the legs could be collapsed into one body part to be explored as opposed to differentiating lower and upper; the same could be done for arms. The main caution for this exercise rests in the clinician's choice of feeling labels. It is important not to suggest a particular feeling for any one body part. Language is chosen so as to open the client's mind to a variety of possibilities, not to guide the client to a specific conclusion about the existence of one particular feeling. Even if the mental-health-care provider is certain that the client is feeling anxiety (as opposed to depression, anger, and so forth), the range of labels and language used in this exercise needs to encompass all emotions to allow the client a choice and to expand the client's awareness of the richness and range of human affects. To show how the instructions are modified for higher-level work, an abbreviated Level Seven sample is included. This abbreviation chooses one body area and shows how the client is directed toward deeper work in the search for an underlying affect. The same basic deeper work can be translated to any other body part by the reader, as dictated by client needs. Usually higher-level work will single out a few specific body parts that have already been identified by client and mental-health-care provider as most relevant and affected. It is rare that the entire body will be "exercised" at higher levels of work. Finally, debriefing directions are provided, first for a Level One client, then for Level Seven to highlight the differences. All cautions noted so far again apply to this exercise.

Introduction to Bodily-Experience Exercise: Level One

"You know the body exercises we have been doing? Today I'd like to change them a little bit again. I still want you to observe what the different parts of the body we'll focus on feel like, but I'll also try to give you some help by every now and then asking you to pay attention to whether certain feelings may be present. I'll give you lots of options and I'm never suggesting that you should feel a certain thing. I am just going to try to help you explore whether certain feelings fit or don't fit for you when you pay attention to different parts of your body. So I'll ask you to note if a part may feel relaxed or tense, calm or exited, still or trembling, hot or cold, good or bad, comfortable or uncomfortable. Just like always, if you feel nothing, that's fine; no need to panic. Just pay attention to the next body part as we move on. Does that make sense?"

The clinician now gives the client a chance to object or ask questions.

"Like always, we'll start the exercise with the breathing exercise that we have been doing and then I'll ask you to just follow my instructions. I will ask you to pay attention to different parts of the body at different times, and then I'll ask you to pay attention to what it is that you are feeling in that body part. Alright?"

The clinician gives the client a chance to ask more questions. Then the following points need to be made if they were not already covered by the client's questions:

"If at any point something feels uncomfortable, just lift one of your hands to let me know to back away from a certain body part and I'll move on. You can do this exercise sitting comfortably or lying down, just like with the other body exercise. Is there anything I need to know about before we start?"

This represents yet another opportunity for the client to ask questions. Once all questions are answered, the clinician moves on to the basic instructions.

Introduction to Bodily-Experience Exercise: Level Seven

"Do you remember that body exercise we did where I suggested different feeling states while you were paying attention to your body? I think that exercise would help us figure what else is going on with you emotionally. Now that we have identified that there is some amount of anxiety, we both seem to agree that there is more; maybe something deeper. How about we do that same exercise, but this time I'll direct your attention to move beyond signs of anxiety, to signs of other emotions that may be there that you didn't notice before. What do you think?"

The clinician now gives the client a chance to object or ask questions.

"Well then, like always, let's start with the breathing exercise that you have been doing and then just follow my instructions. How about you start with the breathing any time you're ready, and when you want me to start with the instructions for the rest of the exercise just raise your hand. Okay?"

The clinician gives the client control of the breathing exercise as this is very familiar by now and the client probably has developed a personal rhythm. No further introduction is necessary. Once the client has found a comfortable breathing rhythm and has raised a hand to signal the mental-health-care provider to start, the clinician will move to the instruction portion of the exercise.

Instructions to Basic-Bodily-Experience Exercise: Level One

"Seat yourself comfortably and close your eyes. Draw your attention to the inside of your body. Consciously focus your mind inside your body and then just follow my instructions. . . . Remember, you don't have to endure anything that does not feel right. . . . If you need to signal me to move on to the next body part, just raise one of your hands. As always, let's start by taking a deep breath in . . . through the nose . . . and then out . . . through the mouth."

Here the clinician takes in a deep audible breath through the nose and then blows out the breath through the mouth. This may be done a couple of times.

"Breathe in . . . "

Clinician inhales audibly.

". . . and out through your nose."

Clinician exhales audibly through the nose.

"And in . . . and out . . . and in . . . and out."

Clinician establishes a comfortable audible breathing rhythm. This should be done without speaking for about twenty to thirty seconds, or whatever period of time is comfortable for the client. When the client has established a good rhythm and appears at ease, the clinician moves on to the next set of instructions.

"As you continue to breathe calmly and in this comfortable way, draw your attention to your feet. . . . Pay attention to the feelings in your feet and toes. . . . Notice the feelings in your feet. . . . Slowly and gently pay attention . . . to all parts of your feet . . . from your heels . . . to your toes. . . . Pay attention to any feelings you might have in your feet. . . . Maybe they're cold, . . . or warm; . . . maybe they're cramped; . . . or relaxed; . . . maybe they're moving; . . . or still; . . . maybe they're upset; . . . or at ease; . . . maybe there seems to be no feeling at all. . . . Just notice the feelings in your feet, . . . Notice what they experience, . . . notice what they feel like to you, . . . right now . . . in this moment. . . . All the while, keep breathing . . . gently and calmly, enjoying your focus on this very unique and special part of your body. . . ."

Clinician gives a slightly longer pause here in anticipation of moving to the next body part. The clinician might want to breathe in and out audibly for a few breaths to remind the client to do the same.

"As you continue to breathe calmly and in this comfortable way, draw your attention to your lower legs. . . . Just pay attention to the feelings in your calves and ankles. . . . Notice the feelings in your lower legs. . . . Slowly and gently pay attention . . . to all parts of your lower legs . . . from your ankles . . . to your knees. . . . Pay attention to any feelings you might have in your lower legs. . . . Maybe they feel stiff, . . . or relaxed; . . . maybe they're agitated, . . . or calm; . . . maybe they feel heavy, . . . or light; . . . maybe they feel good, . . . or bad; . . . or maybe there seems to be no feeling at all. . . . Just notice the feelings in your lower legs, . . . Notice what they experience, . . . notice what they feel like to you, . . . right now . . . in this moment. . . . All the while, keep breathing . . . gently and calmly, enjoying your focus on this very unique and important part of your body. . . ."

Clinician gives a slightly longer pause here in anticipation of moving to the next body part. The clinician might want to breathe in and out audibly for a few breaths to remind the client to do the same.

"As you continue to breathe calmly and in this comfortable way, draw your attention to your upper legs. . . . Just pay attention to the feelings in your knees and thighs. . . . Notice any feelings in your upper legs. . . . Slowly and gently pay attention . . . to all parts of your upper legs . . . from your knees . . . to your thighs. . . . Pay attention to any feelings you might have in your upper legs. . . . Maybe they are resting comfortably, . . . or uncomfortably; . . . maybe they feel tight, . . . or relaxed; . . . maybe they feel cold, . . . or warm; . . . maybe they hurt, . . . or feel good; . . . or maybe there seems to be no feeling at all. . . . Just notice the feelings in your upper legs, . . . Notice what they experience, . . . Notice what they feel like to you . . . right now . . . in this moment. . . . All the while, keep breathing . . . gently and calmly, enjoying your focus on this very important and special part of your body. . . ."

Clinician gives a slightly longer pause here in anticipation of moving to the next body part. The clinician might want to breathe in and out audibly for a few breaths to remind the client to do the same.

"As you continue to breathe calmly and in this comfortable way, draw your attention to your buttocks and hips. . . . Just pay attention to the feelings in your pelvic area. . . . Notice any feelings in your buttocks. . . . Slowly and gently pay attention . . . to all parts of your pelvis . . . from your buttocks . . . to your hips. . . . Pay attention to any feelings you might have in your buttocks or hips. . . . Maybe they are aching, . . . or healthy; . . . maybe they have a sense of ease, . . . or tension; . . . maybe they are up-tight, . . . or relaxed; . . . maybe feel heavy and burdened, . . . or light and free; . . . or maybe there seems to be no feeling at all. . . . Just notice the feelings in your buttocks, your hips . . . notice what they experience, . . . notice what they feel like to you, . . . right now . . . in this moment. . . . All the while, keep breathing . . . gently and calmly, enjoying your focus on this very distinct and useful part of your body. . . ."

Clinician gives a slightly longer pause here in anticipation of moving to the next body part. The clinician might want to breathe in and out audibly for a few breaths to remind the client to do the same.

"As you continue to breathe calmly and in this comfortable way, draw your attention to your hands. . . . Just pay attention to your fingers and palms. . . . Notice any feelings in your hands. . . . Slowly and gently pay attention . . . to all the feelings in all parts of your hands . . . from the tips of your fingers . . . to the palms . . . to the connection with your wrists. . . . Pay attention to any feelings at all that you might have in your hands. . . . Maybe they are warm, . . . or cold; . . . maybe the fingers are trembling, . . . or still; . . . maybe there is pain, . . . or comfort; . . . maybe they are cramped, . . . or relaxed; . . . or maybe there seems to be nothing at all. . . . Just notice the feelings in your hands, . . . notice what they ex-perience, . . . notice what they feel like to you, . . . right now . . . in this moment. . . . All the while, keep breathing . . . gently and calmly, enjoying your focus on this very important and amazing part of your body. . . ."

Clinician gives a slightly longer pause here in anticipation of moving to the next body part. The clinician might want to breathe in and out audibly for a few breaths to remind the client to do the same.

"As you continue to breathe calmly and in this comfortable way, draw your attention to your arms. . . . Just pay attention to the feelings in your wrists, . . . your lower arms, . . . your elbows, . . . your biceps. . . . Notice any feelings in your arms. . . . Slowly and gently pay attention . . . to all parts of your arms . . . from your wrists . . . to your elbows . . . to your up-per arms. . . . Pay attention to any feelings you might have in your arms. . . . Maybe they are agitated, . . . or calm; . . . maybe there's a tight-ness in the joints, . . . or relaxation; . . . maybe they feel comfortable, . . . or uncomfortable; . . . maybe they want to move, . . . or stay still; . . . or maybe there seems to be no feeling at all. . . . Just notice the feelings in your arms, . . . notice what they experience, . . . notice what they feel like

to you, . . . right now . . . in this moment. . . . All the while, keep breathing . . . gently and calmly, enjoying your focus on this very miraculous
and special part of your body. . . ."

*Clinician gives a slightly longer pause here in anticipation of moving to the next
body part. The clinician might want to breathe in and out audibly for a few
breaths to remind the client to do the same.*

"As you continue to breathe calmly and in this comfortable way, draw
your attention to your shoulders and back. . . . Just pay attention to the
feelings in your shoulders and upper back. . . . Notice any feelings in your
upper back. . . . Slowly and gently pay attention . . . to all parts of your
shoulders and upper back . . . from the outside . . . to the inside . . . from
top . . . to bottom. . . . Pay attention to any feelings you might have in
your shoulders and upper back. . . . Maybe they are tight, . . . or
relaxed; . . . maybe they are down, . . . or up; . . . maybe they feel heavy
and burdened, . . . or light and free; . . . maybe they're in pain, . . . or
comfort; . . . or maybe there seems to be no feeling at all. . . . Just notice
your shoulders, . . . notice what they experience, . . . notice what they feel
like to you, . . . right now . . . in this moment. . . . All the while, keep
breathing . . . gently and calmly, enjoying your focus on this very unique
and important part of your body. . . ."

*Clinician gives a slightly longer pause here in anticipation of moving to the next
body part. The clinician might want to breathe in and out audibly for a few
breaths to remind the client to do the same.*

"As you continue to breathe calmly and in this comfortable way, draw
your attention to your throat. . . . Just pay attention to the feelings in your
neck and throat. . . . Notice any feelings in your neck. . . . Slowly and gently pay attention . . . to all parts of your neck . . . from front . . . to
back . . . inside . . . and outside. . . . Pay attention to any feelings you
might have in your throat and neck. . . . Maybe it's choked up, . . . or
clear; . . . maybe it feels soreness, . . . or comfort; . . . maybe it feels heaviness, . . . or lightness; . . . maybe there's tension, . . . or relaxation; . . . or
maybe there seems to be no feeling at all. . . . Just notice the feelings in
your neck, . . . in your throat, . . . notice what they experience, . . . notice
what they feel like to you, . . . right now . . . in this moment. . . . All the
while, keep breathing . . . gently and calmly, enjoying your focus on this
very distinct and special part of your body. . . ."

*Clinician gives a slightly longer pause here in anticipation of moving to the next
body part. The clinician might want to breathe in and out audibly for a few
breaths to remind the client to do the same.*

"As you continue to breathe calmly and in this comfortable way, draw your attention to your scalp. . . . Just pay attention to the feelings in your forehead and the skin covering your head. . . . Notice any feelings in your scalp. . . . Slowly and gently pay attention . . . to all parts of your scalp and forehead . . . from the nape of your neck . . . to right above your nose. . . . Pay attention to any feelings you might have in your scalp and forehead. . . . Maybe they're tight, . . . or relaxed, . . . maybe they carry agitation, . . . or calmness; . . . maybe they hurt, . . . or feel no pain; . . . maybe they feel bad, . . . or good; . . . or maybe there seems to be no feeling at all. . . . Just notice the feelings in your scalp and forehead, . . . notice what they experience, . . . notice what they feel like to you, . . . right now . . . in this moment. . . . All the while, keep breathing . . . gently and calmly, enjoying your focus on this very unique and special part of your body. . . ."

Clinician gives a slightly longer pause here in anticipation of moving to the next body part. The clinician might want to breathe in and out audibly for a few breaths to remind the client to do the same.

"As you continue to breathe calmly and in this comfortable way, draw your attention to your face. . . . Just pay attention to the feelings in your eyes, . . . nose, . . . mouth, . . . and chin. . . . Notice any feelings in your face. . . . Slowly and gently pay attention . . . to all parts of your face . . . from your eyes, . . . your nose . . . to your cheeks . . . your mouth . . . and your chin. . . . Pay attention to any feelings you might have in the features of your face. . . . Maybe there is agitation, . . . or calmness; . . . maybe they feel tight and drawn; . . . or at ease; . . . maybe there's trembling, . . . or stillness; . . . maybe they feel heavy, . . . or light; . . . or maybe there seems to be no feeling at all. . . . Just notice the feelings in your face, . . . notice what all the parts experience, . . . notice what they feel like to you . . . right now . . . in this moment. . . . All the while, keep breathing . . . gently and calmly, enjoying your focus on this very important and wondrous part of your body. . . ."

Clinician gives a slightly longer pause here in anticipation of moving to the next body part. The clinician might want to breathe in and out audibly for a few breaths to remind the client to do the same.

"As you continue to breathe calmly and in this comfortable way, draw your attention to your chest and abdomen. . . . Just pay attention to the feelings in your chest area and stomach. . . . Notice any feelings in your torso. . . . Slowly and gently pay attention . . . to all parts of your torso . . . from your chest . . . through your diaphragm . . . to your abdomen. . . . Pay attention to any feelings you might have in your chest and stomach. . . . Maybe they are comfortable, . . . or uncomfortable; . . . maybe there is

agitation, . . . or relaxation; . . . maybe there is heaviness, . . . or lightness; . . . maybe there is upset, . . . or ease; . . . or maybe there seems to
be no feeling at all. . . . Just notice all the parts of your torso, . . . notice
what they experience, . . . notice what they feel like to you . . . right
now . . . in this moment. . . . All the while, keep breathing . . . gently and
calmly, enjoying your focus on this very crucial and life-giving part of
your body. . . ."

*Clinician gives a slightly longer pause here in anticipation of moving to the next
body part. The clinician might want to breathe in and out audibly for a few
breaths to remind the client to do the same.*

"Keeping your attention on your chest and abdomen, . . . slowly and gently
take a deep breath, inhale and exhale . . . deeply . . . slowly, expanding
your rib cage as much as you can. . . . Pay attention to the feelings evoked
by this deep, . . . deep . . . breath in your abdomen . . . your chest. . . .
Notice all the feelings as muscles move . . . when you inhale . . . and exhale . . . deeply . . . slowly . . . gently. . . . Notice the rhythm of your
breath in your chest and abdomen, . . . the motion of the air . . . circulating through you. . . . Noticing feelings of calmness, . . . or agitation; . . . of
tightness, . . . or freedom; . . . of lightness, . . . or burden; . . . of joy, . . . or
pain. . . . Breathing . . . deeply . . . gently . . . calmly, enjoying your focus
on this part of your body. . . . When you are ready, return to your normal
breathing rhythm and note the feelings in your chest and stomach as they
continue to move . . . gently now . . . up and down."

*Clinician gives a slightly longer pause here in anticipation of moving to the next
body part. The clinician might want to breathe in and out audibly for a few
breaths to remind the client to do the same.*

"Now bring your attention to your breath. Take a few moments to observe
the movements and feelings in your body as you breathe . . . in . . . and
out. Enjoying each breath . . . enjoying the clean air it brings to your
body. In . . . and out, . . . in . . . and out."

Clinician inhales and exhales audibly.

"And in . . . and out."

Clinician inhales and exhales audibly.

"And in . . . and out.
   "Now that you have observed the feelings in your body, I'd like you
to bring your awareness back to this room. . . . Slowly begin to focus your
attention away from your body . . . away from your breath . . . and to the
outer world. . . . Do that by beginning to notice any sounds that you may
hear, and when you're ready go ahead and open your eyes. Take all the
time you need."

Instructions for Basic-Bodily-Experience Exercise: Level Seven

The clinician has received the signal from the client to begin with the instructions. Thus, the client has indicated having found a comfortable breathing rhythm. The clinician starts by moving to the parts of the body that were identified previously as housing anxiety (see introduction to Level Seven example). The purpose is to identify whether any other affects may be hidden in the area. If the client does not appear to have found a good breathing rhythm when giving the signal, the clinician can focus on breathing for a few moments.

"As you continue to breathe calmly and in this comfortable way, begin by drawing your attention to your torso. . . . Pay attention to the feelings in your chest area, your back, and your stomach. . . . Notice any feelings in your torso, no matter . . . how small, no matter . . . how subtle. . . . Slowly . . . and gently pay attention . . . to all parts of your torso. . . . Listen to your chest . . . give attention to your diaphragm . . . watch your abdomen . . . and feel your back. . . . Pay attention to any feelings you might feel in your chest, . . . your diaphragm, . . . your back, . . . and your stomach. . . . Don't just notice the familiar feelings . . . the feelings you know about . . . of agitation, . . . the butterflies in your stomach, . . . the constriction in your chest, . . . the pain in your lower back, . . . the freezing of your diaphragm . . . when you hold your breath; . . . Go deeper this time. . . . Go to unfamiliar ground; . . . notice feelings and sensations that go beyond the tightness and tension; . . . slowly pay deep . . . and complete . . . attention . . . to every single . . . subtle feeling . . . in your torso. Go beyond the usual, listen for the new. . . . Note if there are deeper feelings, perhaps . . . of heaviness, . . . or pain; . . . discomfort . . . or unease; . . . agitation; . . . or doom; . . . Go deeper . . . and deeper . . . into your experience. . . . Pay closer . . . and closer . . . attention. . . . Note anything, . . . anything at all, . . . the smallest hint . . . of feeling. . . . The smallest feeling . . . of heaviness, . . . agitation, . . . discomfort, . . . pain, . . . confusion, . . . explosiveness, . . . excitement, . . . joy, . . . pleasure, . . . pain. . . . Go deeper . . . and listen; . . . go deeper . . . and watch; . . . go deeper . . . and taste; . . . go deeper . . . and sense. . . . Sense . . . and feel anything, . . . anything at all. . . . Notice all the feelings . . . in all the parts of your torso, . . . notice what they experience, . . . notice what they feel . . . right now . . . in this moment. . . . All the while, keep breathing . . . gently and calmly, enjoying your focus on this very crucial and life-giving part of your body. . . ."

Clinician gives a long pause here, allowing the client to continue to explore further independently, before moving to the next body part or closing the exercise with the usual focus on the breath. The clinician might want to breathe in and out audibly for a few breaths during the pause to remind the client to do the same. When the client appears done and the exercise should close, or when it is time to move to the next body part, the clinician moves on. [The sample moves to a closing; with some clients another set of body parts may be explored following the example given so far.]

"Now bring your attention to your breath. Take a few moments to observe the movements and feelings in your body as you breathe . . . in . . . and out. Enjoying each breath . . . enjoying the clean air it brings to your body. In . . . and out, . . . in . . . and out."

Clinician inhales and exhales audibly.

"And in . . . and out."

Clinician inhales and exhales audibly.

"And in . . . and out.

"Now that you have observed the many different feelings in your body, bring your awareness back to this room. . . . Slowly begin to focus your attention away from your body . . . away from your breath . . . and to the outer world. . . . Do that by beginning to notice any sounds that you may hear, and when you're ready go ahead and open your eyes. Take all the time you need."

Debriefing of Basic-Bodily-Experience Exercise: Level One

The mechanics of the debriefing are virtually the same as those for the *Body Attunement Exercise.* The main difference is that a more feelings-oriented language will be used. The focus will be placed on exploring which body part appears to be most readily identifiable as carrying some emotion. It is important to remember that occasionally, body parts that are involved in the most intense (perhaps) traumatic experience of the client may have the least feelings associated with them. Not uncommonly, for example, clients who are victims of childhood sexual abuse may have little to no sensation in the pelvic/buttock area. Pushing the client into experiencing something is clearly not the point of these exercises. Instead they represent a gentle and cautious road to allowing clients to begin to experience feelings as they emerge, at the client's pace. If no feelings are reported within a certain body part, the clinician does not push the client harder next time. This does not mean that the clinician does not inquire about all experience for all body parts. As always, clinicians ask general questions first, and then hone in on all the body parts that were covered in the exercise. Each body part is addressed to gain maximum information about the client's current emotional and physiological state. The more often the exercise has been repeated, the less intense the querying during the debriefing will become as the client will spontaneously disclose which body parts felt something (and what) and which did not. The more information a client offers spontaneously, the less probing the clinician has to do. Clients can be encouraged to practice bodily experience on their own at home. If possible, the mental-health-care provider makes a tape of the exercise as it was conducted in session for the client to take home to use for that purpose, applying the same cautions provided above. As recommended previously, encouragement to practice at home is given as a suggestion, not as a directive.

The debriefing of this exercise is a most important aspect of the experience as this may be the first time that a client has ever listened to inner sensations and tied them to feeling language. Often clients will spontaneously move to Level Three work through this exercise, beginning to identify affect and feelings where they were unable to do so before. This exercise is often a powerful impetus for therapeutic work. With many clients the exercise will not need to be repeated once they spontaneously move to Level Three work, at least not for Level Two purposes. Some clients, on the other hand, open up to experience only if helped by the exercise, and Level Three and Level Two will alternate consistently until a wide range of affects has been identified. Often when this is the case, the clinician will find that only relevant parts of the body are covered in each application of the exercises. The client is the best guide in deciding which parts of the body to explore to continue gaining awareness and insight.

Debriefing of Bodily-Experience-Exercise: Level Seven

Debriefing at Level Seven (and the other higher levels) is usually quick and easy as the client is already quite affectively aware and clear about the focus and purpose of the exercise. Often clients working at a high level will spontaneously debrief, that is, very little inquiry will be needed. Most importantly, the clinician needs to help the client recognize the underlying feelings that lurked beyond the readily identified affect that has already been in the client's awareness. As both client and clinician entered the exercise with that expectation, it is rare that the client does not emerge from the exercise with some new awareness. Despite the brevity of the debriefing, this is of course where the thrust of the therapeutic work takes place. It is in the debriefing that the client clearly identifies and labels the underlying affect. Work progresses from there.

Advanced-Bodily-Experience Exercise

This exercise makes use of spontaneous expressions of feelings that are not identified by clients as such. All clients will leak emotions at least occasionally even when they claim not to be feeling anything or while talking about an issue. This exercise takes advantage of these emotional leaks, using them to draw the client's awareness to the body and to sensations and feelings in the body. As mentioned above, bridge exercises are not yet concerned with labeling a particular affect; they merely increase the client's awareness that sensations exist in the body and that feelings are being experienced all the time, even if they cannot yet be identified (that is, labeled). Given their nature, bridge exercises often spontaneously lead to Level Three work as clients often become motivated to learn labels once they have identified the existence of emotions. This development needs to be initiated by the client, not the clinician, so as to allow the client to set the pace for the affective work.

Advanced-bodily-experience work can happen any time and for as long as necessary. Sometimes it may take moments; sometimes it may preoccupy the remainder of a session. It is difficult to predict exactly where the work will lead or how long it will take as these factors depend largely on the openness and reaction of the client. This work is extremely useful in that it uses body movements and sensations that are clearly already finding expression and merely need to be made conscious to the client. An emotional leak that can be used for advanced work may consist of a client's gesture, facial expression, or other body movement while talking (perhaps rather unemotionally) about a certain topic. A leak is usually obvious to the clinician because of one of several possible traits:

- it is an unusual gesture, expression (facial or voice inflection), or movement that the clinician has not noted in the client before
- it is a quick gesture, expression, or movement that client tries to hide as soon as it occurred
- it is a gesture, expression, or movement that occurs with some regularity, always in a predictable context
- it is a habitual gesture, expression, or movement that the client does not appear to be aware of and may even deny if asked about

Once the leak has occurred, the clinician asks the client to repeat it. Sometimes clients are confused when asked to repeat a certain gesture or movement, as they were not even aware that they engaged in it. The clinician can simply ask such clients to repeat what they said exactly as they said it and to pay attention to their bodies. Clients will then generally repeat and become aware of the movement. If this procedure does not work, it is best to drop the issue and to try again when the next leak occurs. Sometimes, clients may deny the gesture as they appear to be embarrassed by it. The mental-health-care provider then has to make a judgment call as to whether it is worth pushing the issue. A good rule of thumb is that if rapport is secure and the client seems to trust the clinician, it may be worth pursuing the work on the leak. If rapport is still being built or the client feels vulnerable vis-à-vis the clinician, it will not be worth the risks to pursue the issue. Clearly, the faster the clinician can catch the leak and draw the client's attention to it, the more likely the client will not be able to deny or forget it.

If the leak was caught quickly and the client repeats the gesture or movement upon the request of the clinician, she or he is then asked to talk about the bodily expression. Most specifically, clients will be asked what thoughts the movement or gesture evokes, if it is familiar, used often, used by anyone else they know, and what else comes to mind as they engage in the movement again.

Cautious query about accompanying internal bodily experiences can also be useful. If the client can identify physiological reactions, that can be helpful as well. The exercise can also involve asking the client to exaggerate the motion or gesture. With many clients, simple repetition may not have enough impact to help them recognize the emotional expression and experience contained within the movement. Asking the client to exaggerate the motion will increase its emotional salience and may help the client to recognize the underlying experience. Exaggeration is more likely used with clients at lower levels; simple repetition often suffices at higher levels as clients are already more self-aware.

Stopping clients and asking them to become aware of the bodily experiences they have as they speak has the same effect as the basic bodily experience in that it draws their attention to bodily processes and to the fact that feelings may be lurking under behavior and thought. The advanced exercise is best understood by example. Hence what follows are two examples. The first example shows an application of the exercise with a client who is working at Level Two, that is, a client who is still struggling with basic inner experience and is not yet labeling affect. This example will show the application of the exercise with a request for exaggeration of the movement. The second example is applied to Level Six, involving a client who is beginning to recognize the fact that emotions do not necessarily exist singly, but can be mixed across emotional categories. Simple repetition (that is, no request for exaggeration) will be demonstrated here.

Level Two Application of the Advanced-Bodily-Experience Exercise

This example involves a client who is seen in her fourth session, and who was relating an incident that occurred between her and a close female friend. The client and this particular friend have been fighting frequently and yet have remained friends for many years. The client is currently considering breaking off the friendship, in part motivated by the friend's recent announcement that she has discovered that she is gay. The client is showing a lot of affect about her relationship with this friend and her decision making regarding what to do about the friendship. Nevertheless, her voice remained somewhat monotone, though some inflections were notable, suggesting that feelings were just under the surface. In prior sessions the client had denied feeling any particular feelings about anyone in general, and about this friend in particular. She indicated that her family of origin was not very "emotional" or "touchy-feely" and that she did not believe in "making too much of feelings." Thus, the client appeared somewhat closed off from her feelings and seemed to have only occasional awareness of emotionality. This occasional awareness led the clinician to the conclusion that the client was currently struggling affectively somewhere around Level Two or Three, having some rudimentary awareness (or an inkling of experience), but not being quite able to label feelings because of not accepting affect as an important aspect of being human. While talking about the interaction with her friend, the client crossed her legs (a seated position she had not assumed before) and swung her lower leg rhythmically and quite forcefully. When she stopped talking, she returned to her usual position, which consisted of sitting back in the chair, legs (touching each other) side-by-side and both feet on the ground. The following interchange was then initiated by the clinician:

CLINICIAN: Would you sit back the way you were sitting just a minute ago?
CLIENT: Sit how? *(looks puzzled)*
CLINICIAN: With your legs crossed like that *(models the position)* and your leg swinging. . . .
CLIENT: Why?
CLINICIAN: I'd like to try something with you. . . .
CLIENT: Like that? *(shifts to the "leak" position)*
CLINICIAN: Yeah, that was it. Now swing your lower leg, like that. *(models)*
CLIENT: I really did that?
CLINICIAN: Yes, you really did.
CLIENT: Okay, so now what? *(swinging her leg)*
CLINICIAN: When you were sitting like that you were talking about telling Amy that you would like to end the friendship. I got the feeling that you were communicating something else to her with the way you were holding your body. So I thought maybe you could sit like that again and listen to your body. See if you can identify any sensations you are aware of as you sit that way. . . .
CLIENT: Okay. . . .
CLINICIAN: Go ahead and start swinging your leg, like you did before.
CLIENT: *(complies)*
CLINICIAN: What do you notice in your body?
CLIENT: I don't know . . . *(tentative and unsure)*
CLINICIAN: Hang in there with me for a moment. I really think this will help us out. Would you, just to give this a fair try, swing your leg a little harder?
CLIENT: Swing harder?
CLINICIAN: Yea, just put a little more "umph" in that movement.
CLIENT: Okay . . . *(grins and swings harder)*
CLINICIAN: Okay, now what do you notice in your body?
CLIENT: I'm not sure, but it seems like the right thing to do when I think about Amy right now. *(more forceful voice now)*
CLINICIAN: What feels right about it?
CLIENT: Well, it gives me something to do I guess. *(backs off the affect)* It occupies me with something because this is a tough thing to do, you know, to tell your friend you want out.

CLINICIAN: What thoughts come to mind as you do it, as you swing your leg? *(allowing the detour away from obvious affect for now and going to the cognitive plane, which is more comfortable for the client)*

CLIENT: Oh, I got it; it's like—"Hey Amy, I really wanna kick you out right now!"

CLINICIAN: Were you aware of that thought before?

CLIENT: No. But you know what, it's true. I would like to kick her. *(rather emphatic now; more voice inflection than before)* How can she do this to me. Gay? Since when? Next thing she'll wanna be lovers.

CLINICIAN: You really are having a reaction to this.

CLIENT: Yes, I am. I guess I didn't realize how upset I was about this whole thing. Is that it? I'm swinging my leg to kick her because I'm upset?

CLINICIAN: Is that what you make of it?

CLIENT: Yeah. I am. I am upset. My body is upset. I can feel it in my stomach now. Wow, all that from swinging my leg. *(Client moves back to her usual position now, needing to gain some distance.) (Session continues from here.)*

This example shows how a simple exaggeration of a movement helped the client achieve a recognition of a bodily experience or impulse that moved her along the continuum of affective awareness. The fact that she labeled the anger reflected in the swing as "upset" is not important. The label at this point is much less critical than her recognition that she was having a physical reaction to the situation. The session moved from there to more exploration about her relationship with Amy and some work around her beliefs about homosexuality. The client stayed away from affect for the remainder of this session but seemed touched by the experience.

Level Six Application of the Advanced-Bodily-Experience Exercise

This example involves a client who has been seen for twelve sessions. At this particular moment the client was talking about his anger in his relationship with his wife, when he suddenly wiped his eyes and quickly turned his head away from the clinician. The client continued to talk angrily and acted as if himself had not been aware of this brief glimpse of another emotion. The clinician, knowing that rapport was solid, decided to interrupt the client to draw his attention to this emotional leak and an exploration of its potential meaning.

CLIENT: . . . and as always it just pissed me off. *(The "leak" gesture occurs.)* Well, I should say it aggravated me, because it wasn't really as bad as being pissed off. . . .

CLINICIAN: *(interrupting)* What was that?

CLIENT: What was what?

CLINICIAN: That thing you just did with your hand!

CLIENT: Nothing. . . .

CLINICIAN: Nothing?!

CLIENT: Well, I don't know. . . .

CLINICIAN: What do you think. . . . Given all the work we've done paying attention to how you use your body to express your feelings, do you really think it was nothing?

CLIENT: I'm not even sure what you're talking about.

CLINICIAN: I'm talking about that thing you did with your hand and your head right when you changed your mind about how angry you were.

CLIENT: What did I do?

CLINICIAN: This. *(models the head turn and eye wipe)* You do it. What do you feel when you do that?

CLIENT: *(wipes eyes and turns head; remains silent, but looks struck)*

CLINICIAN: What's going on? *(very gentle voice, leaning forward)*

CLIENT: It's like I'm crying, isn't it?

CLINICIAN: *(nods gently, stays leaning forward)* What's that about?

CLIENT: I'm not one to cry . . . but I think of sadness right now. . . .

CLINICIAN: You're thinking of sadness. . . .

CLIENT: Yes, I'm sad. *(voice mirrors the sadness and also betrays some surprise at this recognition)* So much has gone wrong between me and Charlotte. But we used to love each other so much. It's so sad to be fighting.

CLINICIAN: So aggravation isn't all there is. . . .

CLIENT: I guess not. I thought I was just mad, but it's really sad too, isn't it? We have twenty-three years in that relationship. We should be willing to fight for it, don't you think?

CLINICIAN: What do you want to do? Do you want to fight for it?

(Session continues from here.)

This example shows how a very quick and easily missed gesture can open the door to new awareness and inner experience. This client, who had just learned to recognize the varying degrees of his own anger, had never recognized his sadness about the changes in his spousal relationship before. The gesture gave the clinician an opening to invite the client to recognize that he felt more than anger. Interruptions are of course not always a good idea. However, in this case the clinician knew the client well and felt that the current task of affective work was to help the client recognize his mixed emotions. Thus, the opportunity needed to be seized. The client not only recognized his anger but also came to experience his sadness, a profound step in the direction of recognizing and ultimately accepting mixed emotions about the same situation. The whole process only took moments and yet the therapeutic accomplishment was

Skill Development Recommendations

Recommendation 11-4   *Practice the* Bodily-Experience Exercise: Level One *with a friend or family member. You may want to start by reading from the script, and then try it from memory. Pick a friend who is willing to give feedback about your technique. Practice with this person until they report enjoying the exercise and deriving benefit from it. Then try it with another friend or family member before using the exercise with a client.*

Recommendation 11-5   *Make a tape of the Level One exercise for your own use. Practice the exercise a few times until you get an appreciation of what it feels like for the client. If you have a friend or peer who can guide you through the exercise, that may be an acceptable substitute to making a tape. The main idea is for you to experience the exercise so that you can identify with what your future clients will go through.*

---

relatively large. Feeling words were very appropriate with the client as he was already somewhat emotionally sophisticated. He was able to identify a range of affects, was clearly aware of differing levels of intensity at least with regard to anger, and thus was ready to move to Level Six, recognizing and integrating the experience of more than one emotion at a time.

WORKING WITH AFFECT AND EMOTION

Focus on Feelings

People hate the darkness of their negative tendencies just as children hate the darkness of the night, but just as if there were no dark of night we would never recognize the light of day, so also if we possessed no negative aspects we could never recognize our positive ones. Our negative and positive tendencies are thus the valleys and the mountains of a beautiful landscape— there can be no mountains without valleys, and vice versa, so that those who would misguidedly seek to annihilate the valleys must in the same stroke level the mountains. Trying to rid ourselves of negative tendencies, trying to destroy them and eliminate them, would be a fine idea—if it were possible. The problem is, that it is not, that the negative tendencies in ourselves to which we try to shut our eyes nevertheless remain firmly ours and return to plague us as neurotic symptoms of fear, depression, and anxiety. Cut off from consciousness, they assume menacing aspects all out of proportion to their actual nature. We can tame evil only by befriending it, and we simply inflame it by alienating it.

K. Wilber, 1993, p. 196

This chapter continues the work with affect and emotion by focusing on strategies that help clients explore their full range of affects, including subtle nuances of affected, blended feelings, underlying emotions, and their meanings. In the previous chapter, work with the body was used to help clients recognize and gain awareness of their affects and emotions. In this chapter, bodywork is largely used to help clients gain a sense of mastery over their affect and recognize that they need not be victims of their emotions. Overall, the focus of the exercises in this chapter is on helping clients become more sophisticated in their affective experience, teaching them higher levels of affective awareness. As such, the work focuses on helping clients recognize the higher-level affective nuances contained in subtle blends of emotions, coexisting emotions, and underlying affects. It seeks to help clients accept all of their emotions, both positive and negative, and to recognize their meaning and source.

Many examples and instruction are included to help the clinician apply this work directly with clients. As in the prior chapter, in these samples and instructions words that are spoken by the mental-health-care provider directly to the client are placed in quotation marks and blocked format. These words need to be spoken in a well-paced manner. It is better to go too slow than too fast. Some practice may be required here to get the pacing just right. Ellipses, that is, three periods (. . .), indicate places where the clinician best pauses for a moment before moving on. The length of the pause will need to be adjusted as the clinician becomes familiar with a given client's needs. Actions the clinician takes while practicing a particular exercise with the client are printed in *italics*. Basic comments and instructions to the mental-health-care provider are printed in regular typeface. Any directions that need to be tailored to a client's particular affect or body area are placed in [brackets]. The content in the bracket will consist either of an example or a directive as to what to fill in the bracket. None of the instructions (including introductions and debriefings) have to be used verbatim. All transcripts are simply examples and reflect the content that needs to be covered; how this is accomplished will be up to each individual mental-health-care provider. It is best not to work from a transcript while with the client, even during exercises for which the client closes the eyes. The rustling of paper can be distracting and the pacing is often not as attuned as when the clinician speaks from memory. Although this may seem overwhelming at first, none of the scripts is actually very difficult. Memorizing the gist of each is usually pretty easy and just takes a little bit of practice.

FOCUS ON THE EXPERIENCE AND IDENTIFICATION OF AFFECT

The exercises in this category are designed to help clients distinguish different affects and to recognize that the same affect may occur with varying intensities in different situations or even within one and the same situation. Both exercises help clients integrate experience with language, being concerned not only with the inner experience of affect, but also the outer labeling (or verbal expression). This outer labeling helps clients recognize that there are many affects and intensities and gives them an invaluable tool of communication. Identification and labeling also increase affective awareness, the most important aspect of this work. It is crucial to understand that the experience is always more important than the label. If a client is clear about the experience but cannot settle on a specific label, that is no problem. Too often clients jump to the use of labels when the label really does not reflect experience. It is much better to have the client render a description of the physiological reaction and processes than to be presented with a beautiful label. The idea of labeling is introduced because it is useful for communication and over time can turn into a shortcut for client and clinician in terms of talking about what the client is feeling. The label must not be abused as a substitute for experience. This caution, while most relevant here, applies to all affective work. A final note of caution about labeling affect may be indicated. Clinicians can provide *samples* of labels but they do not *choose* labels for clients. The final choice about how to label an internal experience always rests with the client, even if the clinician does not agree with the client's choice. Thus, if a client chooses the word "gloomy" for an affect the clinician would have labeled "defeated," the client's label will be used to talk about the particular experience from now on. The clinician and the client will both know what the label stands for, that is, both are clear about the physiological sensation the label "gloomy" describes. Squabbling over which label "fits better" is irrelevant as all language is relative in any event.

Although only two formal exercises are noted here that deal with or focus on affect, there are numerous therapeutic interventions that can be used to help clients with these same goals. Further, the two exercises covered here are anything but static. They will look different with each client and with each application. Thus, unlike for the exercises covered up to this point, only general directions and examples can be given, no firm outlines or instructions as to what exactly has to be done. These are not step-by-step exercises as much as they are therapeutic interactions that have a clear direction but a meandering path toward their final goal(s). It probably goes without saying that use of these interventions requires affective self-awareness on the part of the clinician. Further, to be successful in helping clients recognize the distinctions between feelings (as in mixed emotions) and within feelings (that is, in levels of intensity) based on the inner experience and bodily sensations that accompany them, clinicians need to have a large affective vocabulary. There are many common labels for feelings that have been so overused that clients may reject them for the simple reason that they ring trite or commonplace. Further, there are many affects that are often stereotyped to a single label (for example, happy, depressed). It may be helpful in differentiating levels of intensity to have a large set of synonyms. To help clinicians develop an affective vocabulary, Table 12-1 lists feeling words that can be used for work with clients at basically all but the very lowest levels of affective experience. This listing is by no means all-inclusive but represents an attempt at compiling a useful listing of the many feeling words that exist. Clinicians are encouraged to add to the list on an ongoing basis.

Here-and-Now Affect Exploration Exercise

The goal of this exercise is to help clients translate inner affective experience into the recognition of emotion and the selection of a label for it. It enriches and enhances the work that was done up to this point by challenging clients not only to listen to their bodily experiences and feelings, but also to begin to recognize what each sensation and feeling may represent. Here-and-now work is used at Level Three for the first time, and is used consistently from here on out in the therapeutic process. In fact, most clients will benefit from here-and-now work regardless of the level of affective experience they have achieved. All here-and-now work is based on an affective experience that occurs during the session, that is, is focused on an affect the clinician perceives in the client, but of which the client appears unaware. The purpose of here-and-now work is adapted to the client's level of affective experience as identified by the clinician, and shown in Table 11-1, but in all cases the ultimate goal is to help clients recognize their emotional state empathically and accurately. What follows are discussions and examples of the application of here-and-now work at two different levels of affective experience.

In reading this information, it is important to keep in mind that clients who function at Level Three and higher may be unconsciously selective in their unawareness, unlike clients who are in need of the Level One and Two interventions. Some clients may be quite aware of their positive affects but have no awareness of negative affects. Thus, they function at different levels in different areas of emotionality. Further, they may have very differentiated experience when it comes to some emotions, but all-or-nothing attitudes about others. For example, a client may be exquisitely sensitive to varying levels of happiness, but perceive anger as rage regardless of intensity. This again represents a client who functions at different levels of affective experience with regard to differing emotions. Here-and-now work can be sensitive to working with clients on varying levels depending on which affect is being dealt with. In all here-and-now work, the clinician keeps in mind that clients lack affective awareness for many reasons. Often understanding the reasons behind the client's affective states helps the clinician tailor treatment, even when the work with the client does not yet address the understanding and acceptance of affect that occurs at Level Seven and Eight. Some possible reasons for lack of awareness follow. This list is not all-inclusive, but should give the clinician food for thought as to where to look.

Possible Reasons for Low Affective Awareness and Experience

- client learned in childhood not to pay attention to affective arousal because the client's affective needs remained unmet
- client had a traumatic experience at some time during the lifespan and subsequently repressed all or certain affects

TABLE 12-1

FEELING WORDS CATEGORIZED BY TYPE OF AFFECT

Afraid	Angry	Happy	Hurt	Loving	Sad	Shameful	Worthless
Aggrieved	Acrimonious	Ablaze	Abandoned	Admiring	Abject	Abashed	Absurd
Aghast	Aggressive	Affable	Abused	Adoring	Alone	Amiss	Contemptible
Agitated	Annoyed	Appreciative	Alone	Affable	Bleak	Amoral	Defective
Alarmed	Bellicose	Blessed	Bad	Affectionate	Blue	Ashamed	Deficient
Anxiety-ridden	Cantankerous	Blissful	Beaten	Agreeable	Crushed	Apologetic	Dense
Anxious	Choleric	Blithe	Belittled	Amiable	Dark	At fault	Despicable
Apprehensive	Corybantic	Bright-spirited	Betrayed	Amicable	Degraded	Attritional	Detestable
Bothered	Cranky	Buoyant	Broken	Appreciative	Dejected	Atoning	Dim-witted
Care-worn	Cross	Cheerful	Broken-hearted	Ardent	Depressed	Bashful	Disreputable
Concerned	Displeased	Comfortable	Collapsed	Attached	Despairing	Belittled	Dull
Cowardly	Enraged	Contented	Crushed	Attentive	Desperate	Blame-worthy	Dumb
Craven	Exasperated	Convivial	Damaged	Benevolent	Despondent	Blushing	Emasculate
Desperate	Fierce	Delighted	Deceived	Caring	Dire	Chagrined	Fatuous
Discomforted	Forceful	Eager	Defective	Charitable	Disappointed	Compunctious	Foolish
Disquieted	Fretful	Easy-going	Defiled	Cherishing	Disconsolate	Condemnable	Forceless
Distraught	Frustrated	Ecstatic	Degraded	Close	Disheartened	Contrite	Half-witted
Distressed	Furious	Elated	Deserted	Compassionate	Dismal	Culpable	Idiotic
Distrustful	Fuming	Entranced	Devastated	Concerned	Dispirited	Degraded	Ignominious
Disturbed	Grouchy	Euphoric	Disgraced	Considerate	Dissatisfied	Demeaned	Imbecilic
Dreading	Grumpy	Excited	Dishonored	Cordial	Doleful	Depraved	Immaterial
Faint	Hateful	Exhilarated	Disregarded	Courteous	Downcast	Derelict	Imperfect
Fainthearted	Hostile	Fervent	Exploited	Cuddly	Downhearted	Disconcerted	Impotent
Faltering	Hot-headed	Fine	Fooled	Devoted	Dreary	Disgraced	Inadequate
Fearful	Hot-tempered	Friendly	Forgotten	Doting	Dull	Dishonored	Inane
Fragile	Ill-humored	Gay	Forlorn	Emotional	Empty	Docile	Incompetent
Fretful	Ill-tempered	Genial	Forsaken	Enamoured	Forlorn	Embarrassed	Incomplete
Frightened	Incensed	Glad	Harassed	Enthusiastic	Frantic	Exposed	Inconsequential
Halfhearted	Indignant	Gladdened	Harmed	Faithful	Gloomy	Flustered	Ineffectual
Haunted	Infuriated	Gleeful	Hated	Fond	Glum	Guilty	Inept

Guilt-ridden	Grave	Friendly			Inglorious
Humble	Grievous	Generous			Insipid
Humiliated	Grim	Genial			Insubstantial
Inexcusable	Heavy	Gentle			Insufficient
Irresolute	Heavyhearted	Good-hearted			Irrelevant
Meek	Hopeless	Gracious			Laughable
Mortified	Inconsolable	Heedful			Ludicrous
Nefarious	Let down	Indulgent			Miserable
Objectionable	Lonely	Infatuated			No-good
Penitent	Lost	Intimate			Pathetic
Perplexed	Low	Kind			Petty
Pusillanimous	Lugubrious	Kindhearted			Pitiable
Regretful	Melancholy	Loyal			Powerless
Remorseful	Miserable	Mindful			Ridiculous
Repentant	Morose	Neighborly			Scandalous
Reprehensible	Mournful	Passionate			Silly
Reproachable	Oppressive	Peaceful			Simple
Responsible	Overwhelmed	Positive			Stupid
Retiring	Pitiable	Pure			Tedious
Scandalized	Poignant	Refined			Tiresome
Self-conscious	Rueful	Regardful			Undeserving
Self-effacing	Saddened	Respectful			Unfit
Shamed	Shattered	Responsive			Unimportant
Sheepish	Somber	Sensitive			Unintelligent
Sorry	Sorrowful	Supportive			Uninteresting
Submissive	Spiritless	Sweet			Unmerited
Subservient	Tearful	Sympathetic			Unseemly
To blame	Tragic	Tender			Unworthy
Timid	Undervalued	Thoughtful			Useless
Unforgivable	Unfortunate	Trusting			Valueless
Unjust	Unhappy	Understanding			Vapid
Wicked	Weepy	Warm			Vile
Withdrawn	Woeful	Watchful			Weak
Wrong	Worthless	Well-disposed			Wretched

Horrified	Irascible	Good	Ignored	
Ill at ease	Irate	Good-natured	Ill	
Intimidated	Irked	Great	Impaired	
Irresolute	Irritable	Gratified	Inferior	
Jittery	Irritated	Happy-go-lucky	Injured	
Jumpy	Mad	High	Maligned	
Nervous	Mean	Impassioned	Minimized	
Panicky	Miffed	Jocund	Mistreated	
Paralyzed	Militant	Jolly	Misused	
Scared	Obnoxious	Joyful	Overlooked	
Shaken	Outraged	Joyous	Pained	
Shaky	Peevish	Jubilant	Put down	
Shocked	Perturbed	Light-hearted	Put upon	
Shy	Petulant	Luminous	Rejected	
Spooked	Piqued	Marvelous	Ridiculed	
Startled	Pissed off	Merry	Ruined	
Surprised	Provoked	Optimistic	Scorned	
Terrified	Quarrelsome	Overjoyed	Shattered	
Terrorized	Querulous	Phenomenal	Slandered	
Threatened	Rabid	Pleased	Subjugated	
Timid	Rankled	Pleasant	Swindled	
Timorous	Raving	Positive	Tainted	
Tormented	Repugnant	Radiant	Traumatized	
Tremulous	Resentful	Rhapsodic	Tricked	
Troubled	Rough	Satisfied	Unappreciated	
Uncertain	Seething	Serene	Undesired	
Uncomfortable	Short-tempered	Sparkling	Unloved	
Uneasy	Snappish	Stimulated	Unpopular	
Unsafe	Spiteful	Thankful	Unwanted	
Unsettled	Testy	Thrilled	Used	
Unsure	Upset	Triumphant	Victimized	
Upset	Vicious	Uplifted	Violated	
Vulnerable	Violent	Wonderful	Wounded	
Worried	Wild		Wronged	

- client grew up in a nonresponsive environment and never learned about affects
- client was raised with a focus on cognition and/or behavior and never integrated affect into the human experience
- client was punished for the expression of certain or all affects in childhood
- client was ignored when expressing certain or all affects in childhood
- client had little guidance during childhood about emotions and their meanings or labels
- client learned little or nothing about expressing and labeling affect as a means of diffusing it
- client did not learn that expressing and labeling affect is a normal part of psychological growth and health

Level Three Here-and-Now Work

At this level, mental-health-care providers focus on helping clients begin to recognize the existence of basic affects by drawing their attention to bodily sensations and changes as feelings arise in the therapy room. Clinicians can recognize Level Three when clients express an affect without being aware of it or talk unemotionally about a situation that would usually arouse affect. When this occurs, the clinician has a perfect opening for here-and-now work that directs the client to sensations or feelings in the body. This here-and-now work will put the client in touch with bodily sensations that were previously ignored and that are clearly tied to affective experience. The client will then be encouraged to come up with a label for the feeling that is being recognized, although this labeling often occurs spontaneously. As this kind of work is best learned through example, an interchange follows that models it. In the following example, the client is relating an incident that is highly suggestive of an emotional reaction, but does so without any emotional expression. The clinician intervenes to help the client recognize his underlying affect.

CLIENT: Funny thing happened this week at work. We had a hold-up. *(grins oddly)*

CLINICIAN: A hold-up?! *(expression of emotion intended)*

CLIENT: Yup. . . . *(matter-of-fact voice, but eyes wide, betraying some emotion)*

CLINICIAN: Tell me about it! *(voice still intense to model)*

CLIENT: Well, I was working the night shift; you know they always joke about us night clerks at convenience stores taking our lives into our hands. But I really never thought about it. Anyway . . . I was working the night shift, and it was pretty quiet so I think I wasn't really paying much attention to what was going on. Don't tell anyone, but I may have nodded off. . . . So this guy suddenly stands in front of me with a gun pointed at my chest. (*grins and pauses*)

CLINICIAN: Oh . . . (*leaning forward; intensely attentive*)

CLIENT: Well, it was just like in the movies—He told me to clean out the cash register for him, then he wanted some booze, and cigarettes. We keep those behind the counter, you know. I guess that's why he asked me for those because then he just started grabbing stuff off the shelves. He was just having a ball.

CLINICIAN: And you?!

CLIENT: Well, I was just watching him. I didn't really know what to do. And then all of sudden he got pissed, started yelling at me for watching him, telling me to lie down on the floor or he's going to shoot. He was waving his gun at me again. I dropped to the floor and then all hell broke loose. I guess something I did just really pissed him off. He started trashing the place, throwing stuff, pushing shelves over. I couldn't see what was going on anymore, and it got to be really something when he started shooting his gun off. I have no idea what he was shooting at, I just was waiting for it to be me. . . . (*voice raised, agitated now*)

CLINICIAN: How awful.

CLIENT: Oh well. (*shrugs; looks away; trying to shut down the affect that was beginning to emerge*)

CLINICIAN: Then what?

CLIENT: I think he finally ran out of bullets, so he starts screaming at me again to get up and bring him that booze. (*very pale now; voice highly pitched*)

CLINICIAN: And?

CLIENT: I got up and there he is right in front of me with this huge blade. I thought for sure he'd slice me right there and then. (*takes deep breath*)

CLINICIAN: Uh huh . . .

CLIENT: And then, right then, a cop walks in. Can you believe it? I coulda kissed the guy. He totally clued into what was going on and had the guy down in a flash! I gotta go to the station tomorrow again to talk to them some more. I'm not sure why. (*voice getting lower and more agitated*)

CLINICIAN: Wow, incredible. So much going on. . . .

CLIENT: Tell me about it! (*flushed now*)

CLINICIAN: Tell me what is going on with you right now?

CLIENT: What?

CLINICIAN: What are you feeling right now?

CLIENT: Nothing much, I guess. (*tries to pull back from his experience*)

CLINICIAN: Look at you—You're at the edge of your seat, your face is flushed, and I don't think I've ever heard you more upset.

CLIENT: Well, the cop even said that I was pretty cool about it all. You know, I'm no wimp. No stupid little crook is gonna spook me. . . .

CLINICIAN: So what would you say is going on in your body right now? Tune in a little bit. What can you sense right now?

CLIENT: My face feels hot. My heart is feeling funny; I guess you'd call it my heart is racing—you know, like it's on speed or something. And you know what, I didn't really put this together before, but my stomach's been upset ever since. It's like cramping all the time and I don't have much of a craving for food. Oh, and I don't know if that has anything to with it, but you know those blood pressure machines at the grocery store? I always use it while I wait for my take-out. Well, today it was like totally off the chart . . . *(pauses; looks up)* What do you think?

CLINICIAN: More importantly, what do you think? Or more to the point, what's your body telling you?

CLIENT: I guess I'm a little freaked out maybe? I haven't slept too well the last couple of nights, so maybe I'm just a little run-down. I don't know . . . *(calming down now)*

CLINICIAN: Would it make sense to be a little freaked out?

CLIENT: I suppose so. I guess I might have actually been pretty scared while it was going down. Just kept telling myself these guys can smell fear, so don't be scared. But I don't know. . . .

CLINICIAN: You don't know?

CLIENT: Well, you know. I think maybe I was scared but then I'm not sure. I was raised to be tough. You know that. My father the drill sergeant. *(grins)*

CLINICIAN: Yeah, I know that. But what you were feeling a minute ago, that was real!

CLIENT: I guess so. . . .

CLINICIAN: And you called it being freaked out . . . or scared. Was it anything like what you felt that night?

CLIENT: Oh yeah. I was actually getting a little freaked here because I got to where it was like I was back there, you know, feeling it all over again.

CLINICIAN: Sure, that makes sense!

CLIENT: It does? *(puzzled)* Why would I get scared now? It's over and done with.

CLINICIAN: It may be over and done with, but the feelings, those can linger; especially since you didn't really pay attention to them at the time. *(Session goes on from here.)*

This example shows how even a client who has blocked his emotions successfully for a long time can be led to recognize feelings. Every human being has a physiological response in situations that are emotionally arousing or stimulating. In fact, if a situation was grave enough, as the one this client was relating, just the telling of the story should result in the same physiological arousal. If the mental-health-care provider can help the client identify that physiological response by drawing attention to the bodily reactions in the here-and-now, the client may learn a valuable lesson about how to recognize and identify emotions. In the example, the emotion involved became fairly obvious once the client realized that he indeed had a feeling response to the situation he was talking about, both at the time of the event and right now. Once the client acknowledged his present arousal (his physical sensations), he spontaneously recognized it as fear (again in both situations), a perfectly normal response given the situation he had found himself in. This recognition and admission of fear was a breakthrough for this client, who had been very divorced from his feelings up to now. No doubt, the body awareness and breathing exercises had primed him to be more in tune with his body so that the recognition of affect, and its subsequent labeling, were allowed to happen now.

Level Seven Here-and-Now Work

Here-and-now work at Level Seven (that is, work on identifying underlying emotions) is highly sophisticated work with clients who are already very emotionally aware and savvy. The work at this level challenges clients to look deeper and to explore levels of experience that may be buried and not easily reached. This work is often not done until a client has been in treatment for a while or is done with a client who comes to treatment without major developmental delays but primarily for personal growth. The goal of the here-and-now work with the Level Seven client is to help the client identify underlying affects, or affects that are at the root of the client's adjustment and behavior. These affects are buried under more obvious and easily experienced or accepted affects, and often their recognition moves the client forward in treatment. Many times when clients become aware of underlying affects, they spontaneously move to insights about themselves that they did not have before, making connections about their emotional life that they had been unclear about until now. Following is an example of Level Seven here-and-now work that leads to such insight. The example clarifies how such work can lead to spontaneous understanding of the origins of certain behaviors or emotions, essentially leading the client to Level Nine work. The example is taken from the beginning of the client's fourteenth session.

> CLIENT: *(client plops down on the couch and immediately starts talking without needing clinician encouragement)* I am so pissed I could scream! *(clearly agitated, flushed face, loud voice)* You would not believe what just happened! Unbelievable! I just got fired. The gall of that woman to kick me out. *ME,* of all the people in that office. I gave the best ten years of my life to her!! I've been loyal; I've been there when she was having

problems—and now this. I am so pissed. No, pissed doesn't even cover it. I am furious!! I don't think I've ever been this mad in my life. Can you believe this? *(takes a breath and pauses for a brief moment)*

CLINICIAN: Wow, what a development! You've been talking about problems at work, but how did this come about?

CLIENT: Well, I got there early this morning. You know how I like to be early. You know, how I like to get there before everyone else and get organized for the day. And there she was, passed out on the floor, booze all over the place.

CLINICIAN: She?

CLIENT: Oh, sorry, my boss, you know, Karyn. *(calming and slowing down a bit now)* Well, I think I told you that I have been suspecting that she is a boozer, but I guess I don't have to suspect anymore. This was pretty clear evidence. She was passed out good and I wasn't sure what to do. So I decided to go to my desk and pretend she's not there. So I did that for a while and then I got worried and so I went back over there and she was still on the floor but it looked like she was awake. So I said "Karyn, I think it's time to get up and get cleaned up. You look like a mess." She just stared at me like she couldn't process what I was saying and then she groaned and started throwing up. So I went and got a garbage can to try to keep some of this crap off the floor because I sure as hell didn't want to have to clean it up. Is this disgusting or what. I really started getting pissed then. You know, if she wants to be a lush, fine. But leave me out of it. She knows I come in early so did she have to be there when I got there? I was getting really pissed and I started yelling at her to pull herself together. I tried to get her to get up and go to the bathroom and finally she did. Of course she left her mess behind, probably expecting me to clean up after her. I tell you what though—no way in hell! I heard her retching in the bathroom for a long time and then when she came out she was white as a ghost. She looked at me like it was my fault and told me to get lost. Told me to get lost! Can you believe it? I said where do you want me to go. And she said to go for a walk or something till it was time to go to work. Then she started yelling why was I early and was I checking up on her. Paranoid stuff, you know. Well, I told her I wasn't gonna leave, but that she should. I also told her I'd have to tell Carl.

CLINICIAN: Carl?

CLIENT: Her boss . . .

CLINICIAN: Ah . . .

CLIENT: Boy, that really got her going. She said it was none of my business what she did after hours and I told her it was if she did it in my work space. I guess I was a little out of line because it's really her work space, but still. . . . Anyway, I refused to leave, told her I had a lot of work and I wasn't gonna get behind because of her drinking. I was steaming by then. You know what a hothead I am anyway. Well, we ended up in a shouting match and neither one of us had any intention of backing down. I kind of forgot who's the boss, I guess. Anyway before I knew it, she told me that was it for me. Fired. She's the screwup and I'm unemployed. I went to see Carl as soon as I could, and he refused to listen. Said something about women not being able to work together! You can imagine that that didn't exactly help my mood. So I ended up yelling at him, too, and threatening to sue the company. He threw me out of his office. Threatened to call security. God, I was screaming mad. I am so glad I had an appointment at lunch with you today because I don't what I would do if I couldn't get this off my chest. If ever I had a murderous impulse, this would be the time. *(grins a little)* Na, don't worry, just kidding. I am pissed, though!

CLINICIAN: Yes, I'm getting that idea . . . *(also grins)*

CLIENT: I guess it is obvious, huh?! *(calming down again)*

CLINICIAN: Yeah, it's hard to miss. But for some reason I am getting a sense that this is more than anger.

CLIENT: *(interrupts)* You bet, it's rage.

CLINICIAN: No, I mean something else. You know, another feeling, not just lots of anger but something more, something else. . . . I'm not sure what gives me the impression. It's just I've seen you angry before, and this feels different; like there is something else mixed into it. . . . Can you help me out here?

CLIENT: Well, you could be right in some ways. I felt like crying on my way over here. You know, like I was hopping mad, but at the same time I had this urge to crawl in a corner and cry my eyes out. That's weird, isn't it?

CLINICIAN: Maybe not . . . maybe it makes a lot of sense. A lot happened here. Isn't it possible that you have more than one reaction to it?

CLIENT: I suppose *(hesitates)*, but what? Crying . . . like I'm depressed or something?

CLINICIAN: Is that what comes to mind?

CLIENT: Not really; it doesn't fit quite right. I just thought of that because of the crying. Isn't that when people cry, when they're depressed?

CLINICIAN: Oh, my guess is people cry for all kinds of feelings. . . .

CLIENT: Okay . . . so what then?

CLINICIAN: Well, let's try to figure it out. Take a deep breath and focus inward, like we do so often. What do you notice?

CLIENT: *(centers, breathes, and closes her eyes spontaneously, being used to this type of work)*

CLINICIAN: What's under the anger *(slow, gentle voice)* . . . what are the tears trying to tell you. . . .

CLIENT: *(keeps breathing and listening internally)*

CLINICIAN: As it feels comfortable just tell me what comes up for you . . . *(quiet, long pause, waits patiently for client now)*

CLIENT: *(after some time)* . . . There is a sense of tightness in my chest that I've never felt before and yet it feels like a grip that I am familiar with. Some old feeling coming back to me . . .

CLINICIAN: Some old feeling? *(gentle, low voice)*

CLIENT: Yes. Something sad, no, not sad, I'm not sure what it is . . . let down, maybe. Like she should be a better person and my insides ache because she isn't. . . . That doesn't make any sense, does it? *(starts to open her eyes)*

CLINICIAN: Don't worry about making sense for now. Just keep listening to what your body is trying to tell you. . . .

CLIENT: Just that tight grip on my chest, my eyes watering *(tears start flowing now)*; oh, and my stomach is soft, gooey; how strange . . . not like anxious, but also not mad anymore. Just soft, like I'm a little girl who didn't get what she earned. . . . *(opens her eyes)* What is this? Wow; this is more intense than anger, and now that I'm in touch with it the anger is gone. Like this is more important . . .

CLINICIAN: Like this is the real feeling and the anger was just a cover?

CLIENT: Exactly. And you know what, that's what's so familiar about it. I think this has always been under the anger.

CLINICIAN: This sense of having been let down?

CLIENT: Yes! Disappointment! Not getting what I deserve. Not being cared for, drawing the short straw. All of that. Oh my . . . *(starts crying softly)*

CLINICIAN: An old hurt feeling . . .

CLIENT: Yes . . .

CLINICIAN: Does it remind you of anything?

CLIENT: Yes, yes it does *(cries harder now)*. This is me as a little girl, isn't it? . . . *(Session continues from here with an exploration of the origin of this underlying affect that had been buried for years by the safer emotion of anger.)*

This example demonstrates how Level Seven work often launches clients into deeper understanding and profound exploration. It also serves to demonstrate why this type of work needs to occur after excellent rapport has been established between client and counselor. Often exploring underlying affects is work that makes clients vulnerable as they begin to explore the deeper aspects of their emotional life. The clinician needs to be able to help the client contain emotion and needs to be perceptive to the client's pain and limits. As in all here-and-now work, the clinician needs to be prepared to deal with difficult affects on the spot and needs to help the client through the experience and catharsis of emotions that may heretofore not have been explored. Not all Level Seven work will prove to be this profound or meaningful. Sometimes underlying affects are easily recognized and understood and do not affect the client on a deep level. But, since the potential exists, the counselor is advised to be prepared for the possibility. Also notable in this example is the fact that when working at this level, clients often need little guidance regarding listening to their bodies. By this time in treatment, they have learned to pay attention to their physiological responses and are skilled about how to listen and attend to their bodies. Simple encouragement by the counselor or therapist for the client to turn attention inward is usually sufficient.

Affect Continuum Exercise

The Affect Continuum Exercise is specifically tailored to work with clients who are struggling at Level Five (that is, with the recognition of affective shades of gray). Clinicians can often recognize clients who function at Level Five by their all-or-none attitudes about feelings. These clients are unable to recognize that any one affect can manifest at different levels of intensity. They conclude that if they have a certain feeling, it is the same each time they experience it. Some clients may shy away from particular affects altogether because of this attitude. They are afraid that once they start the affect, they cannot stop it. This often happens with depression. Clients do not allow themselves the experience of sadness for fear of being completely overwhelmed by it. They fail to recognize that sadness comes in different degrees, some of which are easily managed and endured. This reaction is also common with regard to anger. Often, clients believe that anger is inappropriate because when they think of their anger, they associate it with an extreme behavioral response that they perceive as unacceptable. Then, instead of allowing any expression of even mild forms of anger, they deny the entire affect. The inability to differentiate shades of gray can be addressed through the Affect Continuum Exercise. It teaches clients to recognize subtle differences in their internal sensations and to apply new labels commensurate with these subtle differences, not just one emotion from another, but also differing levels of intensity within the same affective category. This type of intervention shares many of the features of here-and-now work. Thus, all the cautions about counselor preparedness and client readiness apply.

The lists of affects provided in Table 12-1 will be helpful with the Affect Continuum Exercise, although they are not ordered according to perceived intensity within each affect category. Such ordering is a highly personal arrangement. Clients differ greatly in what they may perceive as a continuum of affect. For example, for some clients "furious" may represent more severe anger than "enraged," whereas others may switch their relative ranking. It is best to let each client come up with a personal ranking, assisting merely by providing a list of labels from which the client can choose. The exercise helps clients understand that a particular affect need not be feared because of its potentially intense manifestation, as it can be experienced at lower levels of intensity that are manageable and safe. As such, the exercise can at times result in work that actually represents Level Eight, acceptance of affect. This is not usually the purpose, but simply a useful by-product of the Affect Continuum Exercise.

Affect continuum work can vary widely from client to client and even from affect to affect with the same client. It always involves helping clients develop a hierarchy of labels for a given affect category by providing label options and tying them to physiological arousal. Sometimes this work is done as the client experiences the affect; sometimes the work is retrospective. If the work is done with here-and-now experience, it resembles here-and-now work quite closely, perhaps with the main difference being the more active participation of the counselor in providing label options. If the work is retroactive, the client has to recall feeling states rather than experiencing them in the present. Beyond that, differences are minimal. Following is an example of an Affect Continuum Exercise with a client who is experiencing affect right now. This example highlights how affect continuum work can be used to help clients recognize that a given affect does not always have to be overwhelming or disastrous. It can manifest in milder forms that are of little threat or consequence. Of course, this work is not to be misused by the mental-health-care provider to minimize or belittle a client's emotion; it is merely helpful in assisting the client to gain a sense of control or acceptance of the affect.

CLIENT: I'm afraid I'm about to fall off the deep end . . . *(weepy)*
CLINICIAN: Help me understand . . .
CLIENT: Well, I think I'm depressed, just like my mother was when she killed herself . . . *(long pause)*
CLINICIAN: Tell me more . . . *(gentle but prodding voice)*
CLIENT: I have been in a real funk ever since we figured out last week that I'm depressed. You know that really scares me. My mother was exactly my age when she killed herself. What if I'm next? *(shaky voice, teary eyes)*
CLINICIAN: Do you have thoughts of killing yourself?
CLIENT: Well, not really. But my mother was depressed when she did . . .
CLINICIAN: And so you are wondering if you might do the same?
CLIENT: Yes. It's what depressed people do, isn't it? . . . *(pause)*
CLINICIAN: It's what depressed people do, you think? All depressed people?
CLIENT: Well, all really depressed people . . .
CLINICIAN: Really depressed people . . . What about the other depressed people?
CLIENT: *(looks up puzzled)*

CLINICIAN: Well, if there are really depressed people who kill themselves, are there also not really depressed people who don't?

CLIENT: Like some people who are less depressed?

CLINICIAN: *(nods)*

CLIENT: What do you mean?

CLINICIAN: Is it possible that there is more than one kind of depression? Really depressed, and less depressed? And that one kind of depression is so bad that killing oneself seems like the only solution and that another kind of depression is less bleak?

CLIENT: Hmm . . . *(clearly thinking)*

CLINICIAN: Tell me about your depression, your sadness *(beginning to introduce a new possible label)*

CLIENT: Well, it's like we realized last week. . . . I just can't get much joy out of life these days. And since yesterday it's been particularly bad. I just cried and cried last night after I watched this stupid TV show. No reason, just felt really sad and down. Then I didn't sleep well and then I dreamt about my mother and that's when I got scared that I might follow in her footsteps.

CLINICIAN: So you're feeling sad, down, nothing is fun, and you are having trouble sleeping. . . .

CLIENT: Yes.

CLINICIAN: Is this feeling ever better or worse?

CLIENT: Well, I guess yesterday before that TV show it was better, but then seeing all these people in love just got me all down . . . *(sobs a little)*

CLINICIAN: So in a way, in the last two days you've had at least two kinds of depression; one that was less bad than the other?

CLIENT: Yeah, I suppose. . . .

CLINICIAN: Could we come up with separate labels for these so we can differentiate them?

CLIENT: Like what do you mean?

CLINICIAN: Oh. Like the depression in the morning, before the TV show, maybe that was blue or mellow or sad; and then the depression in the evening after the TV show, maybe it was a little worse, like empty or heavyhearted or in the dumps. . . .

CLIENT: Oh. . . .

CLINICIAN: Could you come up with some labels that would make sense to you to describe the difference?

CLIENT: Well, in the morning I guess I felt kind of sad and then in the evening I felt down in the dumps.

CLINICIAN: *(accepting the client's labels)* So we have at least two levels of depression—kind of sad and down in the dumps. Have you felt other levels of depression? Like what level might you be at now? Worse than down in the dumps or better?

CLIENT: Oh, when I first got here I was worse because I was so scared that I was losing it. But right now I feel better. . . .

CLINICIAN: What might you call what you felt when you came in?

CLIENT: Oh, um, I don't know . . . really, really bad? Is that okay?

CLINICIAN: Any label that makes sense to you and that seems to describe what you feel is fine. . . .

CLIENT: Well, I don't know, that seems too vague. . . . What are some other words . . . well, maybe desperate. Yeah, that's it, desperate.

CLINICIAN: Okay, so we have kind of sad, down in the dumps, desperate. What might you call how you feel now? You said it was better than when you came in. . . .

CLIENT: It's worse than kind of sad but better than down in the dumps, I suppose. Kind of dull in a way, like I can't really think without being made to think—you know, like you're just making me do . . . *(small smile)*

CLINICIAN: *(smiles too)* So we are developing quite a list here. There isn't just one kind of depression, is there?

CLIENT: No, I guess not. I never really thought of it that way.

CLINICIAN: So, your mother, where do you think she was with her depression?

CLIENT: Oh, more than desperate even! She must have been beyond hope! . . . Oh . . . *(looks up with a flash of insight)* I just got what you are doing with me. Not all depressed people kill themselves.

CLINICIAN: *(nods)* No, they don't.

CLIENT: My mother was beyond hope, not just kind of sad or down in the dumps. I'm usually down in the dumps or kind of sad. I'm not even feeling desperate all that often. . . .

CLINICIAN: Right. Lots of levels of depression. You'll probably find that you have many, many other experiences of depression that we haven't even ranked yet. It may be worth it to keep track of how you feel each time you feel depressed and then to try to figure out what that feeling means. . . .

CLIENT: *(interrupts)* Like order my feelings and then not get freaked out if I'm just a little blue and rush in to see you if I ever get to feeling beyond hope. . . .

CLINICIAN: Exactly. . . . *(Session continues from here.)*

This example demonstrates how helping clients differentiate shades of gray within the experience of a single affect not only clarifies their experience but also gives them permission to experience the affect to begin with. It certainly helps clients be more honest with themselves about what they may be feeling. The example also demonstrates that differentiating levels of intensity can help clients evaluate their reactions and physiological responses more realistically.

Skill Development Recommendations

Recommendation 12-1 *Choose an affect you commonly experience. Develop a ranking of labels for the emotions within that affect category. Repeat this exercise for any other affects you experience commonly, or that you anticipate working with frequently. You may also want to try to do this with a friend or family member to get some idea about how people differ in their choice of language or labels.*

FOCUS ON THE ACCEPTANCE AND UNDERSTANDING OF AFFECT

As indicated previously, most higher-level affective work is actually quite cognitive in nature, relying mostly on cognitive strategies to help clients understand why they feel what they feel. This section will highlight two strategies that can be used if clients hesitate in their acceptance of an affect because they feel uncomfortable about it or do not trust that they can manage the affect in its more severe forms. These strategies are focused on helping clients relax their bodies so that they can gain a certain level of comfort and ease. Although these exercises, namely progressive muscle and inner-focus relaxation, have been covered in the literature as strategies to deal with anxiety, they are actually applicable for a wide range of emotions. Not only is it difficult for a body to be relaxed and anxious at the same time, it is equally difficult to feel relaxed and angry, relaxed and depressed, or relaxed and self-conscious. Relaxation will be introduced here as a means of facilitating clients' acceptance of their feelings when their initial nonacceptance was based in the fear of not being able to manage the affect once it emerges. Work regarding acceptance and understanding of affect that is not based in the client's fear of the affect per se is cognitive in nature and is amply demonstrated in the chapters on cognitive strategies. Strategies covered in those chapters that have applicability to higher-level affect work (Levels Eight and Nine) include pointing out patterns, clarification, here-and-now cognitive processing, confrontation, and interpretation.

All relaxation strategies are based on the premise that a body cannot be physiologically aroused and relaxed at the same time. If a client can learn to relax the body willfully and purposefully, this skill can be used to counteract the negative physiological reactions associated with other (negative) affects. If a client has learned to use breathing and muscle tension or focusing techniques to reduce physiological arousal to a tolerable, perhaps even pleasant level, fear of affect is reduced. The affect itself is not squelched, but the physiological arousal is reduced to a tolerable level that reduces the impact of the affect on the body, making it more acceptable and tolerable to the mind. Once fear of affect is reduced, the client can become more accepting of the affect and can learn to cope with it effectively, as well as being in a better psychological place to explore its meaning and origins. Original applications of relaxation were fairly specific to the reduction of anxiety. They focused on the elimination of general anxiety, the reduction of anxiety about specific events, or on dealing with situation-specific fears (for example, phobias about speaking in public), especially if combined with guided imagery or systematic desensitization. The use of relaxation strategies as outlined in this chapter centers around helping clients gain a sense of control over the level of physiological arousal experienced in their bodies to help them tolerate and accept any affect that may be present or about to emerge.

A few cautions apply to the work with relaxation strategies. Relaxation exercises need to be used with caution with clients who have seizure disorders, physical ailments involving pain (for example, arthritis or fibromyalgia), traumatic-stress disorders, or psychotic disorders. The inexperienced clinician may want to avoid altogether the use of these strategies with clients who fall into any of these categories until experience has been gained. Experienced counselors need to be prepared to deal with the possible side effects or consequences that can occur with such clients. They also need to give proper cautions to the clients affected and need to set up a warning system for the client should adverse effects arise. For example, if clients with temporal-lobe epilepsy go through a relaxation exercise, they need to be warned to open their eyes and to signal (in a predetermined way) the clinician to change course, should they perceive colors, spots, or other signs suggesting the possible onset of a complex partial seizure. Similarly, fibromyalgia patients need thorough debriefing after the first experience to assess whether any aspect of the relaxation exercises was uncomfortable physically. It is probably best not to use progressive muscle relaxation with such clients as the tensing of muscles may be quite painful for them. Should they not be able to make successful use of another relaxation strategy and a muscle tension exercise has to be used, it is best to predetermine a signal that tells the clinician that the client is in pain. Traumatic-stress clients may experience flashbacks; both client and clinician need to be ready to deal with dissociative or similar affective crisis states. Psychotic clients who begin to have perceptual distortions during the exercise need to learn to signal the clinician when this occurs so that the course of the exercise may be changed. In all of these cases of caution, once the client has signaled the clinician that discomfort or threat is present, the counselor calmly redirects the exercise to simple breathing and then slowly and calmly brings the client back to the present. The exercise is not abandoned abruptly, rather, a gradual and calm transition is made to allow the client to emerge from the relaxed to the normal wakeful state of being.

Most importantly, the clinician must not panic at the client's signal but behave calmly and with an air of reassurance and safety.

For all relaxation exercises, clients need to be carefully prepared. The cautions outlined above are only one aspect of the information that is shared with the client. Complete and proper preparation involves sharing all of the following information with the client the first time the strategy is used:

- rationale for and purpose of the use of the strategy
- details about what the exercise will involve and how long it will take
- directions about positioning and comfort (lying versus sitting; use of a blanket in case of feeling cold; taking shoes off; closing eyes; and so on)
- details about the fact that the clinician plans to prepare a tape of the exercise, so the client can relax during the exercise without having to focus on remembering what was done for future use
- details about the breathing exercises that will precede the relaxation strategies (see *Breathing Exercises* above)
- reminders that the client can open the eyes or discontinue following the instructions at any point in time or if pain, discomfort, or fear should arise
- cautions about the use of the strategy in the presence of particular presenting problems such as seizures, traumatic stress, pain disorders, or psychosis and exploration of these symptoms in the client
  - seizure disorders: tell client to open eyes if perceptual phenomena, such as colors, spots, or lights, occur
  - traumatic stress: tell client to open eyes or use agreed-upon signal if dissociative state appears imminent or if fear occurs
  - psychosis: tell client to open eyes and use agreed-upon signal if perceptual disturbance threatens or begins
  - pain disorder: tell client to use agreed-upon signal should pain occur
- warnings about possible effects that may occur, along with actions to be taken by client or clinician
  - experience of heaviness: normal experience requiring no action on the part of the client unless it is perceived as uncomfortable
  - experience of lightness or floating: normal experience requiring no action on the part of the client unless it is perceived as uncomfortable or frightening
  - pain in a muscle group of focus: develop a signal for the client to caution the clinician to change instructions
  - perceptual phenomena (for example, seeing colors): normal experience for most clients requiring no action on the part of the client unless it is perceived as uncomfortable or frightening (red flags requiring immediate action with seizure or psychotic patients)
  - falling asleep: normal experience monitored by the clinician and requiring no action on the part of the client

- instructions and agreement about a signal the client will be able to use to communicate with the clinician in a case of need (for example, raising the index finger of the right hand, shaking the head side to side)

Once the client has understood this information, the exercise can begin. During the initial phases of the exercise, some of this information can be repeated in a calm and comforting tone that makes it part of the induction phase of the exercise. For example, the client can be reminded of the options for signaling the clinician—opening the eye or making a special, predetermined signal that cautions the clinician about client discomfort, and of the value of deep and rhythmic breathing. Once the client is in a comfortable position, exercise instructions are delivered in a low, calm, soothing voice that is relatively monotone and perhaps even perceived as boring, due to the lack of inflection. Relaxation exercises always begin with deep breathing (as outlined above) and proceed from there to either progressive muscle work or inner-focus work. Instructions are highly repetitive and monotone; they are easily followed and highly descriptive. Work usually proceeds by relaxing peripheral parts of the body first and slowly moving toward the center of the body. Throughout the work, the counselor gives reminders to the client to retain the relaxation in parts of the body that have already been worked on. Following are instructions for muscle tension and inner-focus relaxation strategies. Many other variations of relaxation work exist, and each mental-health-care provider will ultimately develop a preferred set or two of instructions. The examples provided here are merely to give the clinician some ideas about how relaxation exercises can proceed. Modifications are not only possible, but recommended, based upon clinician preferences and client needs. As is true for all of the structured exercises covered in this chapter, relaxation exercises begin with an introduction, proceed to actual instructions, and end with a thorough debriefing.

Progressive-Muscle-Relaxation Exercise

Progressive muscle relaxation is based on inducing relaxation by contrast. Each muscle group in the body is first tensed, then relaxed, and the client's attention is then drawn to the difference in the tense-versus-relaxed state of each muscle. It is the attention to the difference in the experience of a tense-versus-relaxed muscle that is the mediator of overall relaxation for the client. Progressive muscle relaxation is easier to deal with for most clients in their early attempts at relaxation, though it appears that inner-focus work can lead to deeper levels of relaxation. Thus, it may be best to start clients with muscle tension work and then to graduate to inner-focus work once the client has achieved some success with muscle tension work. For some clients, most obviously pain sufferers, muscle tension work is less than optimal. For them, the tensing of muscles may be so painful as to counteract the relaxing effect. Therapists will have to use their clinical judgment about when not to use this type of relaxation with clients. Muscle tension relaxation exercises can be completed sitting up or lying down based on the client's preference. The instructions that follow are based on a client who is lying down. Only minor modifications are necessary for work with clients who prefer to sit. Some clinicians engage in the muscle tension and relaxation along with the client to get the timing right and to know firsthand what the client is experiencing. This is a personal preference of each therapist or counselor. Regardless of whether a clinician does the exercise with the client, it is probably best to have personally done the exercise at least three or four times before using it with a client. This will give the counselor a better appreciation of what it is the client is feeling as various muscles are tensed and relaxed. It may also prevent the therapist from giving a tensing instruction that is painful. One final note: The first time the exercise is used, the whole session needs to be dedicated to it to give plenty of debriefing time. Thus, if the idea for the use of relaxation comes up toward the end of a session, the client can be prepared for it (some of the introduction can be given), but will not begin the actual exercise until the next session, when a brief review of the introduction will precede the exercise. Debriefing time after the first use of the exercise is essential and this is one caution that is best always followed.

Introduction to Progressive-Muscle-Relaxation Exercise

"One thing that you might find helpful in dealing with [insert client's difficult affect here] is something called progressive muscle relaxation. The exercise helps you relax and calm down when you are feeling [client's affect] and may help you not [fear that affect] in the future. It's also a great exercise to do anytime you feel anxious or upset, or even when you're having trouble sleeping. You can use it for lots of things and in lots of places. Does this sound interesting?"

Clinician gives client a chance to respond; this is important as many clients have already heard of relaxation exercises and may have a reaction (positive or negative) that is best processed before proceeding. Then the introduction continues. Based on client interactions, some portions may be addressed in a different order than presented here. The main point is to cover all aspects; order is irrelevant.

"Great. Well then, let me tell you a little bit about what the exercise involves. The ultimate goal is to get you to be able to relax and feel calm and collected. The easiest way that seems to happen for a lot of people is to pay attention to how their body feels when it's tense versus how it feels when it's relaxed. So what I'll do is I'll talk you through lots of different body parts, asking you first to tense certain muscles and then to relax them. All along I'll give you some things to pay attention to. The exercise is pretty easy—you just follow my directions. And don't worry about re-membering what I'm doing because if this turns out to be something you enjoy, I will make a tape for you that you can take home so that you can practice at home if and whenever you feel like it. So far, so good?"

Clinician gives client another chance to respond; then continues with introduction.

"Also, if at any point I'm giving you a direction and you try it and it hurts or doesn't feel comfortable, you definitely don't have to do it. If I ever get off on my timing and I'm asking you to tense longer than feels good to you, feel free to let go of the tension in the muscle. Do try to give it a fair chance first, though. If you need to, you can signal me that you are un-comfortable. Just [raise your right index finger]. Alright?"

Clinician gives client another chance to respond, then continues with introduction.

"Now, before we get started I want to double check a few things. I think I already know the answers to these questions but I always like to double check. First, do you have any physical problems that I should be aware of that may be affected by this exercise? For example arthritis, fibromyalgia, or any other kind of pain problems?"

Clinician gives the client a chance to respond, then continues checking on all relevant contraindications in the same manner, that is, similar questions are then phrased for seizure disorder, dissociative episodes, and if necessary (it usually should not be), psychotic symptoms.

"Okay, now that I have ruled out that you have any symptoms that may get worse during this exercise, let me tell you about a few things that you may experience. Sometimes people get a floating or a heavy feeling. That's perfectly normal. In fact, it is usually a sign of very deep relaxation. Should this upset you, though, just use the same signal we talked about earlier. So, if you want me to help you out of the feeling because it's un-comfortable, just [raise your right index finger]. Does that make sense?"

Clinician gives the client a chance to respond, then continues by running through all the cautions noted above (for example, pain, colors, perceptual dis-turbances, falling asleep). If the client wishes, a different signal can be arranged for different eventualities. The clinician needs to walk a fine line here between helping the client know what to expect and scaring the client about too many potential dangers of the exercise. Thus, arranging multiple symptoms may be reserved for the debriefing with those clients who did indeed experience some difficulties with the exercise.

"Alright. Now that we have that covered, let me remind you that you don't need to worry about remembering what I'm doing because I can tape this for you next time we use the exercise. Also, this will take about twenty-five to thirty minutes. I'll start the exercise with the breathing exercises we have been doing [describe the breathing exercises as above if they have never been used]. You can sit up or lie down, whichever feels more comfortable. The exercise usually works best if you have your shoes off and your eyes closed. Some of the directions I'll give you will sound funny and you may feel a little self-conscious. Just remember, no one is watching, so go for it anyway. I have a blanket here that you are welcome to use if you might get a little chilly lying still so long. You can also use the pillow, if you'd like. Any questions?"

Clinician provides one final chance for comments and questions, then, once the client is settled into a comfortable position, begins with the actual exercise instructions.

Instructions for Progressive Muscle Relaxation

"Now that you are settled into a comfortable position, go ahead and close your eyes. This will draw your attention to the inside of your body. Consciously focus your mind inside your body now and follow my instructions. Start by taking a deep breath in through your nose and then out through your mouth."

Here the clinician takes in a deep audible breath through the nose and then blows the breath out through the mouth. This may be done a couple of times.

"And breathe in"

Clinician inhales audibly.

" . . . and out through your nose"

Clinician exhales audibly through the nose.

"And in . . . and out . . . and in . . . and out."

Clinician establishes a comfortable audible breathing rhythm. This should be done without speaking for about twenty seconds, or whatever period of time is comfortable for the client.

"Now as you keep breathing deeply and comfortably, direct your attention to your feet. . . . On your next breath in, curl your toes downward. Notice the tension this position creates in your feet. . . . Notice the tightness. . . . Feel the tension, . . . and then let go. . . . Let your toes return to their normal position, . . . and notice the difference. . . . Notice how relaxation feels different from tension. . . . Now, curl your toes one more time. . . . Study the feeling of tension, . . . of tightness, . . . and notice the difference in the feeling in your toes as they are tight . . . and tense. . . . Now let go . . . and enjoy the difference. . . . Enjoy the relief . . . of letting go of tension, . . . of relaxation . . . flooding into your toes . . . as you let them relax into their normal position. . . . Study the difference between tension . . . and relaxation. . . . All along, . . . keep breathing in . . . and out . . . at a comfortable rate."

Clinician inhales and exhales audibly.

"And in . . . and out."

Clinician inhales and exhales audibly.

"Now flex your feet, toes toward knees. . . . Tight, . . . and tighter. . . . Study the tension this creates in the back of your calves, . . . in the bottoms of your feet. . . . Study the tightness, . . . the tension, . . . as you flex your feet . . . toward your knees. . . . When you are ready, . . . relax your feet to their usual position . . . and notice the difference. . . . Notice the relaxation . . . pouring through your feet . . . and calves . . . as you relax your feet. . . . Study the difference between relaxation . . . and tension. . . . Notice the warmth . . . and comfort . . . of the relaxation . . . pouring through your feet. . . . So different . . . from the tightness you felt before. . . . Flex your feet one more time. . . . Notice the tightness, . . . the tension. . . . Now let go . . . and explore the difference. . . . Enjoy the warmth . . . and comfort . . . of relaxation. Recognize the good . . . feeling of relaxation, . . . the ease . . . and peace in your feet . . . when they relax . . . in their natural position. . . . All along, . . . keep breathing in . . . and out . . . at a comfortable rate."

Clinician inhales and exhales audibly.

"And in . . . and out."

Clinician inhales and exhales audibly.

[The clinician now repeats essentially the same instructions, as indicated thus far, for *any or all* of the parts of the body listed below. These instructions need minimally to include:

- the appropriate repetition of each movement
- proper pacing of tension (not too long)
- adequate breaks between tensing of muscle groups
- comparison statements of relaxation versus tension
- reminders to keep other parts of the body relaxed while tensing the targeted muscle groups, and
- refocusing on the breath between body parts

The clinician will work from the periphery of the body to the core; for each body part the following tension movement is recommended:

- thighs: hold legs out straight (either both at same time or one at a time); if too difficult, plant feet firmly on ground and push down as hard as possible
- buttocks: scrunch buttocks toward each other
- hands: make a tight fist, thumb on the outside, keeping arm relaxed
- wrists and lower arms: make a fist and curl hands toward the inside of the elbow joint (do not flex elbow joint)
- arms and elbows: with hands in a fist pointing toward the shoulder, flex lower arm up (curl)
- shoulders: shrug shoulders up toward the ears
- neck: first lean head toward right shoulder; on repetition, lean head toward left shoulder; or drop head to chest
- forehead: wrinkle up forehead only (not eyes), easiest done by raising eyebrows toward scalp
- eyes: clench eyes shut tightly; this might wrinkle up the nose as well
- mouth: purse lips tightly as if about to peck a kiss
- jaw: open mouth wide; may also stick tongue out as far as possible
- entire face: squeeze eyes shut tightly, purse lips, wrinkle up forehead (pucker up whole face)
- chest: after a deep inhalation, hold breath and push shoulders back
- abdomen: stick stomach out as far as possible; or tighten abdominal muscles and sphincter

Then the clinician once again refocuses the client on the breath and proceeds with the following instructions.]

Clinician inhales and exhales audibly.

"Your whole body is relaxed now. . . . Every part of you is calm . . . and quiet, . . . warm . . . and tingly . . . with relaxation. . . . You are relaxed . . . from your toes to your hips, . . . from your fingertips to your shoulders, . . . from your neck to your forehead, . . . from your eyes to your chin, . . . from the outside in. . . . Enjoy this relaxation . . . and the warmth . . . and comfort it brings. . . . Enjoy the difference of relaxation . . . versus tension. . . . Revel in your calmness. . . . Treasure . . . the warmth . . . and comfort. . . . As you breathe in . . . enjoy your restfulness, . . . and as you breathe out . . . savor your calmness."

Clinician inhales and exhales audibly.

"Enjoy your peacefulness . . . as you breathe in deeply. . . . Relish your stillness . . . as you breathe out fully. . . . Calm . . . restful . . . tranquil. . . . Fully and completely relaxed."

After a comfortable amount of time, the clinician asks the client to end the exercise as follows:

> "Now that you have welcomed calmness . . . and peacefulness, . . . experienced the warmth . . . and comfort of relaxation, . . . slowly bring back your awareness back to this room, . . . bringing your tranquillity . . . and relaxation . . . with you. . . . Knowing that you can go back . . . to this relaxed state . . . any time you want to. . . . Slowly begin to focus your attention . . . away from your body and your breath . . . back to the outer world. . . . Do that by beginning to notice any sounds that you may hear, . . . by moving your body in any way that's comfortable. . . . As you do this, . . . I will slowly begin to count back . . . from five to one. . . . With each number I say, . . . you will become more and more alert. . . . When I get to one, . . . you will be fully alert. . . . Then take whatever time you need . . . and when you're ready . . . open your eyes."

Clinician slowly counts back from five to one, increasing volume of voice as numbers decrease, and adjusting the time required to the needs of the client.

> "Five, . . . becoming more alert and aware of the outside world. . . . Four, . . . aware of the sounds [might mention specific audible sounds here], . . . rousing the body. . . . Three, . . . becoming more and more alert and aware. . . . Two, . . . coming back to the here-and-now. . . . One, . . . fully alert and aware!

Clinician now allows the client to pace her or his own return by remaining quiet until the client opens the eyes and makes eye contact with the clinician. Once the client is fully alert and has regained contact with the clinician, debriefing can begin.

Debriefing on Progressive Muscle Relaxation

In the debriefing the clinician attempts to find out how the client responded to the exercise, that is, if the exercise has met its purpose. Often, the simple question "How are you feeling?" is a perfect opening for exploring the effect of the exercise. Timing is crucial. It is best to begin questioning gently and calmly once the client has opened the eyes and has reestablished eye contact with the clinician. Some clients volunteer information spontaneously; that is preferable. Once the counselor has a handle on how the client feels and whether the exercise met its purpose, the therapist explores what, if anything, was particularly helpful to the client and what, if anything, may have been less than conducive to the client's relaxation or comfort. It is important to elicit detail from the client, perhaps asking for specific feedback about a few of the tension movements to make sure the client is responding in a detailed manner.

If a client signaled discomfort during the exercises, the clinician must remember and follow up on the incident to investigate what caused the discomfort, to consider its consequences, and to plan future changes in the exercise to prevent a similar occurrence. It is often helpful to phrase the question in a manner that reminds the client of what was going on at the time of the discomfort. The question may be phrased as follows: "While we were working on [your hands by making a fist], you indicated distress by [raising your right index finger]. What was going on for you right then?" The client is asked if any modifications might be helpful and if anything in the exercise appeared strange or unusual. The client is also specifically asked about self-consciousness about tensing certain muscle groups, knowing of the clinician's presence. It is often helpful to ask about the specific cautions (for example, pain, colors, heaviness, floating), to see if any of these issues arose for the client and how this was dealt with by the client. It is always good practice to be as specific as possible in questioning after the first use of the exercise and not to rely on brief answers about the client's experience. It is crucial to be open to negative feedback from clients lest they not derive necessary benefits from future modifications. For example, if a client indicates that the clinician's voice was too loud or too soft, the clinician must not be offended but be grateful to have this information so that the voice can be adjusted during the next attempt at the exercise. The question "Is there anything I might have done that would have made this experience [even] better for you?" usually works well to elicit such feedback.

Once sufficient feedback has been collected, the clinician can make a plan for future use of the exercise. The clinician may decide to continue to practice the exercise with the client in session for a few more weeks to have a way of monitoring progress in its use. If the client was very successful in the use of the exercise, the clinician may decide only to use counseling time once or twice more and then to encourage the client to use the exercise on private time. If the client is encouraged to use the exercise on her or his own, a tape can be made. If only minor modifications appeared necessary, a tape can be made during the next use of the exercise in session for the client's later home use. If major modifications are needed, the exercise may need to be repeated in session a few more times before taping is in order. All cautions about taping and the recommended use of tapes that were spelled out for the bodywork exercises apply here as well.

Focusing-Relaxation Exercise

As indicated above, clients are usually not introduced to inner-focus work until they have had some success with muscle work, unless there was a reason not to use progressive muscle relaxation. The introduction and debriefing for this relaxation exercise are essentially identical to those for progressive muscle work. The main difference rests on the description of what will be done during the exercise (that is, paying attention to various muscle groups and parts of the body, without tensing and relaxing of muscles). Since the client is completely at rest throughout this exercise, it may be helpful to have a blanket available for clients who have a tendency to feel cold, as coldness tends to distract the client's focus away from relaxation. As was true for progressive muscle work, the client can work sitting up or lying down. The main issue is for the client to find a comfortable position that can be maintained easily for the duration of the exercise. Some trial and error may be necessary. Given the similarity of the introduction and debriefing, following are only the actual instructions for the Focusing-Relaxation Exercise. The reader can use the specifics provided in the instructions to modify the relevant portions of the introduction about what the exercise involves. All debriefing comments (except those regarding muscle tensing) apply to this exercise as stated above.

Focusing-Relaxation Instructions

"Now that you are settled into a comfortable position, go ahead and close your eyes. This will draw your attention to the inside of your body. Consciously focus your mind inside your body now and follow my instructions. Start by taking a deep breath in through your nose and then out through your mouth."

Here the clinician takes in a deep audible breath through the nose and then blows the breath out through the mouth. This may be done a couple of times.

"And breathe in"

Clinician inhales audibly.

". . . and out through your nose."

Clinician exhales audibly through the nose.

"And in . . . and out . . . and in . . . and out."

Clinician establishes a comfortable, audible breathing rhythm. This should be done without speaking for about twenty seconds, or whatever period of time is comfortable for the client.

"Now as you keep breathing . . . deeply . . . and comfortably, . . . direct your attention to your feet. . . . Open yourself . . . to the experience of warmth . . . and relaxation . . . in your feet. . . . Focus your mind on the comfort . . . in your feet, . . . recognizing it . . . as relaxation . . . and noticing it . . . as calmness. . . . Notice the calm . . . and peace . . . in your feet . . . as they rest comfortably . . . on the couch. . . . Enjoy this profound tranquillity . . . in your feet . . . as they relax . . . more and more . . . completely. . . . All along, . . . keep breathing in . . . and out . . . at a comfortable rate, . . . breathing relaxation and calmness . . . deep into your body . . . with each breath in . . . and inviting deeper and deeper tranquillity . . . and peacefulness . . . with each breath out."

Clinician inhales and exhales audibly.

"Breathe in . . . fully relaxed . . . and calm . . . and out . . . peaceful . . . and quiet."

Clinician inhales and exhales audibly.

"Keep breathing . . . deeply . . . and comfortably, . . . keep enjoying the relaxation . . . and comfort . . . in your feet . . . and direct your attention to your calves, . . . noticing . . . that the good feeling . . . of calmness . . . is spreading up . . . from your feet . . . into your legs now, . . . into your calves. . . . Calmness . . . and comfort, . . . warmth . . . and tingling . . . in your lower legs . . . as a profound sense of relaxation . . . and calmness . . . travels through . . . your lower legs. . . . Supporting the comfort . . . and tranquillity . . . in your calves . . . is the peacefulness . . . you breathe in . . . with each inhalation, . . . and the restfulness . . . and release . . . that comes . . . with each exhalation."

Clinician inhales and exhales audibly.

"Breathe in . . . fully relaxed . . . and calm . . . and out . . . peaceful . . . and quiet."

Clinician inhales and exhales audibly.

"Keep breathing deeply and gently, allowing the relaxation to spread further now, up your legs through your knees into your thighs." [The clinician now repeats essentially the same instructions (with the appropriate pacing, breaks, suggestions of calm and relaxation, and refocusing on the breath), as indicated thus far, for *any or all* of the following body parts, working from the periphery of the body to the core:

- spreading relaxation from thighs into hips and pelvis
- spreading relaxation from fingertips throughout the fingers
- spreading relaxation from fingers into the entire hand
- spreading relaxation from the hand into the wrist and lower arm
- spreading relaxation from the lower arm through the elbow to the upper arm into the shoulder
- spreading relaxation from the shoulder to the neck and spine
- spreading relaxation from the neck up the skull across the entire scalp
- spreading relaxation from the top of the head to the forehead and eyes
- spreading relaxation from the eyes across the rest of the face
- spreading relaxation from the face down to the chin and throat and on to the chest
- spreading relaxation from the chest to the abdomen

Then the clinician once again refocuses the client on the breath and proceeds with the following instructions.]

Clinician inhales and exhales audibly.

"Your whole body is relaxed now. . . . Every part of you is calm . . . and quiet, . . . warm . . . and tingly . . . with relaxation. . . . You are relaxed . . . from your toes to your hips, . . . from your fingertips to your shoulders, . . . from your neck to your forehead, . . . from your eyes to your chin, . . . from the outside in. . . . Enjoy your relaxation . . . and the warmth . . . and comfort it brings. . . . Enjoy the peacefulness . . . of relaxation. . . . Revel in your calmness. . . . Treasure . . . the warmth . . . and comfort. . . . As you breathe in . . . enjoy your restfulness, . . . and as you breathe out . . . savor your calmness."

Clinician inhales and exhales audibly.

"Enjoy your peacefulness . . . as you breathe in deeply. . . . Relish your stillness . . . as you breathe out fully. . . . Calm . . . restful . . . tranquil. . . . Fully and completely relaxed."

After a comfortable amount of time, the clinician asks the client to end the exercise as follows:

"Now that you have welcomed calmness . . . and peacefulness, . . . experienced the warmth . . . and comfort of relaxation, . . . slowly bring your awareness back to this room, . . . bringing your tranquillity . . . and relaxation . . . with you. . . . Knowing that you can go back . . . to this relaxed state . . . any time you want to. . . . Slowly begin to focus your attention . . . away from your body and your breath . . . back to the outer world. . . . Do that by beginning to notice any sounds that you may hear, . . . by moving your body in any way that's comfortable. . . . As you do this, . . . I will slowly begin to count back . . . from five to one. . . . With each number I say, . . . you will become more and more alert. . . . When I get to one, . . . you will be fully alert. . . . Then take whatever time you need . . . and when you're ready . . . open your eyes."

Clinician slowly counts back from five to one, increasing volume of voice as numbers decrease, and adjusting the time required to the needs of the client.

"Five, . . . becoming more alert and aware of the outside world. . . . Four, . . . aware of the sounds [might mention specific audible sounds here], . . . rousing the body. . . . Three, . . . becoming more and more alert and aware. . . . Two, . . . coming back to the here-and-now. . . . One, . . . fully alert and aware!

Skill Development Recommendations

Recommendation 12-2   *Practice one or both of the relaxation exercises with a friend or family member. You may want to start by reading from the script, and then try it from memory. Pick a friend who is willing to give honest feedback about your technique. Practice with this person until they report enjoying the exercise and deriving benefit from it. Then try it one more time with another friend or family member before using the exercise with a client.*

Recommendation 12-3   *Make a tape of one or both of the relaxation exercises for your own use. Practice the exercise a few times until you get an appreciation of what it feels like for the client. If you have a friend or peer who can guide you through the exercise, that may be an acceptable substitute to making a tape. The main idea is for you to experience the exercise so that you can identify with what your future clients will go through.*

Clinician now allows the client to pace her or his own return by remaining quiet until the client opens the eyes and makes eye contact with the clinician. Once the client is fully alert and has regained contact with the clinician, debriefing can begin.

FINAL THOUGHTS

The complexity of therapy and counseling has no doubt by now become apparent. There is much to know and do to help clients grow and change. The techniques introduced in this book serve as a solid foundation for clinical work. Combining them flexibly and logically according to the individual needs of each client will mark the successful clinician. Any technique presented in this book can be useful or hurtful depending on how it is used and the context in which it is used. Learning how to apply knowledge in a skillful and caring way is the most important next step in the process toward becoming a counselor or therapist. To take the next step, it is important for the developing clinician to begin to practice, first with peers, then with real clients, and to read, read, read. There are many wonderful counseling and therapy books. Many of them have been referred to in these pages and are listed in the reference section that follows. For those readers who would like to continue to read in the same style as was presented in this book, two other books by this same author may be particularly helpful. These are as follows:

Brems, C. (1999). *Psychotherapy: Processes and techniques.* Boston: Allyn & Bacon.

Brems, C. (2000). *Dealing with challenges in psychotherapy and counseling.* Pacific Grove, Calif.: Brooks/Cole.

For those readers who want to expand their work to include child clients, the following book may be useful:

Brems, C. (1993). *A comprehensive guide to child psychotherapy.* Boston: Allyn & Bacon.

Practice of the Skill Development Recommendations made throughout this book will be an excellent start toward the goal of refining therapeutic skills. In-class exercises (often done in groups) will augment these experiences and will help with the necessary confidence building. Once mastered at these levels, the skills can then be used with clients.

I wish you good luck with these techniques and a happy career in mental health.

References

Adair, M. 1984. *Working inside out: Tools for change.* Oakland, Calif.: Wingbow Press.

Adler, A. 1969. *The practice and theory of individual psychology.* Paterson, N.J.: Little-field, Adams.

Alarcon, R. D., and E. F. Foulks. 1995. Personality disorders and culture: Contemporary clinical views (Part A). *Cultural Diversity and Mental Health.* 1:3–17.

American Counseling Association. 1995. *ACA Code of ethics and standards of practice.* Alexandria, Va.: American Counseling Association.

American Psychiatric Association. 1994. *Diagnostic and statistical manual of mental disorders.* 4th ed. Washington, D.C.: American Psychiatric Association.

American Psychological Association. 1987. Resolutions approved by the National Conference on Graduate Education in Psychology. *American Psychologist.* 42:1070–1084.

———. 1992. Ethical principles of psychologists and code of conduct. *American Psychologist.* 42:1597–1611.

Anderson, B. S. 1996. *The counselor and the law.* 4th ed. Alexandria, Va.: American Counseling Association.

Armour-Thomas, E., and S. A. Gopaul-McNicol. 1998. *Assessing intelligence: Applying a bio-cultural model.* Thousand Oaks, Calif.: Sage.

Assaglioli, R. 1965. *Psychosynthesis.* New York: Viking Compass.

Atkinson, D. R., G. Morten, and D. W. Sue. 1997. *Counseling American minorities: A cross-cultural perspective.* 5th ed. Dubuque, Ia.: William C. Brown.

Atwood, G., and R. Stolorow. 1984. *Structures of subjectivity.* Hillsdale, N.J.: Analytic Press.

Balch, J. F., and P. A. Balch. 1997. *Prescription for nutritional healing.* 2d ed. Garden City Park, N.Y.: Avery.

Bandler, R., and J. Grinder. 1975. *The structure of magic.* Vol. 1. Palo Alto, Calif.: Science and Behavior Books.

Bandura, A. 1969. *Principles of behavior modification.* New York: Holt, Rinehart & Winston.

Barnouw, V. 1985. *Culture and personality.* Chicago: Dorsey.

Barrett-Lennard, G. 1981. The empathy cycle: Refinement of a nuclear concept. *Journal of Counseling Psychology.* 28:91–100.

Basch, M. F. 1980. *Doing psychotherapy.* New York: Basic.

Bateson, C. D., B. D. Duncan, P. Ackerman, T. Buckley, and K. Birch. 1981. Is empathic emotion a source of altruistic motivation? *Journal of Personality and Social Psychology.* 40:290–302.

Bayne, R. 1997. Survival. In *The needs of counsellors and psychotherapists: Emotional, social, physical, professional,* edited by I. Horton and V. Varma, 183–198. London: Sage.

Beck, J. S. 1995. *Cognitive therapy: Basics and beyond.* New York: Guilford.

Bellak, A. S., M. Herson, and A. E. Kazdin. 1990. *International handbook of behavior modification and therapy.* New York: Plenum Press.

Bellak, L., and H. Siegel. 1983. *Brief and emergency psychotherapy.* Larchmont, N.Y.: C.P.S.

Bennet, M. J. 1986. A developmental approach to training for intercultural sensitivity. *International Journal of Intercultural Relations.* 10:117–134.

Berman, P. S. 1997. *Case conceptualization and treatment planning: Exercises for integrating theory and clinical practice.* New York: Sage.

Bernstein, I., and J. Glenn. 1988. The child and adolescent analyst's emotional reactions to his patients and their parents. *International Review of Psycho-Analysis.* 15:225–241.

Beutler, L. E., and M. R. Berren. 1995. *Integrative assessment of adult personality.* New York: Guilford.

Borysenko, J. 1987. *Minding the body, mending the mind.* Boston: Addison-Wesley.

Borysenko, J., and M. Borysenko. 1994. *The power of the mind to heal.* Carson, Calif.: Hay House.

Brems, C. 1989. Dimensionality of empathy and its correlates. *Journal of Psychology.* 123:329–337.

———. 1993. *A comprehensive guide to child psychotherapy.* Boston: Allyn & Bacon.

———. 1994. *The child therapist: Personal traits and markers of effectiveness.* Boston: Allyn & Bacon.

———. 1998a. Cultural issues in psychological assessment: Problems and possible solutions. *Journal of Psychological Practice.* 4:88–117.

———. 1998b. Implications of Daniel Stern's model of self development for child psychotherapy. *Journal of Psychological Practice.* 3:141–159.

———. 1999. *Psychotherapy: Processes and techniques.* Boston: Allyn & Bacon.

———. 2000. *Dealing with challenges in psychotherapy and counseling.* Belmont, Calif.: Brooks/Cole.

Brems, C., and M. E. Johnson. 1996a. Facing reality: The need for masters level accreditation and licensure in psychology. *Administration and Policy in Mental Health.* 23:271–273.

———. 1996b. Comparison of Ph.D. programs in clinical and counseling psychology. *Journal of Psychology.* 130:485–500.

———. 1997. Comparison of recent graduates of clinical versus counseling psychology programs. *Journal of Psychology.* 131:91–100.

Brems, C., D. K. Fromme, and M. E. Johnson. 1992. Group modification of empathic verbalizations and self-disclosure. *Journal of Social Psychology.* 132:189–200.

Brems, C., M. E. Johnson, and P. Gallucchi. 1996. Publication productivity of clinical and counseling psychologists. *Journal of Clinical Psychology.* 52:723–725.

Brislin, R. 1993. *Understanding culture's influence on behavior.* Fort Worth, Tex.: Harcourt Brace College.

Burns, G. W. 1998. *Nature-guided therapy: Brief integrative strategies for health and well-being.* Bristol, Pa.: Brunner/Mazel.

Canter, M. B., B. E. Bennett, S. E. Jones, and T. F. Nagy. 1994. *Ethics for psychologists: A commentary on the APA ethics code.* Washington, D.C.: American Psychological Association.

Cargile, A. C., and Sunwolf. (1998). Does the squeaky wheel get the grease? Understanding direct and indirect communication. In *Teaching about culture, ethnicity, and diversity: Exercises and planned activities,* edited by T. M. Singelis, 221–225. Thousand Oaks, Calif.: Sage.

Carkhuff, R. R. 1969. *Helping and human relations: Practice and research.* New York: Holt, Rinehart & Winston.

Carter, R. T. 1990. The relationship between racism and racial identity among White Americans: An exploratory investigation. *Journal of Counseling and Development.* 69:46–50.

Castillo, R. J. 1997. *Culture and mental illness: A client-centered approach.* Pacific Grove, Calif.: Brooks/Cole.

Choca, J. P. 1988. *Manual for clinical psychology trainees.* 2d ed. New York: Brunner/Mazel.

Chrzanowski, G. 1989. The significance of the analyst's individual personality in the therapeutic relationship. *Journal of the American Academy of Psychoanalysis.* 17:597–608.

Coke, J. S., C. D. Bateson, and K. McDavis. 1978. Empathic mediation of helping: A two stage model. *Journal of Personality and Social Psychology.* 36:752–766.

Corey, G., M. S. Corey, and P. Callanan. 1998. *Issues and ethics in the helping professions.* 3d ed. Pacific Grove, Calif.: Brooks/Cole.

Cormier, L. S., and H. Hackney. 1987. *The professional counselor: A process guide to helping.* Englewood Cliffs, N.J.: Prentice Hall.

Cormier, W. H., and L. S. Cormier. 1991. *Interviewing strategies for helpers.* 3d ed. Pacific Grove, Calif.: Brooks/Cole.

———. 1998. *Interviewing strategies for helpers.* 5th ed. Pacific Grove, Calif.: Brooks/Cole.

Corsini, R. J., and D. Wedding. 1997. *Current psychotherapies.* 5th ed. Itasca, Ill.: Peacock.

Cottone, R. R., and V. M. Tarvydas. 1998. *Ethical and professional issues in counseling.* Upper Saddle River, N.J.: Merrill.

Crayhon, R. 1994. *Nutrition made simple: A comprehensive guide to the latest findings in optimal nutrition.* New York: M. Evans.

Cross, W. E. 1971. The Negro-to-Black conversion experience: Towards a psychology of Black liberation. *Black World.* 20:13–27.

Cuellar, I., I. C. Harris, and R. Jasso. 1980. An acculturation scale for Mexican American normal and clinical populations. *Hispanic Journal of Behavioral Science.* 2:199–217.

D'Andrea, M., and J. Daniels. 1991. Exploring the different levels of multicultural counseling training in counselor education. *Journal of Counseling and Development.* 70:78–85.

D'Andrea, M., J. Daniels, and R. Heck. 1991. Evaluating the impact of multicultural counseling training. *Journal of Counseling and Development.* 70:143–150.

Dana, R. H. 1987. Training for professional psychology: Science, practice and identity. *Professional Psychology: Research and Practice.* 18:9–16.

———. 1993. *Multicultural assessment perspectives for professional psychology.* Needham Heights, Mass.: Allyn & Bacon.

Das, L. S. 1999. *Awakening to the sacred: Creating a spiritual life from scratch.* New York: Broadway Books.

Davis, M. H. 1983. The effects of dispositional empathy on emotional reactions and helping: A multidimensional approach. *Journal of Personality.* 51:174.

Day, J. 1995. Obligation and motivation: Obstacles and resources for counselor well-being and effectiveness. *Journal of Counseling and Development.* 73:108–110.

Dillard, J. M. 1983. *Multicultural counseling: Toward ethnic and cultural relevance in human encounters.* Chicago: Nelson-Hall.

Dolan, Y. M. 1991. *Resolving sexual abuse: Solution-focused therapy and Ericksonian hypnosis for adult survivors.* New York: W. W. Norton.

———. 1996. An Ericksonian perspective on the treatment of sexual abuse. In *Ericksonian methods: The essence of the story,* edited by J. K. Zeig, 395–414. New York: Brunner/Mazel.

Donner, S. 1991. The treatment process. In *Using self psychology in psychotherapy,* edited by H. Jackson, 51–71. Northvale, N.J.: Jason Aronson.

Dorfman, R. A. 1998. *Paradigms of clinical social work.* Vol. 2. New York: Brunner/Mazel.

Education in Psychology. *American Psychologist.* 42:1070–1084.

Eells, T. D. 1997. *Handbook of psychotherapy case formulation.* New York: Guilford.

Egan, G. 1994. *The skilled helper.* 5th ed. Pacific Grove, Calif.: Brooks/Cole.

Ellis, A., and W. Dryden. 1987. *The practice of rational-emotive therapy (RET).* New York: Springer.

Fields, R. 1985. *Chop wood, carry water.* Los Angeles: Jeremy P. Tarcher.

Fogelsanger, A. 1994. *See yourself well: Guided visualizations and relaxation techniques.* Brooklyn: Equinox.

Fox, M. W. 1997. *Eating with conscience.* Troutdale, Ore.: NewSage Press.

Frankl, V. E. 1969. *The will to meaning: Foundations and applications of logotherapy.* New York: World.

Freud, S. 1900. The interpretation of dreams. In *The standard edition of the complete psychological works of Sigmund Freud.* Vol. 485. Trans. by J. Strachey. New York: Norton.

———. 1949. *An outline of psychoanalysis.* New York: Norton.

———. 1959. The future prospects of psychoanalytic therapy. In *Collected papers.* Vol. 2, 285–296. Edited by E. Jones. New York: Basic.

Garfield, P. 1977. *Creative dreaming.* New York: Ballantine.

Garrett, L. 1994. *The coming plague: Newly emerging diseases in a world out of balance.* New York: Farrar, Straus, & Giroux.

Gelso, C. J., and B. R. Fretz. 1992. *Counseling psychology.* New York: Harcourt Brace Jovanovich.

Gendlin, E. T. 1981. *Focusing.* New York: Bantam.

Gibbs, J. T., and L. N. Huang, ed. 1989. *Children of color: Psychological interventions with minority youth.* San Francisco: Jossey-Bass.

Gil, E. 1988. *Outgrowing the pain: A book for and about adults abused as children.* New York: Dell.

Gill, M. 1982. *Analysis of transference.* Vol. 1. New York: International University.

Goldstein, J., and J. Kornfield. 1987. *Seeking the heart of wisdom.* Boston: Shambhala.

Goldstein, J. 1976. *The experience of insight.* Boston: Shambhala.

Greenberg, L. S. 1994. *Process experiential psychotherapy.* Washington, D.C.: American Psychological Association Publications.

Haas, E. M. 1992. *Staying healthy with nutrition.* Berkeley: Celestial Arts.

Hammond, D. C., D. H. Hepworth, and V. G. Smith. 1977. *Improving therapeutic communication.* San Francisco: Jossey-Bass.

Hanh, T. N. 1975. *The miracle of mindfulness.* Boston: Beacon Press.

Hayano, D. 1981. Ethnic identification and disidentification: Japanese-American views of Chinese-Americans. *Ethnic Groups.* 3:157–171.

Helms, J. E. 1990. *Black and White racial identity: Theory, research, and practice.* New York: Greenwood.

Helms, J. E., and R. T. Carter. 1990. Development of the White Racial Identity Attitude Inventory. In *Black and White racial identity: Theory, research and practice,* edited by J. E. Helms, 67–80. Westport, Conn.: Greenwood.

Herlihy, B., and G. Corey. 1992. *Dual relationships in counseling.* Alexandria, Va.: American Counseling Association.

———. 1996. *ACA ethical standards casebook.* 5th ed. Alexandria, Va.: American Counseling Association.

———. 1997. *Boundary issues in counseling: Multiple roles and responsibilities.* Alexandria, Va.: American Counseling Association.

Hirai, T. 1989. *Zen meditation and psychotherapy.* New York: Japan Publications.

Hogan-Garcia, M. 1999. *The four skills of cultural diversity competence.* Pacific Grove, Calif.: Brooks/Cole.

Holmquist, R., and B. A. Armelius. 1996. The patient's contribution the therapist's countertransference feelings. *Journal of Nervous and Mental Disease.* 184:660–666.

Hoy, D. 1978. *The critical circle.* Berkeley: University of California Press.

Iijima Hall, C. C. 1997. Cultural malpractice: The growing obsolescence of psychology with the changing U.S. population. *American Psychologist.* 52:642–651.

Ivey, A. E. 1995. Psychotherapy as liberation: Toward specific skills and strategies in multicultural counseling and therapy. In *Handbook of multicultural counseling,* edited by J. G. Ponterotto, J. M. Casas, L. A. Suzuki, and C. M. Alexander, 53–72. Thousand Oaks, Calif.: Sage.

Ivey, A. E., M. E. Ivey, and L. Simek-Morgan. 1997. *Counseling and psychotherapy: A multicultural perspective.* 4th ed. Needham Heights, Mass.: Allyn & Bacon.

Jackson, B. 1975. Black identity development. *Journal of Educational Diversity.* 2:19–25.

Jevne, R. F., and D. R. Williams. 1998. *When dreams don't work: Professional caregivers and burnout.* Amityville, N.Y.: Baywood.

Johns, H. 1996. *Personal development in counsellor training.* London: Cassell.

———. 1997. Self-development: Lifelong learning? In *The needs of counsellors and psychotherapists: emotional, social, physical, professional,* edited by I. Horton and V. Varma, 54–67. London: Sage.

Johnson, M. E. 1993. A culturally sensitive approach to child psychotherapy. In *Comprehensive guide to child psychotherapy,* C. Brems, 68–94. Boston: Allyn & Bacon.

———. 1994. Modeling theories. In *Magill's survey of social sciences: Psychology.* Pasadena, Calif.: Salem Press.

Johnson, M. E., and C. Brems. 1991. Comparing theoretical orientations of clinical and counseling psychologists: An objective approach. *Professional Psychology: Research and Practice.* 22:133–137.

Johnson, R. A. 1986. *Inner work: Using dreams and active imaginations for personal growth.* San Francisco: Harper.

Jones, W. T. 1990. Perspectives in ethnicity: In *Evolving theoretical perspectives in students,* edited by L. Moore, 59–72. New Directions for Student Services no. 51. San Francisco: Jossey Bass.

Jung, C. G. 1968. *Analytical psychology: Its theory and practice.* New York: Vintage.

———. 1974. *Dreams.* Princeton: Princeton University Press.

Kabat-Zinn, J. 1990. *Full catastrophe living.* New York: Delta.

———. 1994. *Wherever you go, there you are.* New York: Hyperion.

Karoly, P. 1993. Goal systems: An organizing framework for clinician assessment and treatment planning. *Psychological Assessment.* 5:273–280.

Keinan, G., M. Almagor, and Y. S. Ben-Porath. 1989. A reevaluation of the relationship between psychotherapeutic orientation and perceived personality characteristics. *Psychotherapy.* 26:218–226.

Kim, M. S. 1994. Cross-cultural comparisons of the perceived importance of conversational constraints. *Human Communication Research.* 21:128–151.

Knapp, M. L. 1978. *Nonverbal communication in human interactions.* 2d ed. New York: Holt, Rinehart, & Winston.

Knobel, M. 1990. Significance and importance of the psychotherapist's personality and experience. *Psychotherapy and Psychosomatics.* 53:58–63.

Kohatsu, E. L., and T. Q. Richardson. 1996. Racial and ethnic identity assessment. In *Handbook of multicultural assessment,* edited by L. A. Suzuki, P. J. Meller, and J. G. Ponterotto, 611–650. New York: Jossey-Bass.

Kohut, H. 1977. *The restoration of the self.* New York: International Universities Press.

———. 1982. Introspection, empathy, and the semi-circle of mental health. *International Journal of Psychoanalysis.* 63:359–407.

———. 1984. *How does analysis cure?* Chicago: International Universities Press.

Kohut, H., and E. Wolf. 1978. Disorders of the self and their treatment. *International Journal of Psychoanalysis.* 59:413–425.

Kolevzon, M. S., K. Sowers-Hoag, and C. Hoffman. 1989. Selecting a family therapy model: The role of personality attributes in eclectic practice. *Journal of Marital and Family Therapy.* 15:249–257.

Kornfield, J. 1993. *A path with heart.* New York: Bantam.

Kottler, J. A., and R. W. Brown. 1992. *Introduction to therapeutic counseling.* 2d ed. Pacific Grove, Calif.: Brooks/Cole.

Krebs, D. 1975. Empathy and altruism. *Journal of Personality and Social Psychology.* 34:1134–1146.

LaFramboise, T. D., H. L. Coleman, and A. Hernandez. 1991. Development and factor structure of the Cross-Cultural Counseling Inventory-revised. *Professional Psychology: Research and Practice.* 22:380–388.

LaFramboise, T. D., and S. L. Foster. 1989. Ethics in multicultural counseling. In *Counseling across cultures,* edited by P. B. Pedersen, J. G. Draguns, W. J. Lonner, and J. E. Trimble. 3d ed., 115–136. Honolulu: University of Hawaii Press.

Land, H. 1998. The feminist approach to clinical social work. In *Paradigms of clinical social work,* R. A. Dorfman. Vol. 2, 227–256. New York: Brunner/Mazel.

Lane, R. D., and G. E. Schwartz. 1987. Levels of emotional awareness: A cognitive-developmental theory and its applications to psychopathology. *American Journal of Psychiatry.* 144:133–143.

Lauver, P., and D. R. Harvey. 1997. *The practical counselor: Elements of helping.* Pacific Grove, Calif.: Brooks/Cole.

Lazarus, A. A. 1981. *The practice of multimodal therapy.* New York: McGraw Hill.

———. 1985. *Casebook of multimodal therapy.* New York: Guilford.

LeShan, L. 1974. *How to meditate.* New York: Bantam.

Levine, S. 1987. *Healing into life and death.* Garden City, N.Y.: Doubleday.

———. 1989. *A gradual awakening.* Garden City, N.Y.: Doubleday.

Lewis, K. N., and W. B. Walsh. 1980. Effects of value-communication style and similarity of values on counselor evaluation. *Journal of Counseling Psychology.* 27:305–314.

Lum, D. 1999. *Culturally competent practice.* Pacific Grove, Calif.: Brooks/Cole.

Mahoney, M. J. 1997. Psychotherapists' personal problems and self-care patterns. *Professional Psychology: Research and Practice.* 28:14–16.

Mahrer, A. R. 1989. *Dreamwork in psychotherapy and self-change.* New York: W. W. Norton.

Mahrer, A. R., D. B. Boulet, and D. R. Fairweather. 1994. Beyond empathy: Advances in the clinical theory and methods of empathy. *Clinical Psychology Review.* 14:183–198.

Maslow, A. H. 1968. *Toward a psychology of being.* New York: Van Nostrand Reinhold.

Matsumoto, D. 1994. *Cultural influences on research methods and statistics.* Pacific Grove, Calif.: Brooks/Cole.

McGrath, P., and J. A. Axelson. 1993. *Accessing awareness and developing knowledge: Foundations for skill in a multicultural society.* Pacific Grove, Calif.: Brooks/Cole.

Mehrabien, A., and N. Epstein. 1971. A measure of emotional empathy. *Journal of Personality.* 40:525–543.

Meier, S., and S. R. Davis. 1997. *The elements of counseling.* 3d ed. Pacific Grove, Calif.: Brooks/Cole.

Milliones, J. 1980. Construction of a black consciousness measure: Psychotherapeutic implications. *Psychotherapy: Theory, Research and Practice.* 17:175–182.

Millman, D. 1993. *The life you were born to live: A guide to finding your life purpose.* Tiburon, Calif.: Kramer.

Minuchin, S., and H. C. Fishman. 1981. *Family therapy techniques.* Cambridge, Mass.: Harvard University Press.

Monges, M. M. 1998. Beyond the melting pot: A values clarification exercise for teachers and human service professionals. In *Teaching about culture, ethnicity, and diversity: Exercises and planned activities,* edited by T. M. Singelis, 3–8. Thousand Oaks, Calif.: Sage.

Morrison, J. 1995. *The first interview: Revised for DSM-IV.* New York: Guilford.

Moss, R. W. 1996. *Cancer therapy: The independent consumer's guide to non-toxic treatment and prevention.* Brooklyn: Equinox.

Namyniuk, L. 1996. *Cultural considerations in substance abuse treatment.* Paper presented at the 3d Biennial Conference of the Alaska Psychological Association, Anchorage, AK.

Namyniuk, L., C. Brems, and S. Clarson. 1997. Dena A Coy: A model program for the treatment of pregnant substance-abusing women. *Journal of Substance Abuse Treatment.* 14:285–298.

Naparstek, B. 1994. *Staying well with guided imagery.* New York: Warner.

National Association of Social Workers. 1993. *Code of ethics.* Silver Springs, Md.: National Association of Social Workers.

Natterson, J. 1991. *Beyond countertransference: The therapist's subjectivity in the therapeutic process.* Northvale, N.J.: Aronson.

Nichols, M. P. 1987. *The self in the system: Expanding the limits of family therapy.* New York: Brunner/Mazel.

Null, G. 1995. *Nutrition and the mind.* New York: Seven Stories.

Olson, K. R., T. T. Jackson, and J. Nelson. 1997. Attributional biases in clinical practice. *Journal of Psychological Practice.* 3:27–33.

Parham, T. A., and J. E. Helms. 1985. The relationship of racial identity attitudes to self-actualization of Black students and affective states. *Journal of Counseling Psychology.* 32:431–440.

Patterson, L. E., and E. R. Welfel. 1993. *The counseling process.* Pacific Grove, Calif.: Brooks/Cole

Pearce, S. R. 1996. *Flash of insight: Metaphor and narrative in therapy.* Needham Heights, Mass.: Allyn & Bacon.

Pennebaker, J. W. 1990. *Opening up: The healing power of expressing emotions.* New York: Guilford.

Perls, F. S. 1969. *Gestalt therapy verbatim.* Lafayette, Calif.: Real People Press.

Phinney, J. S. 1990. Ethnic identity in adolescents and adults: Review of research. *Psychological Bulletin.* 108:499–514.

———. 1996. When we talk about American ethnic groups, what do we mean? *American Psychologist.* 51:918–927.

Pigram, J. J. 1993. Human nature relationships: Leisure environments and natural settings. In *Behavior and environment: Psychological and geographical approaches,* edited by T. Garling and R. G. College, 400–426. Amsterdam: Elsevier.

Pinderhughes, E. B. 1983. Empowerment for our clients and ourselves. *Social Casework.* 64:331–338.

————. 1997. Developing diversity competence in child welfare and permanency planning. *Journal of Multicultural Social Work.* 5:19–38.

Pitchford, P. 1993. *Healing with whole foods: Oriental traditions and modern nutrition.* Berkeley: North Atlantic.

Pizzorno, J. 1998. *Total wellness.* Rocklin, Calif.: Prima.

Polster, E., and M. Polster. 1973. *Gestalt therapy integrated: Contours of theory and practice.* New York: Vintage.

Ponterotto, J. G., and C. M. Alexander. 1996. Assessing the multicultural competence of counselors and clinicians. In *Handbook of multicultural assessment,* edited by L. A. Suzuki, P. J. Meller, and J. G. Ponterotto, 651–672. New York: Jossey-Bass.

Ponterotto, J. G., and J. M. Casas. 1991. *Handbook of racial/ethnic minority counseling research.* Springfield, Ill.: Charles C. Thomas.

Ponterotto, J. G., and S. L. Wise. 1987. Construct validity study of the Racial Identity Attitude Scale. *Journal of Counseling Psychology.* 34:218–223.

Ponterotto, J. G., J. M. Casas, L. A. Suzuki, and C. M. Alexander. 1995. *Handbook of multicultural counseling.* Thousand Oaks, Calif.: Sage.

Pope, K. S., and L. S. Brown. 1996. *Recovered memories of abuse: Assessment, therapy, forensics.* Washington, D.C.: American Psychological Association Publications.

Reid, D. 1994. *The complete book of Chinese health and healing.* New York: Barnes and Noble.

Reid, W. J. 1998. The paradigm and long-term trends in clinical social work. In *Paradigms of clinical social work,* R. A. Dorfman. Vol. 2, 337–351. New York: Brunner/Mazel.

Richardson, T. Q., and K. L. Molinaro. 1996. White counselor self-awareness: A prerequisite for developing multicultural competence. *Journal of Counseling and Development.* 74:238–242.

Rinpoche, A. T. 1995. *Taming the tiger.* Rochester, Va.: Inner Traditions.

Robbins, J. 1987. *Diet for a new America.* Walpole, N.H.: Stillpoint.

Roehl, E. 1996. *Whole food facts: The complete reference guide.* Rochester, Vt.: Healing Arts.

Rogers, C. R. 1961. *On becoming a person.* Boston: Houghton Mifflin.

Rohe, F. 1983. *The complete book of natural foods.* Boulder: Shambala.

Rokeach, M. 1973. *The nature of human values.* New York: Free Press.

Rosenbaum, R. 1999. *Zen and the heart of psychotherapy.* Boston: Taylor & Francis.

Rossman, M. 1993. *Mind/body medicine: How to use your mind for better health.* New York: Consumer Reports Books.

Rowe, C. E., and D. S. MacIsaac. 1986. *Empathic attunement: The technique of psychoanalytic self psychology.* Northvale, N.J.: Aronson.

Rychlak, J. 1984. *Personality theory and psychopathology.* New York: Prentice-Hall.

Sanderson, C. 1996. *Counselling adult survivors of child sexual abuse.* 2d Ed. London: Jessica Kingsley.

Schiffmann, E. 1996. *Yoga: The spirit and practice of moving into stillness.* New York: Pocket Books.

Schwartz, T. 1995. *What really matters: Searching for wisdom in America.* New York: Bantam.

Sharma, P. and D. Lucero-Miller. 1998. Beyond political correctness. In *Teaching about culture, ethnicity, and diversity: Exercises and planned activities,* edited by T. M. Singelis, 191–194. Thousand Oaks, Calif.: Sage.

Shulman, L. A. 1988. Groupwork practice with hard to reach clients: A modality of choice. *Groupwork.* 1:5–16.

Sigelman, C. K., and D. R. Shaffer. 1995. *Life-span human development.* 2d ed. Pacific Grove, Calif.: Brooks/Cole.

Singelis, T. M., ed. 1998. *Teaching about culture, ethnicity, and diversity: Exercises and planned activities.* Thousand Oaks, Calif.: Sage.

Singelis, T. M., and W. J. Brown. 1995. Culture, self, and collectivist communication: Linking culture to individual behavior. *Human Communications Research.* 21:354–389.

Singelis, T. M., H. C. Triandis, D. S. Bhawuk, and M. J. Gelfand. 1995. Horizontal and vertical dimensions of individualism and collectivism: A theoretical and measurement refinement. *Cross-Cultural Research.* 29:240–275.

Sodowsky, G. R., R. C. Taffe, T. Gutkin, and C. L. Wise. 1994. Development of the Multicultural Counseling Inventory: A self-report measure of multicultural competencies. *Journal of Counseling Psychology.* 41:137–148.

Somer, E. 1995. *Food and mood: The complete guide to eating well and feeling your best.* New York: Holt.

Sommers-Flanagan, J., and R. Sommers-Flanagan. 1999. *Clinical interviewing.* New York: Wiley.

Steinman, S. O., N. F. Richardson, and T. McEnroe. 1998. *The ethical decision-making manual for helping professionals.* Pacific Grove, Calif.: Brooks/Cole.

Stern, D. N. 1985. *The interpersonal world of the infant.* New York: Basic Books.

Strauss, J. S. 1996. Subjectivity. *Journal of Nervous and Mental Disease.* 184:205–212.

Strupp, H. H. 1992. The future of psychotherapy. *Psychotherapy.* 29:21–27.

———. 1996. Some salient lessons from research and practice. *Psychotherapy.* 33:135–138.

Sue, D. W., R. T. Carter, J. M. Casas, N. A. Fouad, A. E. Ivey, M. Jensen, T. D. LaFromboise, J. E. Manese, J. G. Ponterotto, and E. Vazquez-Nutall. 1998. *Multicultural counseling competencies: Individual and organizational development.* Thousand Oaks, Calif.: Sage

Sue, S., D. B. Allen, and L. Conaway. 1978. The responsiveness and equality of mental health care to Chicanos and Native Americans. *American Journal of Community Psychology.* 6:137–146.

Suzuki, L. A., P. J. Meller, and J. G. Ponterotto. 1996. *Handbook of multicultural assessment.* New York: Jossey-Bass.

Suzuki, S. 1998. *Zen mind, beginner's mind.* New York: Weatherhill.

Swenson, L. C. 1997. *Psychology and the law.* 2d ed. Pacific Grove, Calif.: Brooks/Cole.

Takaki, R. T. 1993. *A different mirror: A history of multicultural America.* Boston: Little, Brown.

Taylor, J. 1983. *Dream work.* New York: Paulist.

Teyber, E. 1997. *Interpersonal process in psychotherapy: A relational approach.* 3d ed. Pacific Grove, Calif.: Brooks/Cole.

Thayer, R. E., J. R. Newman, and T. M. McClain. 1994. Self-regulation of mood: Strategies for changing a bad mood, raising energy, and reducing tension. *Journal of Personality and Social Psychology.* 67:910–925.

Todd, J., and A. Bohart. 1994. *Foundations of clinical and counseling psychology.* 2d ed. New York: Harper Collins.

Triandis, H. C. 1989. The self and social behavior in differing cultural contexts. *Psychological Review.* 96:506–520.

Ullman, M., and N. Zimmerman. 1979. *Working with dreams.* Los Angeles: Jeremy P. Tarcher.

Ulrich, R. S., U. Dimberg, and B. Driver. 1991. Psychophysiological indicators. In *Benefits of leisure,* edited by B. Driver, P. Brown, and G. Peterson, 73–89. State College, Pa.: Venture.

Wachtel, P. L. 1993. *Therapeutic communication: Knowing what to say when.* New York: Guilford.

Webb, N. B. 1989. Supervision of child therapy: Analyzing therapeutic impasses and monitoring countertransference. *The Clinical Supervisor.* 7:61–76.

Weeks, G. R., and L. L'Abate. 1982. *Paradoxical psychotherapy: Theory and practice with individuals, couples, and families.* New York: Brunner/Mazel.

Weil, A. 1995. *Spontaneous healing.* New York: Fawcett Columbine.

Weiss, J. 1993. *How psychotherapy works.* New York: Guilford.

Werbach, M. R. 1999. *Nutritional influences on mental illness: A sourcebook of clinical research.* 2d ed. Tarzana, Calif.: Third Line Press.

Wheeler, S. 1997. Achieving and maintaining competence. In *The needs of counsellors and psychotherapists: Emotional, social, physical, professional,* edited by I. Horton and V. Varma, 120–134. London: Sage.

Wilber, K. 1993. *The spectrum of consciousness.* 2d ed. Wheaton, Ill.: Quest Books.

———. 1997. *Eye of spirit.* Boston: Shambhala.

Wirth, L. 1945. The problem of minority groups. In *The science of man in the world crisis,* edited by R. Linton, 347–372. New York: Columbia University Press.

Wolf, E. S. 1988. *Treating the self: Elements of clinical self psychology.* New York: Guilford.

Wolmark, A., and M. Sweezy. 1998. Kohut's self psychology. In *Paradigms of clinical social work,* R. A. Dorfman. Vol. 2, 45–70. New York: Brunner/Mazel.

Young, M. E., and F. Bemark. 1996. The role of emotional arousal and expression in mental health counseling. *Journal of Mental Health Counseling.* 18:316–332.

Zeig, J. K. 1994. *Ericksonian methods: The essence of the story.* New York: Brunner/Mazel.

Zinn, H. 1995. *A people's history of the United States.* New York: Harper.

Author Index

Ackerman, P., 182
Adair, M., 84
Adler, A., 250
Alarcon, R. D., 65
Alexander, C. M., 56, 57, 68
Allen, D. B., 65
American Counseling Association, 42
American Psychiatric Association, 65, 255
American Psychological Association, 42, 56
Anderson, B. S., 42
Armelius, B. A., 33
Armour-Thomas, E., 64
Assaglioli, R., 250
Atkinson, D. R., 61
Atwood, G., 266
Axelson, J. A., 57

Balch, J. F., 90
Balch, P. A., 90
Bandler, R., 250
Bandura, A., 204
Barnouw, V., 64
Barrett-Lennard, G., 28, 184, 188
Basch, M. F., 26, 28, 253
Bateson, C. D., 182
Bayne, R., 75, 92
Beck, J. S., 249
Bellak, A. S., 249, 317
Bellak, L., 317
Bemark, F., 309, 310, 311
Bennet, M. J., 68
Bennett, B. E., 42
Ben-Porath, Y. S., 27

Berman, P. S., 253
Bernstein, I., 35
Berren, M. R., 107
Beutler, L. E., 107
Bhawuk, D. S., 65
Birch, K., 182
Bohart, A., 250
Borysenko, J., 84, 85
Borysenko, M., 85
Boulet, D. B., 192
Brems, C., xix, 11, 21, 28, 29, 33, 44, 66, 69, 70, 72, 99, 131, 151, 184, 188, 200, 203, 226, 248, 252, 255, 265, 311, 312, 398
Brislin, R., 68
Brown, L. S., 320
Brown, R. W., 21, 26, 27, 250
Brown, W. J., 68
Buckley, T., 182
Burns, G. W., 95, 96

Callanan, P., 34, 41, 42, 43
Canter, M. B., 42
Cargile, A. C., 68
Carkhuff, R. R., 199
Carter, R. T., 62
Casas, J. M., 56, 64, 68
Castillo, R. J., 65
Choca, J. P., 26
Chrzanowski, G., 27
Clarson, S., 70
Coleman, H. L., 57
Conaway, L., 65
Corey, G., 21, 34, 41, 42, 43

411

Subject Index

415

TO THE OWNER OF THIS BOOK:

We hope that you have found *Basic Skills in Psychotherapy and Counseling,* First Edition, useful. So that this book can be improved in a future edition, would you take the time to complete this sheet and return it? Thank you.

School and address: _____

_____

Department: _____

Instructor's name: _____

1. What I like most about this book is: _____

_____

_____

2. What I like least about this book is: _____

_____

_____

3. My general reaction to this book is: _____

_____

_____

4. The name of the course in which I used this book is: _____

_____

5. Were all of the chapters of the book assigned for you to read? _____

   If not, which ones weren't? _____

6. In the space below, or on a separate sheet of paper, please write specific suggestions for improving this book and anything else you'd care to share about your experience in using this book.

_____

_____

OPTIONAL:

Your name: _____ Date: _____

May we quote you, either in promotion for *Basic Skills in Psychotherapy and Counseling,
First Edition,* or in future publishing ventures?

Yes: _____ No: _____

Sincerely yours,

Christiane Brems

FOLD HERE

NO POSTAGE
NECESSARY
IF MAILED
IN THE
UNITED STATE

BUSINESS REPLY MAIL
FIRST CLASS   PERMIT NO. 358   PACIFIC GROVE, CA

POSTAGE WILL BE PAID BY ADDRESSEE

ATTN: *Julie Martinez, Counseling Editor* _____

**BROOKS/COLE/THOMSON LEARNING
511 FOREST LODGE ROAD
PACIFIC GROVE, CA   93950-9968**

FOLD HERE